From Heart to Heart

Women's Voices in Ukrainian Literature

From Heart to Heart

Selected Prose Fiction

by

Hrytsko Hryhorenko

and

Lesya Ukrainka

Translated by Roma Franko
Edited by Sonia Morris

Language Lanterns Publications
1999

Canadian Cataloguing in Publication Data

Main entry under title:

Women's voices in Ukrainian literature

Partial contents: v. 4. From heart to heart / by
Hrytsko Hryhorenko and Lesya Ukrainka

ISBN 0-9683899-3-7 (v. 4)

1. Short stories, Ukrainian--Women authors--Translations into English.
2. Ukrainian fiction--19th century--Translations into English.
3. Ukrainian fiction--20th century--Translations into English.
I. Franko, Roma Z. II. Morris, Sonia V.

PG3932.5.W65W65 1998   891.7'93'01089287   C98-920168-6

Series design concept: © Roma Franko and Sonia Morris
Translations: © Roma Franko
Portrait sketches: © Raissa Sonia Choi
Editorial assistance: Paul Cipywnyk
Cover production and technical assistance: Mike Kaweski

© 1998 Language Lanterns Publications
   321-4th Ave. N., Saskatoon, SK, S7K 2L9
   Web site: www.languagelanterns.com

Printed and bound in Canada by
Hignell Printing Ltd., Winnipeg

Women's Voices in Ukrainian Literature

Lovingly dedicated to
our mother
Sonia Melnyk Stratychuk
whose indomitable spirit inspired this series

Titles in Print

The Spirit of the Times, 1998
In the Dark of the Night, 1998
But the Lord is Silent, 1999
From Heart to Heart, 1999

Forthcoming Titles in the Series

Warm the Children, O Sun, 2000
For a Crust of Bread, 2000

Introduction to the Series

The turn of a century marks a pause in time—a pause that impels us to take stock, assess the extent and significance of societal changes, and make sense of our individual and collective experiences. When the end of a century coincides with the millennium, this need to engage in retrospective analyses is intensified.

The purpose of this series is to make accessible to English readers the selected works of Ukrainian women writers, most of whom have not been previously translated into English, and, in so doing, enhance our understanding of women's slow, difficult, and ongoing trek to political, economic and social equality—a trek on which women in Ukraine embarked over a century ago.

The works selected range from vignettes and sketches to novelettes and novels. Together they constitute an unsystematic but compelling social history of an era during which the mortar of social mores, religious beliefs, and gender distinctions began to crumble as successive political and ideological cataclysms wreaked havoc with time-honoured personal and societal relations.

The authors are not equally talented or skilled. What they have in common is an appreciation of the power of literature, be it as an avenue of self-actualisation or a vehicle of social activism. In addition to national, political, and educational issues, they address matters of gender which cut across ethnic and social divisions, and explore the power and often devastating consequences of social conditioning.

They do not, of course, speak with one voice. For some, women's concerns are overshadowed by larger issues of political freedom, cultural autonomy, and socio-economic reform. Their goals range from group emancipation to individual freedom, with many initially defining their emerging status in terms of a synthesis of traditional female roles, immediate community responsibilities, and more general humanitarian imperatives.

More importantly, whatever the subject matter, they observe and interpret experience from a female perspective. They intuitively understand that women forge their identities in the context of relationships, appreciate the power inherent in this need for connectedness and emotional wholeness, and demonstrate a keen sensitivity to both the promise and the human cost of change.

Their voices are loud and strong, what they have to say is worth hearing, and their impact should not be confined to one time or place. Translating their stories into English permits their message to transcend temporal and geographical boundaries.

The difficulties inherent in the process of translation were compounded by textual variations and vexing problems of transliteration. In the case of the earlier works, there were two other problems: archaic and dialectal language, and nineteenth century stylistic conventions. Ultimately, it was the criterion of readability that informed the many difficult decisions that had to be made.

A biographical note about each author anchors her writings in a social and historical context. No other analyses are provided; the works are allowed to speak for themselves.

Sonia Morris, Editor
Former Assistant Dean of the College of Education,
Former Head of the Department of Educational Psychology,
College of Education, University of Saskatchewan

Roma Franko, Translator
Former Head of the Department of Slavic Studies
and the Department of Modern Languages and Literatures,
College of Arts and Science, University of Saskatchewan

Contents

Contents

Lesya Ukrainka
(1871-1913)

Hrytsko Hryhorenko

1867-1924

Biographical Sketch

Oleksandra Sudovshchykova-Kosach, is known in Ukrainian literature as Hrytsko Hryhorenko, the male literary pseudonym that she chose to use. Her father, Yevhen Sudovshchykov, was a Russian with strong pro-Ukrainian sympathies who taught in a private school in Kyiv and undertook the writing of a Ukrainian grammar. Both he and his Ukrainian wife, Hanna Khoynatska, a former student of his, who also became a teacher, were actively involved in collecting Ukrainian folk materials and in enlightening the underprivileged. Because of their involvement in Ukrainian organisations, they were exiled to northern Russia in 1866, and it was there that Oleksandra was born in 1867.

In 1868, Hanna's husband died, and her brother was able to negotiate the return of the young widow and her infant to Kyiv. Prior to obtaining a tutoring position, Hanna and her daughter lived with friends, the Drahomanovs, relatives of Olha Drahomanov-Kosach (literary pseudonym: Olena Pchilka).

Little Oleksandra was much the same age as the children of Olena Pchilka, and she became close friends with them. She was able to maintain this friendship during her childhood and adolescent years, as she and her mother spent their summer holidays in the country with the Kosach family.

After completing high school, Oleksandra continued her formal education in Kyiv and joined the *Pleyada (The Pleaides)*, a literary circle that was organized by the two older children of Olena Pchilka: her son Mykhaylo (literary pseudonym: Mykhaylo Obachny) and her daughter Larysa (literary pseudonym: Lesya Ukrainka). This circle was dedicated to promoting the development of Ukrainian literature and introducing Ukrainian readers to the works of foreign authors by translating them into Ukrainian.

It was as a member of this group that Oleksandra became interested in writing. She wrote poetry in Ukrainian, Russian, and French, and translated Ukrainian authors into French. Drawing on her knowledge of European languages, she collaborated with Mykhaylo Kosach (Obachny) in translating Swedish and English authors into Ukrainian. She also translated French authors into Ukrainian, including such works as Jules Verne's *Twenty Thousand Leagues under the Sea*.

In 1893, Oleksandra married Mykhaylo Kosach who, because of political persecution, was forced to move to Estonia to continue his university studies. For the next few years, she and her mother lived with

Mykhaylo in Tartu, Estonia, where he was first a graduate student, then a professor of physics and mathematics. It was in Estonia that Oleksandra began writing prose fiction and, in 1898, she published, under her male pseudonym, her first collection of realistic ethnographic narratives, *Nashi lyudy na seli (The Lives of Our Peasants)* in which the bleak lives of the Ukrainian peasants were documented.

Oleksandra and her husband returned to Ukraine in 1901 and settled in Kharkiv, where Mykhaylo assumed a position as a professor at the University of Kharkiv. Happy to be back in her native land, Oleksandra continued with her writing and her translations of foreign authors.

In 1903, she had to cope with the tragic loss of her husband. With his death, she lost her soul mate and mentor, and found herself in the same position that her mother had been after the death of her husband. Unable to support herself in Kharkiv, Oleksandra and her young daughter moved to Kyiv where they lived with the Kosach family. During this most difficult period in her life, she received encouragement and support from her sister-in-law, Lesya Ukrainka.

Faced with the task of maintaining herself and her young daughter, Oleksandra completed a law degree and worked for some time in a Kyivan court. At the same time, she became involved in the women's movement, wrote a number of articles supporting the right of women to obtain a higher education, and worked closely with an organization that provided assistance to working women.

During this time Oleksandra became acquainted with many of the prominent writers of the day and embarked upon a new phase of her literary career. Writing in a modern, impressionistic style, she broadened her themes to include stories about the intelligentsia and explored the concept of psychological individualism in her short stories and sketches.

Dissatisfied with her work in the legal profession, Oleksandra supported herself through writing and private tutoring. In 1917, after her daughter completed high school, she moved with the Kosach family to the country, where she lived until her death in 1924.

The greater part of Hrytsko Hryhorenko's literary legacy consists of her early naturalistic works that are devoted to exposing the harsh conditions and moral decay of peasant life at the turn of the century, and to detailing the desperate measures to which the peasants, especially the women, were driven by adversity. Indeed, her works were written with such brutal honesty, that the critics and readers of her day responded negatively to her writing, accusing her of being overly pessimistic and dwelling solely on the dark side of life. Her later writing, in which she examined the impact of technological and social change on individuals from all levels of society, was no less moving and candid.

Old Man — Young Man

(1898)

"Well . . ." Hrytsko Zanuda said in the tavern on the second day after the funeral of his wife, "we've buried my old woman!" And he sighed heavily, as if he had just hauled in a ponderous sack.

He was saying this, perhaps for the tenth time and, with every repetition, he felt more and more liberated, but he did not want to admit as much in front of the others, and that was why he rubbed first his sweaty brow and then both eyes, one after the other.

"Oh yes, yes indeed, old friend, we've buried her," the gathering affirmed noisily. "So tell the Jew to give us whiskey, and we'll drink in memory of her soul."

Yankel, a slight, agile Jew with long red side curls and a face wrinkled like a dried apple, was already pouring drinks without even being asked. He knew that yesterday they had emptied a barrel of whiskey sending a soul on its way and so, today, they needed to drink to cure their hangovers; he knew this and rejoiced, even though he also knew that if the peasants got good and drunk, they would box his Jewish ears. Well, so what? Feh! As long as they drank—profit above all else!

And today he would, perhaps, hide somewhere or ask them to leave before they reached the point that they would most certainly want to "beat up on a Jew"; or, better still, he would let them drink all day long, let them drink until they were all laid out flat, and then, he, Moshko, and the children could quietly, ever so quietly, lug them out into the street. Yankel laughed out loud as he thought about how the inebriated peasants would sleep in the street by the tavern and then, after awakening in the morning, heap abuse on him, his wife, all the little ones, and Moshko—but that did not matter at all! He did not fear them when they were sober.

"Feh! What's there to be afraid of when they're sober? All I have to do is promise a peasant some wagon-grease or some kerosene for a *kopiyka [penny]*, and he's ready to do anything. And even if he swears at me—so what? Feh! He'll still have to come to me, a Jew, for who else will write an official document for him, if not me? Where else will he go? What can he do without me? When they quarrel among themselves, they always come crawling to me. They won't write anything for each other, even though there are those among them who are literate— although not too many as yet, praise God. How can a peasant get along without a Jew? He'd perish!" This is what Yankel was thinking as he took down one quart of whiskey after another from the shelf—because the whiskey barrel was empty—and he began to pride himself for being very good to the peasants, who, he was sure, could not manage without him.

"Drink up, my *kozak [Cossack]*, drink up; there's no need to worry!" he said, turning around and smiling at Hrytsko.

Hrytsko truly did appear to be worried as he sat at the table, propping up his sizeable head, with its luxuriant, greying crop of hair, with his hands.

"Are you really worried?" one of the men in the group asked.

"Oh, there's no need to worry! The deceased was, in fact, quite old for you. Just wait and see—we'll find somebody for you now! Oh yes, indeed! And in the meantime, old friend, let's drink, as it befits us to do, for the repose of the soul of your old woman."

"Let's," Hrytsko replied, pouring himself a glass of whiskey. "It's no use denying it—she really was too old for me."

"She was too old for you, Uncle Hryhoriy?" asked a tall, swarthy man who looked as if he were carved out of leather.

Hrytsko pretended not to hear; he never liked to listen to anything that was said about his age, because he always thought of himself as being young.

A diminutive man, standing beside the tall swarthy one, tugged him by the sleeve and, barely able to hold back his laughter, said: "Of course she was too old for him. Are you trying to say that you don't know how it is, kinsman Mykhaylo? You see, it's like this—the woman lived and kept on living, so how could she help but grow old?"

Hearing these words, everyone roared with laughter.

"And now we'll convince Khveska Kononykha to marry our good friend Hrytsko. What a pair they'll make—oh, yes indeed!" Everyone laughed even more uproariously.

"Take me as your matchmaker, kinsman Hrytsko, and I'll match you up with whomever you want! And we'll drink again and again! God give you good health!"

The diminutive man downed a drink.

"That was a mouthful, kinsman Vasyl; we should drink again and again!" Mykhalyo said, and he too tossed back a drink.

Hrytsko also drank. They all drank. And then they drank again.

Yankel was happy. His beady eyes darted like mice from one empty bottle to another. "Drink, go ahead and drink it all," he thought, "and pay me for it. And if you don't give me money, you'll pay me with eggs, chickens, or your labour—because if you don't, I won't pay off the tavern. That's the way things are!"

The men drank and drank. Some faces turned pale, while others were flushed and flecked with droplets of sweat like dewdrops on flowers; everyone's eyes were murky, and eyelids drooped; hands trembled and, falling on the table, spontaneously formed either fists or insulting gestures.

At first, they all talked loudly, but later, fell silent, all at the same time. Then, some started shouting threateningly; others cried, and still others either laughed or kissed while singing and whooping it up. It was as if another being entered each man and changed him into the opposite of what he usually was. A shy man became bold; a sad one became happy, while a happy one became sad; a quiet man became garrulous and aggressive; still others would have been glad to give their life for another, to give him everything they had. They stopped thinking about their misery; they no longer knew where they were or why they were there. All that mattered was the whiskey!

Then Hrytsko got a strange feeling that he had forgotten about something at home, that someone was waiting for him there, a woman, or something. When the Jew tried to stop him from leaving, Hrytsko gave him a shove, almost toppling him and, breaking free, staggered out of the tavern and set out for home.

A few men followed Hrytsko out of the tavern and turned their steps homeward. Only the inveterate drunkards remained, and they now began drinking in earnest and smashing the glasses.

The Jew, along with his wife, hid on the bed atop the clay oven—the children had long since fled—and trembled like a sparrow held captive in a human hand. Gone were all his wonderful dreams; gone were his glasses and his money! Cursing and swearing at the damned peasants, he decided that when they showed up the next day he would scare them by threatening to take them to court for the smashed glasses; they would then most certainly pay him for everything, just to keep him quiet, just to ensure that he kept the tavern open!

The Jew gradually regained his composure, and the drunkards, after shouting and raising a ruckus, went off to sleep wherever they happened to fall down. And maybe the odd one even managed to make it all the way home.

When Hrytsko entered the cottage, his daughter-in-law Natalka asked sharply: "Where have you been, father? You were in the tavern, weren't you?"

"What's it to you?" he retorted as he crawled up to the bed atop the clay oven to go to sleep.

He did not want to get into a conversation with his daughter-in-law, because she knew all to well how "to reproach him," and there were times when he himself understood that she was right, but he did not like to admit it. He did, however, speak up once more from his bed: "It's not your money I'm drinking with—it's my own!"

"But Stepan doesn't drink," Natalka said, "and you had plenty to drink at home—and that should have done it! Why go to the tavern? We've gone into debt because of the funeral as it is."

"Stepan! Stepan!" The father was infuriated now. "What does your Stepan mean to me? Is a son supposed to tell his father what to do? After all, wasn't it my wife who died? It's my wife who died—mine! And I'm drinking for her, and that's that!"

"You're drinking for her? How is it going to help her, our late mother, if you drink and waste your money? I'm not saying anything about having a drink at home and at her grave for the repose of her soul—that's how it should be, but to go to the tavern . . . Will her sins be forgiven if you drink and sin?"

"Well, you've pulled out all the stops now! That's enough, I'm telling you, you magpie! Because if I crawl down from this bed, you'll see what I'll do!" Hrytsko threatened her. And then he growled: "I'm drinking with my own money!"

"With your own money!" the daughter-in-law mimicked him. She was a fearless young woman, not overly intimidated by her father-in-law, because he rarely got into fights, even when drunk.

"With your own money!" she repeated. "But wasn't it we— wasn't it Stepan—who bought the boards for the coffin, and paid the priest, and . . ."

"That's enough, I said!" Hrytsko interrupted her and, dismissing her with his hand, tucked himself into bed.

But Natalka could not stop talking—she had to have her say, to chide her father-in-law for the money Stepan had spent burying his mother. The old man should have buried his wife with his own money—not Stepan's. What did Stepan have to do with it?

Her father-in-law, staying out of sight, remained silent, but she would have gone on and on, if Stepan, who had been tending to the cattle in the yard, had not come into the house.

Stepan walked in and, without greeting her or taking off his cap, sat down on the bench.

"Well, did Kutsy lend you some money?" his wife asked, just to say something. She felt sorry for him, thinking: "He's not talking, and that means he's sad."

Stepan did not reply to his wife's question.

"He's still not saying anything!" Natalka reflected. "Maybe he's thinking that his father will get married now; because, as soon as his wife fell ill, the old man bragged he would remarry. If he does get married, all our work on the farm will be for naught!"

"Stepan, will we have supper right away?"

Stepan did not utter so much as a word.

Natalka woke up their little five-year-old daughter Onyska who was sleeping on the hearth; she wanted to feed her before putting her to bed for the night. Onyska, all rosy and warm from her nap, was as cheerful as ever. Chattering rapidly, without pausing, she repeated the word "mummy" with every breath.

"Mummy, will we have *halushky [dumplings]* for thupper? Mummy, did you thee the mill Ivanka made? Mummy, is Makthym thleeping?"

Maksym was her little brother, and he sometimes made Onyska laugh because he did not talk yet; he only squealed and cried. She had taken it upon herself to teach him how to talk and walk, saying: "He doethn't know how to walk at all—not at all; you thtand him up—and he fallth wight down. It'th vewy funny!"

Onyska scampered over to the cradle to see if Maksym was sleeping. He was. Turning around and hopping a few times, she looked at her mother, who was standing with a bowl in the middle of the room, and then at her father. She seemed to be on the verge of saying something, but then changed her mind.

Glancing around the room, she recalled something and began lamenting: "Oh dear God! Where ith our gwanny? They've buwied gwanny in a hole—thump-thump! Daddy, why are you thweating?" she asked, snuggling up to her father, who was wiping his eyes and face with his sleeve. "Daddy, are you thweating?"

"No, I'm not sweating, sweetheart, I'm just . . . that is . . . a little . . . Listen, we'd better eat. Give us our supper, Natalka!"

Hearing this, Natalka cheered up, turned around, and began to fill the bowl with *halushky.*

"But where's father?' Stepan asked.

"He's sleeping over there, on the oven-bed, and he's feeling no pain!" Natalka said.

Stepan knew that Natalka was angry at his father; he felt angry himself. Nevertheless, he said: "Why don't you call him to eat?"

"Father! Father! Come and have some supper!" Natalka called.

There was no reply from the oven-bed.

"He's sleeping off his righteous labours." Natalka smiled, waved her hand and, picking up a spoon, took her place at the bowl.

"Mummy," the irrepressible Onyska began jabbering once again after downing a few dumplings. "Mummy, did you thee the mill Ivanka Buhayiv built? Mummy, it turnth and waveth its wingth thith way and that way—did you thee it, mummy?"

Before her mother had a chance to reply, Onyska started in again: "Mummy, why did they bind gwanny'th feet?"

"That's how it's supposed to be—it's a muslin veil."

"That'th how it'th thuppothed to be," Onyska repeated, "thuppothed to be . . . muthlin veil . . . muthlin veil." And she fell silent for a moment.

The father and the mother also ate without saying anything.

"Now it'th a thin for me to wear wed flowerth, I have to wear gween ones," the little girl sighed.

"Why?" her father asked, either not hearing or understanding what she said.

"Becauthe gwanny died—that'th why," the wise little one replied and then fell silent.

Natalka found Onyska so amusing that she had to cover her mouth with her hand to stop herself from laughing.

"Mummy, how tathty the honey was at the funewal dinner!" the little girl continued. "Oh, I can thtill tathte the thweetneth in my mouth! Mummy, why did it thmell tho bad in the houthe when gwanny wath lying on the bench? Mummy, when will gwanny get up out of that hole?"

"Put her to bed, so she doesn't make our hearts ache with her jabbering," Stepan said, rising from the bench.

Natalka began putting Onyska to sleep. The little girl was still chattering; she recalled the market she had recently been at with her father and the gold rings a Jew had been wearing.

"Well, I weally wanted to twy on one of them, at leatht one of thothe bwight . . . gol. . . . den . . . wingth," and, saying this, Onyska fell asleep.

Her granny's funeral, the market, and Ivanka's little mill were all equally fascinating to Onyska, and so it is little wonder that they all came to mind simultaneously.

Natalka and her husband began counting up how much they had spent on the funeral.

"It looks like we'll have to sell the heifer, or something else, in order to pay off all the debts," Stepan reflected. "We'll probably have to sell the heifer . . . First there was the birth of our son, and then mother died—it's impossible to get out of debt!"

"He's the one who should be paying for it," Natalka said, "But you're taking it all upon yourself—God only knows why."

"Well, what can I do, if that's how things have turned out? I couldn't keep mother laid out on the bench here for a week! And he kept saying: 'There's no money!' Where the devil is the money he got for threshing for the lord? He earned a daily wage all fall, flailing grain and working alongside the threshing machine."

"He drank it all up—squandered it foolishly, that's where!" Natalka said angrily. "Now we'll have to sell the cow, and she's already with calf, so we would have had milk soon! And now the children won't have any milk! Oh, I'm so unfortunate, so very unfortunate—from my cradle to my grave!" And Natalka burst into tears.

Stepan interrupted impatiently: "Stop crying!"

"Listen," he continued, speaking slowly, as if talking to himself. "I've been thinking that maybe we should do something like this: the receipt that I'm to give Kutsy for the money—I haven't given him one yet—maybe I should write it in my father's name, as if he entrusted me to get the money, and then . . . Yes, indeed, let him pay it off himself as best he can. It's not up to me to bury his wife. And that's that. He'll remarry, and all that should have been mine will be lost. I'm right, aren't I? But, then again, maybe I shouldn't do that with the receipt?" he asked his wife.

"Of course you should; of course you should do that, and you'll do the right thing if you do," Natalka encouraged him. And then she asked, genuinely alarmed: "Is he really planning to get married?"

"There's no doubt about it. Uncle Vasyl, the scoundrel, is trying to set him up with Khveska Kononykha; he was joking about it when mother was still alive. Where would we and our children go then?"

"But she won't marry him! Not she! She's about half his age!"

Natalka was nonplussed when she thought of Khveska, a spry, cheerful young woman, whose husband had been sent to prison not so long ago for stealing.

"But wait, Stepan; she has a husband, so how can that be?"

"So what if she does? They say he's going to be deported to Siberia, and then she'll be free to get married . . . But that's not the point . . . Where will we and our children go if there's a new mistress in this cottage? Just tell me that, if you can!"

Natalka turned pale and, flapping her arms like a mother eagle, cried: "No, Stepan, that will never happen! I won't let him get married and treat my children unjustly! No!"

Stepan looked at his wife and said: "You won't let him?" Then, after remaining silent for a moment, he added: "Well, we'll see how things work out, but right now we'd better go to bed, because we have to get some sleep as well."

As Natalka cleared the bowls and spoons from the table, she kept thinking that under no circumstances would she allow her father-in-law to remarry; she had faith in herself and her strength, and even looked forward to fighting for herself and her children and, in the long run, getting her way.

Her husband was thinking his own thoughts. He foresaw—there could be no doubt about it—that his father would get married and start a new family. It would become crowded in the cottage; there would be quarrelling, discord, dissension. "Her" children would abuse his, and he would not be able to do anything about it, because it was his father's house.

"Well, let him at least pay for the funeral," Stepan thought angrily. But then he had second thoughts. It became clear to him that he, like his father, had an obligation to pay for his mother's funeral; it was as if two voices were speaking within him: "She was his wife," and "She was your mother."

"I don't want 'him' to squander his money on whiskey instead of using it for the matter at hand," he thought, "but all the same, I'll have to sign the receipt in my own name . . . Natalka says that we should . . . but no, she's just angry with my father . . ."

And Stepan began to realise that he would never do what he had threatened to do. Why wouldn't he do it? The devil only knows! Did he not have enough courage, or what? He cursed himself for being the way he was, but all the same he could not do suddenly, abruptly, in a single stroke, whatever came to mind. At first, he would think one way, but then he would think things over—and in the end he could not do it; it was not fitting. And that was how it always was—he did not do what he at first had wanted to do. He deluded himself.

Natalka made up the bed. They turned out the light and lay down to sleep.

When Hrytsko awoke, the moon was weaving its silver threads throughout the house. He kept turning over on one side, and then on the other—but could not fall asleep again. Finally, he looked up at the moon and began thinking about all sorts of things.

During these past two days he had not given any thought to his dead wife. There were all the problems connected with the funeral, and then there was the whiskey to be drunk, and he was always in the public eye, always in a group—and there was no time to think about her. At night—both on the night of her death and of her funeral—there was the *kanun [a funeral dish of spiced, diluted honey],* the candles that burned all night long, and the people who sat around, talking incessantly, turning his thoughts away from her. In the daytime, his head was befogged with whiskey and so, when he did think about a wife, he thought of a young, healthy, new wife. He did not know yet what this new wife would be like, but he conjured up a woman who looked a lot like Khveska and a little like his deceased wife when he married her— a lively young woman—and he seemed to have forgotten about his old wife who had just died. But now, all of a sudden, he recalled her as a sick woman with swollen legs, who looked frightful—her face had yellowed like leaves in autumn.

How she regretted dying! And yet, it really should not have mattered to her! She had lived long enough already, and her illness had exhausted her completely and was grinding her down as if she were in a mortar dish, but no—she still said: "Oh, how I wish it were some other person who was dying, and I was going to be burying him! It's hard . . . ever so hard . . . I don't want to die!"

"And it may well be that she died more from fear than from anything else," Hrytsko thought, "because her daughter and daughter-in-law, thinking that her end was almost upon her, put a candle in her hands. And, when she saw the candle, she began to shake all over and groaned heavily: 'Oh, what's happened? Have I died already? Oh, what are you doing to me, my dear children? Would to God that you were the ones who were about to die, my dear children, if you're burying me alive in my grave!'

"And she groaned again and actually did begin to die. Otherwise, she would still be dragging it out, and her legs would have gone on swelling . . . Well, now I'll get married, and I'll take myself a young wife, one that's beautiful! I wonder who it will be? A girl or a widow? But she really didn't want me to marry a second time; it got so that . . ."

Something rustled in a dark corner where the moon's rays did not reach; something whispered and scratched, as if dragging its claws over glass . . .

"Is it true what they say, that corpses come at night to visit the living?" he asked himself suddenly, like a bolt out of the blue, and began listening intently.

Something knocked . . . again . . . Now it sounded as if the door had squeaked . . . Hrytsko raised himself on his elbows, and listened even harder—there was nothing more to be heard! And a thought flashed through his head: "What nonsense! It's those damned mice!"

But then something truly did begin to walk around with bare feet, slapping them down on the floor . . .

Hrytsko turned his back to the room and tried to reassure himself: "After all, my children never came to me after they died. It's sheer nonsense! But no, something is actually walking about. What can it be?"

It seemed to him that something was moving across the floor, grabbing at the bench, the table, the oven . . .

"Oh, oh! What's going to happen? No, praise God, I can't hear it any more . . . I'm going to sleep!" Determined to fall asleep, he covered himself well with a blanket, but sleep would not come.

"Why didn't I get her that apple?" he thought. "They say that a dying person's last wish should be fulfilled. So why didn't I get her that apple? Why didn't I buy it for her? Huh? Why?"

He closed his eyes and tried to fall asleep, but the thought continued to plague him. Before his tightly shut eyes, white muslin veils began to float by endlessly; it was as if the entire world were being wrapped in white muslin, first in one direction and then in the other . . . Were these veils, so fine and so silvery, extending from the moon?

Afraid to open his eyes now, he wrapped himself so securely in the blanket that he became very warm, but he crouched beneath it and did not throw it off. There was a buzzing in his ears, as if someone were pacing the floor, talking, arguing . . .

Then he recalled that it was right here—on this oven-bed, in the very same spot where he was now lying—that his wife had died. And it seemed to him that under those veils stretching from the moon into the house, someone's bluish legs appeared, someone's cold legs . . . only legs . . . Legs as long as a woman were lying beside him, right next to him; they were lying there—swollen, and so blue that they were almost black; there was no head, just legs; everywhere there were legs, ice-cold legs, and those icy legs were touching him . . . He tried to move away, but the cold emanating from them pierced him to the bone . . .

And now it seemed to him that these legs were crawling on him, that this "woman-legs" was crawling on him, choking him, shaking him and saying: "How much longer are you going to live?" Just as one time, in a drunken stupor, he had choked his ailing wife and yelled: "How much longer are you going to live?"

Cold perspiration beaded Hrytsko's brow, but he felt hot.

"Oh, save me!" he shouted hoarsely like a madman and, flinging off the coarse hempen sheet, clawed at the collar of his shirt.

Then he sat up and slowly regained his senses.

It was dawning and gradually growing light, but in the cottage it was still dark. Stepan and Natalka were sleeping, and little Onyska, rapidly mumbling something in her sleep, sounded as if she were gurgling. His scream had not awoken anyone.

"You see," Hrytsko thought angrily, "the two of them aren't scared because they're together, and so they're sleeping soundly. Well, it will be daylight soon, and nothing will come now. I'll go to sleep for a while as well."

He lay down again but, as soon as he started to doze, it immediately seemed to him that something cold was lying beside him; he groped around—the oven-bed was warm; he shut his eyes—the cold, swollen legs were beside him again, stretching all the way from his head to his feet!

Hrytsko was overwhelmed by a great need to have something that was alive, something warm beside him. It was terrifying to lie in bed all by himself and so, even though he wanted to sleep ever so badly, he simply could not. Finally, he crawled down from the oven-bed, went outdoors, and roamed about aimlessly until his children got up.

Hrytsko always thought of himself as a young man—eternally young! But then, all of our villagers think they are young, because no one knows exactly how old he is. Who can say for certain if he is thirty or thirty-five? But, if he lives to be old, then he knows he is really old, because his hair turns grey, and he does not want to sing, or dance, or sit out in the street for any length of time. His hands and feet do not move as quickly as they used to, and he is tempted to lie around on the oven-bed. And he begins to cough a bit and does not see too well, or hear too well—and, of course, all of this means that he is old.

But Hrytsko Zanuda never experienced anything like that—he was always young and that was that! He sang, played the *sopilka [shepherd's flute],* and even danced with enthusiasm—he was a convivial man! He sported a flashy buckle, a red shirt, and a vest with gold buttons; he parted his hair to one side, did not grow a beard, joked with the girls—wherever there were womenfolk, he was sure to be there—so what else could he be, but young?

Even as a young man, Hrytsko had not farmed. Preferring to hire himself out, he would give a small portion of what he earned to his father who, during his lifetime, farmed the land with his eldest son; a third son died while serving his stint in the army. Later, after his father and older brother were dead, Hrytsko gave part of his earnings to his grown-up son, who had married and taken over the land. The remainder of the money he would spend on liquor and clothing, and then he would go off to earn some more.

Hrytsko did not like to remain in one place for long, nor did he like to stay at home with his wife and children. He was like a guest in his own house, and when he was away from it he behaved like a bachelor—cheerful, lively, and carefree! He spent time at home only when his brother, father, and children were being buried, and when he married off his daughter and his son. Once his son was settled, he left the running of the household to him and went out into the world, coming home only occasionally to criticise the young man and tell him that he did not know how to do anything—how to plough, or seed, or mow.

And when his son responded by saying: "Then do it yourself; stay home and do it," he just ignored him and went away again.

When he worked nearby as a day labourer, he did come home now and again, but did he stay long? He was there on feast days, on Sundays, and in the evening when he came home to sleep. But, as for the rest of the week, his family did not see him. On the odd day that he did stay at home, he would sit around, think of something that should be done, do it very well, and then brag about it for the rest of the month.

"Just look," he would say to his son, "at the gate that I built (or manger, or whatever); never in the world would you be able to do it as well; this is how things should be done—look and learn!"

But it was too late now for Stepan to learn; moreover, his father did not tell him how to do anything—he just did it himself and then reproached his son for not knowing how to go about it.

Stepan had grown up with his grandfather, his uncle, and his mother, but without his father. His grandfather and his uncle— who did not have any children—often scolded him when he was little, but did not teach him anything. And his mother spoiled him. Not having learned how to do anything properly, Stepan was ridiculed by others when he grew up, and so he became a timid man—he never knew if things should be done this way, or that way. He would think about things and stew over them for a long time before he finally made a decision; or, he would ask his wife and then do whatever she told him to do.

Hrytsko was accustomed to working for others from childhood. His father had hired him out, as the youngest son, so that there would be money coming in to the farm. After the death of the eldest son, the father, complaining that he found it difficult to take care of things by himself, tried to stop Hrytsko from leaving home to find work. Hrytsko, however, continually ran away; he was used to working for other people, to being in a group, to working on the wide open steppe, where he usually worked as a herder.

Ten or more young herdsmen would gather together—and they felt so free, so happy! They would play, sing, and cut *sopilky [shepherds' flutes]* from elder trees. And the boundless steppe rolled away to the horizon, right up to the blue sky, and the cattle dispersed into the distance . . .

My God, how beautiful the steppe is in the springtime, in the summer . . . It is always beautiful! In the spring, the grass grows so quickly that it seems to be vying with itself; the sky turns blue, ever so blue and, over it float fleecy clouds—white as lambs and fluffy as soft feathers—and occasional pink patches tinged with gold and silver. Forgetting about the cold and the snow, about weariness, everything comes to life at the same time—the trees, the grass, the sky, the clouds, and the earth; everything—as if deliberately pruned—grows and thrives, pushing ever onwards.

Every stem, every blade of grass, every tiny weed seems to be bragging: "I'm growing!" "Just look at me now." "I'm ever so big already." "I . . . I . . . I . . ." "I'm growing swiftly." "I'm growing even more swiftly." "And we're blooming already!" And truly, the cherry orchards in the village are completely white, as if they have been dipped in milk. Hastening to catch up with them, the apple and pear trees begin to blossom, and they bloom together amiably, in great profusion! What wonderful blossoms, and what an intoxicating fragrance! You want to take all of them, heap them into a huge mound and, lying down on top of it, press them to your face, to yourself, spread them out and gather them in again, crush them and knead them with your hands! In the village, fruit trees burst into bloom and, out on the steppe, flowers do not lag far behind—with daisies and toadflax rushing into view and stretching in yellow bands across the green fields. There are flowers everywhere! Blooming at first only over here, along the edge of the field, they are now spreading far and wide—racing off into the distance!

Hrytsko would lie down and press his ear to the ground: "By God, it's breathing—the earth's mighty chest is breathing, rising and falling, straining and falling silent again . . ."

This is what Hrytsko thought about the earth, but then he would begin to think about the sun: "What is the sun? Maybe it's a sack filled with gold coins that pour down from the heavens? But if so, they should fall somewhere, shouldn't they? Who gathers them? Probably the lords . . . Where exactly do they fall? But maybe the sun is a lamp hanging in the sky? Is it kerosene that burns in it? Why does it burn so long and so brightly? Who fills it with kerosene?"

Such thoughts about the sun occurred to Hrytsko mostly in the summer, when the sun blazes, blazes intemperately, and when it is possible to say about everything—it is the sun's doing; the kernels, dry and dark, begin to shell—it is the sun; a man, feeling as if he were on fire inside, longs for shade and water—it is the sun; the youths, including Hrytsko himself, lie down and sleep wherever they happen to be—it is the sun; the ground cracks, disintegrates like sand, and pleads daily for rain—it is the sun; it is arid and bright, and the cloudless sky is shiny and hot—it is the sun; the grass burns, yellows and gives off a scorched aroma that drifts over the steppe—it is the sun; the sun is everywhere, and it is always—the sun!

What is the sun? What is it made of? No one knows. When he was little, Hrytsko also did not know, and when he grew up these thoughts of his were pushed out of his mind by his work, his drinking-bouts, and his fascination with girls.

In autumn, the steppe becomes deserted. The peasants gather in the grain, the heavily grazed pasture-land becomes barren, and the ploughed fields, like slashed flesh torn away from its skin, turn black; an odour of sweat hangs in the air. The empty, boundless steppe seems more vast. The wind hums as if it alone is the master here. At times it is so strong that it sweeps up everything and carries it away in all directions; blowing fiercely, racing along, and tearing things up, it turns the very soil itself into a cloud of dust. The trees fight and shove each other, the grass deserts the fields, and dust-clouds rise in columns, whipping up ridges in the road.

Oh, the songs, the songs that the wind sings then, keening in a reedy woman's voice, roaring like a bull, weeping ever so sorrowfully, as if it were being restrained, held back by someone, and then rumbling like two men quarrelling and shouting . . . two men, then three, then four, and then a whole legion of them—like a drunken crowd caught up in a raging lament!

The wind terrifies Hrytsko, especially if he has to be out in the steppe at night, when clouds blanket the sky, hiding the stars and the moon, when all one can see is darkened human backs and looming walls, intent on creeping up on people. And such a fear seizes all the herdsmen that, talking and shouting as loudly as they can, they try to light a huge bonfire; but the wind continues to blow—roaring, whistling, mocking them—and the fire will not burn. The youths are left in darkness. It is cold. A light rain begins to drizzle, and the tiny droplets feel like cold, sharp needles. Everything cools off, grows cold; it is clear that winter is approaching. Soon the grazing will come to an end.

When winter comes, Hrytsko will help to drive the cattle herds to St. Petersburg to sell them there. A large number of hired men will make the trip. They have a good time on their way there and are happy to return with some money—because once the cattle are sold, the master pays them for their summer work. And it is exhilarating to travel through so many different parts of the country, to see all kinds of people.

Hrytsko knew very little about the steppe in the winter, when, after smiling briefly in its green coverlet of winter rye, it loses its strength, lies down, grows dumb, and folds its long feather-like wings—wings that were fresh and green in spring, gold in summer, grey and black in autumn, and white in winter—and die. But what if it did die! Such a death is not terrible because spring will return, birds will fly back, and the steppe will regain its vigour and youthfulness; it will once again come alive, rejoice, and be reinvigorated. And Hrytsko too will be rejuvenated and begin to live, drink, sing, dance, and play anew.

He played skilfully, really skilfully. He had ever so many *sopilky*—short ones, long ones, and some with five, six, and more finger holes in them. He also had a *dudka [a pipe]* that looked like a trumpet; it was fashioned out of wood and had a tin watering can fastened on one end of it. Having made this "apparatus" himself, he bragged greatly about it. And truly, when he blew into it, he could be heard from a long way off.

But Hrytsko not only sang and played well, he was also a marvellous storyteller. In his lifetime, he had heard and seen many things. The stories that he related were always about thieves and robbers, but he narrated them in such a cheerful voice and laughed so often, that everyone listening to him began to feel happy and, because of this, people liked him. And the women and girls liked him most of all. Whenever they happened to be working together, he would always help them, joke with them, and kiss them. When he hired himself out far away from home, few people knew that he was married and, even though they knew he was not so young and heard from his friends that he was married, they found it hard to believe.

But you must not think that Hrytsko knew only how to sing and joke; he was also very dextrous and knew how to do everything. No one could say where he had learned to do things—he must have been born with such a nature that no matter what was required, he knew what to do, how to go about it, and how to get it done. It may be that he learned how to do things by watching others as they worked, but, be that as it may, he knew how to do everything—and he certainly liked to boast about it.

Once he started to brag there was no getting away from him: "I know how to do such and such, and I can do this and that . . ."

All the same, people thought of Hrytsko as a clever, hard-working man. He earned quite a lot of money, but he spent much of it on drinking; indeed, his love of whiskey often cost him his job but—he still did not stop drinking. He would try to do without whiskey for a while, and then he would break down, drink more than enough to make up for his abstinence, and treat all his friends while he was at it.

And so, when Hrytsko came up with a plan to get married, it was quite the plan. The people had many a good laugh at the ridiculous figure that he cut. He purchased an accordion, bought himself a green belt, and began to act like a young man. People laughed and pointed at him when he walked down the street on a workday playing the accordion; they laughed but, at the same time, they drank with his money and courted first this widow and then that one on his behalf.

These widows, while jokingly agreeing that Hrytsko could send matchmakers, laughed and talked among themselves: "May his father go berserk! Who would marry him? He's so old!"

Even those who had a lot of children thought that Hrytsko "was very old already." It was Khveska Kononykha who laughed more than anyone else, and she was so obnoxious about it! She pretended to be nice, as if she would gladly marry Hrytsko and, while drinking with him on the ninth day after the death of his wife, flirted with him outrageously, making him lose his wits completely. When matters came to a head, however, she sharply refused his matchmakers, saying: "Let him go to the devil! I'm not the woman for him!"

Later, when Hrytsko ran into her and began berating her, she put on a great act of being saintly and pious, blaming her refusal on her husband who was in prison.

"I'd marry you most willingly," she said. "But my cursed husband will be in prison for two more years, and I can't marry someone else during that time; I'll be free to get married only after he's been deported to Siberia . . . Otherwise I'd be more than willing . . . But I didn't speak ill of you, God forbid! I would never do that! The people are lying . . . I'd be most willing . . ."

Behind Hrytsko's back, Khveska once again ridiculed him and told the women how he preened in front of her mirror, convinced that he was young and handsome! Khveska, imitating the slight lisp with which Hrytsko talked—he was missing a tooth—told them: "He promised me that if I married him I would have 'heapth of money.' He would buy me a 'prethent,' and I would 'alwayth drink tea with thugar'—he really likes to drink tea, he got this habit from the Russians—and he's saying that even now a certain lord has sent him five telegrams asking him to come and work for him, but he doesn't want to. And this lord 'liveth in a foretht and hath a hundred hortheth and a hundred cowth,' and he told Hrytsko: 'When you get married you can pick the betht cow and any horthe you want; I won't begrudge you anything, becauthe you're a man like no other, because you know how to work! Take both the money and the wallet . . .'"

Some people laughed, but others worried.

Stepan and Natalka most certainly were not laughing. Stepan tried to figure out ways of dissuading his father from getting married, but he never carried out his plans. Should he perhaps ask his father to take pity on his grandchildren? But the old man would never listen to anything like this—of what concern were his son's children to him? Should he demand that his father build him a new house? But where would he get the money to do this? Should he ask him why the devil he wanted to get married in his old age? But did his father not know that he was old? He would just chase him away angrily, and that would be that! Should he demand that he be paid for what he had put into his father's farm? But would his father not say that he too had worked and contributed to it? Should he take him to court? But he did not want to bring shame on himself or his father.

And so, he did not do anything, just looked daggers at his father, and avoided talking to him. Natalka, however, knew how to talk to her father-in-law in such a manner that he had no desire to remain in his own house. As soon as he came home, be it for lunch or for supper, she immediately went on the attack: "Why do you need to get married, father? Do you have little children, or what?"

At first, he claimed that he needed a wife because there was no one to wash his clothes or spin for him. His daughter-in-law vowed that she would be very willing to do all that, just so that he would not bring her family to ruination. Then Hrytsko became angry and said: "Why shouldn't I get married, since I'm still young?"

At this point Natalka could not refrain from laughing: "But father, you're old! Just look, even your hair is grey!"

"It's turning grey, because I grease it with oil," Hrytsko retorted sharply and walked out of the house, thinking all the while: "Why didn't I beat her up, that stupid Natalka, so she wouldn't mention my grey hair again? I'll go and beat her up now . . . Oh, the devil take it! I'll get married no matter what she says, and she'll lose out anyway! Let her talk!"

There were times when Natalka attacked Stepan: "Why don't you tell father that you won't let him get married?"

Stepan would just spread his hands helplessly and say: "But what can I do? Just think about it; he's my father—and I'm his son; so what can I do? If I were the father I'd know what to do, but the way things are—what can I do?"

Natalka would look at him and grow angry; she realised that there would be no help from Stepan. You might say that he was overly timid; but no, he would go into the forest at night and, when he was still a youth, he hauled the mail with such huge horses that another man might not have been able to hold them in check. It was just that he ruminated for a long time and never knew on which foot to stand, or what it would be better to do. Another man might simply say something or do something and get it over with, but to him it always seemed to be this way on the one hand, and that way on the other hand.

Natalka knew very well what was good, what was not good, and what was better. Now, it was up to her and her alone to save their children from misfortune. And so she would approach her father-in-law time and again. She would say that if he did not do badly by them, she would cater to him, as one caters to a little child. And then she would say that all the people were laughing at him because he was acting like a young man, and said that it would be better if he broke that accordion on her head, instead of walking through the village with it and making—excuse the word—a "fool" of himself.

After listening to her, Hrytsko would boil over and shove her away. She would not say another word; instead, she would send Onyska to him. The little girl would begin to cuddle up to her grandfather, chattering away and amusing him. He would put her on his knee and play the *sopilka* for her. And Onyska, slobbering all over the *sopilka*, would also try to play it, making it squeak like a mosquito.

At such times, Natalka would approach Hrytsko again, trying once more to persuade him not to marry.

Onyska, not fully understanding what her mother was saying, would intrude into the conversation: "Don't get mawwied, gwandpa, don't get mawwied—it'th not good." And she would shake her head.

"Why, you silly thing?" the grandfather asked.

"The's going to beat uth," the little girl said with terror in her eyes, even though who this "she" was, she really did not know.

And then the grandfather would begin to brag and tell the little girl all sorts of stories about how rich they would be if he got married—although who knew how it was that they were to become rich?—how they would drink tea with sweet sugar.

"What ith thugar like?" Onyska wanted to know.

"It's sweet, very sweet."

"Like honey?"

"Oh no! It's better than honey," he would reply, "and it's white, like snow. You'll see!"

"Buy me a gingerbwead cookie!" the little girl begged. She had no way of knowing what sugar was like, but she knew very well what gingerbread was and wanted to ask her grandfather for some while he was still in a good mood.

"I'll buy you one when I get married," her grandfather said. "And I won't buy just one, I'll buy ten, twenty—ever so many!"

"Ever tho many . . . ever tho many . . ." Onyska repeated after him and then added: "Get mawwied, gwandpa. Come on, get mawwied wight away . . . buy me a gingerbwead cookie. Oh Lord, I want one tho badly!"

Natalka, hearing what the grandfather was saying, stormed out of the house, slamming the door so hard that the lime fell off the walls. She could not bear to hear such nonsense, to listen to it. She wanted to tell him off, to lash out at him, but, no matter what he said, he was still the father; her tongue itched to say something, and she wanted to quarrel—so it was better to leave.

"Why doeth gwandpa have gingerbwead cookieth when we don't have any?" Onyska continued. "Oh, how I want thome gingerbwead, I want thome . . . Buy thome wight away, gwandpa."

Her grandfather fell silent and did not reply. He was now engrossed in his thoughts about getting married.

At other times, when Natalka began talking, Hrytsko would look long and hard at her without answering. She could see that he had not heard a word of what she had said.

And then he would say: "I need a wife, yes I do!"

Natalka, embarrassed, would think: "Has the old man gone mad?" One time, totally distraught, she began to weep in front of her father-in-law, enjoining him not to treat her children badly.

He consoled her: "Don't cry, silly! What's wrong with you? Everything will be fine."

Her father-in-law then spoke softly to her, saying that she would be better off; a new mother-in-law would help her and take care of the children during the harvest. He said that it would be possible to build his son a new house, a separate one, if they found they could not live together.

It may be that he truly believed that everything would be fine, but Natalka could not believe it. Her heart sensed that it would not be as her father-in-law was saying, and that he would not have enough money to build a new house for his son; and so she cried.

When Hrytsko, ignoring his daughter-in-law's tears, kept on courting women, she became infuriated. Continually cursing her father-in-law, she complained about him to others. Earlier she had referred to him as "weak,"—and said that if any of the womenfolk dared to marry him, she would chase the old codger out of the house with a poker and scratch his eyes out. Natalka wanted to present herself as an evil person, as a usurper, so that all the eligible women would fear her as they feared fire. She swore, using terrible words that she had never used before, and her voice seemed to grow stronger; her eyes bulged strangely, and she attacked the neighbouring women threateningly, as if every one of them intended to marry Hyrtsko Zanuda.

But one thing made Natalka happy—none of the women wanted to marry her father-in-law; all of them considered him "very old." Even those who were getting on in years themselves or were of an age with him, thought of him as being older. This delighted Natalka, and, beginning to think that victory was hers, she was ready to laugh at her father-in-law, saying that "there was no bride for him in the whole world."

Hrytsko was not yet ready to give up; he wanted to carry out his wish and now, more than ever, he believed that he most certainly had to get married, that it was not possible for him to be without a wife.

It was his older sister who contributed a great deal to keeping him out of kilter by saying to him: "A man can't be without a wife; no, he can't be; he simply can't be."

But what good would it do her to have her brother get married? Well, who could tell why she was confusing the man.

Natalka had already quarrelled with her, saying both behind her back and directly to her: "But really, aren't you ashamed? You're so old already!"

But the sister kept on prattling and telling Hrytsko what she thought he ought to do.

When everyone refused him, Hrytsko grew angrier and angrier, but he remained convinced that he would eventually attain his goal. Now he walked around in such a bad mood that even Natalka was afraid to approach him; she bided her time, waiting for him to come to his senses and abandon his courting, since it was obvious to her that no one wanted to marry him. She concluded that the matter would end at that. What she thought, however, was not in line with how Hrytsko behaved.

He courted women everywhere—throughout his own village and wherever his drunken friends, by way of a joke, took him. But he could not win a woman's hand anywhere, regardless of his assertions that he was still young, regardless of the promises he made that he would earn money and chase his son and daughter-in-law out of his house, regardless of how much he complained about his fate that had tied him to a woman—his former wife— who was sickly and ugly, and ten years older. And once he even said that his wife had been a widow when she married him.

But, no matter what he said, and no matter how much the matchmakers extolled his virtues—nothing worked! Hrytsko concluded that the women were afraid of his daughter-in-law—he had heard her bragging that she would rip out the eyes of her new mother-in-law—and he vowed that he would chase both her and his son out of his home as soon as he got married.

More than once he complained that all this would not have happened in days gone by when the lords made the laws. "The lord would immediately have ordered the most beautiful girl to marry me," he said in the tavern, where he now spent much of his time.

Hrytsko had begun to drink so heavily that Yankel was beside himself with happiness. And, when he was drunk, it seemed to him that everyone was insulting him, especially the women who had such a good laugh at his expense. He would have liked to beat them all up; more to the point, he wanted to have a wife of his own to beat up. Well, before long, he would have one!

"I'll beat her, and then I'll pity her and hug her . . . How warm you are, how soft, my sweetheart!" These were the thoughts that preoccupied old Hrytsko.

He wanted to have something alive, something of his own, his very own, something that belonged solely to him, something very dear to him, something he could caress or not caress, depending on how he felt; something he could be master of, that no one could take away from him, and that would not flee of its own accord; something that could not be separated from him, that would be, as it were, a part of him, so that, because of it, he would live twice, three times as vigorously as he lived now. This is why Hrytsko wanted to get married; or perhaps it was because even though he bragged that he was young, the years were creeping up on him, and he wanted to settle in one place, in his own house, with his own wife, in his own oven-bed.

Hrytsko viewed everyone who counselled him against getting married as his enemy, even little Onyska, because she had recently said to him as she hopped about on one foot: "Get mawwied gwandpa, get mawwied tomowwow with a thack." And had instantly followed it up with a question: "Gwandpa, gwandpa, what kind of a thack ith it?"

Instead of answering her, the grandfather pulled her ear, and after that she cried in Natalka's arms for a long time, whimpering: "You thee what he'th like . . . He pulled my ear . . . pulled my ear . . . I don't want him to do that again . . ."

Hrytsko wanted to have a wife but, as he himself said: "The devil take it, where am I to get one?"

Finally he came up with an answer—he would go courting in a distant village.

He went away, courted a woman, and got married! He took as his wife a woman who had five children—three girls and two boys.

If Motrya had not agreed to marry him, then Hrytsko would have died a widower. He had made up his mind that he would try to get married for one last time in another village, and if it did not work out, then that was that! It would mean that Natalka was right; it would mean that he ought to take pity on his son. But Motrya did marry him. So it had been his fate to get married— he was not so old after all.

Hrytsko got married. Where had Natalka been that she allowed such a thing to happen? She was so sure that the father would not get married, that no one would accept him, no matter where he went courting. And when people gleefully told her that her father-in-law had sneaked off to find himself a wife, and that the deal had already been sealed with a drink, and that the wedding would take place on Sunday, she was sure they were lying.

When her father-in-law came home, she tried to find out what was going on, saying: "You can beat me, or even hack me to death, but I won't allow a wife of yours to come into this house!"

Hrytsko smiled grimly and quickly fled without saying anything. That was when Natalka realised that people had been telling her the truth. She pounced on Stepan, telling him to saddle up the mare as quickly as possible, go to the village where his father had found himself a wife, and try to talk the bride out of marrying him. But Stepan said that maybe people were fooling them and that there was no way of knowing in which village it was, or who, or what. Was he to travel throughout the entire district or what? He did, however, tell some other people to pass on defamatory remarks about his father to Hrytsko's bride, informing her that she and her children would be badly off, because his father was a man who promised one thing, but did another, and that he drank a lot. But none of it helped, and his father got married!

Well, if Natalka had been able to confront the father she would have read him the riot act, but he had gone away and vanished, and no one saw him in the village for several days. She was ready to go by horse, or even on foot, to set the father free, but it was cold, and her child was small, and it was far, and Stepan was the way he was. She scolded her husband and railed at him, until he became so angry that he smashed her distaff; a little while later, he was ready to obey her but, before that happened, his father, wasting no time, got married.

Natalka had missed the opportunity, and all was lost!

On the day of the wedding, when the bride was driving home from church, Natalka was furious—so furious that Stepan had to restrain her from creating a scandal and giving the villagers more reason to laugh at them. The marriage ceremony had taken place in the village where the bride lived and, therefore, Natalka could not prevent it. If it had been in her church, do you suppose that Natalka would not have interfered? That she would not have gone to the priest and broken up the marriage ceremony?

All the same, as soon as Natalka saw her new mother-in-law, she began to growl: "Oh, the scurvy woman! She's come to chase other people's children out of someone else's house!"

"What is it you're saying, my dear?" the mother-in-law asked.

Natalka had to fall silent but, in her anger, smashed a few dishes, smacked Onyska, and refused to do anything for the wedding. She did not tidy up the house, or give any of her bread for the wedding meal. Consumed by her fury, she prowled around, constantly on guard, waiting like a dog for a chance to sink her teeth into her new mother-in-law.

The bride, however, did not give her any reason to do so. She appeared to be very friendly and quiet, both on the wedding day and the day after. Always addressing Natalka as: "Sweetheart, my darling, my precious," she asked about everything—how to go about doing things—as if she were the junior person, not Natalka; as if Natalka were the mistress. And the more gruffly Natalka responded, the nicer and sweeter she became.

And the father was ever so happy! He truly appeared to have grown younger! He bought Onyska some gingerbread and sweet buns, gave Natalka a kerchief, and treated the wedding guests with tea—he had to borrow a samovar from the Jew to do this. In short, he fulfilled all his promises.

Natalka finally concluded: "We were fated to have this happen to us. What can you do against fate?"

But if the newlyweds did not leave her alone, she would show them!

Stepan silently gave his new stepmother the once over and did not know what to think.

One time he happened to meet up with Uncle Mykhaylo, the one who liked to call Hrytsko Grandpa Hryhoriy.

"Well," Mykhaylo asked Stepan with a smile, "so you've married off your 'young man.'"

"Yes, we have," Stepan replied. Then he added: "You know what, Uncle? A wife is a stone around her husband's neck, not quite heavy enough to choke him completely, or drown him, but heavy enough to keep dragging him down to the bottom."

"If you beat your wife more often, the stone would disintegrate into sand," Mykhaylo said, with another smile.

Stepan continued: "A man can't be without a wife . . . How can he be without a wife?"

"Of course, he can't," Mykhaylo said.

"But what are women needed for?"

"What for? But don't you know?" Mykhaylo laughed and went on his way.

And Stepan stood there and began thinking very hard. "A wife is necessary. I need a wife, and that means that father also needs one. Why did Natalka and I try to stop him from getting married? It means that I couldn't have stopped him. Just because he's old? But so what if he is? If mother had lived, he would have had a wife, and that means that he needs a wife, so it's a good thing that he got married . . .

"But for us it's not good; so far, things are fine, but in a short time he and his wife and her children—and maybe they'll have their own children as well—may drive us out of the house. How can that be? If father, like all men, needs a wife, and the old one is no longer there, then he should take a new one; but now that he has taken a new wife, he'll chase us out . . . But is it certain that he'll chase us out? Yes, of course, he will, because it will be too crowded for all of us to live together.

"But if I were in his place, would I chase my son out? I don't know. Maybe if the son were like me, I wouldn't. Why? Because every man thinks that he is the best. And yet, is it really so? But if it were too crowded for me in my home, then I ought to chase out somebody. Oh dear, oh dear! Why did mother die? Why did she have to die? Just look at the mess she's created. She was the younger one, but she died sooner than father. Why is it like that? It would have been better . . ."

Stepan stopped to reconsider: "Am I calling down death upon my own father? No! I'm just saying . . . I'm just wondering, why do younger people die before older ones? But if she had lived, and father had . . . Then it would have been different . . . What would it have been like then?"

Stepan went home, taking his thoughts with him.

Everything appeared to be coming along just fine, but there was a fire smouldering under the ashes.

For one thing, Motrya had brought her son Hnat with her, a boy of about ten. Up to now he had lived with an uncle, and she had also stayed there; she had no land of her own, her house had caved in, and it was this brother who ploughed her garden.

It was mainly because she had no place of her own that Motrya got married; it was her brother who had to feed her, and she had quite a few children—five of them. There was Hnat and another son—a youth who was hired out as a servant; one daughter was married, but two others who worked in a factory were supposed to come home to spend the winter with their new father.

As soon as Onyska laid eyes on Hnat, she began to wrangle with him: "Why have you come here to eat our bwead—may the devil take your mother! Get out!"

Hnat struck her. Onyska ran to complain to Natalka, who was spinning. Natalka stood up for her child and struck Hnat. Motrya grabbed an oven rake and lunged at Natalka.

Onyska started screaming: "Don't touch my mother!" And she began cursing Motrya with the worst words that she had been able to learn in her short life.

Natalka ripped Motrya's shirt and almost trampled Onyska, who happened to be underfoot. Hrytsko ran up from the loom where he was weaving and tried to grab his daughter-in-law by her hair. All three of them yelled abuses without pausing for breath. Natalka said that Motrya was a witch, that she "knew something," and that she had used that "something" to turn a father against his son because she wanted to be the mistress in another person's home. And it was true that, even though up to now Motrya had not done anything, she did hope that with time she would be able to convince Hrytsko to turf out Stepan and his wife.

Motrya was shouting that Natalka was lying like a bitch, that the father knew all too well what kind of daughter-in-law he had, and that he would chase her out his house himself so that she would not go around telling the father what to do—because the egg does not teach the hen.

Hrytsko yelled at the top of his lungs: "Shut up, you fiendish bitches! May the devil take your mother! May you go mad! May you never know any peace! May you drop dead!"

Just as Hrytsko raised his fist to strike Natalka, the door opened, and Stepan walked in. Staring wildly at his father, he attacked him, saying: "Oh, no you don't! That's enough! I don't want you to cripple my wife!"

He shoved his father so hard that the old man tottered and struck a post in the middle of the room.

They all instantly fell silent and gaped at Stepan, who, after striking his father, turned on his heel and walked swiftly out of the house. He realised that he had acted rashly and that, at another time, he probably would not have acted on impulse; but all the same, at that moment he had no love for his father and would not have obeyed him.

As soon as Stepan walked out, the father began complaining that his son was a bandit, a murderer; he went on to say how much good he had done for his son, and he made it sound as if he, Hrytsko, had showered his son with gold, but that his son was "a good-for-nothing, a son of a bitch!"

Both women listened silently to the old man and, returning to their work, averted their eyes and avoided looking at each other.

The children had long ago forgotten about their quarrel and the fact that their elders had quarrelled because of them. Onyska cried briefly when her mother was hit, but Hnat just clucked his tongue and almost laughed as he watched how "dextrously" they fought. Now they were sitting side by side.

Onyska picked up a little blue vial that Hnat always carried around—it was one of his prized possessions, along with a bottle, a knife made from a scythe, a few buttons, a little matchbox, a bobbin, and some other treasures like that. She poured some ashes into the vial and then poured them out, puffing out her childish red lips and holding the little container high above the bench, so that the ashes trickled out for a long time in a fine, even stream; this task delighted her.

Hnat watched her; then he started to brag that he knew how to build a mill.

Onyska, enraptured by his words, asked: "What kind of a mill? Do you know how to make a mill like the one Ivanka made?"

"Of course," Hnat replied. "But no! Not like that! I'll build a better one than your Ivanka built. The one he made isn't a mill—the devil knows what it is!"

The truth was, of course, that Hnat had no idea what kind of a mill Ivanka had built—he did not even know Ivanka!

Onyska picked some splinters out of the rubbish by the oven and brought them to him, saying: "Make me one!"

"You're foolish," Hnat said. "Do you suppose it can be built out of this? I'll go and find some real wood in the yard . . . And I know how to make a ram as well!" he added as he walked out of the house.

Onyska gasped in astonishment. "A wam, a wam . . . Thee what he can do!" she finally squealed. And then she ran to tell her mother that Hnat knew how to make a ram.

In the meantime, Stepan was weaving a wattle fence and thinking: "There you have it! He got married! Now, God forbid, there will be strife every day! What's to be done? Who will be chased out of the house—will father chase me, or will I chase him? I've managed the farm; I bought and acquired things. I got us a plough, thatched the roof, traded the old horse for another one, and bought a heifer. And whose bread, whose vegetables are they eating now if not the ones that I provided? They say that you're to honour your father, but how can I honour him if he's so devious? Oh . . . I shouldn't have let him get married. Natalka was right. He might have listened to me then . . . But what now?"

Stepan scratched his head. "What? He'll chase us out, that's what! And especially after what happened today! But he doesn't have the right to do that. Have I worked for nothing all these years? No, he won't chase us out. I'll give that damned Motrya such a smack that she'll stop turning him against us . . .

"But what good will it do if I hit her? It will only make things worse. But maybe she isn't doing anything bad? Still, I did hear her say not too long ago: 'It's crowded in your house, really crowded,' and then she fell silent because she noticed that I was in the yard, doing something. And why wouldn't this bitch try to hurt us? People everywhere are cruel and dream up ways of harming one another.

"Oh, phew! My unfortunate fate! I don't know what to do. Why did they bring me into this world? If I had been able to, I would have told them then and there that I did not want to be born. They bore me out of their own desire, for their own joy, and now I have to live and suffer! But then, I too have children . . . Why did I conceive them, if I myself do not want to live? Why did I have them? Of what use are they, if life is so bad? And I don't love my father; I can see that he is not treating me fairly, and I know that he will chase me, my wife, and my children out of his home because of that bitch. I know this but I can't do anything to change the way things are! Why is this so? What kind of a man am I?

"Take today, for example . . . What will come of it? I'll have to pay dearly for shoving him . . . Another man just gets an idea and acts on it, but not me! I have to know if this or that will happen because of it, and then I lose my enthusiasm for it—for it seems to me that nothing will come of it. Oh, my damned nature!"

But Stepan did not guess correctly. His father, essentially a good man, did not chase him out of his house; instead, growing sick and tired of living with such a large family amidst all the quarrelling and animosity, he said: "May you all get what's coming to you!"

And, without so much as a backward glance, he went away and hired himself out as a guard somewhere. He spent his days joking with the women servants and his evenings in the sweet enjoyment of playing a *sopilka* or drumming on a board. Occasionally, he sent some money home, but he never showed up there himself. Living among strangers, he once again felt young and happy!

Back home, they followed their daily routine of quarrelling, fighting, and making peace with each other.

Who Outwitted Whom?
(1898)

Oh, but Yakylyna Semenenkova was a fine girl—yes, she truly was! She caught the eye of all the young men in the village—and certainly not because she was beautiful! Skinny, with long arms, and legs as swift as an eel, she had reddish hair, freckles, and flashing green eyes; however, as an only child, she had inherited five acres of land, a cottage, and a garden—and that was what attracted them! It was no wonder that her mother's cousins— Yakylyna's closest surviving relatives—the rich and cheerful Opanas Malyutenko and the poor but pious Zakhar Malyutenko both danced attendance on her.

Yakylyna was only five when cholera took away her father and mother. Before he died, her father entrusted his little daughter to Zakhar, a man he liked, as all people did—until they got to know him better. And so, Zakhar, who had just married but had not yet done his military service, became Yakylyna's guardian. The arrangement was not a legal one but, because there were no older relatives, and because Zakhar knew how to dupe people, no one said anything. And so Zakhar took her into his home and began working her land.

At the time, Opanas, who was still a bachelor, lived with Zakhar in their paternal home. Their parents were dead, and their five sisters—all older than they—were married. Opanas disliked his older brother; Zakhar kept making the sign of the cross, reciting the Lord's Prayer, and rushing off to church, habits he had picked up as a youth when he served in a priest's home. He also admonished others, telling them how they should live, even though he himself did not practise what he preached. In the privacy of his home he was cruel and lazy; he mistreated his wife, his brother, and little Yakylyna, making life miserable for them, and even beating them.

If his wife Varka did not prepare the food to his liking, he would order her to stand by the oven with a pot in her hand and stare into the oven until he told her she could stop. And the poor woman, who was a meek creature, would stand there from breakfast until noon; she would stand there and weep, even though her baby was bawling in the cradle, even though she had work to do—and Zakhar would torment her the whole time.

When he fell into a rage, he made Yakylyna kneel on buckwheat groats or prostrate herself in deep bows before him; when he was not angry, he teased her, calling her "a little red bitch."

The little girl, almost beside herself, would shout: "I'm not a wittle wed bitch!"

And he would say: "But you've got red hair, and that means that you're a little bitch."

She would reply: "A bitch has a tail, but I don't."

Then he would tug at her skirt and say: "And what's this?"

And she would say: "A bitch barks, but I don't."

"But you know how to yap some pretty good lies, little bitch!"

He tormented everyone with his words.

"Who are you? What will become of you?" he shouted. "What will you say on Judgement Day, you stupid asses, you damned fools! Oh my heavens! What sins you have!"

And he would goad them like this every day and look at them as if they were completely doomed; or he would read to them, but he read so poorly that no one could understand what it was all about. His father had sent him to a psalmist for a few reading lessons, but he had forgotten most of what he had learned. Nevertheless, he demanded that everyone sit and listen while he laboriously sounded out the words. And he stayed at it for such a long time that even he would begin to yawn and bless his mouth.

Bored with the reading, Opanas would spit and walk away. He was a carefree young man who liked to laugh, play cards, sing with the girls, eat sunflower seeds, and have a turn on the swings. There was no resemblance between him and his brother.

Gaunt and skinny like a penny candle, it seemed that, like a cricket, Zakhar could squeeze through any crack. He was dark, with black hair so shiny that it looked greased, large dark eyes, and thin-set lips that hid, like a fine red string, under the long moustache that he sported even though he was still quite young.

Opanas did not have a moustache. His protruding cheeks, soft and pink, almost concealed his small pudgy nose and his little grey eyes; his lips were thicker than Zakhar's, and his blond hair stuck out all over his head.

Although somewhat heavy, Opanas was agile and very strong. Everything pleased him and moved him to uproarious laughter: "That's wonderful, the devil take it . . . That's striking! It sure is deftly done, may the devil take your mother!"

In the presence of others, Zakhar would shake his head and intone: "O sins, our mortal sins!" But if there was no one around, he would rant and rave: "May he go berserk, the sluggard! May he drop dead, the good-for-nothing!"

And Zakhar was so secretive that even his wife did not know what he had in mind. Opanas, however, told everyone he met what he was thinking and what he was going to do.

Both brothers were poor, landless peasants. Each had a narrow strip of garden like a green ribbon, a cottage that they owned in common, and nothing else. They rented land, and Opanas worked in the manor yard during the winter. They both liked money; but whereas Opanas liked it as a father delights in a healthy child, Zakhar cared for it as one hovers over a sick one. If he happened to get hold of a *kopiyka [penny]*, he was scared to breathe on it and refused to spend it unless he absolutely had to.

Opanas put away only what was left after partying and buying clothes. And, from the time that their father died—he had died right after Zakhar's wedding, while their mother had died when they were little—he gave Zakhar only enough money to cover his share of the rent and not a *kopiyka* more, no matter how cleverly Zakhar coaxed or harangued him, trying to pry loose some extra money. Nor did Zakhar know where his brother kept his money, because even though Opanas would, without fail, tell everyone what was on his mind, he did not tell his brother anything; he did not trust him.

The few times that Opanas did lend his brother money, Zakhar, in spite of promising to return it promptly, spent it all on himself and then lied about it. Once, Zakhar borrowed five rubles, saying that he needed the extra cash to buy a horse. He went to the market, returned without a horse, and publicly said to Opanas: "Forgive me, my dear brother, but I lost your money. You can beat me—here I am." And, walking up close to his brother, he smiled and looked him straight in the eye.

"The devil take you!" Opanas muttered and walked away. He had already heard that Zakhar had not even tried to buy a horse, and he saw the new boots Zakhar was wearing—they caught the eye and affronted the nose—but he did not want to quarrel in front of others. He did not like to meet Zakhar in public, never talked about him with the other servants and, if someone asked about him, all he would say is: "May he go berserk!"

When Zakhar found out, quite by chance, that Opanas was loaning money to earn interest, he suggested that they rent hay fields together. But Opanas remembered all too well that his brother had always tricked him, right from childhood. Zakhar would come up with a scheme, get Opanas to help him do some damage—steal, smash, or break something—and then put all the blame on him, while he himself would come out of it unscathed.

One time when their mother forgot to lock the cottage, Zakhar incited Opanas to crawl in and taste the honey stored in a jug on the shelf. "Come on, brother—let's have some honey! Why haven't we been allowed to try it? What the devil is it there for?"

Both Zakhar and Opanas dipped into the honey and, when they heard their mother coming, tried to run away. Opanas, obeying his brother, was crawling up to the shelf to put the jug back, when it slipped from his hands and shattered; honey poured out on the floor. Opanas began gathering the pieces, raking the earthen floor with his bare feet to hide the evidence, but he got stuck in the honey, like a fly. When their mother walked in and saw what had happened, she struck her hands together, scolded him, and pulled his ears, even though he swore that it had been Zakhar's idea. She did not believe Opanas, because Zakhar had managed to sneak out of the house so adroitly that his mother had not even seen him among the pottery shards.

When Opanas went out into the street with his red ears and teary eyes, he saw that Zakhar, while playing jacks with other children, kept fooling them, always yelling: "I've won," and intentionally bumping the boys' hands so that they could not do well.

Seeing Opanas coming towards them, Zakhar yelled out: "Hey there! Why are your ears all red? Did you get it? Ha, ha, ha!"

Opanas just spit.

Zakhar later told Opanas that he did not feel guilty, because he too had been beaten for the honey.

"When?" Opanas stared at him in astonishment.

"Mother gave me a beating out in the street."

Opanas did not believe him, because his mother had told him: "Dear little Zakhar is such a fine boy! He never touches or damages anything, but as for you, you scoundrel, I'll show you!"

Zakhar, however, stuck to his story, vowed that he had been beaten and, to dupe Opanas even further, suggested they steal some cucumbers from the garden. Zakhar knew how to mould another person as if that person were made of dough and so, even though Opanas, a moment before, had been angry enough to beat up his brother, he now agreed to this new plan, saying: "What a great idea!" And, going along with Zakhar, he once again got into trouble and had to take all the blame, because, as usual, Zakhar was never around when things came to a head.

But Opanas fell into such traps, like a bird into a net, only until he became smarter and stopped trusting his brother. Even then, however, Zakhar was able to get around Opanas by flattering him, telling him how clever he was: "You see, Opanas, I may be clever, but you're far more clever than I. And why do people say that I'm the smarter one? It's all because you're so quiet, while I talk a lot." Opanas's firm resolve would melt like wax in a flame, and he would agree to help his brother by working for him or giving him money.

But, after Zakhar bought himself boots instead of a horse with the money he had borrowed, Opanas refused him any more loans, and became more stubborn, stronger, and tougher, like an apple tree that grows both upwards and sideways, so that it is more difficult to break it. And he no longer was taken in by cunning words or flattery. Like a man who has swallowed too many bitter nuts, Opanas went along his own path, irrespective of what his brother advised him to do.

Before long, Opanas began to gain the upper hand over his brother; he no longer took heed of Zakhar's "admonitions," and even began to yell at him: "Why are you teasing the little girl? Why are you beating your young wife? Why are you gaping at me? Just look at yourself—aren't you wonderful? Just you wait, you'll see what I'll do to you . . ."

Opanas did not know what it was that he would do to his brother, but Zakhar, who had threatened to chase his younger brother out of the house, did not dare to do so now. He was afraid of what people would say, and he also feared that Opanas might reveal to others that he mistreated his family, and that Yakylyna might be taken from him.

And so he began to look Opanas in the eyes and to speak more gently to Yakylyna. He would tease her and then try to ingratiate himself with sweet words: "Well, tell me, why are you crying, why? You're such a darling! You're a fine girl—you're pure gold, and you're beautiful, and smart. What a fine girl! Come here!"

Yakylyna did not believe what he said and hid from her Uncle Zakhar on the bed atop the clay oven, or behind the skirts of her Aunt Varka, or in her Uncle Opanas's arms. She always felt happy when she was with Opanas—he would sing for her, and bounce her on his knees, and then they both would laugh as if they were demented, and even her aunt would have to smile as she watched them. Yakylyna also loved her Aunt Varka, but she found her boring, because she was always crying and hardly ever laughed.

Even though Opanas was as pleasant and generous as always, he no longer trusted his brother and ignored his attempts to ensnare him. "Oh yes indeed," he thought, "the wolf has donned sheep's clothing!" Once Opanas understood how things were, he never forgot or gave in, no matter how he was flattered.

It was true that Zakhar knew how to flatter and ingratiate himself, and to deceive and take advantage of others, and he bragged about this to his wife, who regarded him as a superior being. He claimed that no one could oppose him, catch him in a lie, or outtalk him, and everyone would bow to his will if he so desired, and, therefore, he could do whatever he wanted to.

Even though he was exaggerating, it was true that Zakhar could act as a matchmaker for anyone—even a blind man or a cripple— and get him the bride he wanted. He could also break up any wedding that he chose to; make neighbours quarrel among themselves, even if they had always lived on good terms with each other; find a person a job or have him removed from any position whatsoever; and praise a person so highly that everyone would gape in amazement, or vilify him so thoroughly that the poor fellow would be ostracised.

Zakhar could get anything he wanted from the villagers by pleading eloquently and cheating, and that was why, even though he was poor and reluctant to spend his money, he was not too badly off. Everything that he owned had been given to him outright, or had been begged or borrowed.

Some people considered him to be a most pious and wise man with whom it was a pleasure to do business; others saw him as a clever heathen who should to be feared; and still others viewed him as a quiet, decent, talkative man, with whom it was pleasant to pass the time of day. Everyone helped him and listened to him, and there were those who could not do without him; others, even though they quarrelled with him, asked for his advice; but he, it seemed, did not like anyone except, perhaps, his infant son, Mykyta, whom he rocked in his cradle and, gazing fondly at his spindly body, long and thin as a herring, said: "You're the spitting image of me."

When Mykyta learned how to get up, holding on to the cradle, Zakhar smiled happily: "Why, hello there, Mykyta Zakharovych! Oh, he's going to be so clever, so wise, the little rascal! Was anyone ever able to get to his feet or stand at nine months?"

While Zakhar talked in this kindly manner to his son, he spoke quite differently to his wife: "Come on now, you good-for-nothing, help me off with my boots! Get a move on! Get me some water! Undress me! Cover me! Come on now, quickly, quickly!"

He loved to see his wife cringe and, because she never talked back, he kept her in his grasp as tightly as a little boy holds a sparrow. He knew that she genuinely feared him and would always fear him, and so he could bully her as much as his heart desired.

He often bragged: "You should know that your husband is far better than you deserve! Who are you, after all? You're rubbish! I can twist everyone around my little finger, that's what I can do!"

Varka, a young woman with a small pointed face and eyes that were overly large, remained silent, smiled a trifle sorrowfully, and stared unblinkingly at Zakhar's mouth as he talked. When he talked to her, it was as if he were talking to himself—he never heard a single word of protest. He knew very well that Varka had no thought in her head other than his thoughts, and when she did come up with some nonsense of her own, it was to no avail—he paid no attention to it.

In his view, Varka was very well off indeed to have him as a husband, because there was no other man who knew, as he did, how to talk differently with different people, to use different words, and to speak in a different tone of voice—delicately, roughly, softly, threateningly, cheerfully, ingratiatingly, sharply, briefly, lengthily, stubbornly, or lightly. Like a good musician who plays the violin in all sorts of styles and with all manner of embellishments, he intertwined everything with names, well-known adages, and his own favourite expressions: "O seven angels from heaven! O our sins! May the cross strike me!"

Zakhar talked differently with men than with boys, with women than with girls. When he was with older men, he acted as if he were older and talked about farming matters; with the girls, he joked and talked a lot of nonsense, such as: "there was a lord who kissed all the girls to find out which one was the prettiest"; and with the women, he either praised their snotty children or said in wonderment: "How young the married women of this world are."

And, if he needed something from the children, he enticed them with candies—he never did anything that did not benefit him. Yes, he even knew how to harness these free-spirited butterflies—he knew all their names, even though there were as many children in the village as flowers in the field. If he came across one of the foolish little ones, he would begin to interrogate him: "What's your mother doing? Where's your father?" And he would find out all that he needed to know, because children everywhere are aware of what's going on, and Zakhar trained them to observe things carefully and secretly. If one of them, feeling bored, began to squirm like a fly before the rain and wanted to run away, Zakhar would ask him: "Did you eat a *palyanystya [flatbread]* today?

"Yes, I did," the child would say. "Mother said she'd bake some bread tomorrow. Oh, I really want some fresh, soft bread."

"You probably don't have any more flour."

"What a thing to say! We have ever so many sacks at home — one, two, no lots of them—and we have more at the mill . . ."

That was all that Zakhar needed to know. Now he knew where to go to wheedle some flour. People could not figure out how Zakhar knew everything. They called him "the wise one," and some feared him. Some obeyed him; others did things their own way, furtively, but he always managed to find out and, if they were weaker, intimidated them—but he himself feared anyone who was stronger. And so he treated everyone differently; he would speak haughtily with a man who asked him for something; with another one he would speak sweetly and do what he was told, bowing and scraping before him; with a stingy man he was stingy; and from a generous one he wheedled all he could.

His real nature came through only when he was inebriated, and this was why he rarely drank. If he did get drunk, however, he ran home right away, so as not to blurt out any information. When he got home, he would turn to his wife, whom he considered to be no better than a wall, and ask: "Who am I? Huh? Tell me right now—am I a son of a bitch, or what?"

Varka just trembled and said nothing, and Opanas rarely stayed home when there was a party in the village.

Zakhar knew how, in a twinkling of an eye, to say something that turned a foolish man into a wise one, or a thief into an honest man, and he did it in such a way that the man himself believed that he was like that, and that it was other people—not he—who were foolish, and that others were taking advantage of him and not the other way around. For this insight, the villagers pressed gifts upon Zakhar; and, if they did not give him anything, he simply took something from them, in the same way that, as a child, he used to take away a pretty bauble or a tasty treat from other children.

Back then, he either promised to give back something better in return, pulled it away, or even stole it—if the child happened to look away for a moment; or he lied, saying that a boy's grandfather was calling him and, when the boy unthinkingly dropped whatever he was holding, Zakhar would grab it and refuse to return it, all the while hopping about on one foot, and boasting: "Aha! Aha! Aha! It's mine now!"

There was no point in complaining about Zakhar to the adults, because you could never expose him; he knew how to squeal so poignantly, to swear in the name of God, to cross himself, and to cover his tracks like a rabbit. What the children hated most of all was that Zakhar made fun of them and laughed when they got into trouble, and their fathers beat them, or their mothers pulled their hair. And so they much preferred to get into fisticuffs with Opanas, than to tangle with Zakhar. Opanas liked to fight, unlike the meek

Zakhar, who was afraid of physical altercations and dared only to cuff the ears of smaller children in quiet corners.

It was even worse when Zakhar began teasing one of them, patting the shoulder of a child who was busily making mud pies.

"Go away," the child would say. "Leave me alone."

Zakhar would not say anything; he would just smile and pat the child on the shoulder once again.

The child would repeat: "Go away!"

Zakhar would step back and then pat the child's shoulder again. Once, twice, three times, four times, ten times, innumerable times, he would gently, ever so gently, pat the child's shoulder, always with a slight smile on his face, until the child would leap to his feet, try to slap him as you slap a mosquito that buzzes and annoys you, and then return to what he was doing.

But Zakhar would once again creep up to the child and start doing the same thing—simply patting his shoulder.

The child would begin to plead and cry in annoyance: "Zakhar, go away. Honest to God, why are you bothering me?"

But Zakhar would not desist; he would reach out, pat the child's shoulder, and then quickly jump away; and he continued doing this over and over again . . .

The child would begin to scream as if he had lost his mind, pounding his feet on the ground, twisting this way and that, and yelling: "Don't touch me, or I'll beat you up!"

Zakhar did not let up until the child either ran home or, as if possessed, began to pelt Zakhar with anything he could lay his hands on—stones, lumps of earth, and sticks. But, even though Zakhar had made the child angry, he had not beaten him or hurt him, so there was nothing that the child could complain about. And it was only when he had succeeded in driving the child to distraction that Zakhar would calmly go home.

Just as he liked to torment children, so too did he like to torture butterflies, snails, flies, and other insects. He would catch one and begin to tear it apart bit by bit—first one little leg, then its wings, and then he would tear off its head, and all the while he would stare at it with wide eyes, his cheeks flushed, and his thin rosy lips stretched still more finely in a smile.

Opanas had always known him to be cruel and manipulative, but had only recently recognized the full extent of his duplicity. But other people did not see through him, because, like glass sparkling in the sun with a variety of colours, he assumed whatever guise suited the situation.

All day long, whether it was a work day or a feast day, Zakhar bustled about the village gathering information—where a deal had been sealed with a drink, where matchmakers were wooing a girl, where down payments were being paid to a factory, where people were quarrelling. He insinuated himself everywhere, giving a scolding here, making peace there—whatever was more convenient for him, but always in such a way that no one could accuse him later of causing an "incident." He always came out smelling like a rose.

As a boy, he had served for a couple of years as a lackey and, during that time, had learned a lot—how to tell lies and how to cheat, but the people had forced him to leave his post, for he had not yet learned how to dissimulate, and told the lord everything.

Zakhar could convince the entire community—it was strange that the older people would listen to such a young man—to borrow money at a high rate of interest or on the basis of working it off. The man who loaned the money was grateful to Zakhar and, initially, when the people received the money, they also gave Zakhar a drink to seal the deal. Afterwards, when they had to work it off, they cursed him and his scheme, but he knew how to wriggle his way out of that kind of predicament as well. He would either teach them how to avoid the work by pretending to be "sick" or saying they would do it "tomorrow"—until it was time to harvest and, as the grain could not wait, others would have to be paid to take in the crop. Or Zakhar would begin to speak ill of the good man who gave them money in the winter for work to be done in the summer, convincing the villagers that the man should not be demanding that they work so hard to settle their debt.

"O sins," he would say. "There's always a thief who will skin his brother alive."

If word of what he was doing got back to the rich man who had lent them the money, Zakhar would cleverly whitewash himself: "Oh my goodness! O seven angels from heaven! Would I ever say something like that? May my tongue fall off if I said that. They're all lying! Does it take much to heap lies on someone else? O sins, our mortal sins! That's what people are like! Well,

God be with them. I forgive them because I'm a poor and peaceful man. O God! What people won't say!"

To make matters even worse, Zakhar might even take the initiative and inform the rich man that the people were planning to work poorly for the money he had given them; and once again the rich man would be grateful to Zakhar, while the villagers would thank him for instructing them how to go about their work.

And so Zakhar knew how to trap everyone in circles from which they were unable to free themselves. He always seemed to be weaving nets and entangling people in them. The dimwitted villagers did not like Zakhar, even though they did not really understand what he was doing; they only knew that he managed to retain control over them. It was not in vain that he wandered through the village in the dead of night and spent his days hiding under a willow or in someone's shed, without eating or drinking.

He would spread a malicious lie about a man he disliked and then say: "Oh my goodness! That poor young man! I feel so sorry for him! I didn't know anything about it, but people are saying that he has a very serious illness. Oh my goodness! O sins, our mortal sins! Well, there's nothing that can be done about it. Now there isn't a girl in the village who would marry him! Oh, that unfortunate young man! No matter how hard he tried to hide it from others, it still came out into the open."

And Zakhar would bewail the fact like an old woman until everyone knew about it, and when he met the young man he would say: "So you're still sick, are you? Oh, I feel so sorry for you, so very sorry!"

"But why?" the young man would ask, his eyes bulging in astonishment.

"Oh, what's the use of trying to hide what's wrong, when everyone knows what kind of sickness you have?" And Zakhar would wink slyly.

"Who's been spreading lies like that?" the young man would say, turning deathly pale. "Oh, if I could only lay my hands on the son-of-a-bitch!"

"So it's all a lie, is it? But I thought it was true, and I felt so sorry for you, so very sorry for you! O sins, our mortal sins!" Zakhar would say with a smile, gazing directly into the young man's eyes.

And the latter would turn cold with fear upon seeing that smile and hearing that sweet, cunning voice.

The rich and the wise respected Zakhar because they needed a man like him, who was clever and never refused to help. For example, if a rich man was in dire need of money, but did not want to face the poor family from which he wanted to get it, he would send Zakhar.

And Zakhar would badger the family until he squeezed the money out of them, while repeating over and over again: "O sins! What poverty! How sorry I am for you, but it can't be helped. O seven angels from heaven! He's as firm as steel and won't let go of what is his. Give me the money, because if I don't get it from you, he'll make manure out of me. Oh, my goodness! O sins! Let me sell your boots or your sheepskin coat, or anything else that you might have. You're lucky that I'm the one who came for the money, because if it weren't for me, what would you do? Come on now, give it to me . . . O seven angels from heaven!"

And no matter how the woman cried, or tried to say that without the sheepskin coat she would have nothing to wear in the wintertime or to cover her children at night, Zakhar assured her that it was their good fortune that he could sell their sheepskin coat for them at this time.

This is how Zakhar lived, meddling in people's affairs, both helping and hindering them, until he was called up to serve in the army. He was not too concerned about this turn of events, for he knew he would have an easy life wherever he went. His only fear was that there might be a war—he feared this as much as he feared a rifle and fighting. But they did not ask him if he wanted to join the army or not; they just came and took him.

Varka grieved mightily, because such was her nature—she enjoyed crying. She never stopped to think that her husband was unkind to her, because she truly believed that, as he always reminded her "she was not worthy of him." No one else felt sorry to see Zakhar leave, and his brother was even glad that he would have some respite from the constant: "O sins, our mortal sins!' and "O seven angels from heaven!"

Zakhar was away from the village for a few years, and during that time everything changed.

Opanas got married and assumed the guardianship of Yakylyna. Before leaving, Zakhar had placed her with another family and had seen to it that the grain from Yakylyna's land would go to his wife. But Opanas, concerned that the new guardian was squandering Yakylyna's inheritance, took his place. He took away Yakylyna, along with her land, built a house, and began to lead a good life, because his wife was well-off and smart, and he himself was not completely stupid.

Opanas's wife, Mavra, came from another village. She was quite homely—sallow, as if moulded out of clay, with a long nose, no eyebrows, ugly grey eyes, and pale lips. But, in Opanas's view, she was wonderful. She was lazy, mean, slovenly, and a heathen, but Opanas thought she was truly wonderful, so wonderful that he was not ashamed to brag among the men out in the street that there was not another woman like her, the devil take it.

The men laughed at him and teased him: "Hey, come on, tell us what kind of a wife you have, Opanas."

"What kind? Oh, she's wonderful!" Of course, almost everything seemed "wonderful" to Opanas—except for his brother Zakhar. He even thought of himself as wonderful and, no matter what happened, it was all wonderful. Even if the weather was so bad that the sparrows hid, the villagers shivered from the cold, and the wheat was flattened by the rain and the wind, Opanas would still maintain: "The weather's wonderful!"

And that is probably why his wife was dear to him, even though she bore him only three daughters and no sons, and even though, the whole time they were married, she did not learn how to cook him a decent bowl of borshch or sew him a pair of pants. She was, however, rich, and had come into her money in a clever and devious way.

She nursed an aunt of hers through a lengthy illness and, after the aunt died, she took all the money that this woman had hidden away—her husband, a tavern keeper had died earlier, and she had run the tavern herself for a while. Mavra took this money without even informing the aunt's only son, who served elsewhere as a shepherd, that his mother had fallen ill. This boy was a bit slow and, when he showed up for the funeral, did not look for any money; he simply believed Mavra's story that she was paying for the burial with money she had earned in the tobacco fields.

And she lamented over her dead aunt: "Oh, woe is me! My aunt has died and there's no money to bury her. O God! Why have you forsaken us, auntie? Why have you left your young son without a penny, without a shirt?"

Mavra had not only known how to ingratiate herself with her aunt so that the latter told her where her money was hidden, but she had also sworn to look after the aunt's son after her death, to sew his clothes for him and do his laundry, knowing full well that he would go back to being a shepherd after the funeral. Not only did she take her aunt's best clothes, but she was clever enough not to tell anyone—including her father, her mother, and her sisters—anything at all about the money she had found. She told only Opanas about it when they met while threshing, and so Opanas married her, even though she was getting on in years.

Of course, all this caused talk among the people; Mavra was censured, while the orphaned boy was pitied, because rumour had it that Mavra's aunt had left a lot of money.

But no one could prove anything, especially when Mavra, in response even to her mother's questioning, stuck to her reply: "I don't know. There was no money, and there is none."

Opanas, who by now had learned to be discreet, let it be known that he was the one who had money in the family, because he loaned people money and earned interest. Following his wife's advice, he did not throw his money around and presented himself as being too poor to even buy another horse. He always did what his wife told him to do, and he was convinced that if she were elected village chief, she would tell everyone what to do and put things right in short order.

No other man tried to please his wife like Opanas. Every morning and every evening he fetched water for her, led the cow home from the pasture, put the pitchers of milk in the cellar and brought them out as they were needed, fed the pigs, pulled straw from the stack, and even kneaded the dough in the kneading trough if Mavra made it too stiff. And to top it all off, he carried the baby in his arms, threw it playfully up into the air, and sang to it: "Where's our mummy? Oh, where's our mummy? Oh, that mummy! She's wonderful!"

Mavra took his help for granted and even scowled and grumbled: "M-m . . . How are you holding the child, you scoundrel? Why are you sticking both hands into the kneading-trough, you dimwit? Just look! You've spilled the milk again, may you be damned! I told you to crawl down the ladder slowly."

Whatever had to be done, Opanas always asked his wife: "How? And what? And when? And is it this way, or that way?"

Well, this is not all that bad yet, for men often listen to women without admitting it, saying all the while: "The woman is stupid."

And what man, other than Opanas, praised his wife directly to her face: "You gave me some wonderful advice back then, when you told me not to buy a horse, because horses are much cheaper now, and for the same amount of money, and just a bit more, I can buy a pair. That's really wonderful!"

Mavra grumbled: "Oh sure, it's always 'wonderful' as far as you're concerned, but how are you going to feed a pair?"

Opanas whistled: "Phew, phew! I'll get some grass in return for some work, and I'll take the straw from Yakylyna's rye. It's always succulent—it's wonderful!"

"Oh sure, you'll take the grass, and when it's time to work it off, your own rye will be ready to harvest, but you'll be working for some son-of-a-bitch."

"But I'll take the grass for doing the mowing; the grass will be ready for mowing before the rye ripens."

"Oh, sure it will. And what if one of the horses dies, what then? The money will be lost!"

"Why should it die? The one that we had didn't die. And if it does die, I'll sell the grass for ten or twelve rubles and buy a light bay colt. That's my favourite colour—it's just wonderful!"

"You're a fool. Who'll give you twelve rubles for some grass?"

"But what if there's no grass anywhere? And in the winter you can sell hay by the yard."

Opanas would roar with laughter, but Mavra would be annoyed, because she always saw the dark side of things and never trusted anyone. She often berated him, telling him that he behaved as if he had gorged himself on honey—everything seemed so rosy and golden to him.

Mavra often grieved and complained without cause: "O Lord, what will we do, whatever will we do if the crops are hailed out like they were last year?" Or: "The cow isn't chewing its cud—it must be dying! What will I do then, God forbid?"

Opanas always tried to cheer her up, saying: "Don't be afraid. Everything will be fine. The grain will be wonderful, the cow will be healthy, and if it isn't, God forbid, we'll buy an even better one, you'll see!"

"Oh sure, I'll see. Where will you get the money to buy it?"

"But we have it—praise God—we have the money!"

"Oh sure, but where is it?" Mavra could not believe that they had more money than a hundred villagers; to her it always seemed that they did not have very much. "And if you spend it all, then there won't be any!"

"But we have thirty rubles owing to us in interest alone!"

"Oh sure we do. And where are they, these thirty rubles?"

"If I want them, I can collect them right away."

"You always say: 'I can collect them, I can collect them,' but you never do, and the money will vanish. I know these 'paupers.' You let them off today and the next day, and eventually they trick you out of our money altogether. As sure as I'm standing here, our money will be lost. You'd do better to collect at least some of it now, so we can see that there really is some. And if they don't want to pay the interest, then take back the money you lent them. It's as simple as that!"

Opanas set out for the village to exact the money owing him. He knew that his wife was very stingy. Before she would buy him or the children something new, she would sew a patch on a hole ten times over, or mend an old bowl with clay before she bought a new one. He knew that she was sending him to collect money just to hold it in her hands, to feast her eyes upon it, and then she would give it back to earn interest on the interest. Opanas himself thought that money was not to be fooled with. If you had money you could do everything; without it, you could do nothing. The only thing that money could not buy, he thought, was your own father. But then again—who could be sure even of that? As for children, however, there was no doubt that they could be bought!

He was on his way to collect the money to assure himself, as well as his wife, that he actually had it. There were some people who returned his money, but there were also those who begged him, in the name of Christ and God, to wait until market day when they could sell their only horse or cow in order to pay off their debt. And then there were those who borrowed money, but had no means at all of paying it back, because their cattle died, or there was an unexpected funeral in the family, or a birth, or a wedding, and they were completely entangled in debt. At first they had at least a faint hope that they would be able to repay it, but later there was not a peep out of them.

In those cases Opanas regretted that he had not listened to his wife, who said that if people had no assets they should not be lent any money—that you may as well give them the money outright. But how could he help it? These people were such "good fellows"; they made all sorts of promises that they would repay the money, claiming that they could get money if they had to—they had things they could sell or pawn—and pleading so earnestly that Opanas simply could not refuse them.

And now, walking into the cottage of one of these fellows, he saw tiny children with wizened little faces and bodies, crawling around on the floor in grimy torn shirts, sucking dry crusts of bread covered with dirt. He saw a scrawny, bedraggled cat—the only "cattle" the owner now had. And he saw the householder himself sitting at the table, his hair all dishevelled; there was nothing to thresh, and so he had no work to do, and there was no horse, so there was nothing to attend to. And he saw the young wife, who sat spinning without raising her head, while tears rolled down her cheeks and fell on her hands, on the yarn, on her skirt.

He saw all this and said: "Good day to you. Come on, Semen, give me back my money."

"Where am I to get it?" Semen—or Trokhym, or Mytro, or whoever—would cry out, almost in tears.

"Well, but you . . . that is . . . Give me at least some of it. Well, maybe a *poltynyk [a fifty-cent coin],* because I lent you ten rubles with interest at six percent a year. And now the year is over, and you haven't given me anything. I haven't seen either the money I lent you, or the interest. Give me at least a *poltynyk.*"

"But do you see this?" Semen pointed at the children.

"Tut-tut . . ." Opanas clucked his tongue. "Yes, it's truly wonderful how you've ended up. I see what I see, but I can't go on like this either—my money wasn't stolen money."

Semen bowed so low before Opanas that his long stringy hair reached the ground, and his wife began to lament. "Oh what a damned murderer, what a 'stingy miser!' He's ready to skin people alive, to choke them for his money . . . May you not live to see your children! He wanders like that damned cholera from house to house . . .''

Opanas looked silently at the young woman, and even smiled. Then he bent down to a little child. It had crawled right up to his feet and, wetting its finger, was rubbing something on his boot while he was talking.

A moment later, Opanas quickly rose to his feet and walked out of the house, sternly admonishing Semen: "See to it that I get the money when the overseer makes the payments for the harvesting! And come to help with the threshing."

If the poorer people did not have the money, Opanas always made them work off the interest that they owed him and, in this way, minimised his losses.

Opanas had not gone far beyond the gate when the child shrieked: "It's so pretty! It's so pretty!" It had found two silver coins in the hem of its shirt.

"You see, you scurvy woman, and you were cursing him."

"Oh, dear mother of mine! How could I have known that he was that kind of a man?"

And Opanas continued on his way, thinking: "Well, this Semen has done a wonderful job of it this time. He used to be a wonderful householder, but now he has no bread to eat and, after such a cold snap, his house is still unheated."

When Opanas went to collect money from well-to-do people, who could repay their debt, he approached them as if he were holding a knife to their throats, and no matter how a rich man squirmed, Opanas would get what was owing to him by repeating: "Give it to me, give it to me—you have the money."

The rich man would disclaim that fact, swearing to God that is was not so: "Honest to God, I . . ."

"You have the money," Opanas would say once more.

He would repeat the same words over and over again and follow the man everywhere. If the rich man went into the barn, Opanas would follow him; if he went into his house, Opanas would go there as well; the rich man simply could not get rid of him and had to give him the money.

But, all in all, he did not collect much money. Mavra was dissatisfied and said: "If ever Opanas or one of our daughters

should happen to die, there would be nothing to bury them with!"
She did not consider the possibility that she herself might die,
because she had a great fear of death and always took great care
not to catch cold in freezing weather, and not to strain herself if
she was doing any hard work.

When Mavra began asking Opanas why there was so little
money, he replied that it had been impossible to collect any more.

"Why is that?" Mavra stared at him in astonishment. "Why
didn't you get any from Semen?"

"Because they're living in complete poverty!"

"Oh sure, and you believe the sons-of-bitches," Mavra said.

"Well, but what if a man hanged himself because of our money?
What would happen then?"

"He's lying. He wouldn't hang himself, the son-of-a-bitch."

"Oh sure, he wouldn't hang himself. But he even had the rope
ready, when I was there," Opanas lied.

And Mavra had no choice but to fall silent again, because,
according to Opanas, all the poor people to whom he lent money
were ready either to hang or drown themselves if he tried to
recover his money. Besides, Opanas assured his wife that he would
collect the money soon, that he would collect it without fail;
moreover, they had enough money now, and enough of
everything, and everything was wonderful. He laughed, displaying
his healthy white teeth, and his shaved ruddy cheeks quivered.
He still had not grown a beard and, with his clean-shaven face
that was as round and firm as an apple, looked like an unmarried
young man.

Opanas rarely worried. And if he ever became angry at all, it was
at his axe or scythe when they became dull, or at his horses when
he was harnessing them. But he almost never lost his temper with
people and, even if he did, he would boil over, get rid of his
venom, and instantly cool off. As for his wife and daughters, he
never got angry at them. He would take one of his little girls in
his arms and fuss with her all day long, sitting on the earthen
embankment abutting the house and rocking her. And it was hard
to tell who was happier—he or his daughter.

"Get into the house already," his wife would shout. "It's going
to rain."

"No it isn't. It's wonderful; it's so bright," he would reply.

When the rain actually did come down in a rush, Opanas would finally jump up, prattling: "Oh, it's raining! It's really raining! Oh, how wonderful it is!"

And the little girl, as she tried to catch the streaming rain in her hands, would also cry out: "It's wonderful! It's wonderful!"

Then Opanas would open his mouth, throw his head back, and drink in the rain, and both he and his daughter would get even more drenched, and when they finally came into the house, they were so happy and wet that even Mavra, who was angry, could not help but laugh.

Mavra was not pleased that her husband often fooled around with the children or became so involved in conversations with other men that he forgot about everything else. She was an envious woman and did not enjoy being with people. Whenever she went out, she either sat and pouted, or gossiped about how other women got along with their husbands. And she made nasty remarks about them—that a certain woman's breath reeked, that another one had boils on her legs, and that a third had a rotting nose. And at home she assigned all the women such comical nicknames—the wet chicken, the spotted heifer, the coverless pot, the fly swimming in cream, the bedraggled heron, the potbellied one—that Opanas rolled with laughter. Mavra also tended to criticise other women for faults that she herself had.

"You should see," she would say, "how disgusting Yaryna's housekeeping is, and how slovenly she herself is. In their house, they eat lice with their bread."

But at the same time, in her own home, the dishes would go unwashed for a week, and cockroaches and mice scurried over the unwiped benches.

"What a scurvy woman she is," she would say. "She's always sick. And she does nothing, just lies around like a pig, and when her baby fills its diaper in the cradle she won't even change it."

Yet there were times when she herself was so lazy that she made her husband and Yakylyna do everything. She would not even get up to get a drink of water, and they would have to fetch it for her. She enjoyed pretending that she was sick, but she hated with a passion anyone who actually was ill.

If she saw someone with a boil or a bloody sore, she would squeal in revulsion: "Oh! I can't look at that, I simply can't."

And if she saw someone who was ailing, she would immediately say: "Phew! How sallow she is, how flabby, how odious, and how she shakes—just like gelatine, and she can't even reach for anything herself. She's absolutely disgusting!"

If Opanas fell into a fever, she would bawl him out soundly, yelling: "Well, now you've come down with something! So, why are you always crawling around among people? Go ahead and be sick, for all I care! I won't even so much as look at you!"

If Yakylyna hurt herself, Mavra lost her temper. "You fool, you devil's seed. You don't even know how to hold a knife. Run as fast as you can and get some plantain to put on your wound. Why are you still standing here? Off with you!"

Mavra was not pleased that all the women did not listen to her, or bow and scrape before her, and so she rarely sat with them out in the street. She preferred to stay at home and chat with women whose husbands borrowed money from her and Opanas, and who came to her home to work off their debt by helping her plaster the house, or wash clothes, or spin.

At those times she would loosen her tongue and tell them how she had made a match between a worthless young man and a good young woman, or vice versa. Mavra liked to be a matchmaker. She found it amusing to dupe young women so that they too—as she put it—would have a taste of honey. And she found it interesting to observe how these new couples, as the days and months went by, began to quarrel, heap abuse upon each other, and fight with increasing frequency.

She also liked to tell them her long, drawn-out dreams that had no beginning and no end, while her neighbours listened silently or sighed: "Yes, yes indeed." Or: "So that's how it is!" Or: "Oh, my goodness." Or: "You're quite a woman, dear in-law! Who could have guessed it!" Or: "Be so good as to tell us." And so on and so forth.

Opanas often laughed and said: "It's wonderful! It's wonderful!" But there were times when he restrained her, saying: "You know, you seem to be . . ."

"Oh sure! What do you know?" Mavra would retort. "You'd do better to go and rock the baby!" Or she would simply chase him out of the house, saying: "This is woman's talk. Why are you sticking your nose into it?"

And Opanas would leave, thinking: "Well, my woman—the son-of-a bitch—has a tongue as sharp as a razor. She's a smart one, she is. Oh, the scurvy woman—she's wonderful!"

Mavra did not like it when Opanas interfered in matters that were none of his business. And she also did not like the fact that he treated Yakylyna as well as his own daughters, and maybe even better, because their daughters were still small and foolish, whereas Yakylyna was almost a grown girl already and quite amusing. She was very witty, and so Opanas often joked and talked with her.

"What reason can there be to pay so much attention to someone else's child. Leave it alone and let it live—and so much for that!" She herself was a mean stepmother to Yakylyna. She beat her and made her work from a very young age, all the while favouring her own children.

It was only when Zakhar came back from the army that she began to treat Yakylyna better.

Zakhar was stunned when he learned what had happened in his absence. He immediately resolved to undermine his brother Opanas who had become rich and corpulent.

Yakylyna first caught sight of her uncle one day when she was running down the street pulling Mavra's little daughter Katrya in a wagon. It was her job to amuse the child.

"Hello, Yakylyna!" her uncle Zakhar said to her. And he tried to pat her carroty red hair that was pulled back into a thin, unkempt braid, leaving straggly wisps hanging in her eyes.

Darting backwards, Yakylyna looked ready to run away.

"Don't you recognise your own uncle?" he asked, as if he truly were a close relative and not just her dead mother's cousin. "Aren't you ashamed of yourself?" he added.

The girl came to a stop farther away from her uncle and, looking at him obliquely, asked sharply: "Why should I be ashamed?"

"I'm you're uncle—your uncle Zakhar," he informed her.

Yakylyna looked closely at this uncle, especially at his bright red shirt and narrow trousers, the likes of which she had never seen before.

"O sins, our mortal sins! She didn't recognise her own uncle! O seven angels from heaven!"

His voice, his sighing, and his words—even though she did not recall them exactly—now seemed familiar to Yakylyna, as if she had heard them before. She became bolder but, keeping her distance, asked: "Are you the one who's a soldier?"

"Yes, yes indeed, sweetheart. But now I'm home, and you'll be better off; things won't be like this for you any more."

"Like what?" Yakylyna gaped at him.

Just then, little Katrya began to screech, begging to be pulled again: "Come on . . . Go! Go . . ."

"You won't have to tend the children of others, you poor girl," Zakhar said, shaking his head sympathetically. "Aren't you sick and tired of it?"

"It would be strange if I weren't," Yakylyna pouted, replying in a harsh voice.

"Yakylyna! Yakylyna!" Mavra's voice rang out from the house. Looking through the window, she had seen everything, and possibly even overheard what had been said. "Come into the house to have some *halushky [dumplings]*."

In a flash, Yakylyna clattered off with the wagon, disappearing from her uncle's sight.

"Well, well. My little brother has certainly done well for himself. I'll have to rein him in a bit." Zakhar smiled and continued on his way home.

From that day on, Yakylyna began to eat *halushky* with cheese, dried pears, *palyanytsya* with honey, and other treats that she and Mavra enjoyed and on which Mavra did not mind spending money, but which Yakylyna had rarely seen before the return of her uncle Zakhar.

At first Yakylyna did not understand why things had changed for the better; she was only aware that her aunt Mavra was kinder to her now and no longer abused or beat her.

The next time Zakhar tried to trick Yakylyna into approaching him, he asked her if she knew her prayers. "Come with me and I'll teach you the prayer 'Our Father.' Come along now."

Yakylyna once again looked intently at this uncle, examining him from head to foot. She noted his black hair smeared with grease like a boot, the slim cigarette in his hand, and the shiny buttons on his trousers, and then said: "I don't want to."

And she slowly made her way home.

Eventually, Zakhar thought of a way of enticing Yakylyna. One day, after dinner, he stood in the doorway of his cottage and, from a distance, waved red, yellow, and green snippets of paper at her as she grazed a calf in a pasture close to their home. She looked at him and thought: "Maybe uncle has some candies?"

And her uncle continued calling her: "Come on, now. Come here, Yakylyna."

Yakylyna abandoned the calf and ran towards him like a pebble rolling down a hill.

Her uncle persuaded her to go into his house, placed her on his knees, and gave her some candies. It was then that she found out everything—that her uncle Opanas was taking advantage of her inheritance; that her aunt Mavra, the damned scurvy woman, was forcing her to be a nanny; and that she would be ever so much better off if she moved in with her uncle Zakhar.

Yakylyna spent that night at her uncle Zakhar's. The next day, however, curiosity got the better of her. She wanted to see how her uncle Opanas and aunt Mavra were getting along without her, so she dropped in to see them.

"Where have you been?" Mavra, grimacing, asked her sternly.

Yakylyna smiled, looked her aunt straight in the face, and said: "At my uncle Zakhar's. He gave me some candies."

Opanas yelled: "Well then, why have you come here? Go and live with him, if that's what you're like!"

Yakylyna was about to leave when her aunt Mavra said: "You're a foolish girl! He's giving you candies today, but tomorrow you'll get a goose egg. What does he have? He's a ragged beggar, like a tattered whip made out of hemp! He's telling you all sorts of nonsense and lies, and you believe him." She turned around to her husband and, taking some food out of the oven, asked: "Do you want to eat?"

Nonplussed, the little girl fell silent. She was surprised that her uncle Opanas, who was always even-tempered, had become so angry, and she believed her aunt Mavra that uncle Zakhar was a liar. And so, when barley cooked in milk appeared on the table, and her uncle Opanas, having regained his composure somewhat, asked her: "And as for you, my little wanderer, are you going to eat with us, or with your uncle Zakhar?" she slid quietly behind the table and replied softly: "I prefer to eat with you."

After dinner, Yakylyna played with the doll that belonged to Natalka, aunt Mavra's oldest daughter, and decided to remain with her uncle Opanas. It was not long, however, before Zakhar once again won her over.

Now that Yakylyna began to understand what was going on, she began living for a week with one uncle, and then with the other. If she got tired of looking after the children at her uncle Opanas's home, she ran off stay with uncle Zakhar. And when she tired of eating porridge at uncle Zakhar's, she ran back to uncle Opanas. And both of them welcomed her gladly. They forgave her many things now, and she grew bolder and more clever.

One time at the dinner table, when her aunt Mavra asked her why she was wasting bread by eating only the soft part and throwing away the crusts, Yakylyna said; "So what? Isn't it my bread that you're eating?"

Mavra bit her lip and did not say a word.

And now Yakylyna often pestered both her uncles to buy her things: "Buy me a cross, some ribbons, a coral necklace, a wreath; get me some fabric for a jerkin and a skirt; and I need some *rushnyky [embroidered linen ceremonial cloths],* and a hope chest, because I'm no longer a little girl!"

Uncle Opanas could not refuse Yakylyna now, and uncle Zakhar kept promising to get her everything—O seven angels from heaven!—as soon as he became her guardian and got her land away from Opanas. And he began to work towards this end, spreading the word that Opanas was treating Yakylyna badly—that he was using the orphan's land but not taking care of her, that he had not provided her with a hope chest, and that his wife Mavra was abusing her and making her work very hard.

"Is it fair—O seven angels from heaven!—that Opanas is a man of property because he uses land that is not his, while I am left landless, completely landless?" Zakhar repeated again and again.

After his stint in the army, Zakhar was even more persuasive. He had been smart before, but now he was even smarter, ingratiating, and as smooth as butter. He often complained that he had suffered a lot, and that the only joy left to him was to hear people in church pray for the "Christ-loving soldiers." Hearing this, some villagers, believed him and rose up in his defence.

There were those, however, who liked Opanas for the whiskey he bought them and for his belief that everything was "wonderful." And so, even though the people agreed with Zakhar that an orphan should not be abused, they wriggled and squirmed and, trying to please both brothers, left Yakylyna in Opanas's care, while promising Zakhar to look into the matter. In reality, they all kept their distance, saying: "Actually, it's none of my business."

Then Zakhar tried to undermine Opanas in another way. He alerted the authorities that Opanas was charging a high rate of interest; however, the people who borrowed the money would not disclose what interest they paid, and so the matter ended there.

Now Zakhar began to drive wedges into all of Opanas's dealings. When the latter wanted to buy a mill, Zakhar found another buyer for it. When Opanas wanted to sell a horse, Zakhar became involved, saying that the horse had glanders, and the deal fell through. When Opanas wanted to organise a work bee to haul his straw, Zakhar dragged all the people to a bee at another rich man's place; Opanas could not haul in his straw, and it got soaked in the rain. And things went on like this for quite some time.

When Zakhar met Opanas on the street, he asked him in the presence of others; "Well, my dear little brother, did your straw get soaked? Didn't you manage to haul it in? Oh, how I pity you!"

Opanas just spit: "Get away from me! Go to the devil's mother!"

It is too bad that he could not beat Zakhar up for his "kind" words, as the people truly could not figure out who was in the right and who was in the wrong, and were ready to say nasty things about Opanas for cursing his brother.

In his own mind, Opanas was truly astonished: "Well, the son-of-a-bitch has done a wonderful job of doing me in, may he come to no good!"

As for Opanas, he did not know how to get back at Zakhar, except, perhaps, to let his pig run loose in his garden—but then he would have to pay for the damage that the pig did. And so, no matter what he tried to do to Zakhar, he was paid back tenfold.

More than once Opanas told his neighbours: "Don't believe that son-of-a-bitch, that brother of mine."

But when Zakhar came out once again with his: "We are the Christ-loving soldiers for whom the priest prays in church," and when he found some money at a lower rate of interest than

Opanas charged, and when he gave good advice about what to do so that mice would not gnaw at the straw, then the villagers listened to him once again, and forgot what Opanas had said.

Zakhar was sure that if it were not for Mavra, he would be able to undermine Opanas and ruin him. "That damned woman," he said, "is like a cataract in my eye. She's smart, that scurvy woman, and she stands in the way of getting at Opanas just like caragana bushes stop you from getting into an orchard to pick the apples."

Mavra, it is true, could surmise when Zakhar was up to his tricks, and, darting in all directions like a bitch, defended herself tooth and nail. When he spread the word among the villagers that Yakylyna still did not have a hope chest, Mavra sat in the village common and, picking nits from Yakylyna's hair, declared: "It's really strange, but I love this girl more than my own daughters."

Of course, pretending to be kind and good was more difficult for Mavra now than it had been when she took care of her old aunt, because she had become accustomed to having people try to please her; she understood, however, what lay in her best interests, and became incensed when Opanas once said: "Perhaps we should give up our claim to Yakylyna? Let Zakhar take her in, because as it is, there's nothing but trouble. We have enough money— we'll get by without what belongs to her."

"You're an idiot! I won't let Zakhar catch a whiff of her wealth."

And Mavra, to get the people to side with them, ordered her husband to lower the rate of interest at which he lent out money, even though she later complained: "What will become of us because of this brother of yours, this son-of-a-bitch? We'll end up going begging."

And it was this damned woman who was always standing in Zakhar's way, and he cursed her roundly, saying that she was a so-and-so, and she, for her part, laced into him even more maliciously. And soon everyone knew about the possessions Yakylyna's mother had left her, possessions that had been taken by Zakhar and his wife, even though Zakhar swore that, after Yakylyna's parents died, all that had been left was an empty house.

When a blind baby was born to Zakhar, Mavra made sure that everyone knew who was in the right, and who was in the wrong.

"That's how God punishes people!" she said over and over again.

It was true that a great misfortune befell Zakhar—a little son was born to him, but he turned out to be blind. For a long time, Varka did not realise that her little Vasylko could not see, even though she saw that he did not turn his face to the light, or smile at her until she touched his cheek, or grasp at anything that was handed to him. He turned first one ear and then the other in the direction that people were talking, and when he began to crawl, he moved straight ahead, no matter what was in his path—the oven, or the tub for washing clothes, or the loom, and it was only when he bumped into things, that he tried to avoid them the next time by groping in front of himself with his little hands. And his eyes, like those in a painting, were always fixed on one spot.

Varka noticed all of this but did not understand what it meant.

And then, she happened to meet Mavra on the street one day, and her sister-in-law, taking a good look at the baby, struck her hands in horror and shrieked: "Oh, my goodness! Your baby is blind!"

Varka raced home, screaming: "He's blind! He's blind!" She ran into the house where Zakhar was sitting and smoking, grabbed him by the shirt, and gasped: "Look! Oh, look! He's blind!"

"What's wrong with you? Have you gone mad? Who's blind? Where?" Zakhar attacked her as if someone had stuck a needle into him, without fully realising what was happening.

"Our Vasylko is blind!" Varka screeched, her voice grating and breaking, like glass being scratched.

Zakhar turned cold, and Varka raised the child up to her husband and looked closely, very closely, into his small eyes, round and dull like drops of cold oil, clutching at him and shoving him away at the same time. Terrified, Vasylko began to cry.

"And what am I to do with you now? Well, what? What? Tell me," Varka implored.

"Oh you scurvy woman, you damned creature, why are you crawling to me now?" Zakhar shouted, dumfounded. "What do you mean, he's blind? Where is he blind? Why are you lying? Who said so?"

"Oh, now I can see myself that he's blind! I can see it myself! O dear God! What are we to do now?" Varka burst into tears.

Up to now, it had never occurred to Zakhar that Vasylko was blind. Beset by problems and pressed for time, he had not doted on this child as he had on Mykyta. Only once had it struck him that his son's eyes were somewhat dull, but then he forgot all about it. Now he felt as if someone had placed a huge chunk of ice on his head; he froze and sat down, staring for a long time at his wife, who was rushing about the cottage with her infant. Both she and the baby were crying and screaming; she simply could not stop shrieking: "What in the world am I to do?"

Finally he said: "Nurse the child; you can see that he wants to eat." And he walked out of the house.

"Why has such a misfortune befallen me?" Zakhar thought, sitting down not too far from the house. "Am I worse than others? No! There are many people far worse that I am, but their children aren't cripples. That man there doesn't even go to church. And that one beat his father so viciously that the old man died. And what about me? I'm better than they are . . . Why has this happened to me? Why am I the only one who is being punished? Take my brother Opanas—he's tearing the hides off people with the interest that he charges . . . Mavra abuses Yakylyna . . . an orphan . . . But as for me . . . I've never sinned . . ."

He sat and thought for a long time. He knew how to prove things to himself as well as to others. And finally Zakhar concluded that this was not a misfortune and tried to convince his wife that if the child was blind, well, that was that. After all, some blind people were better off than people who could see. He reminded her how much money blind Zinko collected wandering from village to village—even his brother and father lived off what he earned.

But Varka could not be consoled, and every day she wept and cursed herself: "Why did I give birth to such a child? Who is to blame for it? I'm the one to blame—I'm the cause of our misfortune. What am I to do? Oh, cursed soul that I am. I can see, but I gave birth to a blind child, oh my, oh my, oh my! I gave birth to an ill-fated cripple, may I be damned!"

"But he might have been unfortunate even if he wasn't blind," Zakhar said.

"So what? He might or might not have ended up unfortunate, but now he's unfortunate from the very outset; he'll never see the world. I may as well be dead! Oh, woe is me, woe is me! He's blind, and I am to blame."

"It was God's will."

"God's will? But why did he pick me? He picked me, so it means that I, scurvy woman that I am, must be to blame. Forgive me, Zakhar! Oh, forgive me! Our Vasylko is blind, blind!"

Often now, Varka begged Zakhar's forgiveness and, the more he mistreated her, the more she clung to him. Zakhar had never played the saint with his wife, or talked to her in sweet tones—for he did not fear her any more than he feared a cockroach that he could squash under his boot . . .

So, when he came home angry, and she rushed to him to help him off with his boots, her hands trembling and her wide eyes staring at him, he would kick her in the face once, twice, with his filthy boot, so hard that the mud flew into her mouth, and she, thinking that he was punishing her because of Vasylko, would stretch her hands out to him and kiss his hand, moaning: "Forgive me! Forgive me!"

At these times, her words infuriated Zakhar, and he shouted; "Go to the devil's mother! You've become odious to me!"

And she would cry; her dark eyes shone with tears, her tiny face turned yellow and, looking like a brown-eyed Susan, she bowed her head like that flower and kept repeating: "Kill me, Zakhar. Why did I bear you a blind son? What am I worth?"

Zakhar would once again become convinced that it was Varka who was to blame, and that he himself was without sin. And at those times he would feel sorry for her, turn towards her and say: "There, there, that's enough. Are we the only ones who have a blind child? There are plenty of them in the world. That's enough, that's enough. After all, we have Mykyta as well."

"Mykyta," Varka would repeat, as if she did not know what she was saying. "Oh yes, there's Mykyta."

And she would feel somewhat better, and even though she still wept, it was not as bitterly as she had wept earlier, and she would smile at Zakhar through her tears. In time, she too began to get used to her little blind Vasylko, and she became even kinder to him, because who else would show him kindness now?

Whenever the opportunity presented itself, Mavra said: "If that ever happened to me, I'd choke the child to death, because what is he good for? He's of no use to himself or to anyone else."

But still, advising Varka to rub his eyes with a blue stone that she gave her, she stopped by every day to see if it had helped.

At the same time, Mavra was able to undermine Zakhar more effectively than earlier when she had spread lies about him. She managed to do this quietly, like water washing away a stone, by turning his wife against him.

Varka often wailed: "Why did I give birth to a blind child? How am I to live if, because of me, such a terrible thing has happened? If, because of me, my child will never see the sun?"

At those times, Marva yelled at her: "You idiot! Are you the only one who is to blame? Did you bring him into this world alone? What about Zakhar? After all, he's the father—so it's his fault too. And Opanas says that there was someone in their family who was blind, so there you have it . . ."

"No, no," Varka gesticulated. "It is I, I who am to blame, because I'm the mother. I was the one who was pregnant. I carried him—a blind child—and I gave birth to him. O my God, my dear God, why are you punishing me so terribly?"

"Why you, exactly? For what sins? Do you really think that you are sinful? You don't have any more sins than a little lamb, but as for Zakhar—he does not live righteously; even I know this."

"How?"

"Well, he abuses his own brother; he's tormenting him to death."

Mavra spent a long time telling Varka all about it, and the latter began to see things in a new light. She changed; before, she was like a blade of grass, but now she burgeoned into a shrub; she became more aware, comprehended more, saw her husband in a different light, and did not seem to believe him any more.

Zakhar did not notice this; it was all the same to him what his wife thought—she belonged to him, just as his cottage did. And so, even though Varka still blamed herself for "the little blind child," she now could also see the guilt of her husband before his brother.

One time Varka got up the nerve to say: "Zakhar, stop what you're doing . . . after all . . . he's your brother . . . and you're always against him . . . it . . . you know, shouldn't be like that."

Varka, like the mute grass, had trouble expressing herself.

Astonished, Zakhar could not understand what had come over her; and then he railed at her: "How dare you, you scurvy woman! Shoo! Sit still! Why are you flapping your mouth? Who's taught you how to do that?"

"No one . . . I . . . I . . . only . . . because we'll be in big trouble, Zakhar. You can see already, our Vasylko . . ."

"Go to the devil's mother! I know what I'm doing!"

Zakhar caught on that it was Mavra who had put her up to this, because formerly his wife had not dared to say a word to him; and so he ordered her: "I don't want to see so much as Mavra's foot in my house!" And then he thought; "Oh, if only I had a wife like that, may the devil take her!" And even though he hated Mavra, whenever he met her he turned to her with the sweetest words, as if he were sucking honey. And she also responded in a friendly manner, while thinking to herself; "May you drop dead!"

When Mavra heard what Zakhar had said about her, she was delighted and began to visit Varka as often as she could, as often as the sun appears in the sky—but on the sly at first, so that Zakhar would not see her. When Varka's husband was in the army, Mavra thought of her only infrequently and had no idea how difficult life was for Varka, or how hard she had to work to earn enough to feed herself and her son. But now she befriended Varka and kept trying to heal her son until red rings appeared around his eyes, and they began to look like the eyes of a fish.

Over time, Mavra took control of Zakhar's house, ordering his wife around and passing on to her whatever she knew. Zakhar was furious, but powerless. He tried beating Varka more often, but the seeds of discontent had been sown within her.

It seems that Yakylyna was of the same mind as her aunt Mavra—that a blind person was of no use in this world, and so she often abused Vasylko, pinching him and putting all sorts of rubbish in his hands, and then asking him what it was. Sometimes she would shove him into a hole and watch as he crawled around, trying to figure a way out. In the meantime, Yakylyna would walk around the edge, teasing him: "Peek-a-boo! Peek-a-boo! Where are you?" Just for laughs, she painted his face with dyes used to colour *krashanky [Easter eggs dyed in a single colour],* and the little tyke walked around with such a red face that his mother became alarmed; but he could not tell her what Yakylyna had done while she was caressing his cheeks.

Yakylyna had a lot of fun with Vasylko, but she did not always just tease him. There were times when it occurred to her that she should teach him something, and she would tell him: "This is a flower, you see—a poppy."

"A poppy," he repeated after her, running his fingers along the flower, from its stem to its blossom, feeling every leaf, and poking his finger into its crown of petals. And then he asked: "What's it like?"

"It's red. And here's a marigold—it's yellow. Sniff it, and see how it smells."

"It's yellow—it smells," Vasylko said.

"Yes, indeed."

"And the red one, the poppy?"

"It also smells, only not the same way."

He thought for a long time, and his eyes trembled like dewdrops, but he could not see the flower, and he asked: "What's red like?"

"It's like my jerkin."

Vasylko clutched at her jerkin.

It was difficult for the young girl to explain the word, and she said: "Red? Well, it's like the sun, when it's going to be windy."

"Where's the sun?"

"Where? Up in the sky. Way up there. Look!"

Yakylyna turned Vasylko's head directly towards the sun; she closed her eyes, but his eyes, like glass buttons, did not even blink. Yakylyna moved her finger from Vasylko's eyes way up high, and then brought it down again, saying: "So, the sun's up there . . . Way up there, far away, high in the sky! Do you see? Oh, it's impossible to look at it."

"I see," the little boy replied. "But why can't you look at it?"

"Because it's piercing."

"It's piercing," the boy replied. "It pierces you like a knife."

"Yes, but it pierces your eyes, not your finger."

"Yes, just the way my eyes feel when mummy rubs them with something." Vasylko made the connection and was delighted with himself. He now understood what the sun was, and that it pierces your eyes.

"The sun pierces, the sun is red, it pierces . . . Red is something bad," he said.

"Oh, no, it's wonderful, really wonderful! Red is the most wonderful colour there is," Yakylyna said.

"But it pierces the eyes."

"Why do you say that?"

"Aren't you the one who said that the sun is piercing?"

Yakylyna laughed: "Yes, because it's the sun, because it burns like fire, and it's red, and hot, and you can't look at it, but it's still wonderful, because when it shines it's bright and warm, and we can see, and when it's not there, it's rainy and cold . . . And a coral necklace is red, and my jerkin is red, and berries are red, and ribbons are red—and they're all wonderful!"

Vasylko was completely confused now. It had seemed to him that red was something bad, but apparently it was something wonderful. He had touched everything that was red—the jerkin, the coral beads, the flowers, and ribbons, but he had not touched the sun, because Yakylyna said that it was far away and very hot. But all these things were so unlike one another, that he simply could not understand what "red" was.

In the end, Yakylyna did manage to teach Vasylko where the sun was, and he knew on which side it was and, after looking up at the sky many times, it seemed to him that he was beginning to see it, that he could see some bright spots and shiny stripes with his unseeing eyes—and when there was no sun, everything seemed darker to him, and he complained to Yakylyna: "Today there doesn't seem to be any sun, because I'm cold!" And even if it was not cold, as soon as there was no sun, he felt cold.

"But look, it's coming out from behind a cloud. Look!"

And Vasylko looked and saw it through Yakylyna's eyes. And he rejoiced that the sun was there, and that it felt warm again.

"But it doesn't pierce me when I look at it," he said laughingly.

"It doesn't pierce you, because you're blind," Yakylyna said. "You can't see it."

Vasylko argued that he could see it: "I do so see it! I do!"

"You little fool," Yakylyna remonstrated, pulling him by the ear. Crying, he ran to his mother, and she, beside herself, lifted him, hugged him, kissed him, and consoled him, trying everything in her power to stop his tears. But before long, he hurried back to Yakylyna, as if he had forgotten that she had hurt him.

And so this was how Vasylko lived, seeing and not seeing, but hearing things that others did not hear. When it was completely silent in the orchard, the field, or the house, Vasylko still heard a soft creaking, squeaking, grating, and squealing. He heard all sorts of sounds, and he recognised people by their voices or by the way they walked, and he could hear them when they were still a long way off, when no one else could hear them coming.

Vasylko's father had long since accepted his son's blindness, because he could see how ably he could weave little ladders, sleighs, and all sorts of other things out of straw. And he could also spin—Yakylyna had taught him how to do that. And Zakhar concluded that Vasylko could be taught to weave, and that he could earn money this way. And then he thought that it might even be better to buy him a lyre when he grew older, and let him go to the markets and sing. He could earn a lot of money that way, more than if he were a farmer. He already had a voice that was crystal clear like glass, like water running over pebbles, and his singing was wonderful, and he sang about everything:

> "Yakylyna's pretty because she's red, red.
> Red as a ribbon."

and about what Yakylyna said:

> "Yakylyna said the blind boy can't see,
> He can't see—but he can hear
> The sun shine, the stars twinkle,
> His mother spin.
> Yakylyna said when white threads go,
> Red flowers grow . . ."

Vasylko's father had very little time now to spend with him or to think about him, and no time at all to worry about him. He had begun to teach his older son Mykyta how to read and write for, more than anything, he wanted his son to become the village secretary. He found this task difficult, however, because he himself was barely literate, and the boy kept fooling around. Zakhar wanted him to learn quickly and was cross that not much progress was being made. He beat the boy, who, taking a violent dislike to books, began to hide both from the books and from his father.

Zakhar himself had been named as the village secretary and, together with the village chief, he confused the community, moving the beads on the abacus so swiftly that no one could follow what he was doing, and always saying things like: "That's how it, my dear in-law." "That's how it is, my friend." "That's how it is, my little one." And, whenever people attacked him, demanding that he use the abacus and tell them what he had done with the money the Jew had given him for the tavern taxes, he would wriggle his way out with his "O seven angels from heaven!"

Zakhar would insist—O seven angels from heaven! O Christ-loving soldiers!—that no one had ever been able to accuse him of being a dishonest man. But just take a look at that man over there. Where does he get the money to live like that? And he would say all sorts of things, maintaining all the while that he, Zakhar, had served his country earlier on, and now he was serving the community faithfully and truthfully. But let the people criticise him, if that was what they were like . . .

And Zakhar would pull a long face, lower his eyes, and gesture hopelessly.

When they said that he was counting incorrectly, that he was leaving out rubles and *kopiyky*, he was insulted: "God be with you. Count it yourself then, as you best know how, and relieve me of my duties. If I don't please you, I'll go away."

Then, even though they all should have been happy to see him leave, they said: "Now, now then, in-law Zakhar, stay on for a while longer. What's the matter? If you've counted it correctly, then let it be so. May the devil take it all, that money!"

And so Zakhar stayed on as the village secretary. He counted the community's money and levied taxes, and the highest taxes that he levied were on his brother, and his brother paid them, for what was he to do? They could not get rid of Zakhar; the people thought that he was very well-educated, while Opanas was completely illiterate.

Yakylyna had barely turned sixteen when young men began courting her. Her uncle Zakhar came up with a fine scheme, wanting to marry her off to his older son Mykyta—a lad who still played with the boys out in the street and whom Yakylyna teased as one teases a child, shoving his cap down on his nose, or throwing dried peas at him, or dousing him with water.

Opanas and his wife were not concerned that Zakhar would win Yakylyna for his son—by the time he would be old enough to get married, Yakylyna would be an old woman already. All the same, afraid that Zakhar might try to marry her off to someone else, they took matters into their own hands, drove her into the city, and found her a position as a servant.

After two years in the city, Yakylyna, with the assistance of her uncle Zakhar—whom she rewarded generously for his help—fled back to her village. She was sick and tired of serving others, because even when she had lived in the village, Opanas had always shoved her out to work in the tobacco fields of the Jews and the lords.

When Yakylyna returned, Mavra took it upon herself to find her a husband. Yakylyna had taken a liking to her aunt Mavra, who liked to talk and told such interesting "stories." It was as if she knew everything in the world—how everyone lived, what they did, and what they said.

And so, perhaps, Yakylyna would have obeyed her aunt Mavra, if the latter had told her whom to marry. Mavra would have liked Yakylyna to marry the dimwitted young shepherd, the son of the rich aunt she had buried. But she could not bring herself to give her such advice, because he was far too old for her.

At that time, a young man who was an orphan—Makar Tarasenko—began to woo Yakylyna. A small man with a big nose and a healthy crop of hair, he was slightly cross-eyed and had avoided serving in the army. He was tractable and often worked for Opanas, either for pay, or just to help him with this or that. No matter what he was told to do, he did it with a big smile, saying: "What's true, is true."

Mavra did not think he was overly smart, because he never knew what to say when he was asked; "What are you going to do?" Or: "What do you think?"

He always replied: "I don't know. What do you advise me to do? You're like a mother and father to me."

There was something else about Makar that appealed to Mavra—he ate very little, hastened to fetch things for Mavra or to hand them to her, and did not talk to Yakylyna at all. He worked hard, only occasionally raising his eyes from his work to say sternly to Yakylyna: "But your aunt told you to bleach the cloth. Why don't you do what your aunt tells you to do?"

He said that he had never seen such a fine married woman as Mavra, and that "Opanas was a lucky man." He also stated that he, Makar, would be happy if they would adopt him as a son—because they had no son of their own—and he would feed them and look after them until the day they died.

And so Yakylyna was engaged to Makar. Opanas was happy that they had broken free from Zakhar, and Mavra was confident that Makar would live with them in their home. In this way, they would have their own worker, and Yakylyna's land would remain in their hands.

After Mavra succeeded in her matchmaking, and Yakylyna and Makar were married, Makar bowed to Mavra and said: "Thank you auntie. We will share your bread. May Yakylyna never forget that you took the place of her mother."

At first Makar did not appeal to Yakylyna. She used to chase him away at the *vechornytsi [evening party for young people]*, shoving him and reviling him, but he just kept repeating: "You're wonderful!" And: "You're wonderful! Just look at me."

She kept chasing him away, but he continued to stand by her fence every evening, whispering that she was wonderful. As soon as the stars began to shine, as soon as Opanas and his wife went to sleep, Makar would slip into the house and whisper: "Come with me, Yakylyna. I want to tell you something."

At first she went because she wanted to know what he had to say. And then she went without being called, just like that. Who can say why she went? She followed him like a thread follows a needle. He went out of the house, and so did she. They would stand by the fence, hidden by the shadows.

"Well, what do you want? Why did you call me?" she always asked him.

He would stroke her back saying: "You're wonderful, like a dainty little egg, like a *paska [braided circular Easter bread]*, like a shiny hazelnut."

"Why are you lying?"

"No, I swear to God that it's true . . ."

And his arm, hard and firm as the branch of a tree, would insinuate itself around her waist.

Yakylyna pretended not to notice anything, but then a warm feeling would flow through her body from her head to her feet, her heart would thump once and then fall silent, and she would lean back, murmuring softly and breathlessly: "Oh, why are you choking me?"

Then he would perch on the fence on one side of the willows, and she would sit down on the other side and say: "How can I be wonderful when I have so many freckles?" Her freckles were her sore point.

"Well, so what? It's nothing, and you can hardly see them, but you're wonderful! Marry me. Listen, and I'll tell you how we'll live. We'll have all that we need to eat and drink, and dress attractively . . . Come on, listen to me . . . Come here and sit down on this side . . ."

His arm would once again encircle her waist, and Yakylyna, no longer resisting, would just ask him: "But will you beat me?"

"Never! Never in the whole world!"

"But aren't there prettier girls than me?"

"No, there aren't," Makar would say, falling silent.

"Well, go on, tell me more," Yakylyna pleaded.

And he would begin to tell her a story, and Yakylyna would listen. His arm held Yakylyna firmly, but she did not complain that he was crushing her. Her eyes closed, her head leaning on his shoulder, she dreamt sweet dreams as she listened to Makar.

The stars smiled down from the dark sky, and it seemed that every one of them was trying to peek through the green tresses of the willow in order to see who was standing there beneath them, and the warm light breeze tossed the willows' curly locks, but nothing could be discerned in the darkness.

No matter how many young men Yakylyna's uncle Zakhar tried to match her up with after he realised that she would not marry his son, she did not want to marry a single one of them—"not for anything in the world!"

After Makar married Yakylyna, he became a different man. His attitude towards Opanas changed completely. He not only stopped agreeing with Opanas and Mavra, and praising everything that they said and did, he even ignored Opanas's advice as to how to build a new cottage on Yakylyna's land to replace the dilapidated old one. Using Opanas's money, he did everything his own way, and occasionally even laughed in the older man's face.

"Am I to build a house here? Why, every fool knows that if you build a house in a ditch it's going to be damp."

One time he had the temerity to tell Mavra that she was old and ugly; another time he called Opanas a greedy Jew; and then he took away Yakylyna's land from him and railed at him, because it had not been left fallow for more than ten years.

As for Opanas, he could not help but praise Makar: "The scoundrel did a wonderful job of deceiving us; it rips my innards apart to think how he duped us!"

It was hard for Opanas and Mavra to lose the land that they were accustomed to ploughing as if it were their own. Oh, it was very hard indeed. Mavra seemed to shrink, and her face changed, and she vowed that if ever again she believed anyone in this world, then may she be damned.

Zakhar of course was delighted that Opanas had been taken in. He chortled, crowing gleefully: "Oh yes indeed, a cat doesn't always dine on meat—there's Great Lent as well! O sins, our mortal sins!"

He took it upon himself to advise Makar, telling him to make Opanas accountable for the money he had received for the tobacco from Yakylyna's land and for Yakylyna's earnings when she worked as a servant. It ended with Makar suing Opanas. Zakhar agreed to be a witness against his brother; he knew that he would not receive much from Makar in return for this—Makar was not that kind of a man—he did it just to delight his own heart.

Now Zakhar walked around in a happy frame of mind and pitied Opanas to his face, saying; "O seven angels from heaven! Who would have thought earlier that the son-of-a-bitch that you accepted into your bosom would turn out to be such a scoundrel? And Yakylyna's a fine one too; there's no doubt about that! She won't say as much as a word in her uncle's defence. O sins, our mortal sins! Now she's saying that she never even saw any soft bread in your home, that she always had to eat dry crusts. Really, it's hard to believe!"

"Get away from me, Satan!" Opanas said, turning away from Zakhar. But the latter, whenever he met Opanas, always bemoaned the way Makar and Yakylyna had repaid Opanas for all that he had done for them.

Mavra also taunted Opanas, saying: "Well, there you have it, you idiot! Why did you trust that cabbagehead? So now you'll have to pay him a lot of money, you sure will! I told you: 'Don't believe people! Don't ever believe them!'"

"But you yourself . . ." Opanas started to say.

"You yourself, you yourself," Mavra mimicked him. "It was all because of you, you blind fool. And even if I had . . . Why did you listen to me?"

It appeared now that Mavra was not to blame, and that all the fault lay strictly with Opanas, even though she had formerly said: "He's a fine young man; we can certainly give Yakylyna in marriage to him."

The day before the trial was to take place, there was such a hubbub in Zakhar's home that Mavra, curious to see how Zakhar was beating up on his wife, jumped from her house into that of her sister-in-law—their homes stood side by side, very close together. She liked to watch people fighting or heaping abuse on each other. But no one was fighting in Zakhar's home, and Mavra froze on the threshold, unable to fathom what was happening.

Varka, as if she had gone mad, was rushing about the house holding the blind child and shouting: "Help! Oh, help!"

The little boy was shrieking frantically, and Zakhar was darting around his wife, trying to take the child away from her, but she kept turning away and would not let him.

"What's going on here?" Mavra cried.

"Well you see . . . The boy has scalded himself, but she won't let me see him . . . Do you think she's gone mad?" Zakhar asked in a terrified voice

Mavra stood in Varka's path and snapped: "Give me the boy!"

Startled, Varka let go of Vasylko.

Mavra took over. She ripped off the boy's pants and shirt. His legs, from his waist to his feet were red and already covered with large blisters filled with water.

"Is there any oil?" Mavra asked authoritatively. "Give it here!"

It felt wonderful to be able to yell at Zakhar, and she could see that both of them, fools that they were, would not be able to do anything without her assistance. Zakhar did not know how he found the oil in the icon lamp and gave it to her. Mavra silently dipped the torn shirt into the oil and began dabbing it on the boy, who was still screaming with pain.

Mavra said sternly: "Hush, now! Hush!"

All the while, Varka was trying to take back the child, crying: "Help! Oh, help!"

Mavra did not let her near the child and tried to protect it with her hands. Finally she yelled: "Be quiet! Get away from here!"

At that very moment, Opanas walked into his brother's house. One of his daughters had told him that Mavra was there—she herself had run over to see what was happening. Opanas glanced at the scalded boy and said: "That's wonderful. It sure will leave a permanent memory!" Then he looked over at his brother who sat dumfounded, as in a stupor.

Zakhar found it strange to see Opanas in his home, because although he often dropped in to see his brother—at times to tease him with "pleasant" words, and to call him "my dear, beloved little brother"—Opanas never visited him. And he also found it strange to see his brother's wife busying herself with their little boy. A single thought bolted through his head like flash of lightning: "Is it God who has punished me with this child for my sins? But for what kind of sins?"

This thought had occurred to him before, but not as sharply, perhaps because his wife Varka had taken upon her soul the sin for the blind Vasylko. "For what sins?" Zakhar thought. "We're all sinners before God . . . O sins! O . . . Oh my, oh my!"

Zakhar no longer saw or heard anything. He did not see Opanas leave, saying: "I'll go to the *khvel'shar [assistant doctor]* for some medicine," and then reappear, bringing back with him a paste or powder that he and Mavra used to ease the little boy's pain.

He regained his senses only when Vasylko stopped shrieking and fell asleep, and neither Opanas or Mavra were in the house. There was only Varka sitting by their son, looking at him and whispering softly: "Help! Oh, help!" And from that time on, no matter what she said, she always added the phrase: "Oh, help!" Thus, she would say: "Hello. Oh, help! And have you finished harvesting? Oh, help!"

Some people thought that Vasylko had scalded himself accidentally by sticking his foot into a cauldron of boiling water when he was climbing down from the bed on top of the clay stove, while others thought that it was his father who was to blame; that it was because he had sinned—for having sided with Yakylyna against his own brother, even though Varka had pleaded with him not to.

The next morning, as Zakhar was setting out for the village office for the court case, he met Opanas. The latter wanted to flee from Zakhar's "pleasant" words, but Zakhar said: "Wait a moment . . . You know, my brother, I think that . . ." and he hesitated for a moment. "I think that . . . I'm going to tell the court that Yakylyna wasted her own money . . ."

Then, without so much as a backward glance, Zakhar continued on his way, while Opanas rolled with laughter. "That's wonderful. Really wonderful!" His words could barely be understood through his laughter, and Mavra ran out of the house to ask what was going on. Opanas just waved his hand and laughed so hard that his cheeks shook like red apples hanging on a branch when they are tossed by the wind. Then, having had his laugh, he followed Zakhar to see the chief.

Makar lost his case.

After the court hearing was over, Opanas paid Zakhar some money, and the brothers no longer quarrelled, because two dogs do not bicker when a third one is taking away a bone and running off with it. Zakhar looked at the matter this way: Opanas was a force to be reckoned with, and it was better to harness this force, like the wind in a mill, than to let it rush about unchecked on the steppe. Moreover, Makar was blaming Zakhar for taking money that belonged to the community. In addition, the brothers were on an equal footing now—they were both landless, and so, banding together, they rented more land. And they both turned against the people—Zakhar squeezed out sweat from them whenever he could, and Opanas continued gouging interest from them.

When Vasylko recovered, Varka, her eyes big and dark, said: "Oh, thank goodness—Oh, help!—that he didn't die."

Mavra, as always, quarrelled, cursed her fate, and, whenever her husband said his "wonderful," she said: "Hush! And spit, so that you don't cast a spell. It could be that she's watching us, spying on us . . . And then she'll laugh at us. Evil has come upon us."

"But who's spying on us?"

"Who?" she whispered. "Fate! She's everywhere. When things are going well, she creates evil, and if anyone decides to do something and says: 'It will certainly be that way,' or: 'I will do thus and so,' she turns everything upside down. And if a poor soul thinks to himself: 'Everything's wonderful—I'm a fortunate man,' fate is watching him and will bring him down the very next day."

"Who cares!" Opanas whistled. "I don't believe in all that. If I'm lucky today, then I'll be lucky tomorrow."

"Oh, sure, you idiot! And why was it that when we had that mud slide, that everyone, all who were there—Maksym, and Mykhaylo, and others—they all died, but Ivan stayed alive? He was in deeper than all the others, but he came out alive; he didn't think he'd come out alive, but he did . . . That's fate. And when Mykyta climbed the cherry tree, and the branch broke, and he fell down and was killed . . . Well, what's a cherry tree? It's not a high tree, and no one has ever fallen out of a cherry tree, or been killed that way. But Mykyta was killed—that was his fate!"

And so Mavra feared her fate; but fate did, after all, indulge them. She and Opanas lived in harmony, did not experience poverty, and only one thread snapped—when Yakylyna's property was taken from them. Because of this, Mavra railed against Yakylyna and spread rumours about her throughout the entire village, saying things that it would be shameful to repeat.

Yakylyna led a fairly good life with her Makar, but there was one promise to her that he did not keep: that he would never—"in the whole world"—beat her.

The Madwoman
(1898)

It was a warm, quiet night. The stars streamed out and shimmered like silver dew in the sky. There was no moon, and so, as soon as the sun set, it became so dark that it was difficult to see who was walking on the other side of the street. Clouds gradually moved across the stars, and a darkness, thick like honey, flowed over the land, veiling everything like a cobweb, turning the houses into shapeless piles of coal and transforming the trees into shadowy figures with arms lifted upwards, as if in weariness, or fright.

The evening sounds of the cattle, horses, and pigs that drifted in from the fields had died away; children's laughter—fine, like coral beads, and tinkling like the ringing of scythes—had faded on the street; and the foreman had already galloped through the village with the reminder: "Girls! Women! Come to work at the lord's . . . Come to weed the tobacco . . . for a gold coin per day . . . Come!"

It grew still darker, as if the village had been stowed away in a black sack. Lights were lit in the cottages, as if stars had streaked down from up above—one for every dwelling. Supper was over. Night fell, and it became even quieter in the village than during harvest time when everyone leaves for the day to work in the fields.

Everyone lay down to sleep. Today neither the young men, nor the young women, were shouting out their songs in the village common because it was a working day, and now, after relaxing for a while, the exhausted people were sleeping—unless perhaps, someone hiding behind a house laughed quietly, like water dripping off a roof, and then it became still once again, and no one could be seen, because there was no moon, only the tiny, blinking, unseeing stars . . .

Now it was completely silent—not even a leaf fell from a tree; it was so quiet that even the dogs were not barking, because their masters were in their houses, and there were no strangers walking about. Suddenly there was a creaking sound . . . a rustle . . . Something sneaked out of a house . . . Then there was another creaking sound at the other end of the village . . . a rustle . . . And something leapt into another house.

A light was still burning in this house, but it was not visible from outside, for the window was tightly blocked with a black kerchief, and the lamp was not on the table, but on a bench in the corner. Near the lamp, a fairly young married woman was bent over, laying out some soiled, tattered cards.

The woman was not old yet, but so many wrinkles had puckered the skin around her eyes and mouth that she looked like an old mushroom when its rosy flesh turns so dark that it is almost black, its white cap becomes ragged, and its thin covering yellows, peels off, and dangles. The young matron looked withered and, like mown grass, she seemed to be growing more withered by the minute; her nose was long and pointed, her eyebrows were dark and wide, her narrow grey eyes seemed to be hiding behind the bridge of her nose, and her blond hair kept creeping out from under her cap and falling in her eyes.

Her hands, grey and tough, like bark, were quickly dealing the cards, while her lips whispered: "Yes. . . yes . . . I'll show you . . . You did steal it . . . the black one . . . Yes, yes . . ."

When the door creaked, the woman turned around, shuffled the cards, and said: "Is it you, Khrystya? You really scared me . . . I thought it was someone else . . ."

Khrystya stared fixedly at the cards with her round eyes—also grey, but more pronounced than the other woman's; her thin eyebrows grew in a jagged line just above her eyes. She replied: "It's me, auntie."

Then she stopped for a moment and added: "Is your husband at home?"

"Oh, no! He's gone off somewhere, the devil take him!" She had a deep, hoarse voice, even though she herself, like a heron, was neither big nor plump.

Khrystya walked around the room and, except for four children's legs—dirty and scrawny like those of a cricket—sticking out from the clay bed atop the oven, she did not see anyone other than the young matron.

"So, you see, auntie, I've come . . . Are we going to lay out the cards right now? How is it possible to tell from the cards what the future holds for someone? Oh, I would really like to know—which card is it that divines who has stolen something? I'd really like to know!" Her eyes gleamed. "Come on, auntie, let's deal the cards right now."

Khrystya said all this very rapidly, tearing off her words the way calico is ripped for a shirt. Her rosy cheeks became even redder, like a poppy when it peeks out at the sun from behind the house or a willow.

"You don't say!" The mistress of the house said hoarsely. "I'm to tell you everything at once . . . See how smart you think you are! Do you suppose it came that quickly to me? No, first ask the one I had to ask, and then hurry to learn the rest . . . Just imagine! She already wants to tell fortunes!"

Khrystya fell silent.

It was evident that she was more than a little afraid of this woman called Kateryna Kandzyuba, a good fortune-teller who "always told the truth and knew everything." How was it possible not to be afraid of her?

Khrystya fell silent, even though her lips were still open—so wide that her small white teeth could be seen—as if she had not finished speaking, or wanted to ask something, but did not dare. A small mole near the corner of her mouth quivered, and her eyes became sad.

Kateryna glanced at her, and then spoke more quietly, staring straight into Khrystya's eyes—and the latter could not turn away, almost as if she were nailed to the spot: "It's like this: if you want to tell fortunes, then . . . But swear you won't tell anyone."

Khrystya began to swear and cross herself.

"No, not like that. Are you wearing a cross?"

"Yes."

"Take it off."

Khrystya removed the little yellow cross from her neck and gave it to Kateryna.

"Do you have icons in the house?"

"Yes."

"You'll take them down when you get home and hide them in the pigsty, you hear? If you want to be the kind of person I am, if you want to know everything that was, that is, and that will be, then you have to do this . . . So that you can get to know "him" . . . Now take a vow like this . . ."

Kateryna leaned over to Khrystya and began to whisper something directly into her mouth, gazing continually into her eyes from so close up that Khrystya's eyes became crossed. All the same, however, Khrystya was unable to leave the spot where she was standing and move away from Kateryna.

She only squeaked once—like a fly caught by a boy—"Oh, I'm afraid, auntie, I'm scared," and then she obediently began to repeat Kateryna's words in a whisper, even though, with every word, it seemed to her that she had stepped on a sharp hoe or was passing her fingertip over a knife.

Finally, Kateryna stopped whispering into Khrystya's mouth, leaned away from her and, still without lowering her eyes, began speaking: "When he runs up to you tonight, you hear, you hear now . . ."

Kateryna continually repeated the words "you hear," and Khrystya also repeated "you hear" without being aware that she was doing so. Now she was sitting, and she looked sleepy—her eyelids were half lowered, and her eyelashes, appearing unnaturally long, covered her eyes and cast a fine shadow that stretched far down on her cheeks.

"So then, you hear?"

"You hear," Khrystya said.

"Yes, indeed, when he comes running to you . . . I will send him to you tonight . . ."

"Who is he?" Khrystya asked, wriggling restlessly as if she were awakening from a dream.

Kateryna looked at her sharply and repeated: "Well, 'he'—on black horses, a four-horse team."

Khrystya said: "Oh, yes, 'he,'" and she seemed to doze off again.

"Well then, you hear, you will travel far, far away, but you will have to return on foot, you hear, through a forest and through a swamp . . . There will be many different creatures there . . . You'll see many creatures with horns, with tails . . . And this will continue until the cock crows, you hear? But don't say anything; remain silent—remain silent, because if you get scared and scream, it will all vanish, and you will never know anything; it will mean that you are unfit. You hear?"

She was silent for a moment, and then added: "Well, get up now and go home." Kateryna blew on Khrystya.

Khrystya jumped up from where she was sitting and looked around in a daze, as if she could not immediately grasp where she was and what had happened to her.

She stood like this for a long time in the middle of the house until Kateryna said: "Well, Khrystya go home now, you hear?"

"You hear? Go home?"

"Yes, go home."

"I'm to go home?"

"Of course, you hear, I'm saying: 'go home'."

Khrystya turned around and quietly walked away. She was stumbling—and did not say good-bye to Kateryna.

Afterwards, Khrystya could not remember how she finally made her way home.

Along the way, she kept seeing all sorts of things—horns, green tails coiled into rings, and small, split hooves that danced before her eyes. Yellow and red flames, seemingly bound into spheres, leapt upwards; somewhere close by, strong teeth were clacking, and green eyes as big as apples gleamed in the dark. Well, it was exactly like what she had seen once in a picture that a Hungarian was selling—but no, it was even more terrible than that!

Dashing into the house where her husband and children were soundly sleeping, she rushed up to the bed-bench, lay down, and covered her head with a quilt.

Who can say if she fell asleep or not, but before the break of dawn she frightened her husband with such a terrible shriek that he thought the house was on fire. He jumped up like a madman, and, groping around, found his wife sitting up with her arms widespread, as if she wanted to catch someone.

"There, over there . . . See . . . Oh, how green he is! Oh my, is something else peeping out? And does he ever have good horses—they're so swift! I know, I know! What else? Yes, indeed!"

"What is it, what are you prattling about?"

Khrystya continued: "But I didn't scream; you didn't hear me, did you? You're lying . . . Oh, I'm scared, I'm scared! What's this? To ride again? Oh, oh, oh!"

Roman tried to soothe Khrystya as best he could, but then, seeing that she was going on in the same vein, as if she were talking to a third party, he slapped her a few times for not letting him get a good night's sleep. He liked to sleep.

It was then that Khrystya came to her senses and said: "What's this? Is it almost daytime? Oh, the roosters are crowing . . . Well, he certainly tried to scare me, but I wasn't afraid."

Roman just spat in disgust and got up.

From that night on, Khrystya began going to see Kateryna, the fortune-teller, both during the day and at night—it was as if she had been charmed.

The people were surprised. The old women said that Khrystya was learning how to tell fortunes and that was why she was seen so rarely in church.

Khrystya, however, said: "I'm so poor that I have nothing to wear to church; I've worn out the clothes I had before I got married, and my husband is the kind of man—may no good ever come to him—who never buys me anything. Who goes to church in ragged clothing? I'm ashamed to!"

We can assume, it is true, that Khrystya began to lay out cards but, for some reason, she could never lay them out properly the way Kateryna did. She only learned how to tell what each card meant—tears, or a wedding, or money. But she did not know how to tell a person's fortune; even though she laid the cards out— she could not guess what would happen and to whom. Most of what she said was just something she made up.

She did not hit the mark with her sister, or with any of the young women who asked her to tell their fortunes when they saw cards in her home. Someone had stolen her sister's yarn. Khrystya said that a dark-haired man had taken it and gone away towards the rising sun. But, as it turned out, no one had stolen it; her sister's little boy had dragged it off somewhere and then brought it back.

And it was the same with the young women; if she said: "Such and such a man is going to ask for your hand in marriage," it never came to pass—a completely different man would become her betrothed.

Why was it like this? Why could Kateryna tell fortunes so skilfully that, even when she was hauled into court for her fortune telling, she was able to guess during the trial exactly how much money the judge had in his pocket? And Khrystya once asked Kateryna how she could divine things so accurately.

You see, before all this happened, Khrystya had never visited Kateryna, because the fortune teller lived at the other end of the village, but she had heard from others how skilfully Kateryna could tell fortunes, how much money she earned doing this, and that every Sunday there were as many people at her house as there were at the market, and they all came carrying bags with them—they brought her all kinds of goods just to have her tell them their fortunes.

Then, one day Khrystya lost a ruble she had stealthily taken from her mother—her mother was old and did not need the money, but Khrystya needed a new jerkin. She searched and searched for it, but could not find it; she thought that someone had stolen it and so, for the very first time, she went to Kateryna to have her fortune told.

Kateryna asked her all about it, and then, after laying out the cards, she said: "No one has stolen your money; you'll find it. I won't tell you where, but you'll find it. Look for it—and you'll find it . . . Was it a lot of money?"

"Well, just wait, I'll fool you," Khrystya thought. The little mole by her lips quivered, and she said confidently: "Of course it was a lot, auntie! It was five rubles!"

Kateryna looked at her and said: "Why are you lying? What five rubles are you talking about, when it wasn't so?"

Astonished, Khrystya turned beet red: "It seems she really does know everything," she thought.

Khrystya's belief in Kateryna grew stronger when she found the ruble in some rubbish as she was cleaning the house before Easter. It was then that she got the urge to learn how to tell fortunes, so that she, like Kateryna, could sit around, do nothing, earn money without sweating, and have everyone fear her, believe her, and look up to her as if she held some mysterious power in her hands.

Unfortunately, divining did not come easily to Khrystya. No matter how hard she applied herself, she still could not guess what had happened, or what would happen, and she did not know how to speak convincingly.

Khrystya did not realize that Kateryna, having taught her to lay out the cards, had not taught her how to read a person's face, to see who was happy, who was sad, who was kind, who was angry, who was lying, and who was not. She had not taught her to ferret out information, to spy, to eavesdrop, to make inquiries—as she herself did. And her husband and children also found out about things for her and told her all about them. It was only then that Kateryna took everything that she knew, put it all together, reworked it, and told fortunes.

Many times, when Khrystya came to her at night, Kateryna would look her straight in the eye and order her to do certain things: "Tomorrow you will go to the house of Ivan Naydonenko; you'll crouch by the window so you can't be seen, and you'll listen to what is being said in the house. But if someone should ask you why you're there, don't tell anyone—anyone at all—that it was I who sent you. You'll only say: 'I just happened to be here!' You hear?"

"You hear," Khrystya, looking drowsy, gave her usual reply. And she would assiduously do everything exactly as Kateryna had instructed her to do, and then she would tell her everything, but why and for what reason—she did not know; nor did she ask; nor did she tell anyone.

Kateryna knew about all sort of thefts. At times, she was threatened by thieves to remain silent—not to tell fortunes. When that happened, she would tell a man whose horse had vanished when and how it had been stolen, and where it had been sold, but she did not say who had stolen it, or else she just said: "It was a tall, dark man." And since there are many of those in the world, the thief was satisfied because he had not been unmasked, and the man was also satisfied, because the fortune teller had told him much that was true about the theft.

Kateryna only had to see a person once, and she would never forget either him or his name.

People were amazed when she would turn around to someone and say: "Why, hello, Yarema!" And yet it seemed to this Yarema that he had never laid eyes on Kateryna before, and he wondered how she knew what his name was.

Kateryna needed to hear only a word or two to grasp who was related to whom, and who did not like whom.

One time, a couple of young ladies came to her because they had heard about her great skill at fortune-telling. When Kateryna saw the team of four horses near her window and the young ladies dressed in silk on her doorstep, she initially became alarmed. But then she calmed down, went outside, and welcomed them. And, after finding out why they had come, told them she would gladly tell them their fortunes, but, alas, she did not have cards that were suitable for people of their rank.

"These peasant cards are not at all appropriate. You have to get new ones," she said.

The young ladies left their footman at Kateryna's home and went to the priest's house to get some cards. When they returned, Kateryna took the new cards, laid them out, and divined everything about them: how old they were, and how many members there were in their family; that one of their brothers was an officer, while another one was married, but did not live with his wife; what kind of "suitors" they had, and which one they liked the best; and that they would soon get married because both of them were "beautiful," and that the younger one would marry first . . . And she told them many other things, and the young ladies were amazed.

This is how skilfully Kateryna could tell fortunes! It was easiest of all for her to tell girls their fortunes, because she arranged for evening parties for young people to be held in her home. When the girls began to chatter like magpies, they did not hold anything back; they gossiped about themselves, and their friends, and the young men. They withheld nothing—everything poured out of them like water through a sieve, and when auntie Kateryna began dropping questions in the way that only she knew how, or when she put a bottle of whiskey on the table—she found out about absolutely everything that was going on in the village, both with the peasants and the lords.

Kateryna learned a great deal about other people from the girls, but they talked even more about themselves. They teased one another, laughed, and then stared in amazement when Kateryna would say to one of them: "Your stomach's empty, but you're dressed finely; it doesn't matter that you sit hungry at home because that doesn't show on your face, but if your jerkin is new, then all the young people can see it." Or: "If you've kissed a young lord, it's no use being fussy about who you marry." Or: "Do you think I don't know who your heart desires?" Or: "Well, there are three embroidered linen betrothal cloths in your chest, one sheepskin coat, and two skirts—it's time you were married."

The girls could not figure out how she knew all this, and they were astonished at how well she could tell their fortunes. It was as if she could see through wood and hear through walls what had only been whispered to someone, or had only been thought— yes, they were truly amazed at how skilfully she told fortunes.

Khrystya could not tell fortunes in the same way. What Kateryna did was incredible, and did Khrystya really suppose that Kateryna would share all she knew? The latter only led her on from day to day, and that was it, whereas Khrystya ran over to Kateryna's every day and told her everything.

There were times when she did not want to go, but something seemed to pull her there. She would begin doing something, and a voice within her would start up: "Go, go!" And she would experience such an urge, that no matter how hard she tried to overcome it, she would drop everything—her work and her children—and run to see Kateryna.

Kateryna, sitting at the window and looking out, would smile shrewdly and say: "Why have you left your work and come here?"

"You know, auntie, I myself don't know why I felt such a strong desire to come and see you; it was such an urge, such an urge, that it almost hurt! I had just one thought—I'll go to auntie Kateryna's! It seems to me that even if the house had caved in, or no matter what else might have happened—I still would have had to come to see you."

Kateryna smiled the same shrewd smile and said: "Do you know why you felt this urge?"

"Why?"

"Because I wanted you to feel it . . . I sat down by the window and started thinking: 'That cloud won't pass over the sun before Khrystya runs over here.' And it happened just as I said it would. It's always like that—whenever I think of someone—no matter who it is or where she may be—she will immediately come flying to me. She'll leave what she's baking or boiling, abandon her baby in the cradle, and appear before me—just like that!"

"Oh, dear mother of mine! How do you make people do things like that, auntie?"

"You want to know, do you? You're too foolish to know everything. Do you think this is all I can do? You have to go through what I've experienced, and only then will you know. But I can see that you're not suited to learning our ways of doing things, so why should I waste my time telling you about it?"

"I won't be a coward," Khrystya asserted, but still, she always quaked with fear when Kateryna gave her a sharp look.

Khrystya really did fear Kateryna. She feared her toothless mouth, her narrow grey eyes, and her hair that was completely dishevelled and looked as if it were strewn with ashes; she feared her long, dark fingertips with their big nails, like the claws of a hawk. Who can tell what else she was afraid of, but she certainly did fear the fortune teller from the night that she took the cross off her neck and gave it to her.

Khrystya feared Kateryna and did not like her, but she obeyed her in everything, as she would obey her mother. She probably would have listened to her if she had been ordered to steal something or kill someone—even though there were times when she argued with her, or thought: "You can rage all you want to, I won't do as you say."

Nevertheless, she would do it, and she herself would be surprised that she had done it.

Kateryna could tell at once when Khrystya did not want to obey her—it was as if she could read her thoughts—and then she would say: "Well, why are you being stubborn—you're still going to do as I say!"

Embarrassed, Khrystya would obey her.

There were times when Kateryna told her to do something just for a lark: "When you get home, you'll cook some borshch, but when you all sit down to eat, you'll pour the borshch into the slop pail, you hear?"

Khrystya would laugh and think: "Am I stupid or what, that I would do such a thing?"

But when she got home, she would have a great urge to pour out the borshch, and she would do it, even though her husband shouted: "Ugh, you stupid woman! What are you doing, you stupid bitch!"

And she would reply: "I just did what I felt like doing!"

If Kateryna had so desired, it is possible that Khrystya would have given her all her money and everything that she owned, but, thank God, she had nothing to give her. She was poor. They had managed to put up a house only quite recently, and it had already begun to crumble, because it was constructed with rotten wood, and the clay oven was not built well.

Khrystya gathered all sorts of news for Kateryna and told her absolutely everything about what was happening, where and how people were living. There were times, however, when she did not want to talk at all, but Kateryna only had to say: "Well, speak up!" and she would scoop everything out of Khrystya—all of her thoughts—just as if she had used a spoon.

At times, Khrystya complained to Kateryna about her fate and how unfortunate she was. Her husband was not like other people—he was not making any headway. It was as if he did not want anything more out of life—yes, it was thus and thus, but nothing better was needed. When she had lived at her mother-in-law's, she had been willing to give up half her life to clamber her way into her own home, but as for him—he had not cared at all! She was always arguing and quarrelling in the hope that her father-in-law would chase them out of his home.

Who would want to live in a house where one had to work hard for other people's children, where one's own children were mistreated, where the mother-in-law was continually scolding— praising one daughter-in-law one day, and then, the next day, saying that the other one was the good one. If you said anything, you were "stupid and inept," but if you were silent, you were asked: "Why are you pouting?" And you were told: "Since we've accepted you into the family, you'd better behave yourself!" And it would be better not to hear how they swore at her father!

"Oh, auntie," Khrystya said, "you're lucky. You haven't known any misery; you haven't lived in your in-law's house!"

"No, I know about this as well, even though it's true that my father-in-law and mother-in-law didn't beat my eyes out, and I didn't have to listen very long to their nagging: 'Where are you off to? Why? Stay at home! You're such a lazybones, you don't do anything!' I didn't have to listen long, because I wasn't stupid, because I knew 'something.'"

"How? What?"

Kateryna waved her hand dismissively, raised her eyebrows, and said: "They both died."

Then, after remaining silent for a little bit, she added—who knows why she did so: "If you really want something, it will get done. That's how. But what's the use . . . Well, are you living better now that you're alone with your husband?"

"Oh, no, auntie. The house is rickety, there are lots of children . . . You know how it is, you know . . . It hasn't been six years yet, and there are five of them already . . . They've drained me completely . . .

"Do you think I was always like this? Like this? I was an attractive girl! Oh, the jerkins that I used to make for myself—I dreamt them up myself, and all the girls were envious; but now—look at this—is this a jerkin? It's nothing but patches . . . It's enough to make you go begging, for there's no money to make yourself one.

"And do you think the children are dressed as they should be? So we're all in tatters, and I have to do everything myself, all by myself, and the children are so small.

"Oh, I'm so unfortunate! It seems I'm always flying around in circles like the arms of a windmill out in the field—cooking, and washing, and sewing, and when the harvest comes, there's no one to leave the children with, and so I drag them along and go to the field with children hanging on to me like pears dangling on a pear tree."

"Of course, that's a woman's lot in life—you can't do anything about it," Kateryna observed. "It's no wonder that when one of the children happens to fall ill, you think: 'Oh, if only you would die.' Because, in any event, another one will come along to take its place, or maybe two, or even three instead of one, and there's no time at all for them!"

She knew this "woman's fate" very well, and even though she herself was not too badly off, she still pitied other women. She began to feel sorry for Khrystya, who had been harnessed in a yoke when she was still very young.

Khrystya sighed: "Yes, yes." Then she whispered rapidly and softly: "I want to tell you something, auntie, but I don't know if I should."

"Well, tell me, go ahead and tell me, why not?"

"Well, it's like this . . . How can I . . . say it . . . My husband . . . has become . . . repulsive to me."

"So that's it," Kateryna smiled. "See when you've realized this—after you've been with him for six years already, you foolish woman!"

"No, no, even back then . . . I found him revolting." Khrystya was speaking even more rapidly and softly now, so that it was difficult to understand her.

"Because you know, auntie, my mother forced me to marry him . . . Someone said he was a fine young man . . . But I didn't want to, I didn't want to . . . It makes me shudder to think of it!

"At that time, Kyrylo—he's now in the army—used to go to evening parties with me, and he promised to send matchmakers. But, everyone kept saying: marry Roman, marry Roman! They went at me for a week or more and, in the end, they married me off to him . . .

"Oh, auntie, I ran away to my mother soon after the wedding, and he laid a complaint against me in court . . . The court ordered me to go back home, because my husband had not beat me. Afterwards . . . when I had to live there among all those strangers—the father-in-law and all the brothers-in-law beat their wives just like grain is threshed on the threshing floor—then he did not seem so bad to me, and he was the only one close to me among all those strangers, so somehow it wasn't too bad . . . But now . . .

"Oh, auntie! I can't tell you how repulsive I find him!

"If it weren't for the children, I would go away . . . anywhere at all . . . When he talks and I hear him drawl his 'e-e-e,' I can't stand it, auntie. I don't want him . . . Well, you know, so why am I telling you all this? You know . . ."

"Wait a moment. Should I tell you your fortune to see if you're going to live with him for a long time?"

Khrystya sprang to her feet: "Tell me my fortune, tell me, auntie!"

Kateryna laid out the cards and began narrating: "Look here, you poor dear, the red suit is showing up . . . It's all so happy, so pleasant! There's money . . ."

"From where?"

"From a blond, grey-haired woman; it must be your mother, it can't be anyone else . . . Oh, a red card has turned up again. Expect a guest to come . . . You will buy a good mare . . . You're going to have a good time at a christening . . . And there's going to be a wedding in your family . . . A blond woman—queen of diamonds—and a blond young man . . ."

"Yes, yes, Karpo has asked my father-in-law for the hand of his daughter, Natalka . . . And he is blond. . . The wedding will probably take place quite soon . . . Well, what else is there, my dearest auntie?"

"Well, let's see . . . Hush . . . My husband is coming . . . Where can I hide the cards?"

Kateryna hid the cards as quickly as possible in her pocket.

She always acted as if she were intimidated by her husband, and he truly was frightening in appearance. He was cross-eyed, his face was unshaven, and he was an asthmatic; but the truth is that he was such a gentle man that he never so much as raised a finger to his wife. He lived under her protection and would never say a word against her. Kateryna, however, always pretended in front of others that she was afraid of him, that he would kill her for her fortune-telling if he caught her with the cards. And all this was done to help her wheedle more money from the people whose fortunes she told.

Khrystya was ready to flee as soon as Kateryna's husband walked in, and Kateryna, like a fly in boiling water, began to circle around her husband, asking him in sugary tones: "Will we have supper now? Today, I've only cooked some soup, Maksym, and I don't know if you'll eat it. Well, what are we to do—such is our poverty."

Upon hearing these words, Khrystya thought: "So you live in poverty—may the devil take your mother!"

But then, she immediately became frightened that Kateryna could read her thoughts, and so she said: "Good-bye, auntie, I'll drop in again some other time."

"Come, do come, sweetheart, in the evening sometime, when the children are asleep, and you'll help me sew some shirts. Just look how terribly tattered he is! I'd like to make him at least one new shirt . . ."

Khrystya shrugged her shoulders and left.

She was well aware that Kateryna knew how to make herself look poor. She kept saying everywhere that she had nothing; she never had enough of anything, and as soon as she saw a bright blue or checkered kerchief on another married woman, she would immediately say: "Look, how the bitch is prancing! If only I could ever have something like that to wear!" Or: "That one has put on a jerkin with five yards of material in it, and two pockets, but I have to walk around in an old, torn one," even though there were many jerkins and kerchiefs stashed away in her chest, gifts that people had brought her, and she dressed so finely on holidays, and put on so many ropes of coral beads that she buzzed like a bee when she walked.

But all the same, when someone said to her that she had a lot of everything, she would reply: "What do I have? This is all there is, cheap merchandise—I bought eight at one time." And she always cut the price by a half or a third.

When Khrystya returned to Kateryna's that night, she once again began to complain about her fate—that it was difficult, so very difficult, for her to live; that she simply could not go on this way any longer, she simply could not . . . Soon it would be harvest time, but her hands ached, and her feet hurt. She had lost all her strength, and that was it!

"Oh, I can't go on working like this every day and every night for a scrap of dry bread—oh my unfortunate fate! If I could rest for at least a minute, at least a tiny bit! There's always something that has to be done, there always is, there always is, and you can never finish it all except when you lie down in your grave—then you can finally rest . . .

"I don't have any strength, and if only the children did not break my heart, but there are five of them, and what is there to eat? We had one cow, but Mokryna spoiled her . . . It used to give us a bit of milk, and there were times when I could cook some porridge, but now Mokryna, that damned soul, has made it so that it won't give a single drop, and that's that!

"If you work or don't work—it's all the same. There's always poverty, and grief, and my damned fate! I'd leave everything— the house, the children—and go to the ends of the earth. Let everything go to ruin, let the house burn down, let the children die! Because all the same, when they grow up they'll be just as unfortunate as I am now. They'll have to work, and work, and then they'll perish in a yoke from hunger and the cold!

"I just can't work any more, I can't; I don't have the strength; I don't have the energy! If only I could rest for a week! My hands and feet ache . . .

"No one takes pity on me! My mother has once again gone into town to serve as a nanny . . . Why? God! Oh, where can I go? Where can I go in my grief?"

Khrystya wrung her hands and began muttering angrily to herself: "So, where are you going to go, you stupid bitch? You've brought five children into the world, and now you think you're going to go someplace? Stay at home! Work at home! And who's going to pity you?

"Everyone has the same fate! The devil only knows how women can work like cattle and know nothing but suffering and more suffering. They sit there, like in an ant hill, and work keeps plucking at them from one side and the other, screaming: 'You have to do me, you have to!'

"And then there are the children, and some of the women have husbands who are drunkards—and they beat their wives with whatever is handy. Ugh! It's horrible! They're pulled and shaken like hemp, but they just remain silent, or they scream and curse for a while, like dogs barking, and then they're quiet once again. It's utterly ridiculous!

"The men finish their work in the summer, and then they lie around on the clay bed atop the oven during the winter, and the children don't beset them, but still, the swearing that they do. . . It makes me feel both so sorry and so angry that my heart aches!

"I haven't any strength . . . I can't go on like this . . . If only some sickness would attack me or something—at least I could stay in bed for a while! It's fine for you—you tell fortunes, you earn money . . ."

"Well, not so very much," Kateryna snapped.

Khrystya, biting her lip, said: "Well, auntie, when will I learn how to do it? Am I so stupid, or what? Oh, I would want to . . ."

She put her hands together as if she were imploring Kateryna.

Kateryna remained silent for a moment, and then said: "Take a look—is there anyone near the window?"

"No, there's no one."

"Look behind the door—perhaps there's someone standing there?"

Khrystya opened the door, fearfully glanced out into the street for a moment, and said: "No."

"Well, then, listen now. It will be very difficult for you to tell fortunes . . . You won't learn how . . . But I'll tell you something . . . You want to rest, to stop working; you want everyone to listen to you, to fear you, to do what you want them to do; you want someone to look after your children, to work for you during the harvest; you want your neighbour Mokryna to be afraid of you and not dare to do anything against you. Is this what you want?"

"Yes, it would be strange if I didn't want it." Khrystya nodded her head. "But how is this to be done?"

"Here's how. Listen. There's a madwoman, Paraska, who wanders through the villages. You've seen her, haven't you?"

"Yes, of course I've seen her."

"Well, that's good. See, she's free as a bird—she doesn't work, she doesn't feed any children. All sorts of people give her food and do everything that she wants, just so she won't set their homes on fire . . . Do you understand?"

"No! What does this have to do with anything?"

"Stupid! Wouldn't you be able to be like that?"

"Like what?"

"Like what?" Kateryna mimicked her, and then she rolled her eyes like the madwoman Paraska. "Like this!"

"But it's God who made her like that."

"Some were made by God, and some, if they're smart, make themselves like that . . . They don't want to work, just like that cursed soul, and, well . . ."

"Yes, yes. Oh, auntie! Yes, of course . . ."

"Well, hush, hush! Go now . . . In case of anything, you can come to me . . ."

Khrystya went mad.

The women could not figure it out—why had Khrystya gone mad? Some said it was because of Kateryna—she had cast a spell on Khrystya because she had been teaching her to tell fortunes. She had sent her into the swamp in the dead of night, and Khrystya had seen all sorts of terrible things there and had become so terrified that she had run home all upset, and then kept waking her husband all night, screaming, seeing something or somebody, most likely "him."

Others thought that Khrystya had gone mad because of her troubles and her worries about her tattered children; because of her life in her father-in-law's house, her attempts to claw her way to freedom, to be the mistress of her own home, and then— because of the new house. They had managed to build it only with a great deal of difficulty, and when they moved into it, the indoor oven collapsed, and they had to live like that—in the cold—the entire winter. And because of the fact that a woman bragged that she had seen someone place small bones wrapped in a rag under Khrystya's house when it was being blessed, which meant that they were not to live there, that one of them would die soon.

And then, to top it off, Khrystya's cow had lost her milk, and it was Khrystya's neighbour, Mokryna, who had done this— everyone thought so—because she was always quarrelling with everyone, and most of all with Khrystya.

Mokryna did not overlook a single chicken of Khrystya's that went into her garden and, furthermore, she swore at her and promised: "Just you wait, I'll show you! I'll play such a trick on you that you'll remember me! I'll turn you back to front, you bitch!"

Any other man would have taken Mokryna to court, but not Khrystya's husband. He either did not pay any attention to Mokryna, or said: "Oh, why bother. She'll talk and talk for a while, and then she'll stop. It won't end with this, and if you start suing her over every chicken, you'll never put an end to the matter . . . As for spoiling the cow, there are no laws to cover that— they don't judge things like that in court!"

Khrystya was infuriated that there was no one to take her part, but there was nothing she could do! Her husband would just say: "Well, fine, let me look into this later; I'll say something . . ." but it was not clear when that "later" would be, and that "later" never came . . .

Someone said that Khrystya's husband was to blame that she had gone mad. But no, how could that be! The neighbours did not believe this because he did not beat her very often, and he listened more to her, than she to him.

Well, be that as it may, the fact was that Khrystya went mad. First of all, she stopped nursing her little baby, Natalka, and when the neighbours tried to talk her into doing it, shaming her, and putting the infant girl to her breast, she laughed loudly or assumed such a strange expression that the pupils of her eyes became elongated. She would hold Natalka crossways with only one arm and let her droop like a flower on a bush, and the infant's legs and head hung so limply that it was terrifying.

Then Malashka, the godmother of Khrystya's children, took the infant away and began to feed her herself. This woman—notwithstanding the fact that she had four children of her own—ran over to look after Khrystya's children, cooked for them, and did the harvesting with Khrystya's husband from the time that Khrystya went mad. It was a good thing that she was a widow—her husband had just died and left her with four children, the youngest of which was still nursing—because a husband probably would not have allowed her to run like a skein of thread between Khrystya's house and her own.

Other women also said to her: "Don't you have enough work of your own? Why are you unravelling yourself like this, Malashka?"

Malashka only smiled. She often smiled, and then her plump and shiny face, like a fritter with grease on it, grew still broader.

Then they really began to attack her: "Stupid woman, why are you running over there? Are you her mother or something?"

But she would just say: "Well, fine, I'll say: 'Am I her mother?' And you'll say: 'Am I her mother?' And in the meantime poverty will devour the children. Let's say that something should happen to me at some time, then what?"

"You're only wasting your time!"

"That's nothing," Malashka laughed. "I do it this way—one foot here, and the other foot there!"

Malashka did not know how to explain what was driving her to help Khrystya. She could say it was because she was the children's godmother, but she would have helped anyone in the same way if her assistance had been required. Did she feel sorry for them, or did she not have enough work of her own? She was spinning, like a dumpling in boiling water, first here, and then over there.

Khrystya herself silently laughed at Malashka, as the plump little godmother distractedly and hurriedly tidied up the house for her. And she fooled her more than anyone else—told her all sorts of tales, or stuck her tongue out at her, or added ashes to her salt, or diced cucumbers into her borshch.

And when Malashka said to her, in a slightly alarmed voice: "Softly, softly, Khrystya," Khrystya stared in her eyes and roared with laughter, while thinking quietly to herself: "Well, this godmother Malashka is really something! She's working both for herself and for me, just like an ant that pulls a straw bigger than itself—as if someone were forcing her to do it—and she doesn't even swear!"

And then Khrystya would feel a trifle ashamed and stop laughing, and the odd time she would rush to help Malashka. However, she did not go back to work completely—no, not yet—because she would quickly grow tired and leave everything to the devil and, without giving any thought as to where she was going, would wander through the village and into the fields.

She watched the men mowing and the women tying the sheaves. All the people, arched over into bows, had sweat running down their faces, and the sun was driving everyone on as if it had a golden whip: "Work faster, faster, because I'll be setting any moment now, and you won't have finished. And tomorrow, when I begin to burn everything, when I disperse all the clouds in the sky, then the grain will shell out, and you'll spend the winter in hunger and in the cold!"

There was no time to sleep; there was no time to rest; there was no time to worry that your arms and legs felt as if scalding water had been poured on them, that your lips were dry, your mouth was parched, and the child in the cradle was wriggling and trying to clamber out of it like a little red spider because it wanted to eat—but there was no time.

There was a lot of grain; the earth appeared to be covered with gold as far as the eye could see—right up to the azure sky—and, if you went farther, there would be still more grain, so ripe that the wind was blowing the kernels to the ground.

Up above, there was the sky—so blue and boundless—but who was gazing at it? Up above, the birds were singing—but who was listening to them?

Down below, there were fragrant flowers—but who was sniffing them? There was no time, no time. Hey, hey, it was time to work!

Only Khrystya was free.

Others worked as if they had been attached to their work with a needle—they were working like slaves. Khrystya breathed easily. It was as if she had been carrying something very heavy for a long time, and now had thrown it down and was walking empty-handed.

And now she said to everyone she met: "Leave your work. The devil take it!"

The people looked at her as at a madwoman, but she just laughed, picked some flowers, and sat down like a little child to make garlands out of them. Now she was happy—there was nothing to do, and everyone was afraid of her.

When she had been a young girl, she had always thought about what she might do to make everyone fear her and listen to her. And often, when she used to gather the children around her, she was blissfully happy, and she kept them at her side like fish in captivity, either with a fairy tale or some sunflower seeds. Now, however, even a strong man feared her and looked scared when she chased him.

Malashka often tried to tell Khrystya that she should not do things "like that"; that "it was a pity to leave Natalka hungry"; that "Khrystya would lose her milk"; and that "she was spoiling both herself and her child."

Khrystya herself would sometimes say sorrowfully, as if she were talking to herself: "Yes, indeed, the child is to be pitied. It's my Nata-a-a-alka, my dearest li-i-i-itle one! But how do you know that she's called Natalka?"

Malashka would stare at her in disbelief: "God be with you, what's wrong with you? I'm her godmother!"

"Her gaw-aw-awdmother . . . How's that?" Khrystya would drawl. Then, she would laugh, seize Malashka in her arms, and twirl her around the house, but she still would not feed Natalka.

She would go away and do nothing but wander around from morning until evening. She would walk into a house, sit down, start talking about something, and the people there would give her something to eat. She would forget all about her children, as if they did not exist, and Malashka would put them all to sleep before their mother finally returned home. This went on for quite some time.

There were days when Khrystya would sit down to do some work, some sewing or something, but as soon as she began it, she would abandon it, get up, and go outside to roam around. She wandered to other villages, and she walked over to the church. Her husband Roman would wait and wait, and then he would jump to his feet and go looking for Khrystya. He would bring her home, but the next day she would once again dress herself in her very best clothing and walk away—just vanish.

Roman was at a complete loss as to what he should do. All he could do was look for her every day. He blamed Kateryna the fortune-teller for what had happened to his wife. Khrystya herself—if anyone mentioned Kateryna to her—always defended her, and said that she was "such a good person, that there was not another one like her."

And Kateryna said everywhere that "something had happened to Khrystya," and she would "wander as much as she had to, and when she had endured it all, she would be so wise that she would be wiser than anyone in the village. She would know everything, and everyone would be afraid of her!"

Everyone was already afraid of Khrystya, and perhaps most of all Mokryna, her evil neighbour.

One day Khrystya rushed at her and began choking her when she found her alone in the house, screaming all the while: "Give me back my chicken!"

Mokryna was now willing not only to give back the chicken, but to do whatever else was necessary to free herself from her clutches! Khrystya took the chicken and started to pluck it alive. All the while, her eyes were so crazed and terrifying that Mokryna was completely unnerved.

After this incident, Khrystya often dropped in at Mokryna's to eat dinner. There were times when she laughed uproariously, saying: "Ha-ha-ha, what a cow I've got! It gives black milk! Have you ever heard of such a thing? Tell my cow," she directed this at Mokryna, "that it is to give milk immediately! Why is there so little milk?"

Mokryna shook with fear and swore that she did not know why Khrystya's cow was not giving much milk.

"Oh, so you don't know, you scurvy woman, why it's giving so little? Then I'll twist your child's arms out of their sockets, ha-ha-ha!" Khrystya laughed.

Mokryna's heart grew numb as Khrystya rose to her feet, calmly walked up to the cradle, and picked up the baby.

A moment later, she put the infant down, saying: "Well, I'll come by later. There's no need to do it now." And she casually walked out of the house as if nothing had happened.

Mokryna complained to her husband that she was afraid of Khrystya, because she had threatened to maim her children.

Mokryna's husband went to Khrystya's house. Khrystya was playing with coral beads—threading them and letting them fall on the bench, while her children stood around her like jackdaws with their little red mouths opened wide—and her husband was bent down low repairing something. He looked at them and said: "Good day to you! Perhaps you could take her," nodding at Khrystya, "and just tie her up with a rope and that would be that! Why is she roaming like an apparition around the village, scaring all the womenfolk?"

Before Khrystya's husband could reply, Khrystya's laughter rang through the house like a bell; then her eyes became absolutely terrifying and she said: "I know what you're thinking . . . But that will never happen . . . Oh, take care, uncle 'fornicator', evil will befall you . . . They'll tear your skin off, like . . . Ha-ha-ha, you're saying that they tie . . . Perhaps you should be tied up?"

The man stood undecided for a moment and then fled, muttering through his teeth: "The bitch! She knows everything . . . May no good ever come to you!"

And so, everyone was afraid of the mad Khrystya. Now Khrystya not only took whatever she wanted—everybody gave her things just to get her out of their homes. Not only did she not do anything—others worked on her behalf, like Malashka the godmother or some other neighbour when she spurred them on: "Sew me this, do this for me."

Malashka was a bit afraid of Khrystya, and her heart fluttered like a sparrow when she looked through the window in the morning and saw Khrystya coming to her place. It seemed that now Khrystya did not walk towards you, but just sprang out of the ground before your very eyes—or at least it always seemed that way to Malashka, and she was inevitably startled. Despite this, Malashka still went to Khrystya's every day and helped her. She laughed merrily, both at what Khrystya said and at her caprices, as when Khrystya would seize her out of the blue and begin dancing with her, playing on her tongue as on a fiddle, and even leaping into the air and stamping her feet while dancing.

"What are you doing?" Malashka would sometimes ask as she stared fearfully at Khrystya.

Khrystya would glance sharply at her, stand still for a moment, think, and then say in a strange, high-pitched and sorrowful voice: "I really can't say."

This is what she always replied, or else she would say: "Someone told me that this is what I should do . . . That I ought to do this . . ."

There were times when Malashka felt like fleeing from Khrystya, and when the latter pulled at her saying: "Come on, come on!" she would say: "I can't. I don't have time, there's no time. I have work to do."

Khrystya would laugh and wave her hand: "Work? You'll never do it all . . . No matter how much you work, you'll never get it all done . . . Forget about it! Let's go!"

Malashka had to go, because she was afraid of refusing her and felt sorry for Khrystya's children. Sometimes, when Malashka was bustling about the house, Khrystya would begin to sew or spin, but she would soon stop in the middle of her work and begin to think. Then she would start to do things backwards, or she would fold her hands and say: "Oh, my death is hateful to me, it's hateful! But soon there will be a wedding—a frog and a mouse are engaged . . . Ha-ha-ha . . ."

The children would begin laughing too, and it was painful to watch them—they were like fledglings that chirp when lightning strikes the tree in which their nest is perched.

Every day Khrystya came up with something new. She would sow kernels of grain in the house—it was painful to step on them with bare feet—or she would let down her hair and walk down the street like that. It was truly scandalous.

People advised her husband to beat her. He did beat her once, but she bit him and scratched him like a crazed cat. She found such strength within herself that she seemed to be stronger than he was, and her eyes became so fierce and so dark—almost navy—and when she vowed she would burn him and his children and the entire village so that not a single person would be left, he walked away and did not touch her again.

After that, he began taking Khrystya to both male and female healers. Her mother came from the city and grieved greatly for her when Khrystya jumped up in the middle of the night, stretched her arms out in front of herself, and screamed: "It's over there, over there. Oh, save me, save me! Aha . . . It's you . . . It's the Mother of God who is punishing me . . . You see, she's sitting on a silver chair in a golden cloud."

All the healers agreed that Khrystya was under a spell, and even though it was possible to help her, it would be difficult. And so they poured water over her and did all sorts of other things, but nothing helped—Khrystya remained crazy and did not get better.

Kateryna the fortune-teller said: "That's how it has to be—she's fated to keep on wandering as long as necessary. Maybe she'll die, and maybe she'll live through this . . . If she lives through it, she'll know everything that literate people know . . . She'll know everything . . . a lot. Who knows how much?"

To prevent people from gossiping, Khrystya did not go to see Kateryna very often now.

One day Kateryna ran into her and asked with a meaningful wink: "Well, how is it going?"

"Well, it's like this," Khrystya replied, "every day is a holiday for me!"

They both laughed and parted.

Life was easy now for Khrystya—easy and merry. And as she looked at the other women, she thought: "Oh, look at how the fools are working! They labour until their spines are twisted! Why don't people sleep through the winter, like flies . . . Do your work in the summer, and sleep in the winter!

"Oh, how I always wanted to sleep, Oh, how I wanted to! Because this is the sixth year that I have not slept even once, it seems, through a whole night . . . And who needs those children? May that work be damned! My hands and feet hurt . . ."

Khrystya did not have any real physical ailments, and her face was full and rounded. When she worked hard, however, her legs and arms ached and, during the harvest, sleepiness assailed her as if someone were swaddling her like a baby, and she could not move either her arms or her legs.

"And the children will also have to work hard day after day," she continued. "Oh, to hell with it. I'm not going to think about it. I have my freedom now—I'm on my way!"

She would rise from her spot and leave, even though her older daughter, Halya, would be holding her by the hand and asking: "Mummy, oh, mummy, how long are you going to be wandering around like this?" She asked this so often that it sounded like the branch of the lilac tree that grew next to the house tapping gently and monotonously on the window.

Most of the time, Khrystya did not even notice Halya. At times, however, she shoved her away and heaped abuse upon her. Then she would clutch her head in her hands and begin to wail: "Oh, my dear little children, oh, my dear little ones, what am I to do with you?"

"How long are you going to be wandering around like this, mummy, oh, mummy?" The tiny voice tapped again like a little branch.

"For a long time, my daughter, for a long time, because it's easier for me like this, because I don't have any strength," Khrystya would say as she went away.

And the little one would run to her Aunt Yivha and tell her everything.

Yivha was the only one who was not afraid of Khrystya, no matter how terrifying her eyes were, no matter how she roared with laughter, no matter how she cursed or shouted.

Yivha would only look directly at her and say very quietly and calmly: "That's enough! That's quite enough!"

She always spoke in the same tone of voice, and she never shouted, or swore. She lived as if she were spinning a thread—a fine, smooth, and long thread. She walked, and turned, and did everything in the same way—always evenly, always quietly. But she was proud, and she did not fear anyone or anything—not laughter, nor the judgment of others.

She did not ask anyone anything; she did not listen to anyone—more often, others listened to her. They would stop quarrelling or heaping abuse upon one another when she looked at them with her clear eyes and raised her long eyebrows, or twisted her thin lips and said: "Why call sin down on your soul?" Or: "Is it really impossible to forgive?"

She liked everything to be in order, and she had it all planned out as to when everything should be done—when to sew, when to bleach the linen cloth, and so on. She apportioned groats, lard, and bread over the months and weeks—and she always put away a portion for beggars as well—so that, in their family, everything always lasted until the new crops were ripe.

She knew exactly when to sow the crops and when to gather the hay, because she looked carefully at the sun and observed the birds, watching how they lived when it was cold, when it was raining, and when they felt the warmth—not like other women who are ashamed to know how many sheaves of grain there are on the fields because that's "a man's" business and not "a woman's."

Yivha had learned much of this from her father, but some of it she had learned through her own observations.

She knew a little about healing as well. You were to drink milk with whiskey for a fever, put tallow mixed with wax on sores, sniff grease or garlic for intestinal worms, drink mint drops or pickle brine for a stomach ache, apply a herring to a sore throat, rub your eyes with juice made from honey-covered worms for cataracts, use unsalted butter on the spine, beat a fractured arm or leg with nettles or rub it down with gasoline, and sprinkle broken glass to get rid of mice.

She knew all sorts of other things as well, and she sometimes did help herself and other people; however, she never told fortunes—she did not like fortune-telling. She did not like anything terrifying, wondrous, or abnormal, and she did not really believe Kateryna the fortune teller, saying: "Can anyone really know what will happen? It's all up to God, after all! She's just lying!"

Yivha often discouraged Khrystya from going to learn how to tell fortunes, because it was "both a sin, and a joke." Now, after Khrystya had gone mad, Yivha was convinced that this had happened to her because she had wanted to be smarter than she was and dupe people.

Even though this is what Yivha thought, she never chased Khrystya from her house, and she never locked her out. Other women, upon catching sight of Khrystya's red skirt through the window, quickly barred their doors and hid on the clay bed atop the oven, leaving Khrystya to either shout for a long time or break the windows in anger. If Khrystya succeeded in forcing her way into a house, the women fed her and gave her things as quickly as possible, just so she would leave.

Yivha always talked with Khrystya respectfully, as if she were not demented. And when Yivha, looking at Khrystya's dishevelled hair, said in a voice as even as a ribbon: "Khrystya, you should do up your headdress, or give it to me and I'll tie it for you," for some reason, Khrystya, who now never listened to anyone, would obey her.

Khrystya went to see Yivha quite often. She found it both strange and amazing that Yivha was not in the least afraid of her, and she wanted to find out what this Yivha was like.

Earlier, she had not known her brother's wife all that well; she had only known that Yivha worked hard, lived quietly, and was rarely seen out in the street. Khrystya did not like one thing— that once Yivha said something, she never took it back, no matter what; she was not hewed from a supple tree!

When anyone asked Khrystya where she was going, she would reply: "To the Mother of God," that is, to Yivha's. She always bowed down low to Yivha in public, or kneeled in front of her window and crossed herself.

If Yivha happened to glance out just then, her face would flame and she would rush outdoors to raise Khrystya to her feet, saying: "God help you, what are you doing?"

She would then stroke Khrystya gently and quietly on the cheek, and lead her into the house.

It was in this way that Yivha accustomed Khrystya to herself, and people began to talk, saying that it was she, and not Kateryna, who had cast a spell on her. As has been said, however, Yivha did not care what others were saying, as long as she was in the right, because she liked everything to be as it should be: if you're a woman—be a woman, if you're a man—be a man.

According to her, everyone had his own fate and his own work, and a person could never be unhappy unless he himself desired to be so. If you're sick—get well; if you die—that's how it had to be; if you're poor—there are those who are even poorer; if you're old—the reason for living was to grow old. This is why she simply could not understand Khrystya when the latter complained that she was so "tired out," that it was "hard for her to live and to work!"

Yivha said: "If you were born, then you have to live, and if you have to live, then you must work."

She herself found work easy, and it seemed to her that there was not much to do. She was pleased she had six children who were still among the living, because, as she said: "We'll have many good workers, and they'll give us a lot of help."

"Those workers of yours will be just as unfortunate as we are," Khrystya said, gesturing hopelessly. "They'll live in poverty and work until they die."

"That's nothing; as long as they're born, they'll be fortunate, and they'll find a niche for themselves," Yivha said, and rolling up her sleeves on her reddened hands marked with blue veins, prepared to wash the clothes.

Khrystya often had conversations like this with Yivha. The latter would be busy doing something, while Khrystya, sitting on a bench with her legs tucked under her, watched her and carried on as usual. It was hard for the two women to understand one another, because they were very dissimilar—one was like a trembling star in the sky, while the other was like a swift river on the earth.

Khrystya always talked with Yivha as if she were a completely normal person, but if anyone else walked into the house, she instantly changed. Her eyes would remain fixed on a corner of the room, she would look through people as through glass, and begin to babble: "The smell of roasted meat—of people's flesh—is stifling me!"

And she would begin to sing: "Oh, the people with peace, and dumplings with cheese!"

Then she would cross herself repeatedly and say: "Oh, God, help Khrystya and Yivha, but that bitch doesn't need any help . . ." and she would keep on prattling all sorts of nonsense.

Yivha noticed all this and thought to herself: "What does it mean that Khrystya acts differently with me than with other people? Why does she nurse Natalka at night—Halya has seen her do it—but shove her away when there are people present?

Why is it that Khrystya's eyes are bright at times, and then turn cloudy? Why does she talk sensibly at times, and then babble all sorts of nonsense?"

Yivha began to observe Khrystya more closely. She carefully noted Khrystya's behaviour when they were alone, and she asked her directly: "What did you do today?"

Khrystya would look at her obliquely and begin to babble: "Where am I? I really can't say . . . Oh, I don't know . . . Oh, I don't know . . . Oh, my God, I've come to the Mother of God! And just look at the child! Its hands and feet are so small, oh, so very small!"

And so Yivha would not find out anything in this way. When the conversation turned to something else, however, Khrystya would forget herself and tell her everything as it should be. Why was this so?

"What can be wrong with her," Yivha thought. "I think I should look into this."

Khrystya, as if to spite others, listened to Yivha in public. Taking advantage of this, Yivha often told her not to worry and to "go home and do her work." In this way, she hoped to train Khrystya to begin working again. Khrystya would go, but in a short time she would once again wander over to see Yivha.

The latter would say: "Well, why have you come again?"

Khrystya would reply: "I really can't say . . ." And after remaining silent for a while, she would ask: "What am I to do? Tell me!"

"Are you saying you don't have any work?" Yivha would respond in an even voice. "Go and tend to your garden—you've really neglected it."

"Yes, indeed," Khrystya would say, hanging her head.

"And nurse the baby, because it will wake up soon."

"Yes."

"Well, go on, then. Why are you standing here?"

Khrystya would twirl on one foot, then once again stand still, all the while looking at Yivha with strange eyes.

"What are you doing?"

"I really can't say . . . But Natalka is a sweet little baby . . . She must be fed . . . She must be . . ."

"Have you nursed her today already?"

"Where? Of course! Oho-ho . . ." Khrystya sighed. "I really can't say . . ."

"Well, get going already," Yivha would say impatiently.

Khrystya would go, and then she would return quite soon to say that she had weeded the garden, and to ask what she was supposed to do now.

"Go away, I don't have time to talk with you," Yivha would say angrily.

She already knew from Halya, who had run over to find her mother, that Khrystya had pulled out the carrots instead of the weeds, and had yanked out the potatoes and thrown them aside, and had then gone off somewhere. This was how Yivha figured out that Khrystya did not obey her at all, but just pretended to, and so she did not want to talk with her anymore.

Khrystya, however, still came to see her, and Yivha did not chase her away. Khrystya would come in her best clothes, sit down, fold her arms, and tell her how she had got up that morning, washed, had her breakfast, and nursed Natalka—but this was a lie, for Yivha knew from Halya that Khrystya had not nursed the infant . . .

"Then something seemed to push me," Khrystya would continue. "'Go, go,' and so I went . . . I walked and walked. I really can't say where I was going . . . Then I went past the church . . . I can't go to church on a feast day . . . I don't have a jerkin."

Yivha did not say anything, even though she saw Khrystya was wearing a new jerkin. She waited to see what she would say next.

"I saw the bell, and I thought: 'I'll ring it.'

"Then I thought: 'People will come running, I'll be in trouble, so I must go quietly around it and go home, so that not a single soul sees that I was here.'

"And I took hold of the rope, and said to myself: 'Softly, softly, don't touch it!' And I began to ring it, once, twice . . .

"I rang it many times until the cantor came running, and the priest came running, and they said: 'What are you doing? Why are you here? Get away from here! Go away. Why are you stirring up the people?'

"And I said: 'I really can't say . . . Where am I to go? If someone would lead me . . . I really can't say."

"'Go by yourself,' the cantor cried.

"I just looked him straight in the eye, saying: 'You must lead me.'

"Well, he was very alarmed, and then he said: 'You go first.'

"And so I went, and the cantor followed after me, and in this way he led me to my own home; but I passed by my house and went farther, and he tried to turn me back: 'Your house is right here. Where are you going?'

"And I said to him: 'Thank you! Your wife has been born just now, and she's lying in the cradle . . .'

"And I began to laugh loudly, and he ran way."

Khrystya laughed.

"Why did you drag the cantor around the village?" Yivha could not help asking.

Khrystya looked straight up, stopped laughing, and said: "I really can't say . . . Someone told me it was time to harvest the cabbage because the frost will soon be here . . ."

She rose from the bench, took off her headdress, loosened her hair, and walked out of the house.

The next time, Khrystya told Yivha how one girl was so scared of her that when Khrystya walked up to her she started screaming and ran away. Most of all, Khrystya bragged about how she told people all sorts of things at night—many of them used to gather in her cottage—and they would gaze at her in fear and amazement but, nevertheless, they still listened to her and believed her.

"I tell them, I really can't say where I get it from, but it's as if I know everything, see everything, hear everything; and they look at me like fools, and I find it so strange, so funny, that I could roar with laughter," Khrystya bragged to Yivha. "Malashka is the funniest of all of them. She stares at me with her frog-like eyes, and just keeps sweating and sweating, but nevertheless, she does listen . . . Ha-ha-ha!"

It was true that Malashka found Khrystya amazing and always sighed: "Oh, my God, how does she know this? It's as if she were reading a book."

Malashka had liked Khrystya previously as well, as she liked all young women who—as she said—"like a new grindstone, had not yet been ground down," and that was why she pitied Khrystya even more now, and always said: "When Khrystya begins saying those things during the night about Christ, about the Mother of

God—and she does it all so well, and her own face is so small and red, and her eyes are shiny, and her notched eyebrows grow darker, and her headdress falls off, and her long black hair tumbles down her back—she seems so wonderful to me, and so beautiful that it's just as if she were a child!"

Malashka would tell her own children: "Come on, eat more quickly, eat and go out and play, for now I have ten of you, and I have to get going."

"Where to?" they would ask.

"To Aunt Khrystya's; she's mine now."

"But why is Aunt Khrystya always wandering around? Halya always says: 'Oh, my mother is such a worry to me; she just wanders and wanders.'"

"Well, that's just the way it is with her now," Malashka would reply and, taking the smallest child in her arms, she would go to Khrystya's, thinking: "No, Khrystya is not like all the others, not at all! No wonder they say she's not one of the 'common people.'"

Every night now, people gathered in Khrystya's home, and men took turns bathing her. After a doctor had suggested pouring cold water on her head to try to cure her, Khrystya's husband and Malashka—who thought that a sick person, like a dead one, had no sense of shame—came up with the idea of bathing her in a tub of cold water, in the hope that this might help even more.

Khrystya would not let them do it, and that was why they had invited the men, who forcibly undressed her and placed her in the tub, making her sit in it until she began to shiver from the cold.

"Doing that to her might really make her mad," Yivha said.

Yivha was very proper—even as a girl when she worked in the tobacco fields, she never gathered up her skirt almost to the waist in the dense tobacco plants the way the other girls did.

"How can one sit naked like that in front of all of those men!"

That is why there always were many people in Roman's cottage. The light stayed on there all night. After her bath, Khrystya would crawl to the clay bed atop the oven and begin to tell her stories from there . . . The people listened, and they wondered where Khrystya had heard it all.

Then she would cut short the narration, stretch her arms out, and begin to speak softly, in a sing-song voice: "Well, come here, come here, I'll rock you . . . No, no, not you, not you . . . I didn't

call you . . . Get away, get away! You're not needed . . . See—
there, over there, it's 'his' shadow on the wall . . . Oh no, you
can't fool me! Run away, my good people! From his flame . . .
He'll burn you . . . Run away! Oh, what red streaks there are
where 'he' has scratched with his nails . . . See the blood that's
there, it's black . . . It's sinful blood . . . And he's dangling his
tongue through the entire house . . . It's red . . . Oh! . . Oh! . . .
Oh! Don't touch me, don't you recognize me?"

The terrified people would look at each other in dumbfounded
silence, and Khrystya would stop talking and, still sitting, suddenly
drop off to sleep.

Sometimes, she tried to get away from the people, to flee—who
could say where, so late at night. She scratched, bit, and grabbed
the hair of the first person she came across.

The next day she would tell Yivha what had happened in her
home; however, she laughed when questioned about it, and
pretended that she was insane.

"Fine," Yivha said to herself. "Khrystya is not mad."

And once, taking Khrystya by the arm, she told her directly:
"Khrystya, Khrystya, that's enough wandering around!"

Khrystya was taken aback. She forced herself to smile and said:
"Is it my will to do so? I'll wander as long as I wander."

"Of course it's your will."

Khrystya tore herself free and ran away. After this, she did not
visit Yivha for a few days.

One morning, however, she once again appeared before Yivha,
holding Natalka, who was completely naked, like a wet, newly-
hatched baby dove. Even though the infant was trembling—her
whole body was covered with goose bumps—she was still smiling
and reaching for everything with her swollen little fingers.

"I'm going away," Khrystya said.

"Where are you going in such bad weather, you foolish thing,
and with a naked child at that?"

"To the city."

"You'll go to prison, because you don't have a city permit."

"That's fine," Khrystya replied, wanting to be on her way.

Yivha detained her, pleading with her to reconsider: "Think again,
Khrystya. You're better off to stay at home . . . Well now, you've
had your rest, and that's enough . . . You could go to work . . . or

you'll see—your husband will send you to a hospital, if you make him angry enough."

"Oh, sure, to a hospital!" Khrystya was so furious that her teeth chattered. "He won't orphan my children—all five of them!"

"Why, you've made orphans of them yourself—do you think you're a mother to them now? It's all the same if you end up in a hospital, or if you die. All you do is wander around! Think it over, Khrystya!"

Khrystya turned away, thinking: "The scurvy woman knows everything." And she walked away infuriated.

That night, as she was lying on the oven bed, she heard her husband conferring with the men, asking them how he should go about putting Khrystya away, into a hospital. He was saying: "It's just as if I did not have a wife now. It would be better if she died."

But Khrystya was not taken to a hospital, because she got better on her own and became her old self again. It is true that she never worked very sincerely and, after working for a little while, would become very angry, begin to scream, fling things around, slam doors, and slap the children.

Sometimes she would take ill once again, and then Malashka, like a shuttle in a weaver's loom, would begin running from her home to Khrystya's cottage. In the meantime, Khrystya would rest, because she truly was smarter than the other women—she wanted to change her fate, even though she could not!

"Women do not know how to free themselves from their work," Khrystya thought. "Even though they curse the entire world, they keep on working until they are ground into flour by a fate that does not pour more kernels into the hopper. And their work is so hard, so very hard!"

Yivha thought it was a sin not to work, but she did not tell anyone what she knew about Khrystya. She just said to her husband: "Your sister is behaving badly." And she instructed Khrystya's husband to scare her with the hospital, but she did not tell him anything more: "Let him figure it out by himself, as best he can."

Malashka was of one mind with Yivha; but Kateryna's views coincided with Khrystya's, or rather, it was she who had led Khrystya astray, into idleness . . .

The Father
(1898)

"Oh, how starry the heavens are! O dear God, how starry!" old man Myron said, gazing at the clear sky in which stars were lit as densely as candles in a church. And, on this warm summer's night, it was as quiet as in a church when no one is singing. The sun had taken away, along with its golden warmth, all the clamour of the day, and the earth was sleeping sweetly, like a well-fed infant in its cradle. It was quiet, except for the occasional call of a quail and the infrequent neighing of horses grazing in the pasture.

The moon rose, bathing everything in a silver glow. Brilliant waves rolled over the grainfields, and dew glittered on the grass. The village and the orchards, outlined in a darker silver hue, gleamed in the distance, and the road running through the steppe stretched in a white swath, as if dusted by snow in the middle of summer. The entire sky brightened, the stars dimmed slightly, and the grain and roadside flowers emitted a stronger fragrance.

Old man Myron walked over to where the horses were grazing—he had a pair of horses himself, and two of his sons had one apiece—chased all of them, his own as well as those belonging to the other villagers, away from the grainfields, retied their fetters, and then returned to the men who had herded their horses there for the night. Sitting in a group, they were carrying on a desultory conversation before going to sleep. The focus of the small talk was the wedding that Bozhyk had hosted when he married off his son on Sunday.

"What kind of 'fashion' has taken over now, that youths are marrying at such a tender age?" old man Myron asked. "He hasn't even done his time in the army yet, and they've already ensnared him. He doesn't know how to handle a scythe, and he's already a married man; he's called a 'husband,' and he swaggers before his wife, and shouts at the village tribunal: 'I'm a householder,'"

Myron imitated mockingly. "But he's not a householder at all! And he'll never know how to mow properly, because who'll teach him if he didn't learn how to do it as a young man? And it's the same with the girls. They don't know how to bake bread, they've never harvested—and they up and get married! And that's the way it always is; it's as if they were playing house with dolls! It's all so silly, so foolish!

"No, it was better when the lords ruled over us; the lord wouldn't let us marry until we were twenty-five, and that was how it should be. A man would grow in wisdom and in strength, find a nice girl, and get married. All the people were solid citizens back then—every last one of them; there aren't any like that now."

Myron's companions were all younger than he was and did not remember what life was like under the lords. They asked him to tell them more about those times.

And old man Myron recounted many experiences, good and bad.

They talked about the lords for a long time, and then the conversation turned to witches and other such topics.

Myron asserted that he had seen not only a witch, but even "that one" himself—may his name not be mentioned at nightfall. Then they talked about the evil eye—how there were people who did not want to have an evil eye, but all they had to do was look at an animal or a person, and a spell would immediately be cast on the unsuspecting victim. There were people who were feared by every kind of animal because they had the evil eye, and there were others who knew "the word" that would ward off mice, mosquitoes, and things like that.

And then Myron began telling a story about his lord's beekeeper, an old man whose grey beard reached to his knees, and who drank three glasses of whiskey every day but always remained sober. This man knew "the word" that kept bees from biting him—he used to rake them out of their hives with his bare hands—and, when he sent them off to gather honey, they always flew in the direction he told them to go, and . . .

At this point, old man Myron noticed that all the men were dozing already and, covering himself with a blanket, he settled down beside them. But he could not fall asleep because all manner of thoughts kept creeping into his head. He had always had a head like that; it was as if a weaver lived in it, flinging his thoughts around like a shuttle, this way and then that way, weaving new patterns with them. Others did not think as much in a month as old man Myron thought in a day or a night. He probably thought more than anyone else in the entire village and, because he did not like to sleep, he went into the steppe to graze horses at night when he could have just as easily sent one of his sons.

He had not slept as a young man because of all the work he took on and the partying that he did, and he did not sleep now that he was old. Restless by nature, he always felt like working, talking, or thinking. At times he did not lie down to sleep until midnight, but he still got up at the break of dawn. No one knew how he could get by with so little sleep. Others were only too happy to sleep on a Sunday, both before and after dinner, to recoup their strength, but Myron—God forbid—never did that; nevertheless, he was the best mower in the village, mowing better than his three sons. He was still quite youthful in appearance—tall and straight as a poplar, with long black hair that did not have a trace of grey in it, and dark eyes that glowed like embers.

It is sometimes said that thinking drains a person, but it certainly had not drained Myron. Some people do not think because they are too busy coping with life's problems; they just exist from one day to the next. Others do not know how to think, and no idea ever crosses their minds; and then there are those who believe that it makes no difference whether you think or not, because you cannot change a lacklustre fate.

But Myron liked to think, and so now he tucked himself more comfortably into his sheepskin coat, looked up at the stars once again, and thought: "How unequal they are—over here, they're huge, really huge, but over there, they're just tiny specks. And it's like that with everything in the world. Take this rye—it's ever so much shorter than a bush or a tree; and the grass is still shorter, and people trample it with their feet, but as for the tree—birds alight on it to sing. And that's the way it is among people . . .

"Our people don't like to be bothered with anything, neither for the good of their souls nor for the sake of honour," Myron continued with his thoughts. "For example, when it comes to electing a chief, or an elder, or assistant bailiffs, or tax collectors, they immediately back away and push their neighbours to the fore instead, and it's often done out of sheer malice . . ."

As for old man Myron, even though he cursed the community, he had been elected twice to serve as an elder and once as the chief; now he was a tax collector, and a good one at that. He collected the money on his own time and in a highly organised fashion. Even though he was illiterate, he kept track, either with crosses or sticks, of how much money each household owed, and he never once made a mistake or improperly took a penny that did not belong to him. And he knew how to deal with people; he possessed a certain strength—like the wind that bends willows— to make people bow to his will and get what he wanted. People would follow him the way whiskey runs into a hole. Everyone trusted him, and he was able to explain things in such a way that they all understood that he was right and took his advice. And he was very proud of this.

Of course, it has to be admitted that there were times when the people took the side of stentorian orators who mesmerised them with honeyed words. At times like that old man Myron became incensed and shouted that, as far as he was concerned, all his work could go to the devil's mother, and they could all drop dead and perish, and that anyone who tried to do something for the community was a fool, because it was as useless as trying to eat stones, and may he be thrice damned if he would so much as lift a finger on their behalf, even if they promised to pay him in the hundreds.

Old man Myron would say this but, after a day, a week, or sometimes a month, the villagers would end up pleading with him, and he would once again borrow money from the rich on behalf of the community, on his personal guarantee. And he would call the council together to announce that a third of the community land would be turned into a pasture, or that the lord's herder would work off services they had provided for the lord, or that he was digging a new well in the village. And then he would enjoy himself in the tavern with his "enemies."

Old man Myron was not a heavy drinker, but if he had some spare money he enjoyed having a drink in good company. And it just so happened that he did have some extra cash. He had thought that he would have to pay five rubles for a pair of boots, but they had cost only four rubles and fifty *kopiyky [pennies],* and so he was left with fifty *kopiyky* in change that he could spend on whiskey. The money could have come in handy in the household as well, as his daughter-in-law—his youngest son's wife—often told him, but he thought of it as "spare" money, and so that was how he treated it.

Even though Myron was not well off, he did not care about money. He always said that money did not guarantee happiness, because he had witnessed a rich lord's child die. The lord had sought treatment for it, and hovered anxiously over it, and was prepared to give doctors all his money, all his wealth, to save its life, but despite all his efforts—it had died! In Myron's opinion, a peasant ought to have land, a horse, and some cattle, but as for money—the devil take it! Of course, old man Myron understood that you could not live without money, because with what were you to buy kerosene, salt, oil, and other things like that and, most of all, with what were you to pay "the state taxes?"

Whenever old man Myron began to think about money, he recalled how much evil it gave rise to, how many people made life intolerable for others because of it, how the rich sucked out the blood of the poor with high interest charges, and how tax collectors duped people out of their savings and stooped to injustice for the sake of money.

"Money is a sweet narcotic," Myron decided. "Whoever loves it—lives like a corpse. He works all his life to pay for his own coffin, because when he dies, his money stays behind, but he has not lived, or enjoyed himself, or anything . . ."

"Oh, Oksana, Oksana!" Myron suddenly exclaimed out of the blue, astonishing even himself.

Oksana, Myron's only daughter, was married. He also had three sons—the two older ones lived in the homes of their mothers-in-law, while the youngest one lived with him. He did not have enough land for three sons, so he saw to it that the older sons married into widows' households, thereby ensuring that they had their own land while remaining under his control. They worked as a team and, with everyone pulling together, there were many hands to do the work and four horses to do it with, and so everything was done better and more quickly. The sons, accustomed to obeying their father—the youngest one was virtually Myron's shadow—stayed under his thumb after they got married. And they realised that it was better this way.

Not long ago, Myron had given his daughter in marriage—or rather, she had married the man of her choice. Oh, how he had wanted to see her marry a rich townsman! He had wanted this, even though he knew that money is the root of all evil, because every father would like to see his daughter married to a man who is not just a simple peasant, but a townsman—a man who has a tobacco plantation, four horses, a wide gate, and a cottage with a shingled roof and richly decorated windows; every father would want to see his daughter sleep in a soft bed, eat *halushky [dumplings]* filled with cheese every day, and keep a servant. But it was no use! Oksana refused to marry a townsman, and that was that; instead, she chose to marry a poor man . . .

"And what did she find so appealing about him?" Myron pursued his train of thought. "In my opinion, he's downright ugly! He has red hair, not like the rest of our kin, and he's small, and always rushing about, like a spinning wheel—oh, the devil knows what he's like! He's certainly not her equal . . .

"O Oksana, my Oksana! No girl can even come close to matching her . . .

"What came over her? She stubbornly insisted that she would marry him and no one else. Can she really have been so much in love with him? They came to an understanding at a *vechornytsi [an evening party for young people]* . . . The rogue must have filled her head with a whole lot of nonsense! All a man has to do is say to a girl 'my darling, my sweetheart, my precious,' embrace her firmly but gently, and kiss her—and she, rejoicing, will blossom like a cherry tree and believe every word he says. 'Oh, this man will treat me kindly; I'll marry him!' Would that it were so! If only it were accepted among us peasants, as it is among the nobility, that a girl does not have to get married at all; she just continues to live in her father's home and knows no grief!

"But no, that can't be—a girl has to get married; that's how it should be. Oh, if only our men would fall head over heels in love with women, like our young lord, who recently got married. He kisses his wife's hands, gazes into her eyes, and once, I swear to God, I even saw him down on his knees before her, as you kneel before an icon—what a comical sight!

"Among us peasants, you may show a woman some kindness now and again, but you never let her have her way; after all, a woman is not as smart as a man, not as smart, and weaker. It's true that occasionally a man takes his wife seriously and repeats at the village meeting what she said at home, but even if he does listen to her, he still retains control by yelling at her and beating her when he's angry. Given the lives that we lead, it's impossible not to quarrel and fight; everyone becomes quarrelsome because he doesn't have this, or needs that, or his horse has died, or the grain did not yield well.

"But the main point is that women are stupid; they're stupid and garrulous—may they all perish! I certainly wouldn't want to be a woman—it's the worst possible fate. Every misfortune descends on her shoulders, and then there are the children. If Oksana's husband Andriy were at least a good worker, but as it is . . .

"Granted, he's literate, but what good is that? Those schools of ours—who knows of what use they are? For one thing, what's a man fit for once he's been in school? He turns his nose up at being a herdsman—but not everyone can become the village clerk. He learns to read a bit, and then promptly forgets most of what he learned, and all that he's left with is the glory of having studied.

"And, for another thing, the woman teacher that's there now goes for walks with young gentlemen, while the lads get into fights, pulling each other's hair and knocking each other about. At one time, the teacher would beat them so they'd study, but now they beat each other up. And that's the kind of schools we have!

"It would be different if he were well-educated, but as it is, he's of no use to either God or the devil. And our people are ignorant, really ignorant; when a document of some kind arrives they waste ever so much time before they figure out what's in it. And when the village scribe begins flinging around the beads on an abacus, they all stand around like gaping idiots . . . It's not difficult to dupe one of our brethren . . ."

Myron thought for a long time and finally fell asleep. When he awoke, the sun was beginning to spin its red and gold threads over the steppe and among the trees. Concluding that it was getting late, he took his horses and went home.

When he got there Maryna, his daughter-in-law, was already working busily by the oven. Today was a minor feast day, and she had decided to fry pancakes to be served with cheese. The house was neat and attractive; beautiful icons, each draped with a *rushnyk [embroidered linen ceremonial cloth],* graced the walls, the table was spread with a clean cloth, and on it was a bowl of soft, fresh cheese.

Near the table stood a little girl of about six; she was washed and combed—her fine hair, greased so heavily that it stuck to her forehead, looked quite dark—and her rosy face looked like a *krashanka [an Easter egg dyed in one colour].* Smiling in anticipation as she stared at the bowl of cheese, she did not dare to approach any closer to it because she feared her mother, who tended to be strict. But the moment her mother moved to the oven to tend to the borshch, she quickly reached over and dipped almost her whole hand into the bowl; then, looking obliquely at her mother, who still had her back turned to her, she began to suck her tiny cheese-covered fingers.

At that moment, a boy ran into the house. He resembled the little girl so closely that you could tell at a glance that he was her brother. Hopping up to the table on one foot, he looked into the bowl and, speaking so rapidly that he swallowed his words, asked: "What's this—lime, salt, flour, or cheese?"

"Get away from there," the mother shouted, turning from the oven. "Why have you come here? Who called you?"

"Grandpa will soon return with the horses," the boy replied, eyeing the cheese like a cat.

"Well, so what if he returns? It's still too early to eat breakfast. Go see to the calf. Get going!"

The boy made a face, and then, glancing at his sister, roared with laughter: "Boy oh boy! You've got cheese all over you— just look at your white moustache! Ha-ha-ha!"

Little Tetyanka squinted and rolled her eyes, trying to see what her moustache looked like, but she could not see it and quietly said: "You're lying."

Hrytsko shouted even more loudly that Tetyanka had eaten some cheese. He wanted their mother to hear him. He wanted her to scold his sister, because if he could not have any cheese, then she should not have any either.

But his mother did not react as he had hoped; she remained by the oven and shouted: "Get out of the house, both of you! Why are you bothering me here? Get out, before I . . ."

The children vanished in a flash.

Hrytsko was not happy with his mother; he had wanted her to give Tetyanka at least a good shove for eating the cheese, so on his way out he grabbed an onion from the bench and gnawed away at it, gloating, while Tetyanka stared longingly at his mouth.

This bit of revenge did not satisfy him, however, and yelling: "You . . . you . . . you . . ." he shoved her so hard that the little girl toppled over in the middle of the yard and began to cry.

As luck would have it, their grandfather Myron, having handed the horses over to the herdsman, was making his way to the house just then. Seeing that the boy was mistreating his little sister, he yanked him by the ear.

Hrytsko's ear really hurt, and his eyes filled with tears, but he controlled himself and muttered: "Why is she bawling so loudly? When I was little I never bawled. She's just an old woman!"

The grandfather picked up Tetyanka and, consoling her, carried her into the house: "O my precious, my little darling! Where does it hurt?"

And Hrytsko, holding his onion, ran out into the street with a reddened ear to tell the boys what a sly "vixen" his sister was, and how she had wheedled her way into her grandfather's favour.

Granddad Myron entered the house, sat down on the bench, and placed the little girl on his knee. It was then that she told him that she really wanted some cheese. The grandfather drew the bowl nearer, picked up a spoon, and began to feed her.

Maryna glanced at him from the oven and said with feigned severity: "You're always spoiling her, father. She should wait until we all sit down to eat. I'll finish frying the pancakes right away."

"Oh, it makes no difference; the child wants to eat," the grandfather replied. "But where's Ivan?"

"He went to spread the hay; you said it had to be done."

Old man Myron lowered Tetyanka to the floor, rose to his feet, washed up at the washstand, and walked out of the cottage, saying: "I'll go help him."

Having eaten her fill of cheese, Tetyanka—her face looking like a cherry dumpling speckled with cream—had to get to work. Her other brother, Mykola, was whimpering in his cradle, and her mother ordered her to rock him.

When grandfather Myron and his son Ivan came in for breakfast, the pancakes were ready. Hrytsko, without having to be called, also ran in, just in time. They all sat down and silently began to eat. Myron never talked much with Ivan, and there really was nothing much to talk about. Hrytsko's munching resounded through the house; he was thoroughly enjoying the pancakes.

They had hardly settled in to eat, when a pretty young woman burst into the house, calling out: "Good day to you!" Then she laughed, sniffed, and said: "Oh, how delicious it smells! You were frying pea flour pancakes, weren't you?" And she laughed again.

Maryna looked at the young woman the way a cat glares at a dog, and thought: "Oh, my God, she won't even let us have our breakfast in peace."

Rising to her feet, she went over to the oven to begin tidying up. Whenever Maryna was annoyed, she worked very hard and very fast, and the work proceeded with such a clamour and such a thumping that it seemed that she wanted everything she touched to speak out on her behalf; it was as if, in her fit of anger, she could finish all the work in the world. Because of this trait of hers, whenever her father-in-law wanted to bring in the harvest more swiftly, he would deliberately annoy her. And then just watch out! She would bind the sheaves so quickly that two mowers could not stay ahead of her. And, as she bound them, she did not say a word—she just breathed heavily and made the straw crackle.

And so now, without saying a word, she began to wash the dishes and put them away, working very quickly and banging everything with abandon.

"Sit down, daughter," Myron said to Oksana. "Sit down and have some breakfast with us."

Ivan, moving over on the bench, also spoke up in his soft voice, quietly inviting his sister: "Sit down, Oksana."

Oksana strongly resembled her brother. Like him, she was dark and tall, but instead of an elongated face, she had a round, happy one. Ivan tended to be sad, and his eyes turned downwards, while Oksana's eyes, like birds on the wing, were opened wide to the world.

Grandfather Myron, seeing that his daughter-in-law had left the table, said sternly: "Maryna, bring us some more pancakes, if there are any. And sit down yourself. Why have you run off?"

Maryna replied through gritted teeth: "I don't have time." But she did bring some fresh pancakes to the table.

Oksana, looking unabashedly at Maryna's angry face, her frowning blond eyebrows, her lips—clamped so tightly that they appeared to be stitched together—and her grey eyes that avoided any contact with her, laughed merrily. Maryna threw down the plate of pancakes so hard that it almost broke.

Old man Myron thundered at her: "What's wrong? Have you gone mad?" And then he turned to his daughter: "And why are you laughing? Are you rejoicing in your foolishness?"

"I'm laughing at Tetyanka, daddy," Oksana quickly came up with an excuse. She did not want to rouse her father's ire today, even though the anger of her sister-in-law amused her, and she was always more than ready to tease her. From childhood, she had enjoyed teasing—be it kittens and puppies, or her brothers.

Everyone looked at Tetyanka. She had finished eating and now, leaning her head to one side and sticking out the tip of her red tongue that looked like a strawberry, was striking her cheek with a spoon and listening to the slapping sounds as if they were music.

Everyone laughed, but Tetyanka said seriously: "It's like a cooper beating a barrel."

They all laughed again, and even Maryna smiled, but then she immediately turned her back to them and began feeding the baby in the cradle. Grandfather Myron regained his good humour and asked Oksana what was happening at her place.

Oksana hurriedly gulped down a couple of pancakes and said: "Well, you see, daddy, my Andriy wanted to come to see you himself, but he was dragged off to the village meeting. Uncle Semen came for him, and they went together."

"What's going on there?"

"Who knows—it's about money, some kind of business; he wanted to take care of it himself, and I don't know, I swear to God . . . He just said: 'Go to your father, and beg him most urgently to come.'"

Myron began to speculate what it might be about. "Aha, it's probably about the interest . . . right?"

"I don't know; I swear to God, I don't know."

"Well, in that case . . . Fine, I guess I'll go, I . . ." Myron looked askance at his son and daughter-in-law—even though he had no reason to do so—and hastily repeated: "Yes, yes, I'll go. Yes, I will. What can it possibly be?"

"And I'll be on my way. Good-bye. I have to go," Oksana said anxiously. She leapt to her feet and vanished, like a star flashing across the sky.

Old man Myron paced the room for a while, and then, because it was only a minor feast day and, according to church tradition, you could work with a pitchfork and a shovel, but not with a scythe, he turned to his son and said: "The rye should be winnowed and taken to the mill." And, like smoke rising from a chimney, he disappeared in the same direction that his daughter had gone.

After he left, Maryna rushed to clear the table, and there ensued such a banging and clanging that Ivan's ears began to buzz.

"Why are you so annoyed?" he asked.

"So, he's gone," she nodded her head towards the door. "He's gone to free his 'dear' son-in-law; to take his debt on his shoulders . . . Be quiet!" she yelled at the children.

Hrytsko, having said to Tetyanka: "Come on, I'll do a 'cooper,'" had struck her on the cheek so hard that the little girl screamed with pain.

After hearing their mother's "Be quiet!" the children settled down like flowers after a rain.

Ivan quietly asked: "Oh?"

"Of course," Maryna retorted. She was angry at her husband, and so she added: "And why does the bitch come crawling here if she's married? For a father, a married daughter is like a slice of bread that's been cut off once and for all, but she keeps clinging to him like tar sticks to a boot! She has a husband—what else does she need? And, of course, she doesn't have to wash her father's clothes, or clothe him, or feed him—but the old man is still drawn to her like a bee to honey. Imagine—a daughter is dearer to him than his son. Phew!"

"Yesterday," Hrytsko said, "granddad gave Oksana a kerchief . . . a red one, a bright red one . . ."

"No, you're lying; it was a yellow one. I saw it," Tetyanka interrupted him.

Hrytsko shoved her, and their mother once again said: "Be quiet! Both of you!" And then she continued: "What is this? How long is this going to go on? Are we her servants, or what? Things can't go on this way! She laughs at me, the slut! Do you suppose I don't know why she was cackling like a hen at the breakfast table? All the treats are for her, and the trips to the market are made with her. Their fields are ploughed first, and their land is seeded first, even though the horses are ours. Really, what is this? Whoever saw anything like it?"

"Let it be!" Ivan said quietly.

Maryna slammed a dish down and mimicked him: "Let it be! You're always saying: 'Let it be!' You'll be working as a servant for your brother-in-law until . . ."

"But what am I to do?"

"What? Tell him that you don't want things to continue like this. Let him set us up on our own, that's what!"

"Oh sure, that's just what I can say to him! Don't you know father better than that?"

"You really are . . . spineless," Maryna said severely. But then she thought: "Granted, it's much better for me that he is spineless, but . . ." And she fell silent.

"He is the father, and that's that. There's nothing that can be done about it. I'm going to go and winnow the rye." Ivan got up to leave. Stopping in the doorway he added: "But I won't take his son-in-law's debt on my shoulders; he can do whatever he wants to and get the money wherever he can. I simply won't do it!"

He walked out of the house and, while winnowing the rye, wondered if he truly could separate himself from his father and live independently. And he decided that he could not, because his father took care of everything, knew everything—when it was time to do things—and could do everything. And as for himself— what did he know? He only knew how to do whatever his father told him to do; he did not know how to think these things through for himself.

"No, I can't get along without father, even though, as Maryna says, he does not act fairly when he cares about his son-in-law and ignores his own son. But, what of it? After all, he is my sister's husband. It's really too bad, though, that Maryna gets so angry and upset. It would be far better if we could all get along more amicably."

Maryna, however, was convinced that they could live very well without the father, if only her husband were a little bolder. The way he was, however, he would soon become no better than a slave.

She was certain that the father would make Ivan assume Andriy's debt and make him pay it or work it off, putting an additional burden on his already stooped back. No, it could not go on this way! But she also could not change things around by herself—her father-in-law had the right to chase her out of his home, and her husband would stick up for his father; moreover, she had to admit that it was better and easier to live with the father . . .

Well, she would have to find a way to distance the father from his daughter. But how? Maryna could not solve this knotty problem. Should she try casting aspersions at Oksana? The father would never believe her. Should she try to make Andriy appear in a bad light? The father was fully aware that Andriy was a ne'er-do-well, and it was only for his daughter's sake that he pretended not to realise it. There was no way out! She had to wait until the father died. But he was still hale and hearty, and he did so love to spoil his grandchildren—Lord Almighty!

"But still," Maryna thought, "how dare Oksana laugh at me? Whenever we meet, you can tell from her face that she's laughing at me—as if she thinks she's smarter than I am."

Maryna could neither forget how Oksana slighted her, nor forgive her for doing so. And she thought Ivan was like a dog—so accustomed to living on a leash that even if you untied him he would not budge. And her father-in-law, who in other ways appeared to be a wise man, wise and stern, doted like a fool on his daughter.

There was no one Maryna could confide in, no one to whom she could voice her grievances. It was not seemly to tell others about her plight. She did not trust her neighbours, because what they said to her face was quite different from what they said behind her back. It was only when her sister Mariya asked her if the father still catered to Oksana's whims that she could come right out and say: "Oh yes, he sure does! And what can he be thinking—that a daughter is better than a son? But, my dear sister, God forbid that you tell anyone what I've told you."

And, if the truth be told, Maryna berated Ivan for being spineless, but she herself did not dare to oppose her father-in-law.

By the time Myron arrived at the meeting, a large crowd had gathered. Everyone was talking, shouting, and attacking a beardless, dishevelled young man with large grey eyes, full red lips, and overly long blond hair, who was writhing before them like a lizard. The man was Andriy, Myron's son-in-law, and he flung himself at Myron like a terrified child.

"Daddy, daddy, save me," he whispered in his father-in-law's ear. "I'll do whatever you say, but now . . . I'll be grateful to you the rest of my life."

"Get away from me," Myron said brusquely, shoving him aside. Pushing his way through the crowd as if he were making his way through bramble bushes, he shouted: "What's going on here?"

They all pointed at Andriy and began talking at the same time.

Myron lost his temper. "Speak one at a time! You're all screeching like magpies."

Everyone quieted down, and then, a robust, red-haired man, with such a broad back that you could drive a sleigh over it, began to shout. Glaring threateningly at Andriy, he said that Andriy had wanted to buy a small garden plot from him and had given him a down payment with some borrowed money, but now the man who had lent Andriy the money was demanding interest on it, and Andriy, who was unable to pay it, was demanding the return of his down payment. In other words, Andriy was unable to pay him what was required and, in the meantime, he had lost a reliable buyer for the garden who had been willing to pay even more for it. He wanted Andriy to recompense him for his losses, but Andriy refused to do so, saying that he did not have the money, all the while prattling all sorts of nonsense like: "Of course I know that a contract is more important than money."

Another man—a fat man with a contented, happy, pumpkin-like face—reproached Andriy for not paying him interest on the fifty rubles he owed him. He claimed that Andriy was behind in his payments, and that he should either repay him the money or give him the interest—and he did not want to hear any more excuses.

Then another man with greenish eyes—and grey as the earth— came forward and, strenuously waving his arms, claimed that Andriy (may he be damned!) had pawned his land to him and received money for it and then (may the son-of-a-bitch be damned!) he turned around and pawned it to another man and received money for it from him as well. And now Andriy had better return the money owing to him, or else!

And there were still many others who censured Andriy for the small loans they had made him. Andriy, almost in tears, darted here and there, but could not find a way out. The villagers were all yelling and attacking him.

Andriy liked to deal in both horses and land and, in his own mind, thought things were going very well. He would borrow money here, pay some back there, buy something else over there, and everything would turn out just fine. But this time he had dug himself in so deep that it seemed unlikely he could find a way out. He had not expected all of them to attack him together, at the same time, and threaten to sue him. Prior to this incident, things had always worked out one way or another.

Myron looked long and hard at Andriy who, unable to squirm his way out, dropped his hands in defeat and spoke like a fool: "Well, where am I to get the money? I'd be only too happy to return it, if I had it."

Although he was embarrassed that he had a son-in-law who knew how to trick people out of their money, but did not know how to repay it, Myron knew that he had to rescue the scumbag—the frayed, hempen whip! He absolutely had to, because . . . he had to. And so he began to set matters right.

He told the sturdy man with the broad back, who had sold Andriy the land, that he should keep the down payment because Andriy would soon get the rest of the money and pay him for it. He promised the man with the pumpkin face that he would pay the interest himself and, in a year, God willing, he would pay back the loan as well, just as he would repay the six rubles to the man who had lent them to Andriy for the land. And he let another man use Andriy's land because it had been pawned to him earlier.

And, in this way, Myron settled accounts with all of them, and everyone was happy. Andriy, of course, was happiest of all. All flushed, he could not find the words to thank his father-in-law. He wanted to kiss his hand, but Myron, snarling: "Well, just watch what you do from now on, you son-of-a-bitch," turned around and stalked off, without extending his hand to him.

Where did Myron intend to get the money? He had never had that much money in his hands at any one time, and he would never—not for anything in the world—consider selling his cattle and horses. Well, there was a simple and straightforward solution—

he would hire himself out. He—a landowner who could have sat with folded arms while his sons worked for him—decided to become a servant. He had dubbed as a fool a certain man who worked as a servant, giving his money to a woman whose husband had left her and maintaining her children, even though he knew that in his old age they would not feed him. He had called that man a fool—but was his decision all that different?

When Myron informed his family about his decision, Maryna began banging things around. The cups, bowls, and spoons rang out in chorus in her hands, but, not daring to give voice to her anger, she turned to persuasion.

"But you're old. Why would you want to hire yourself out? Why crawl willingly into hell?"

"It's none of your business," Myron retorted. But all the while he was thinking: "There's no denying she's right, but it can't be helped. I simply have to hire myself out."

"I know you're planning to harness yourself because of that Andriy, but I swear to God, he's not worth it . . ."

"He's a son-of-a-bitch," Myron said.

"There, you see. And here you are . . . Spit on him, and let him go to the devil! You're going to waste your strength on him!"

Myron just dismissed her words with a wave of his hand.

"And how are we to manage without you, daddy?" Ivan interjected with his own concern.

"I'll come by to see how things are coming along," Myron snapped curtly.

Maryna could see that her words had stung the father, and so she ranted on, arguing that it was not worth his while to break his back because of his son-in-law's debts; that it was pointless to give him any money, because he would just let it slip through his fingers once again; and that Andriy was not worth as much as Myron's little finger, and that he would simply throw his father-in-law's hard earned money to the wind.

"Yes, he will," Myron groaned as if someone had just pressed down on a boil. "I know only too well that he will."

Despite everything, however, he hired himself out and, after serving for a year, gave Andriy the money—or rather, gave the money to the people to whom Andriy was indebted. And he bought Andriy a small garden plot, even though, in his opinion, it was better to have less land and work it well by spading and fertilising every foot of it. In a word, he secured his son-in-law's household, and Oksana became more cheerful.

Everything had turned out just fine. And to keep things that way, Myron would have been willing to hire himself out for another year and have the overseer yell at him and push him around as if he were a young boy. And he would have put up with people finding fault with his work, the landowner complaining because Myron was stubborn and did things his own way, and the other workers protesting because Myron was a demanding taskmaster and made them work until they were exhausted, as if he were trying to curry favour with the lord.

Myron not only worked as a servant for a year to assist his son-in-law, he helped him out every way he could. He ploughed for Andriy and Oksana with his horses, hauled grain for them, gave them seed grain and flour when theirs ran out; he gave Oksana money to buy salt, lime, kerosene, and soap; he gave them vegetables, wood, straw, and reeds; he bought fabric at the market for a jerkin and a skirt for Oksana; he fixed their thatched roof, built a threshing floor, a gate, and plaited a fence . . . There was not much that he did not do for them.

Oksana became accustomed to receiving his help. Whenever she needed something, she ran to her father. He would give it to her without fail, no matter how loudly Maryna clattered the dishes. He could not refuse Oksana; everything that was his was also Oksana's. Oksana had realised this as a child and took it all for granted, without so much as a thank you.

But what kind of bond could there possibly be between a father and his daughter? As much as between a bird and a stone, as between the wind and the grass; one flew or blew freely, while the other was bound to the ground, unable to go anywhere. It was true that Myron was "a bit" of a mother as well as a father to Oksana, because, after the death of his wife, he had nursed Oksana with a bottle. But so what?

For a man, a daughter was such that, when the time came, she broke free of her father's care and, like steam rushing through the door of a sauna, fled from him. And this meant that there was no use in growing attached to her. She would never feed her father in his old age; she would work for and try to please someone else's family, forgetting all about her own. She would have a new family, her own worries, her own joy, and therefore it was not becoming for a father to grieve for a daughter, because she was as alien to him as a star in the sky. A son, however, was another matter. A son was also a man, who worked, thought, and looked upon things as he himself did.

It was only Myron who clung to his daughter like a mushroom growing on a birch tree, and he was very sad when he gave her away in marriage. And even though he did not know how to converse with her, he liked to listen to what she said, and kept encouraging her: "Come on, tell me, more!" It seemed to him that, without her songs and her laughter, the sun did not give off any warmth, and he felt an urge to go and find out—to see and hear for himself—what she was doing and how she was getting along. It was the same urge that makes a farmer go to see if his rye is blossoming, or to check if it is heading.

Perhaps Myron hovered over his daughter because she bore a strong resemblance to her mother, and the memory of his deceased wife was so dear to him that he did not marry again, for as he often averred: "The first slice of bread is the sweetest."

It was said that after they had become engaged, his wife had waited three years for him before they finally married. This fact was considered quite remarkable, because nowadays the young men made the rounds of all the houses when they were courting, and the young women, when they tired of partying, married the first young man who asked for their hand in marriage.

Or perhaps Myron felt attached to Oksana because she needed his help, while his sons could manage on their own. She was fragile, like a blade of grass, and he had to support her. Perhaps he loved her because she had been taken from him, though in truth, she herself had left him, because it was her choice to marry Andriy.

Myron had not wanted a son-in-law like Andriy; he had not wanted to give his daughter in marriage to such a young man, and he fumed and swore and threatened to beat her, but nothing had helped—Oksana insisted on marrying him. Myron did not want to forbid the marriage, and so he held a wedding for them and gave Oksana a heifer, a few lambs, and a piglet for her new household. He should have done what another man did—tied his daughter by her braids to the wagon of the young man that he had chosen for her and dragged her off to the altar.

But Myron was not in the habit of beating Oksana; he had done so only when she was still a child, but even then it had usually ended with him stamping his feet and shouting, and that would be the end of that! And he could not stay angry at her for long, because as soon as she saw that he was upset she would turn away his anger either with a joke or some silly remark—just as you would turn a screw-nut with pliers—and he could not help but laugh and get over his annoyance.

"Let her not blame her father," Myron said. "She chose her husband herself, so let her live with him as she best knows how. She saw what she was buying, so now let her eyes feast on him until they burst out of their sockets. It's all the same to me!"

This is what Myron said, but he simply could not accept the fact that Oksana had a husband who, compared to her, was like stinky kerosene compared to milk, or like mud compared to clear spring water. He did not like to look at his son-in-law's bulging grey eyes and his flabby red lips, and that is why he rarely appeared in Oksana's home, preferring to have her come and visit him by herself, even though Andriy tried his best to curry his favour.

"If only he were more attractive; if only he had more brains!" Myron thought; and he often said to Oksana, both in jest and in anger: "Don't believe him; he's a liar."

But Oksana would immediately try to prove that he was wrong.

And Myron would regret his words, thinking: "Would I truly want to part them? No, no. Let them live in peace."

One time Oksana had run to him all in a fright, crying that Andriy was seriously ill and that, to save his life, they would have to call in a woman healer from the next village who, it was said, knew what to do in such cases.

Myron could not refrain from saying: "Oh, just spit on him. Let things take their course."

"Oh, no, my dearest daddy . . . He's groaning, groaning so terribly, that . . . O Lord! He may die! Go for her as quickly as you can."

She bowed down to the ground before her father and tried to drag him out of the house to harness the horses.

Myron felt sorry for his daughter when he saw her tears, but then it occurred to him that she would never be that concerned about him, old as he was, and so he did not want to go.

She saw his reluctance and began to wail: "Oh, my God, my God! What am I to do?" Then, clutching her head in her hands, she tore off.

"Where are you going?" her father shouted after her.

"I'm going to Stepan's—maybe he'll lend me a horse . . ."

Stepan was her older brother.

"Why, you silly little fool, I'm already on my way," Myron thundered. And so he drove off, brought back the woman healer, and saved his son-in-law's life.

What saddened Myron the most was the fact that Oksana was no longer as cheerful as she used to be; she appeared to have wilted, like a cut flower. One reason lay in the crushing poverty in which she lived, and the other in her malicious mother-in-law who persecuted her as a hawk harasses a chicken.

Oksana had married in the spring and, by summer, she came to know true indigence. There was no grain left from the previous year, there were no cattle, the clay stove was crumbling, and the cottage was leaning to one side. In her father's home she had complained about everything: if the bread was left over from the day before and was no longer soft, she pouted and threw it on the table—but now it was quite a different story.

As things stood, the situation was still tolerable, because the father helped the daughter. He managed to do whatever was needed—as if he had ten hands with which to do it. The problem was that Oksana had to work hard, and she had no one to help her.

A delicate girl, who had never had to help with the harvest, Oksana had grown up in relative luxury and had worked in the tobacco fields, while Maryna had done all the work at home. Whatever she earned had been hers to spend, and she had outfitted herself in beautiful clothes. Now, as she slaved away, all these fine garments were wearing out and falling to pieces, and no one saw to it that she got anything new. Hard times had truly descended upon her and, to make matters even worse, her mother-in-law abused her on a daily basis.

This mother-in-law—a fairly young woman with three children younger than Andriy—was stingy and malicious. She continually tormented Oksana, striving to humble and break her, so that she would stop boasting about her rich father and flaunting her youth and attractiveness. Seizing upon the most trivial matters, she would beat Oksana and swear at her, using the most terrible language, and cursing—right in front of the icons—Oksana, her mother, her father, and even her own son, upon whom Oksana appeared to have cast a spell. No matter what Oksana did, it was never good enough. If she cooked some borshch, her mother-in-law peppered her with questions: "Why is it so salty? Why is it murky? Why did it boil over?"

And then the cursing would start anew. "The devil take your mother! You don't know how to do anything. You're a good for nothing so-and-so! Get out of my house! Beat her, Andriy! And as for you, you worthless daughter-in-law, you must have cast a spell on him . . . What did you use to charm him, you rotten so-and-so? May you go mad; may you never know good fortune; may you break your neck! May you . . ."

It was impossible to hear her out. Like a grindstone in a mill, she went on and on without end, cursing nonstop, criticising and swearing, until she vented her spleen. It is true, of course, that it was not entirely without cause that she attacked Oksana, because the young woman really did not know very much about household chores. But why did the mother-in-law boil over like that, jump at her, and swear at her so roundly? And, instead of showing her or telling her what to do, why did she scold her for the slightest misdeed—even for something minor, like putting a pot on the bench instead of on the shelf? And why did she teach her younger children to call Oksana "a little bitch"? And why did she order Andriy to beat his wife?

At first Oksana did not pay any attention to all that. She either laughed and did things her own way, or retorted angrily and swore at them in turn. But then she began to cry and grow sad, and her heart turned cold, like that of a person who slowly freezes to death in winter out on the deserted white steppe. And there were times when Oksana had to admit that her mother-in-law was right, that she, Oksana, truly did not know how to do anything, and then her arms would drop at her sides, and she would do nothing.

Infuriated, her mother-in-law would jump at this chance to attack her: "Let's see how you'll manage to do this—how you'll bake the *paska [braided circular Easter bread]* all by yourself, you bitch. Just let me see! I won't say anything at all, not a word. Do it yourself as best as you know how."

"Why are you making fun of me?" Oksana, bursting into tears, would scream as if she had lost her mind.

What bothered Oksana most of all was the fact that her mother-in-law considered her inept. When she had worked in the tobacco fields, everyone had called her dextrous and swift, but here—just imagine—she was called clumsy. Oksana herself could see that she was somewhat "inept;" she could not keep up to her husband when tying the rye that he mowed into sheaves; the dough that she mixed was either too soft or too stiff; and sometimes she even broke a pot accidentally. At times like that she would run to her father and furtively plead for a pot of some kind. And her father would stealthily take one of Maryna's pots, wrap it in a kerchief, and give it to her.

At first Maryna could not figure out where her pots were disappearing, leaving her nothing in which to cook borshch, but she soon figured things out and, incensed, asked the father: "What am I to cook in?"

"Just wait. I'll buy you a new pot, never fear," Myron replied.

Maryna, sensing that she could get away with saying anything now, muttered: "Oh sure, you'll buy me one. I know you—you'll buy one and then give it away again."

Of course, Myron knew very well that it was not a good idea to give away one's possessions, and he sympathised with Maryna. He saw how much it pained her to part with what was hers; but there was nothing he could do about it. After all, Oksana could not live in poverty!

In a sense, Myron was stealing from himself now, but that was not the real problem! He was also stealing from his son, his daughter-in-law, and their children, and he felt uneasy. Like a tree frozen by winter's frosts, he creaked, leaning to one side, but he still could not do otherwise, just as a sunflower cannot help but turn to the sun.

Oksana did not want people to know that she had brought trouble down upon on herself. Proud like her father, she hid her problems from others for a long time and did not complain to anyone about her mother-in-law.

At first she did not want to tell even her father about her miserable fate, but he soon realised it on his own, even though Oksana's mother-in-law did not dare to scold her on the rare occasion that he visited her. He could see his daughter's pale face and the terror in her eyes, and one time he asked her why she was always so sad. Oksana was unable to hold back and tearfully told him everything. From that time on, he pitied her even more and tried to figure out how to free her from her situation; and she began to visit him on the sly, to cry and complain to him in secret, because she did not want Maryna to see her tears.

Maryna had also advised Oksana not to marry Andriy, because he was poor, and now she could not accept the fact that her property was being transferred bit by bit to Oksana. She began to grumble more boldly about her father-in-law. Once, when she found only half a sack of flour when it should have been full, she confronted the father: "The entire household will be brought to ruin! Everything is continually being carted off; soon there will be nothing left for us to eat ourselves."

Myron did not shout or thunder at her; he just quietly walked out of the house. He was a lot more subdued now, and tried to conceal his meetings with his daughter. She usually came to see him in the evening and talked with him softly, outdoors.

He would ask her: "Well, how are things coming along?"

"Oh," she would reply, "she's tormenting me for accidentally spilling the borshch, and, O God, she curses both me and you so viciously!"

"Yes, I see," Myron would say. "Something has to be done about this . . . Let me think about it a bit."

And then he would bundle something into a kerchief for her, and she would go home.

Myron now continually blamed himself for permitting Oksana to marry Andriy. Even if he would have had to tie her braids to a wagon, he should not have permitted her to marry him.

Only one joy befell Oksana in her marriage—she gave birth to a son, and they named him Myron in honour of his grandfather. Old Myron thought that his grandson was the spitting image of him—even though no features could be discerned as yet on his beet-red, shrivelled little face; Andriy thought that his son looked just like him, while Oksana was sure that little Myronchyk—or

Myros, or Myrok or whatever she chose to call him—did not resemble anyone except his mother.

And what a grand feast Myron held to honour the birth of his grandson. He even procured a bucket of whiskey—he must have borrowed money for it.

All the relatives gathered to celebrate the birth, including Oksana's older brother Stepan. A husky, swarthy, and gloomy man with frowning eyebrows, he resembled his father. Taciturn by nature, he drank a lot and kept trying to curb the tongue of Domakha, his overly talkative wife.

Domakha, an attractive young woman, was also robust, and as dark as a gypsy. She always dressed in red, and tied a fiery crimson kerchief on her head in such a way that she looked like a flaming log in a stove. It was rumoured that she was a thief, and she was blamed whenever something disappeared—a shirt, yarn that had been hung out on a fence, a rake that had been forgotten out in the field, a pitchfork, and other things like that.

When she visited people's homes, everyone was immediately on guard, hiding the salt, soap, and lime. It is true that she had been caught stealing only once. While still single, she had stolen a slab of pork, a pig's shoulder blade, from the lord's manor—otherwise she was very clever and did not allow herself to be caught. She had spent some time in jail for this theft, but what of it? She had served her time, and that was that! Not the least bit ashamed of what she had done, she strutted through the village like a queen, just as she had before, dressed in the same way, and looked just as cheerfully and candidly into other people's eyes.

Domakha liked to party and dance, and she talked a lot, "with a caustic tongue," letting loose a volley of words like a hail of peas, and that was why her husband always tried to rein her in like a colt tethered on a rope.

Did Stepan know that his wife was a thief? No one was sure. He probably did know, because everyone knew, but even so, he covered for her—she was as safe with him as behind a stone wall—and even though he would not take so much as a thread that did not belong to him, he stood up for her and did not wash the family's dirty linen in public. He also refrained from saying anything about the fact that his wife was slovenly and lazy, and that she did not look after the children properly.

Stepan never spoke to his father about his miserable home life and, in answer to his father's question if there was any truth in what the people were saying, he invariably replied: "It's all lies and nothing more! Don't you know what people are like? They're more vicious than snakes."

And so even Myron was convinced that Stepan had a fairly decent life.

On this festive occasion, Domakha, having had quite a bit to drink, lost any inhibitions that she had, and began dancing, singing, and shouting: "For an old woman's hemp you need a crane like this, like this." And she kept calling out: "Ukh, okh, okho-kho! Heh-heh-heh!"

"That's enough, that's enough," her husband tried to stop her, glancing obliquely at the other guests. No matter how much he drank, Stepan never got drunk and always kept his wits about him.

Domakha did not listen to him; she continued dancing and began to sing another song: "Oh, some may drink, and some may not, but we'll just keep on drinking . . ."

At the table sat Domakha's mother, a shrivelled little old woman with a black kerchief reaching down to her beady eyes. Her red, sunken cheeks appeared to have been hollowed out with a spoon. She sat silently with her arms folded on her chest, but her eyes bored into everyone; she looked long and hard at people in order to pass judgement on them later, saying that this was not as it should be, and that was not quite right, and that this one had said this, and that one had said something else. She was a clever woman and a great gossip.

And was it not she who took note of what was lying about unattended, so that her daughter could take advantage of the situation? She had only this one daughter—her husband was dead, and all her other children had died young—and so she had a very close relationship with Domakha. The two of them criticised Stepan and, more often than not, did not listen to him.

Korniyikha, Domakha's mother, often censured him, saying: "M-m . . . Is that how things should be done?" And she demanded that Stepan tell her exactly how much money he had spent on what and why. Domakha, understandably, supported her mother. Whenever he said anything to Domakha, the old woman would intrude, asking what it was all about. She had to know everything.

Stepan would hold his tongue for a long time, and then he would finally shout: "May the devil take your mother, and may you all go berserk! I'll leave everything and take off—and then you can do as you see fit." This outburst would make both of them pull in their horns and lie low for a few days without bothering him.

Now Korniyikha was sitting quietly, looking closely at Mar'ya, Oksana's other sister-in-law, the wife of her middle brother Yehor. Mar'ya, like Domakha, was feeling happy, both because of the whiskey and because the men were ogling her. She liked to have them admire her; she liked men—especially young ones, and this greatly angered Yehor. He beat her often, and brutally, almost killing her.

More than once, she ran away and left him, but it seemed he could not live without her; he always begged her forgiveness and brought her back, as if he really needed her—even though their three children had died. And she would once again begin to party, and go to dances and to the swings, like a single girl.

There were times when she would even take off her married woman's headdress in front of the young men, and, because she was a small woman, her lush hair would stream down her back like golden cobwebs, covering her completely. And she would break into gales of laughter, and everyone would laugh helplessly with her.

Like his father, and all the Chayka family, Yehor was well-built, tall and swarthy, and it may be that Mar'ya had charmed him simply because she was not at all like that; she was small and fair, like a lump of cheese. Yehor found his wife's behaviour embarrassing and flushed brick-red whenever she was up to her tricks, drinking to someone's good health or doing other things like that. He was ashamed of her, but he would not part with her for anything or throw her out, as other men would, even though Myron said to him one time; "Spit on her and let her go to the devil! If she's left you, let her go!"

Mar'ya had no father or mother, and her single sisters had sold their small plots of land to Yehor and taken off to the city to work as servants, and when one of them occasionally showed up to visit Mar'ya, there was nothing but trouble. They prattled such nonsense about the city that they threw her completely off balance. She would begin to throw in some "cityfied" words when she spoke, and she wore a jacket, even though the villagers laughed at her, and her husband beat her.

And he truly did beat her; he slammed her as you slam a sunflower until all its seeds fall out; but she did not hold a grudge against him; if she had, she would have kicked him out of her house long ago. As it was, she was the one who kept running away from him, leaving him the cottage and everything else. She longed to move to the city, but Yehor had decided that as long as he was alive, this was not to be, and when the Chaykas made up their minds, they would never change them. And so every day there was a scene in their home.

Mar'ya, wanting to leave, would shout: "Who are you to stop me from going? I'm a free person, just as you are."

And he would box her ear—that was once; and then wallop her on the neck—that was twice.

She: "I'm not afraid of anyone, except God. Get away from me! Leave me alone! I'm a person, just as you are."

And he would strike her again—slap, slap—and she would flee, streaking like a flash of lightning through the garden, through the swamp, running far far away, until she could no longer hear him. She would hide somewhere, and the next day he would set out in search of her, begging her forgiveness until she returned home again. And then, after a few days, he would beat her up again, because he would be angry with himself for having asked her to come back.

Yehor's father advised him to take in a little boy as his own child because "a man can't survive without some help in his old age." But Yehor did not listen to him in this instance, even though he always obeyed his father in everything else.

And people advised Mar'ya to throw Yehor out of her house, but she would not agree to that, saying: "All in all, he's a good man; another man might have killed me by now."

There were times when they made up and lived together peacefully for a week or more, and it was a delight to see them then. They went everywhere together and kept smiling at each other, and Yehor would peer intently at Mar'ya as if he had never seen her before.

And now too, as Mar'ya danced, Yehor, holding his head tightly in his hands as if he were afraid that it might break or fall off, sat and stared—his big eyes bulging and murky from whiskey—only at his wife, and at no one else.

Who else was at the feast?

Of course it goes without saying that Maryna was there with her husband. She was not at all happy, because she still had not come up with a plan to wean the father from his daughter, and she was angry at her husband, who tried to console her by saying that everything would be different when the father died, but that for the time being they had to put up with things as they were.

Now she was even more upset, because the father was walking around in such a happy daze at this feast celebrating the birth of Oksana's son, that you would think he had found a pile of money. He smiled at everyone, as if he had dreamt a wonderful dream, and then he became so generous that he presented Oksana with a lamb and a calf, and made note of this by drawing them on the wall with a piece of charcoal. And he kept talking to Oksana, holding her by her sleeve: "If you like them ver-r-r-ry much, you can have them but if you don't like them ver-r-ry much, I'll keep them."

She replied: "Why, thank you, dear daddy."

And he repeated: "Only if you like them ver-r-ry much, you know—then go ahead and take them, but if you don't like them ver-r-r-y much . . ." and he rolled his r's until it sounded as if a wagon was rumbling along, and then he shouted: "Come on, fellows, let's go to the whiskey barrel!"

More than half the guests trailed off after him.

Maryna returned home in an angry mood. She had just found out how much the father had earned working as a servant. He had never revealed his pay to them but, having had too much to drink at the feast, had inadvertently let the amount slip out.

"Well, father sure is the clever one," Ivan laughed. He too was slightly tipsy.

"It's too bad you aren't like that."

"Like what?"

"Oh, you're such a fool!" Maryna retorted. "And who would have wanted his money? He's keeping it a secret from us!" she said angrily. "It's all for his Oksana, that little doll, that rotten good-for-nothing! But when you suggested buying a third horse to deliver mail, the answer was no!" She turned around.

Ivan, his attractive head lolling on the table, was already fast asleep.

"Phooey on you!" Maryna muttered and began to make up the bed.

The father came home late. The next day he walked around like a thundercloud; he liked to party and drink, and he did not begrudge the money for it, but in the morning he was annoyed with himself for having wasted the money and for not being able to work well because of the buzz in his head. But nevertheless, when another opportunity arose, he drank and had a good time, cavorting like a stream in the springtime that breaks all the dams.

Ivan, however, could not tolerate whiskey. His head swam after a few shot glasses—even in this he could not equal his father.

Oksana was very thrilled with her little child. For his godmother they chose Mar'ya, Yehor's wife; Andriy wanted her because she was wealthy and childless, while Oksana simply liked her better than her other sisters-in-law. The godfather was the man who had lent Andriy the money, and who now was on good terms with him again.

To his mother, Myronchyk seemed to be more beautiful than any other child she had ever seen, mainly because, as she said: "He's so tiny! Oh, so very, very tiny, but he's a perfect replica of a human being, right down to the fingernails on his teeny fingers."

It is true that Oksana did not always know exactly what to do with him. There were times when she exhausted herself before figuring out what it was that he needed, and she often overfed him to the point that he threw up, because it seemed to her that if he cried that meant he was hungry; and she wailed senselessly over him when he was ill instead of thinking of a way to make him better. She herself was often to blame for his colds, because she would rush right at him after coming in from the cold river. But all in all, he brought her more joy than grief.

She was thrilled beyond words when he made his first sounds: "Ba, ba, dya, dlya," and she continually talked with him as if he were an adult.

The baby gaped at her and played with her coral beads, while she went on and on: "We must buy a little horse; yes, indeed, my golden darling, my sweetheart, my teeny little fish, yes indeed!" She called him whatever came to mind, whatever struck her fancy. "We'll buy another little piece of land . . . We'll sow some tobacco on it . . . and now, as you know, we need a little horse, because you can't run a farm without a horse; yes indeed, my teensy weensy darling." And she smothered her teensy weensy darling with kisses.

Even her mother-in-law had to smile when she heard Oksana talk this way, and she would say: "You're being foolish. Do you really think he understands you?"

"Of course, he understands," Oksana would retort without turning around. And she would continue talking to her little boy.

Myronchyk babbled more and more: "Dlya, lo, la, ma-ma."

"What is it, my little one? What is it my sweet little nightingale? Do you want to go and see grandfather? Grandfather gave us some money, grandfather saved us . . . Grandfather will give us a treat."

And she would wrap the child in her skirt and run off to see her father and brag about how much the child was saying. "Just listen, daddy, listen."

And the child would babble for him: "Balo-o-o . . . Go! Gup!" He was telling them that he wanted to go for a ride, saying "Gup" for "Giddy-up!"

And Oksana was ecstatic: "How clever he is, the little darling. Oh my God, look how he's stretching out his arms!"

And she would begin kissing the child so passionately that he would cry in vexation, and she would become alarmed: "Boo-boo? Where's the boo-boo? Oh, it's your foolish mother that's given you a boo-boo, my poor little dove." And she would begin to kiss the nonexistent boo-boo.

The grandfather would chuckle, and Oksana would begin to laugh as well. She was once again beginning to laugh. It is true that even earlier, in between her mother-in-law's reproaches and her own crying, there were times when she laughed and sang like a single girl, until the house echoed, but that was only when she forgot about her poverty. But now, even though her mother-in-law continued to torment her every day, every hour, every minute—reproaching her, rebuking her, cursing her, and scolding her with words that fell evenly and persistently like the autumn rain—nothing seemed to bother Oksana as long as the child was fed and was not sick or crying.

At times it seemed to Oksana that her mother-in-law was forcing iron rings down over her head or pounding nails into it; it was as if she were constantly wielding a threshing flail and beating her with it: "Thump, thump, thump!" Oksana could no longer discern what the words were—there was only a pounding in her head and in her heart. If only the older woman would stop her incessant nagging for at least a second! But no, it was not in her nature to do so.

Occasionally Andriy stood up for his wife saying; "That's enough, mother. Why are you tormenting her like that?"

Then his mother would lash out at him: "So, you're turning against your mother, you so-and-so! Why don't you beat her? Why? May your eyes crawl out of your head, may . . ." And she went on and on, clattering away like a fanning mill.

She also attacked her own daughters, verbally ripping them to shreds, as one tears feathers. And there were times—when Andriy was not at home—that she would chase Oksana out of the house at night, and the young woman would have to wait by the house or in the barn until her mother-in-law fell asleep.

One time she even tried to abuse little Myronchyk, but Oksana grabbed a knife and yelled: "If you don't shut up at once, I'll throw it at you!"

Her mother-in-law clamped her lips tight, as if she had a mouth full of water that she did not want to spill.

But now that she had Myronchyk, Oksana was not troubled as much by her mother-in-law's anger. Overriding the older woman's ranting voice, she would tell her little son fairy tales she made up about a wolf, a fox, Little Ivan, and others, like this one:

"The flowers in the garden were talking about the stars, saying that they were very beautiful and wondering if you could buy them with money. And a certain lord, who was very rich and had golden houses, heard this and came up with the idea of buying a star for himself. He wanted to fasten it on his wall so that it would hang there instead of a lamp and shine for him at night. But he did not know how to do this, and so he went to a very old man to ask him if he could tell him how to go about it.

"Now this old man was very virtuous, and he lived in a well so deep that the eye could not see into its depths. The lord knocked and knocked on the well.

"'What do you want?' the old man asked from the mouth of the well, without climbing out of it.

"He had not shown himself to anyone for ages, and they say that he was completely silver, but who knows if it's true, because he was never really seen.

"The lord said: 'I've decided to buy a star, but I don't know how to ask God for it.'

"'Pile your money on the ground,' said the old man. 'When you build a pillar with it that reaches to the star, order your servants to fetch it. You will buy the star, but it will cost more than one measure of money.'

"The lord went home and began piling the money the way the old man had told him to; he kept piling it higher and higher until it was as high as the bushes, and then as high as the trees, and then as high as his buildings, and then all the way up to the very clouds.

And then the lord died. He cried bitterly before his death, for he had become very weary of his task, but had failed to buy the star. He told his servants to take all his money and hide it in a chest.

"But no one knew where the pillar of money had disappeared. It had sunk into the ground like a copper pole, and soil had covered it, and it was impossible to tell where the money had gone, or even where the hole was. And so, even though all that money had been spent on the star, the lord was buried without having bought it.

"If someone finds that money he will become a very, very rich man, but no one can say where that money is. Perhaps the old man could be asked, but his well has also been covered with soil, and he was probably taken alive into heaven—that's what he deserved . . ."

Or Oksana would tell Myronchyk about the quarrel between the nightingale and the cuckoo. As they argued about whose voice was sweeter, a cat caught both of them while they were singing and choked them, so that neither one of them heard the other.

And Oksana made up all sorts of stories like that, cheering up both herself and Myronchyk, and making her life a little happier by blocking out her mother-in-law's scolding.

Oksana rarely came to her father's house when Maryna was at home, but one time she ran in when her sister-in-law was there. The entire family was seated at the table eating dinner.

Without even saying "hello," Oksana bowed to the ground before her father and, gasping for air, said: "Have mercy, have pity!"

"What's the matter?" the father asked. "Has the child fallen ill, that you've rushed in like this?"

"No, dearest daddy, it's Andriy." Oksana became disconcerted. "He wants, he's asking that you . . . He's asking for some money . . . for you to defend him."

A horrible grimace contorted Myron's face and, leaping up from the table as if he had picked up a red-hot iron, he shouted: "May his father go mad! I'm not one of his drinking buddies."

He wanted to go, but Oksana clung to him: "Oh save us, daddy, dear daddy!"

Freeing himself from her grasp, he shouted once again: "Am I to become a swindler for a hundred rubles because of him, that son-of-a bitch? I've never been a swindler! So much money that belonged to others has passed through my hands, and now . . . May you all be damned!" And he stormed out of the house.

Oksana collapsed on the bench and burst into bitter tears.

The children fell silent. Hrytsko stared at Oksana without taking his eyes off her, and Tetyanka, sitting as still as a drop of water that froze before it rolled off the roof, gaped at her. Never before had she seen her aunt Oksana cry, or heard her grandfather shout at her.

Ivan began to console his sister: "Father is just saying that; he'll take care of everything. Just don't cry. That's enough now."

She did not listen to him and kept repeating: "Oh, woe is me, woe is me." This time she was weeping as if she wanted to cry out all her tears at once, as if someone had unlocked all the floodgates behind which she had concealed her grief from the eyes of others, as if now she were finally free to weep.

Maryna was amazed. Just as she had never seen a black rose, so had she never seen Oksana like this. Before Oksana got married, she had always been happy and joking, and was able to make everyone laugh if she wanted to by teasing them or making up songs. Maryna still remembered two of the songs that Oksana had composed. The first one went like this:

"People say it's a flute that's playing
But it's my heart that's singing with joy.
People say it's a star that's shining,
But it's my heart that's flaming with joy.
People say it's a flower that's growing
But it's my heart that's blooming with love."

And the second one went as follows:

"He circled above her like a teal-blue dove,
She looked at him, looked and laughed.
He twined about her like periwinkle green,
She looked at him, looked and laughed.
He bent before her like a blade of wild grass,
She looked at him, looked and laughed."

And that is what Oksana had been like as well. She laughed at Andriy when he came to her bearing rings and ribbons, and said he was hairy, and uncombed, and that his mouth was red like that of a jackdaw; but then she married him and stopped laughing. Life was probably not too sweet for her if she was crying like that.

Maryna had heard from others that Oksana's mother-in-law was mean, but she had not believed that it was true; besides, how could you not scold Oksana if she did not know how to do any household chores. When she was still single, she would come home from the tobacco fields and not do anything at all in the house. She would either go off to have a good time, or sew or weave something for her hope chest. And so she had not learned to do anything, despite the fact that Maryna had been angry and reproached her for not wanting to help with the housework. But Oksana had simply ignored her, laughed, and even made Maryna laugh when she began to sing:

"Oh the lord walks, the lord walks,
And eyes the young girls.
The lady finds offshoots
And berates him and berates him.
The girls are like cranberries,
The lady's an old fossil;
The girls are like raspberries,
Love me, you old fogies."

It is no wonder that her father nicknamed her "the rainbow," for she was always happy and laughing.

"Some 'rainbow' she's turned out to be," Maryna thought and, having thought this, she too began to console Oksana, even though it had always seemed to her that, as long as she lived, she would never forgive Oksana for laughing at her. "Don't cry, dear sister. Come now, don't cry! Listen to what I'm saying: 'When all this is finally ground—there will be some flour.' Don't grieve, because your breasts may lose their milk; that's how it is. Does Myronchyk have a lot of teeth already, dear sister? And he's so nice and plump—like a little lump of earth."

Listening to her, Oksana gradually stopped crying. Then she slowly began to reply and, finally, regaining her good humour, laughed and ran home to see to her child.

"And we'll talk father into it," Ivan said in parting. "He'll do everything, never fear. Just don't worry."

Maryna almost called him a fool, and when Oksana left, she stated sternly: "There's no reason for you to go crawling to your father. He knows what he's doing. If he doesn't want to be a swindler, then there's no use forcing him to be one. That scumbag must have really burned him good and hard this time, if he's renounced him."

"Well, fine, let him do as he sees fit. What's it to me? It's just that I feel sorry for Oksana."

"He knows what he's doing," Maryna said once more. "Come, we'll have our meal now, and I'll keep his dinner warm for him in the oven." And they all started eating.

Tetyanka reflected on what had happened. "Why was auntie crying? Does she have a boo-boo? Grandfather didn't beat her, did he?"

"He said 'damned soul,'" Hrytsko said. "Didn't you hear him?"

"Yes, yes, I did," said the little girl. "But what of it? Where's the boo-boo?"

"Hush now, you two," their mother shut them up.

Maryna was still thinking about Oksana, and how she had revealed herself today. When she heard Oksana crying, she realised that she was not weeping just because of her father's words, but that she was sobbing out all her pent-up grief.

That meant that what people were saying was true—that Oksana led a miserable life with her vicious mother-in-law. But Oksana had married Andriy of her own free will, and surely her father, who was attached to her like a hop vine around a willow, would not have given her away to have someone injure her. Apparently, however, life was not a bed of roses for Oksana—and Myron was being punished for transferring the property of Maryna's children to his daughter.

In her heart, Maryna rejoiced, but at the same time she could not help but feel sorry for Oksana, for she was sure that her father had abandoned her. He had damned her and renounced her, and he rarely went back on his word. Well, that Andriy must have really become odious to him if he had yelled at his daughter so harshly. No, he would not be reconciled with them, just as a branch that has been cut off will not grow back on a tree.

But how happy Oksana had been in the past! Even Maryna conceded that the house was darker and gloomier after Oksana had been given in marriage; it was as if a window that looked out into the street had been blocked off. The children also loved their aunt Oksana and missed her, because she spoiled them, petted them, and bought them treats.

Myron, forgetting all about dinner, paced the riverbank beyond the gardens, thinking: "Am I to become a swindler?" He knew all about the matter that Oksana had mentioned. He knew that not long ago, Andriy had rented land from the lord on behalf of the community, and he also knew that Andriy had duped everyone. He had taken five hundred rubles from the peasants, given the lord two hundred, and received two receipts from the lord on the same day—one for two hundred and one for three hundred. But he had put the three hundred rubles back in his pocket, thereby fooling both the lord and the villagers.

Myron guessed that now Andriy wanted him to stand up before the people, who had elected Andriy as their "plenipotentiary," and to testify that Andriy had not taken the money but had given it all to the lord, even though the latter claimed that there was a shortfall in his books.

"I'll never do it as long as I live," Myron thought. "May you drop dead!"

Even though Myron knew that his son-in-law was being blamed for this chicanery he did not want to get involved. Not thinking that Andriy would actually send Oksana to him, he had left him to squirm his way out of the situation as best he could.

Myron knew very well how much money Andriy had collected, and he also knew that the lord from whom they were getting the land wanted only what was owing to him. And he was well aware that Andriy was the kind of man who could not see someone else's money without becoming entangled in it.

He was also aware that from the day that Andriy began gathering the money, he had quite unexpectedly become rich—buying a horse, striking a bargain for a cow, sowing his fields with tobacco, and hiring older girls to work on his "plantation." And where was he getting the money to do it all? Myron knew all this; he knew it, but he remained silent.

Deep in his heart he was angry with his son-in-law for using other people's money to live a good life, but he thought that the young man might be able to wriggle out of this mess on his own. He could sell the tobacco and pay back what he owed.

But it had not turned out that way. Apparently, Andriy was not prepared to admit that he had taken the three hundred rubles and, just as before, had sent Oksana to get her father to stand up for him, knowing full well, the son-of-a-bitch, that he could not refuse her.

"Oh, I'll help you, all right! I'll go and tell the community everything I know," Myron growled to himself. "Those people are truly stupid—they still can't figure out if they gave Andriy five hundred or two hundred rubles. They can't get things straight, and the secretary is probably in Andriy's pocket, as well two or three other loudmouths who drink with his money. Well, just you wait! I'll expose you to the world!

"But really . . . Why did I yell like that at Oksana? Is she to blame that the devil's son sent her to me? She doesn't understand what's going on. She's probably crying. You know, I saw the most beautiful piece of fabric in the Jew's shop . . . Yes, indeed . . .

"Well then, what am I to do? I guess I'll have to go to the meeting . . . to reveal . . . Today's a minor feast day as well—probably everyone has gathered there by now . . . Yes, yes indeed! They must have attacked him there, and that's why he's sent for me . . . He's afraid . . . He's cowering behind me . . . Well, just you wait, you fiend, I'll show you . . . But what if he gets angry and starts beating Oksana, and . . . Oh dear, oh dear . . . Well, what am I to do? Should I go, or shouldn't I?"

Myron finally made up his mind and strode swiftly to the gathering. When they asked him if he knew where the three hundred rubles had disappeared, he said that there was no way he could know, that he had no information, and that Andriy probably did not take the money, and that the lord probably had made a mistake because he had given him a receipt for two hundred, but really, he did not have any way of knowing, and he did not know!

The gathering was confused, and everyone began shouting at the same time. Andriy cheered up and led the crowd to the tavern for a drink.

After this incident, Myron sternly ordered Andriy to sell his tobacco field and return the money to the community. But Andriy forgot about it, and so did all the other people. They collected another three hundred rubles to pay for the land a second time and soon forgot the entire "story."

Myron was the only one who did not forget, but he thought: "It's a good thing that the son-of-a-bitch at least bought Oksana a cow. Now she'll have milk for the child, because she was always complaining about it, and it's impossible to make Maryna part with any milk that we have."

Myron was angry with himself. All week he walked around as if he had been drenched in cold water. Even in the tavern, when his son-in-law was treating the villagers, he sat gloomily and drank silently. And a few times he asked haltingly: "Tell me, I'm an honest man, aren't I? Oh, for the sake of honour, I'd . . . So what kind . . . What kind of a man am I?"

"Of course you're honest, we're all honest people here," Andriy picked up on his words. He poured him another drink, danced attendance on him, and broke into a song; "Let's drink, my in-law, the whiskey is good."

Other songs followed: "He drank away his oxen, he drank away his wagon, he drank away the yoke and even the shafts . . ."

Finally even Myron became cheerful. The next day, however, he walked around black with anger. He recovered only when he found himself a new problem—and forgot about his old ones.

He had long been thinking how to get at Oksana's mother-in-law, but he could not find a means of doing so. It would be best if she would die. How long was she going to make life difficult for Oksana? But no, she did not want to die! Myron could not even give her a good tongue lashing, because it would just make things worse. And it would do no good to tell Andriy; Oksana said that his mother also railed at him for all she was worth.

Myron would have liked, best of all, to take Oksana back home, but what would people say? He was not afraid of anyone, and did not bow and scrape before anyone, but Oksana would be afraid and, moreover, she would not want to leave her husband—she still trusted this strutting stork, this lying devil! Well then, what was to be done? He would see to it that the mother-in-law got married, and that would be the end of that!

As soon as he came up with the idea, Myron began looking around for a prospective groom. At one time he had heard about an old bachelor who had not managed to get married earlier, and now no single girl or young widow would have him. His name was Danylo Siryy, and he lived in another village. Myron had never laid eyes on him. But he found out where his cottage was and went to see him.

As soon as Myron walked into the yard, he saw what kind of a "householder" lived there. The area around the cottage was strewn with last year's rotten straw; the haystacks were badly formed, and hay had been pulled out haphazardly from all sides; in the middle of the yard there was a large puddle that reached right up to the threshold; the earthen embankment abutting the house was crumbling, and the thatched roof was overgrown with grass; two young willow trees, planted near the windows, had withered long ago, and only bare trunks protruded; there was no fence next to the street; and pigs wandered in the garden rutting the soil with their snouts.

When Myron stepped into the house, he saw that things there were even worse. The walls were black with soot; there was garbage, filth, and putrid decaying matter near the threshold; a pile of ashes was heaped next to the stove; a pair of wet, torn pants dangled from a rope; and unwashed pots and dishes were strewn on the bench, along with mouldy pieces of bread. Amidst this clutter scurried countless beetles, and a mangy reddish cat sat looking at them, occasionally scattering them with its paw.

Not far from the cat sat Danylo Siryy, mending a shirt that he had just taken off. He truly was a *"siryy [grey]"* man, as if he had been fashioned out of dirty grease. He had white hair growing in tufts on his head, and pale, drooping cheeks. He had neither a moustache nor a beard, and blue circles outlined his pale, rheumy eyes.

"Good day," Myron said.

"G-good d-d-day," the other replied. "S-so wh-what's n-n-new?"

What was Myron to say? He could not start by trying to act as a matchmaker; he was ashamed to do so, and furthermore, he did not know how. He thought for a moment and then said: "People were saying that you have some straw to sell, so maybe you could sell me sixty bundles. I want to fix up my barn."

"F-f-from wh-wh-where are y-y-you?" Danylo asked.

"I'm Myron Chayka; perhaps you've heard of me?"

"Y-y-es, I h-h-heard . . . y-you w-were a v-village ch-ch-chief."

"Yes, I was. So, will you sell me some straw?"

"N-n-no, I n-n-need it m-m-myself . . . and th-th-there aren't any g-g-good b-b-bundles th-th-this y-y-year."

He rose to his feet, and Myron could see that he was unsteady; he wavered this way and that way like a distaff, or like unbaked, soft dough that flops first here, and then there.

"S-s-sit d-d-down," Danylo said.

Myron could not find a spot to sit and, glancing all around, asked: "So this is how you live all by yourself?"

"Y-y-yes . . . It's n-not t-too b-b-bad . . . I'm u-used t-t-to it."

"Why don't you get married?"

"Ha-ha-ha!" Danylo roared with laughter. "All th-th-the w-w-women l-l-love m-m-me anyway."

Myron was tired of this conversation, but he did not know how to broach the topic of Oksana's mother-in-law, so he said curtly: "Well, good-bye." And he walked out of the house before Danylo could answer.

"G-g-good l-l-luck."

Myron now seized upon his friend Mytro Pynchuk—a friend for partying, and not for working—the most adept matchmaker in the entire village. He talked so much and so "forcefully," that no young man or young woman could hold their own against him once he decided on his own, or in response to a request, to match them up. He was so convincing, so overpowering, so persuasive, and fastened his bulging black eyes at the person he was talking to so intently, that the latter had to agree with him, if not right at that moment, then in a day or two, or a week after Pynchuk set his sights on him.

And it was this Pynchuk that Myron set loose on Danylo and Oksana's mother-in-law. It was difficult to explain the situation to Pynchuk without dragging Oksana into it. When Pynchuk asked why it was necessary to dupe this woman, Myron had to lie.

"It's . . . just for a joke." Or: "She's still young; let her live a little! Perhaps there will still be some children, and the more children there are, the more workers there are."

Having lied, Myron felt as if he had drunk a potion brewed from wormwood. He had to waste a lot of whiskey on Pynchuk, but the latter had Siryy and the mother-in-law paired off before a month was up. He convinced Oksana's mother-in-law that she was still as young as a willow, and that everyone lives in pairs: a dove with his mate, a rooster with a hen, and that she too should get married. And he told Danylo Siryy tall tales about the large sums of money that this woman supposedly had. "She has so much money that you should carry her around in your arms."

Danylo gave in to this compelling argument and moved into the cottage of Oksana's mother-in-law. He lived there for a while, fattened himself up on her food—the older woman cooked the meals herself now, instead of making Oksana do it—tricked her into giving him a bit of money, and then, one morning, without waiting for either the wedding or the birth of his child, vanished as if the earth had swallowed him. They rushed to the village where he lived, but could not find him there. They did find out, however, that he had pulled such stunts before, with both younger and older widows.

One young woman had wept openly that she wanted a man in the house—and because the people had advised her, and because she had grown weary of struggling by herself with her four children like a fish stranded on the ice—she agreed to marry Siryy. Danylo lived with her for a month and then abandoned her before the marriage ceremony. And so now the woman had even more grief. She had been poor, but virtuous, but now she had fallen into shame, and there was an unwanted child, may the devil take it! She hated that child with such a passion, that she was ready to kill it, and she cursed it every day.

Another woman, a soldier's wife, also complained that Danylo had "spoiled" her, and how was she to show herself to her husband when he came back home?

This was how Danylo shook every pear tree without ever having his hands bound.

The wedding of Oksana's mother-in-law was undone. But now she railed less against Oksana and cursed Danylo and the unfortunate child that she was carrying. In her anger, she wanted to choke or starve to death the child within her, or to have a miscarriage by working too hard, so she did not eat and did not spare herself, dragging the heaviest sacks alongside Andriy. But it was all in vain; the child was born, and Myron and the mother-in-law took Danylo Siryy—who finally had reappeared in his village—to court to either make him get married or pay for the child's upkeep.

It seemed to Myron that, in defending the mother-in-law, he was defending justice, because in his view it was not right to bring children into this world and then abandon them and not feed them, especially as they were expected to feed their father later on in life. So he defended Oksana's mother-in-law vigorously, tried hard to make Danylo take her to live with him, took great pains in the courthouse, testifying on her behalf as if she were his daughter.

He hated Danylo and deemed him the worst swindler in the world; however, when Danylo refused to listen to the court and took neither the child nor the woman to live with him, Myron tried still another tactic. He went to him and, bowing before someone for the first time in his life, pleaded with Danylo to get married.

Danylo replied: "Ha-ha-ha! If I m-m-married all th-th-the w-w-women wh-wh-who t-t-try t-t-to l-l-latch on t-t-to m-m-me, th-th-then h-h-how m-m-many w-w-wives w-w-would I h-h-have? And wh-wh-why d-d-do y-y-you w-w-want m-m-me t-t-to?"

"Phew," Myron spit and went home. He was so upset that he had bowed before such a piece of shit that he felt as if he were breaking into pieces or chopping himself into kindling wood.

Before long, Danylo's child died, and he once again was as free as a jackdaw. The mother-in-law remained in Andriy's cottage.

Oksana, understandably, found it very vexing that it had not been possible to get rid of her mother-in-law. And Andriy—even though he rarely spent any time at home now because the cursing and quarrelling had become repugnant to him—would probably have been more tractable if his mother had not been there.

Only Maryna was happy. She surmised whose idea it had been to marry off Oksana's mother-in-law, and she was happy to see Oksana left with her grief; she was happy because she was jealous that Grandfather Myron was favouring little Myronchyk over her own children, and because she could see that Oksana's life was improving. The latter now had a horse, a cow and a tobacco "plantation."

Myron was convinced that all was not lost, and that it might still be possible to find someone who would marry the mother-in-law.

Maryna, however, was sure that no fool would marry the older woman—it was impossible to patch iron with wood.

But Myron kept saying to himself, over and over again: "No, come what may, my daughter will be happy. As long as I'm alive, I'll see to it that she's happy."

"Go ahead," thought Maryna, "catch the wind in the open field!"

They Lived for Themselves Alone
(1899)

Khvedir Turpak was a tall man, slender like a whitefish, with a sharp beak for a nose, steely and piercing grey eyes, yellow straw-like hair that hung in even strands on either side of his face, and a short coarse beard and moustache that jutted out like stubble. He never laughed and, for most of his life, rarely sat still; holding himself erect like a crane, he was always in motion, bustling and rushing about. Taciturn by nature, he spoke only when it was absolutely necessary; otherwise, he remained silent and applied himself to his work.

And he was a first-rate worker, who did everything swiftly. He knew how to thatch a roof, was a skilled carpenter and cabinet maker, and when he built window boxes they were so splendidly decorated and painted, that people gasped in amazement. He knew how to do everything; in a word, he was a man of many talents!

Kharytyna, Khvedir's wife, was equally skilled at women's work. She not only knew how to weave, but also how to sew jerkins—a skill that was considered quite remarkable in our village, as all the tailors and cobblers were men. Before he died, her brother had taught her how to sew, and now she earned a lot of money plying her trade. As Christmas or Easter approached, every girl in the village, no matter what her means, wanted to have a new jerkin. Tearfully imploring her parents or assailing them with reproaches, or borrowing money that she would have to work off later, she would scrounge up enough money to buy some fabric. And then she would hurry with it to Kharytyna's cottage and ask her to sew a jerkin.

And then the pleading would begin: "O auntie, my dearest auntie, sew me the jerkin as soon as you can, and it must have five pleats at the back, and two pockets, and little gold buttons. And sweetheart, my pet, sew it as quickly as you can, for I need it as soon as possible!"

"Stop screeching like a magpie," Kharytyna would say angrily. "You can see how much work I have! Am I to drop all my baking and cooking just to sew you a jerkin, for God's sake? If I get all my work done, then I'll sew it, but if I don't, then I won't." And she would tell the girl, in no uncertain terms, to leave.

But the girl had no need to worry, for Kharytyna, without fail, would finish her work and sew the jerkin. Like her husband, she delighted in money, and would never sew on credit, as others did.

Kharytyna was not a cheerful woman; she seldom said anything, and whoever talked with her was left feeling as if he had eaten strong horseradish or stuck himself with a needle, for every word of hers was stinging and offensive, as if it had been sharpened or salted. Some people who talked with her did not realise at first what she was up to, and it was only later that it dawned on them that she had been making fun of them.

Because she always knew what was happening everywhere, Kharytyna was thought to be a witch, even though she did not look like one. Witches are supposed to be as black as coal, but she was blond, and her eyes—well, I really can't say what her eyes were like, because when she talked she either veiled them, or looked in corners, or at the ceiling, or at the floor, so that it was impossible to tell what colour they actually were: grey, or green, or, perhaps, even blue. You could only see that they were small, almost imperceptible. Her lips were thin as threads, her nose was pudgy, her cheekbones were high and prominent, and her large head sat on her withered, spindly neck like a pot on a peg. Kharytyna was a heavy-set woman, as any good worker should be; she never got tired and, even if she had, there was no one to help her. They had only one daughter, and she had left home to work as a servant.

It is often said that, just as an apple does not roll far from an apple tree, so does a child resemble its parents. If that is so, then why was Marta, the daughter of Khvedir and Kharytyna, so different from her parents—like heaven and earth—that she did not resemble them in the least? Beautiful from childhood, she had curly black hair, eyes dark as plums, full rosy lips that looked like strawberries growing in the steppe, a fair face, and a thin, amusingly pointed chin that reminded one of the leaves of a pansy. She was slender and delicate, like a star in the heavens, and just as silent.

Even as a child, she was unusually quiet. Sitting in a corner without saying a word, she played with remnants from the jerkins her mother sewed. If anyone spoke to her, she flushed like a poppy and bashfully hid her face in her tiny hands. All day long, she spread out scraps of woollen, velveteen, or velvet fabric, and pieced together the slanted, narrow, long, short, and notched bits of cloth until a lovely pattern emerged, like on a leaf.

But why was Marta so silent? Perhaps because she was always alone, like a bird in a cage, or maybe because she was afraid of her parents. Her father looked right through her, as if she were not there, as if she were not needed at all. And her mother was always preoccupied with her work and did not like it if the little girl spoke to her, scattered things about, or made any noise.

Kharytyna liked everything to be in order, and she taught Marta to be like that as well. She would give her a spindle, and say: "Spin." And the little girl would spin and, even if she held the spindle the wrong way, she still spun. Or, to teach her how to sew, her mother would tell her to stitch together scraps of fabric. If Marta wanted to go outdoors to play, her mother would not let her, saying: "Don't go outside, daughter; the boys will beat you up." Or: "Where do you think you're going? Stay where you are!"

To tell the truth, Marta was somewhat afraid of going outdoors. The children called her mother "a witch," and the boys and girls, who were always fighting and quarrelling, were all uncombed, soiled, and dirty—and she was greatly repulsed by anything grimy. From her earliest childhood, she was attracted to what was clean and white. She also liked everything that was dainty or satiny, and if she came across a remnant like that, she would hold it in her hands, finger it lovingly, and then match it up with other colourful scraps. In this respect, she probably took after her mother, who was also attracted to shiny and pretty objects, and who was most adept in matching up colours and coming up with her own beautiful borders and decorative trims.

Oh, if you could only have seen how splendidly Kharytyna decorated her house. O Lord! It was simply dazzling! Almost all the walls were covered with pictures and decorated with tapestries and all kinds of paper flowers. On the windowsills, there were bouquets of live flowers from her lush garden, including some that were so exquisite that no one knew what to call them, because they had never in their lives seen anything like them. There were also numerous icons made out of silver and encircled by golden wreaths; and, in front of them, on a long triple chain, hung a silver lamp in which a red flame flickered every Sunday.

The dishes on the shelves were not at all like the ones found in other women's homes—two or three plates and a chipped glass—oh, no, not at all. Here there were as many as three cups trimmed with gold, six white plates with designs on them, a teapot, a shiny samovar, a lot of glass containers—some with narrow necks and some that were squat—and all sorts of other things like soup bowls, serving platters, and mixing bowls.

There was also a large mirror in a black frame, and such beautiful pictures that you simply stood and gaped at them; there was the tsar, and the tsarina, and generals decorated with medals; and there was a scene of the Judgement Day—with a blazing red fire in hell, and saints smiling down from a blue and green sky; and pictures of young ladies dressed in crimson, sky-blue, and gold gowns; and no end of marvels like that. It was no wonder that Marta could not stop looking at these pictures, and there were times when she pressed herself closely to them and kissed them as if they were her very own sisters. But God forbid that her mother should ever see her doing this, because she would give her a good tongue-lashing; she took great pains to see that no harm came to the decorative objects with which she adorned her house.

And, just as Kharytyna kept her house neat and tidy, so did Khvedir keep his yard in order. The kindling wood was neatly piled, the garden had a ditch around it, the trees were trimmed, and any fresh cuts were pasted over with soil, the sleigh had a good ladder-frame, and the wagon was decked out with iron bolts and wheels. The manure was stacked in an orderly pile that looked like a cottage; the spades, hoes, rakes, flails, scythes, pitchforks—all made of the best wood—were scraped clean and hung in a neat row. It truly was a joy to behold! No wonder Khvedir's brother Andriy smacked his lips and said: "Hm! You keep everything so neat, Khvedir, that it looks as if it's in a painting!"

Khvedir rejoiced, thinking that Andriy was bursting with jealousy. But Andriy was not at all like that; there was not a more candid, open-hearted man in the entire village. It was true that Andriy's yard was not at all orderly, and that something or other was always missing. But that did not matter! Whatever was needed could be borrowed. Of course, Khvedir might not lend it to him, but one of the other householders most certainly would.

Andriy was a trifle lazy and did only what absolutely had to be done—the seeding, mowing, and threshing—and nothing more. He did, however, like to work alongside others during a work bee; then he twisted and turned as swiftly as an eel, until he broke into a sweat and, because of that, drank more whiskey than all the others. He was the kind of man who liked to have a drink in decent company, did not let his poverty bother him, and did not envy Khvedir in the least. Always cheerful and contented, he lived as if there was nothing at all that he lacked.

Andriy was a very handsome man, and he was the one that little Marta strongly resembled, except, of course, his dark eyes, red lips, and black eyebrows were coarser. He had no moustache and no beard, and always looked like a youth—fresh-faced and agile. There was something childlike in his look, and he laughed as heartily and as long as only children can laugh. And he liked to play with children—he built them mills, dreamt up games of tag, told them fairy tales and, along with a whole gang of boys, hopped about on his heels calling out: "Kva, kva!" until you were embarrassed to look at him. Who would have believed that he was married and had a whole nest of children—four in all?

If it had not been for Andriy's wife Motrya, there would not have been any order at all in his household. A woman of pure gold, she managed to take care of everything. She did whatever she was told to do by her father-in-law, a mean old man who lived with them and never stopped grumbling, and she fed the children, washed their clothes, and sent them outdoors to play. After completing her chores, she either worked as a day labourer to bring in extra money, or weeded her own garden and fields—and she put her husband to bed when he came home drunk.

Even though she did not do all this very skilfully or "perfectly"—it was Kharytyna's opinion that: "The devil take it, but she sure makes a mess of things!"—she did it quietly, without a fuss, and always with a smile.

Motrya was not overly bright, but she never harmed anyone. When her husband scolded or beat her, she did not talk back or complain about her fate. When he died, she wept as much as the occasion called for, and, before long, married again. And why would not a woman like that get married a second, and even a third time, seeing that she was so quiet, so submissive, so healthy, and so buxom; her broad backside made it easy to spot her among all the other women.

Kharytyna often said, while looking obliquely at Motrya: "Hm . . ." (She always prefaced what she was going to say with a drawn out: "Hm . . .") "The bench in the house is too narrow; we'll have to get a wider one."

All the women would roll with laughter, and Motrya, not understanding that this barb was directed at her, would also smile and stare unblinkingly at Kharytyna with her large grey eyes.

Kharytyna also never failed to make fun of Motrya's legs, because Motrya wore her skirt raised almost to her knees, baring her legs that were as red as pumpkins, and so fat that her calves jiggled when she walked.

As soon as Kharytyna caught sight of Motrya she would say: "Hm . . . It must be that their cottage stands in a swamp, and because it's awful to soil one's skirt, it's better to buy six yards of fabric for a skirt instead of nine."

And at times she would badger Motrya about her pale face. "What is it with you, dear in-law? Do you powder yourself with lime, or with flour?"

And she would wrinkle her nose so comically as she was saying this, winking at her neighbours and nudging Motrya, that the latter would be ashamed and, flailing her hands, would defend herself: "God be with you, in-law! Why are you saying that? Do you think that I . . . What a thing to say! Really!"

"Hm . . . If only someone doesn't mistake it for sugar and chomp it up, because if it's white, then it must be sweet!"

And all the women who happened to be gathered around the cottage roared with laughter.

But Kharytyna did not forget to get a dig in at everyone and, moving on from Motrya, she turned and looked directly at Marusya, a diminutive woman who was laughing more gaily than all the others, and who was known to burst into gales of laughter if someone so much as moved a finger. Eyeing her soberly, Kharytyna commented: "Yes, that's the one who should be laughing—the one who has such splendid teeth!"

Unfortunately, Marusya had gaps in her teeth, a fact that greatly troubled her. Flushing, and in tears, she leapt to her feet and fled.

And Kharytyna calmly continued her spiel, as if she were talking to herself: "Money should not be hidden in a niche in the hearth, because anyone can find it there—he'll grope there for a match and find it right away . . ."

"Huh, the devil take your mother! How did you find out about our money?" a sallow old woman with a long face shrieked.

"Just be quiet, dear sister," Kharytyna smiled at her, "because I know even more about you. Do you want me to reveal it?"

The old woman just spit and stalked to her cottage without saying anything. The other women exchanged glances, silently asking each other: "Is this Kharytyna really a witch?" And then they dispersed before some calamity befell them as well.

None of the women liked Kharytyna, not only for what she said, but also for the nicknames she gave them, like: "a fly in cream," "a bug-eyed frog," "a spotted heifer." But they did not dare to do anything about it for two reasons—they were afraid that she really might be a witch, and they borrowed money from Khvedir that they had to repay with interest.

Not too many people liked Khvedir either, even though he never harmed anyone. He lived apart from the villagers and never attended the village assembly. And why would he go there? He was an upright man who paid his land taxes, gave money to the church, and honoured all assessments against him. Moreover, had he not seen enough fools that ran, like sheep into a fire, wherever one of the "bellowers" led them? Had he not heard how they quarrelled and senselessly recalled all sorts of grievances? And did he not know that the secretary and the chief twisted things to make them work out to their benefit, so that they could peck away at the community's money? And later, when shortfalls were revealed, they either gathered up their relatives and in-laws, who shut up everyone else with endless shouting, or blinded the villagers with whiskey, taking them to the tavern and buying drinks until they all saw themselves as relatives or in-laws.

Khvedir was not a drinking man and, because of this, he was disliked even more. Who had seen anything like it? The whole village would be drunk on a feast day, and only he would be sober, walking among them like a dead man among the living!

His brother Andriy was not like that at all. Oh, that one knew how to drink and have a good time! Always generous and cheerful, when he got drunk he became incredibly well-disposed towards everyone.

As he walked along, he accosted every girl and every young married woman, greeting them and calling them sweetheart, or kissing them and praising them: "Oh, what a beautiful girl, I . . . I've never seen one like her before in my life!" "Oh, what a house, what a house! Whose house is it? It's a splendid house, isn't it?" "Well, dear in-law, I really like you, may the devil take you . . ."

At other times he would stop, teeter back and forth, peer ever so closely and intently at the person he encountered, think hard for a moment, reach into his pocket, take out whatever money he had, and give it to the startled passer-by: "Here, take it . . . It's yours! Here you are . . . I don't begrudge it!"

Dumbfounded, the other person would take the money, because otherwise he could not shake Andriy off. And then he would go home laughing, saying that he had found the money.

When talking about his brother, Andriy said: "Leave him alone, fellows. He's taken his vows and become a monk."

And so Khvedir was stuck with the nickname "the monk." And he was also taunted with the name "old hundred eyes," mostly by the working girls, who hated him, because when he served as a foreman in the tobacco fields—he was clever enough to work for others as well as run his own farm—he was constantly breathing down their necks. He was very strict, cursed the girls soundly, made them work on church holidays like the Feast of Boris and Hlib, did not let them go home until it was late, and kept track of everything they did.

If anyone hid in a ditch or behind a cherry tree to finish embroidering a flower on a sleeve, he immediately shouted: "Why are you hiding there? Come back here!"

And he always made them work faster, saying: "Come on now, quickly, quickly! Come on, faster faster! Come on, get to work—don't be lazy!"

He never stopped, and he did not nap, even after dinner, and so the girls could not fool around or pick lice in each other's hair. As soon as the noon meal was over, he rose before them like a crane and shouted: "Come on, get a move on! Get to work!"

When the tobacco leaves were being harvested, he saw every stalk and every leaf in every girl's hand, no matter how many of them were seated side by side. And as they threaded the leaves, he watched to see if any got crushed, and if they remembered to remove the side-shoots. In a word, he was "old hundred eyes!"

And the devil knows why he worked so hard for the lords. It would have been better if he had given the girls a bit of freedom— it would have been easier on him, and the girls would not have cursed him. But no, oh no! He did his best for the honour of being called a splendid "tobacco foreman," and, perhaps, because he had very little pity for people, especially women and girls, about whom he always said: "Women—they're just fools!"

Because Khvedir and Kharytyna had only one daughter, who as a young girl went to work as a servant, the two of them lived by themselves and only for themselves—and the strangest thing about this was that this did not concern them in the least.

Kharytyna looked after her work in the garden, sewed jerkins, wove, spun, cooked, and, on a feast day, either annoyed other women in the village common, or told fortunes with cards, divining everyone's fate. As for Khvedir, he was always in the yard, or in the fields, or in the orchard, and he had his job as a tobacco foreman.

The two of them lived comfortably; they had money and everything they needed: bread and all that went with it. They had cattle—two cows and a heifer, three horses, and two hogs that they raised to have their own lard; but no—one of the hogs they fattened up for sale, and they got a lot of money for it, as much as forty or forty-five rubles, and, in their opinion, there was nothing better in this world than money.

And that was why they had shoved their daughter Marta into the living hell of servitude.

As it turned, however, Marta was well off where she was. She was fascinated by the large rooms with their red silk beds, the pink glow of lamps in the evening, the velveteen throws on the floor, and the pictures that were not at all like the ones her mother had. These paintings were huge, bigger than she was, and she really could not tell what was painted on them. She looked at them and said: "O God, O my God—how marvellous!" And there were ever so many mirrors in those rooms—so many that they filled a whole wall and, no matter where Marta turned, she seemed to see Martas walking everywhere: one Marta, a second one, a third one, and a fourth . . . It was really quite amusing! And when the young ladies played the piano, Marta felt as if someone's hand had seized her heart—clutching at it, and then letting it go again, until the tears swirled in her eyes!

And what splendid gowns the young ladies had. They gave her remnants from them, and some fabrics were so fine that you could see through them, while others were heavier silks that rustled like straw in bundles; and their colours were so intense—blue, crimson, and yellow—that no flowers could rival them! And there was so much of everything! It seemed to Marta that she did not want to eat or drink, but just gaze forever at all these riches.

How had Marta ended up as a house servant? Well, she had been assigned to work in the tobacco fields, but one day the young ladies caught sight of her and shrieked; "Oh, what a charming girl!" or something to that effect, and right then and there took her off with them to serve as their chambermaid.

It would have been silly of her not to be happy in such a paradise; but at first she walked around like a fool. They would shout to her: "Pass me this, and bring me that," but she did not know where it was, or what it was, or what it looked like. Of course, after a while she matured, grew accustomed to her surroundings, became adroit, clever, smart, and changed so much that no one could recognise the old Marta in her; just as when snow turns into water—it is the same thing, but it looks totally different. And so it was with Marta. When she broke away from her old life and began to blossom, she became talkative, cheerful, and thought only about clothing and enjoying herself. The young ladies liked to pin ribbons and earrings on her, and so, from all sides she heard: "Oh, how lovely she is! How lovely!"

She began to scrutinise herself more closely; her jerkin now looked old-fashioned to her, and she began to go to the village dressed like the young ladies. The villagers poked fun at her, but she, like the willow that had grown taller than all the others, neither heard their laughter, nor wanted to hear it. Even when her mother instructed her to "live modestly, or there might be trouble," she only smiled to herself.

And her mother, even though she said what she felt she had to say, was happy that it was her daughter, her very own daughter, who was such a beauty, so haughty, and so elegant. When the other women viciously hinted that an ugly rumour was circulating about Marta, she said: "If anyone dares to say something like that to me again, I know a word that will make her walk on the earth as a pig for seven years." And all the women fell silent.

She did, however, warn her daughter that she should maintain her "honour," or else, God forbid, she would choke her with her own hands. Marta kissed her mother's hands for this advice and swore that she was "fine."

Marta had not blossomed long when the bloom came off. The inevitable happened—the lord's lackey led her astray. She found him attractive; he was so pale and delicate, washed his hands with scented soap, walked around in a starched shirt, wore a watch, whispered sweet nothings to her, kissed her passionately, and caressed her face, and her chest, and her back . . .

She had thought he would marry her but, as it turned out, he was already married, and had abandoned his wife. He turned the poor girl's head, and now she was ruined, like an apple tree ravaged by caterpillars.

For a long time, Marta hid from everyone, taking refuge in her work during the day, and weeping through the night. She avoided going home, relaying messages through other serving girls that the lords were detaining her, and her mother did not suspect that anything was wrong.

But the day came when Marta could no longer hide, and she was chased out of the lord's manor. She wandered in the swamps, afraid to go home to her mother; as night fell, however, she had no choice. Not daring to enter the cottage, she sat down on the doorstep and wondered what in the world she should do—whether she should drown herself, or hang herself.

And all the while, she kept hearing in her head the voice of the lackey, who had said in his honeyed tones: "Well, sweetheart, you can go wherever you want to . . ." And her brain throbbed from these words, from her thoughts . . .

Then her mother came outdoors and stumbled over her on the doorstep. "Oh, my goodness! What is this?" The mother's heart turned numb. She was shocked, but she was not sure if it was her daughter or not, and if she was actually seeing what she thought she was seeing.

Marta began to roll around on the ground, wailing: "Oh, my dearest mother! What am I to do? I can't think of anything. Oh, I don't know, I really don't know. Perhaps I should hang myself? But I still want to live! Oh, my dearest mother, take pity on me. Oh, how he betrayed me . . . May he not live to see . . ."

Kharytyna had not wanted to believe the rumours because, after all, Marta was her daughter. Khvedir had warned her as well: "Watch your daughter closely!" It was only now that she believed everything and, giving Marta a vicious shove, she hissed: "Be quiet! Get into the house . . . People will hear . . ."

Marta was so terrified when she heard the low hiss that she jumped away in fear from her mother. Kharytyna shoved her again, and they entered the cottage together.

It was then that Kharytyna lost all semblance of self-control. She tore at her grey hair and, in a low, hoarse voice that was worse than if she had shouted, she kept repeating: "So, you snake! So you've brought shame down upon us . . . So . . ."

Finally Kharytyna could no longer breathe; she clutched her chest and wailed: "A-a-a-a-a . . . I can't, I can't . . . A-a-a-a-a-a . . . I can't . . . A-a-a-a . . ."

Marta became frightened and passed her some water.

Kharytyna pushed her away and knocked the cup out of her hand. She was shaking like a leaf on a poplar tree.

The mother and daughter did not turn off the light or go to sleep that night. Marta had to tearfully explain who, and how, and what, because her mother kept saying: "Tell me!"

And Kharytyna kept swaying and groaning: "A-a-a-a . . ."

It was fortunate that Khvedir had gone into the steppe to graze the horses. If he had been home, he would have beaten his daughter viciously!

From that night on, Marta did not stop crying. There was no end to her tears, because she saw that both her father and mother despised her. Her father's eyes turned dark if he happened to catch sight of her, but usually he just spit and turned away from her. Her mother did not stop railing at her and reproaching her, but she did it softly, hoarsely, as if she were talking to herself, as if she did not want Khvedir to hear. But Marta heard her.

And this is the way it was for three months, until the baby was born dead. Kharytyna buried it and settled down a bit. Khvedir wanted to sue the lackey but, fearing a scandal, settled for cash; he needed money just then, because he was planning to buy a mill. He went to the manor, intercepted the lackey, and stood before him, tall and erect, his right leg jerking, and his hands in his pockets.

"You owe me fifty *karbovansti [dollars]*, you son-of-a-bitch!" he said. "Give them to me before the Feast of St. Mary the Protectress."

"For what? How? Why?" the lackey tried to squirm out of his predicament.

"You know very well for what. There's no need to talk about it. Or do you want me to take you to court?" Khvedir turned around and stalked off.

"No, no, no," the lackey ran after him. "I'll pay you, I . . . I swear to God . . . I . . . ."

Khvedir went home without hearing him out.

But the lackey duped him. After paying out less than half the money he had promised, he left the manor and drifted off.

This was when the people could have repaid Khvedir and Kharytyna with ridicule for their arrogance and haughtiness. But even now it was difficult to approach them. And no one ever saw Marta, because she did not go outside, even for a minute.

Their house was on the edge of the steppe, and the windows, always draped with towels in the evening, now remained covered during the daytime as well. When curiosity got the better of a woman and she tried to enter the house, she either found the door locked, or came face to face with Kharytyna, who came out, shut the door behind her, and asked what it was that she wanted.

"How are things with you? How's Marta? How is she? Is she ill?" the neighbour lady would ask.

"What is it that you need?" Kharytyna would ask in turn, rolling her eyes in anger.

"Well, you see, I came to borrow some matches. Do you happen to have any?" the woman would ask fearfully, even though a moment before she had strode forth boldly to find out everything.

"We don't have any!" Kharytyna would retort sharply, slamming the door in her face.

One day, a daring young woman, who ran across Kharytyna by the river—the mother no longer joined the women in the village common—asked her: "Rumour has it that your daughter is not ill at all, that she's pregnant . . ."

In reply, Kharytyna simply said: "Really? That's news to me."

And the people said that from that day on, the young woman's cow stopped giving milk, her dog started hacking and died in short order, her chicks all died off, and she herself became ill.

After that, no one bothered Kharytyna—the devil take her!

They married Marta off to Nechypir Kotlubko. He had just returned from the army and, catching sight of Marta in church, took a liking to her. He heard that her father had a lot of money and, being landless himself, realised that he could live with his in-laws, as they had no son. And so he began to court Marta.

Even though Nechypir liked to brag that he, like the lucky fellow in a fairy tale, could get whatever he wanted, this was not the reason that he won Marta's hand in marriage. It was more because her parents were finding it difficult to find a suitor for her. The youths in her village would have nothing to do with her because of the ugly rumours about her, and because she, who had formerly been so haughty and unapproachable, was now as shy and easily startled as a quail in a field of rye and ran away from everyone. Moreover, the young men feared the taciturn Khvedir.

But Nechypir was a bold young man—he did not fear anyone or anything. Oh yes indeed, it would have taken a lot to scare him off! It was more likely that he would strike terror in others!

He was also very arrogant, always saying: "I," and "I," and "I," shoving his "I" into everyone's face. And he was very quick-tempered. If something did not go his way, he threw the first thing that came to hand—if it was a knife, he flung it, and if it was an axe, he hurled it. He did not take kindly to jokes, because he was quick to take offence, and would instantly fall into a rage.

He did not know how to do anything, and liked to have things done for him. Being lazy by nature, and having become alienated from village life during the five or six years that he served in the army, he wanted to live like the birds, who neither sowed, nor harvested. That was the way he had lived in the army, because he had been one of the army musicians and had got away without doing the usual army work. He liked to dress in a red shirt, walk down the village street like a dashing young Lothario, and play on the accordion—and that was all he was prepared to do.

He was not the kind of a son-in-law that Khvedir would have wanted. Khvedir was a first-rate farmer, while Nechypir was just a shiftless good-for-nothing! If Khvedir could have had his way, they would have dispensed with all the trouble of a wedding. They had lived by themselves all this time, and now they were taking a wretched lout into their home—into the house where, if you please, he, Khvedir, had pounded in every nail with his own hands.

Khvedir did not need any help. He still had his health and was not all that old, and he did not like it when anyone interfered in his work or stuck his nose into what he was doing. He was convinced that no one could do things as well as he could.

And he did not like babies; to him they seemed to be like the white of a broken egg—slimy and repulsive. Moreover, from the beginning of time, it had always been understood that daughters were to leave home after being given away in marriage. As Khvedir liked to say: "Women—they're just fools!"

As things turned out, however, they did marry off Marta, or rather, they accepted a son-in-law into their home.

Well, why did they not send their daughter to live in someone else's home, if Khvedir did not like to have children in the house? It was because he was practical—it would be more convenient if he had his own worker; he was getting into bigger ventures like building a mill, and he had to keep hiring help, and it would be cheaper if the worker were his son-in-law, because a son-in-law would have to do as he was told.

It is true that Khvedir did not think of all this by himself— he did not want to think about it at all. It was Kharytyna who kept nagging at him, saying over and over again that they had to have a son-in-law who would live with them, until finally Khvedir came around to believing that it would be for the best.

Kharytyna did not want to hand over her daughter to another family; it was like giving away a piece of yourself! Even though she herself had not had lived with her in-laws—Khvedir's mother had died before he got married, and his father had lived with Andriy—she knew all too well what kind of in-laws there are in this world. And so she worked on Khvedir, as if she were pouring her ideas into his head.

Whenever she talked to him, Khvedir remained silent, as if he was not listening to her, or he would just say his usual: "Women— they're just fools!" But then he would turn around and do what she had told him to do.

They had never talked much. Sometimes Khvedir would say: "Wife, it's time to eat." And she would say: "Yes, it is; so let's eat." Or something to that effect. In all the time that passed from their marriage day to that of their daughter's, they had said less to each other than other couples say in a day. Khvedir had even courted Kharytyna silently. He had spotted her by the threshing machine, taken just one look at how her nimble, dark, blue-veined hands untiringly pitched sheaves and, a week later, on a Sunday, sent matchmakers.

Kharytyna was an orphan who lived with her brother. He was agreeable to the proposal, and so she gave the matchmakers her *rushnyky [embroidered linen ceremonial cloths]*. Parting company with Andriy, Khvedir moved into his own home, and he and Kharytyna began to live their isolated lives. They never quarrelled and always accommodated each other, even though Khvedir pretended that he did not listen to her, and Kharytyna also hid the fact that she tried to please him. Even when faced with Marta's troubling condition, they had not talked.

Kharytyna chased Motrya out of the house in the morning, and then, standing by the stove with her back to Khvedir, and gazing into the fire, said dully: "Khvedir, how am I to tell you this?"

"Well, what is it?"

Kharytyna drew nearer to the clay oven. "It's uh . . . The lord's damned lackey turned Marta's head . . ."

She grew redder than the flames.

"Phew!" Khvedir spit and strode out of the house.

From that day on, he could not look at Marta. And that was that.

The wedding they held for Marta and Nechypir was not an overly happy affair. There were not many guests, and most of the women stood in the porch, quietly poking fun at the bride. Among the few relatives that attended, only Andriy, forgetting that he did not like his brother, enjoyed himself to the hilt, carousing and taunting Nechypir: "Tell me, why are you so handsome?"

Nechypir became offended and shouted: "Go to the devil! I'll show you! I'll . . . You know what I'll do . . . Yes, absolutely!"

This last word was his favourite one. He lunged at Andriy with an iron rod, and the onlookers had a hard time pulling them apart.

In actual fact, it was only because Andriy was seeing Nechypir through drunk eyes that he could have called him handsome, because the latter was a short, slightly built, pockmarked man with reddish hair that stood straight up like porcupine quills. And his cheeks were always ruddy, as if sunburned. But, what was to be done? Marta was fortunate to be getting even a man like that—and the poor girl was well aware of it.

Well, they certainly got more than they bargained for when they accepted a son-in-law into their home! They had hurried into the match without finding out more about him. But there really had been no time to do any digging, because Kharytyna had wanted to see her daughter married as quickly as possible and, even if Khvedir had asked anyone about the young man, no one would have told him the truth.

The discord started in Khvedir's house on Monday, the very first day after the wedding. The son-in-law could not bring himself to obey anyone, and he stuck his nose into everything, saying that this was not the way it should be, and neither was that. And all the while he kept bragging like a fool: "Oh, I know how to do this, and how to do that, and that . . . Here, I'll do it . . . There you go! Isn't this how it should be done?"

It annoyed Khvedir greatly to listen to that kind of talk, because he was used to being the head of the household, and everyone said that he did the best work. But here was this young pup—a greenhorn—who dared to yap at him and tell him what to do.

Every so often, Khvedir chased him out, and then Nechypir would settle down and not say anything for a week or so. He did not want to hire himself out and give up an easy way of life, even though he often bragged: "Do you think I can't find a position for myself? Oh, boy, I sure can! The lord knows me, and Kvedka, the Russian foreman, wants me to work in the melon field. Yes, absolutely!" And he would reel off the names of all who knew him and liked him, boasting about himself until it became tiresome to listen to him.

It finally reached the point that Khvedir did not let Nechypir do any of the work on the farm. "Lie atop the clay oven like an old woman for all I care, but don't came to work with me, because you only make a mess of things!"

And Nechypir was only too happy to obey him. He played his accordion, sang, and told tall tales, some of which were so far-fetched that even his father-in-law had to smile. One of his stories was about three fools who wanted to learn to speak like the lord by standing beneath his window. One learned the word "we," the second learned to say "if not for this, then for that," and the third learned "admit it." Well, one day, they found a body in the forest, and the police commissary, who happened to be driving by, asked them if they had killed the man and why. And they replied, using the lord's language that they had learned: "We," "if not for this, then for that," "admit it."

Kharytyna also took a dislike to Nechypir, because Marta, no matter what he did, stood up for him. It was so vexing! Marta had always been so silent, but now she let loose all the stops, as if he were dearer to her than her own father and mother; and yet, all the while, she insisted that she did not love him and, when she talked about him with her mother, criticised him for being "ugly," and "a liar," and "stupid," and "lazy," and complained that he kept pinching her at night.

Nechypir truly enjoyed "bullying" his wife, even though he liked her and bore her no malice; but he was young, and she now belonged to him—like a cow—and so he had every right to torment her, especially when he was angry at Khvedir! Marta would tell her mother all this when they were alone, but when matters came to a head, she would swear that Nechypir had not broken the hoe—or some other implement—even though he had indeed done so, and then she would claim that he had mowed enough for 180 sheaves even though it was only enough for 120.

Kharytyna would boil over with anger: "So, now you're siding with a stranger, a worthless dolt, instead of with your own father and mother!"

Marta herself did not understand why she seemed to be two different people now, railing, at times, against Nechypir in front of her mother, and then defending him when her mother attacked him; and yet later, when she and Nechypir were alone, she would attack him with the same words that her mother had used just a moment ago. Marta felt close to him and was sorry for him, but she did not love him; she did not love him because he was, as she put it, "ugly and repulsive."

And then—who would ever have believed it?—Nechypir robbed his father-in-law! He stole the money that Khvedir had hidden in a hole dug in the barn. How had it come to this? Very simply.

Khvedir had not allowed Nechypir to help him with the farm work, saying: "Don't touch that. Go away. I'll do it myself. It's none of your business."

At first, Nechypir was happy not to do anything, but later, he grew offended. "What am I—the cholera or something, that you're always hiding from me and locking things up? The devil take you! I'll leave you—yes, absolutely—I'll just take off!"

At the same time, Kharytyna began taunting him for eating too much, saying: "You know, sonny, you should eat with two spoons, because you can't fish enough out of the bowl with just one." Or she would say: "There was a time when we baked only seven loaves of bread a week, but now even ten aren't enough, and it's all because such a good worker has come to live with us. He works for two people, and eats for three."

"You know, the fact that you're reproaching me for the bread I eat doesn't sit well with me at all!" Nechypir finally said one day in a fit of anger. "Just tell me—what kind of a wife did you saddle me with? And yet, you're . . . May you live in misery! I'll go away . . . I'll go away and I'll never come back . . . Yes, absolutely!"

Marta froze and then jumped to her feet: "Nechypir, what's wrong with you? God be with you!"

Khvedir and Kharytyna shouted in chorus: "Get out!"

And Nechypir left.

As it later became clear, he had the nerve to leave their home only because, earlier on, he had secretly observed where Khvedir had stashed his money.

Not too long after throwing out his son-in-law, Khvedir needed some money; he went to his hiding place, but found neither the money, nor the box in which it had been kept. Who could have taken it? It must have been Nechypir—he was the stranger in their home, and recently he had gone on a drinking spree, carousing in the village, treating the men to whiskey, and hiring musicians for the girls' dances. There could be no doubt that it was he who had stolen the money.

But still, it seemed impossible; Khvedir always locked the barn himself and carried the key in his pocket; moreover, only he knew where the money was hidden—in a corner by a post. So who could be blamed? Khvedir remembered very well that even when he had still thought that Nechypir was a good man, he had never given him the key, and the lock to the barn was not broken or knocked off—but the money was gone. What the deuce was going on?

Nechypir strutted arrogantly around the village like a black stork, shouting for all the village to hear that if his in-laws accused him, he would sue them for slander—yes, absolutely!

One time, while Nechypir was still roaming around the village—sleeping here and eating there, but spending most of his time in the tavern—he came to see Khvedir and laughed in his face, saying that no matter how smart his father-in-law thought he was, there were people who were smarter. People like the thief—yes, absolutely—because his father-in-law had toiled for so many years with his back bent to earn the money, but the thief had become a rich man in a single night.

"And now I'm going to leave you for good," Nechypir added. "Do you think I won't find a place for myself? Yes, I will, absolutely; you better believe it! And you can just go and keep on locking yourself up, for all I care!"

Khvedir lost his temper and yelled: "Get away from here, you thief! Leave my house and go to the devil! I don't ever want to lay eyes on you again!"

"Oh, so I'm a thief, am I? So that's what you . . ." Nechypir leapt to his feet and, grabbing a knife that Marta had left on the table where she was cleaning cabbages, threw it at Khvedir.

The knife struck Khvedir's hand, nicking it.

Before Khvedir could scream, and before Marta and Kharytyna could begin wailing, Nechypir vanished.

Khvedir decided to sue his son-in-law, using as evidence what his son-in-law had tried to do to him. And then, as luck would have it, Kharytyna looked in Nechypir's small chest where he kept his comb, a book, and some buttons, and found a wooden key there that was made to fit the lock in the barn. And so the thief was uncovered!

Now, no one in the world could say that Nechypir was not to blame. It was too bad he had tripped himself up like that, as if his memory had failed him He had done everything so aptly, so cleanly, but he forgot about the key that he had hidden in the chest, thinking he would destroy it at some later time—but could he not have broken it right on the spot, by the barn?

It was the chest that Nechypir had come back for that last time, but then he had lit a cigarette, got into an argument, flung the knife at Khvedir, and run away, forgetting all about it. And when he did think of it, he just waved his hand and said: "What the devil do I need it for? Let it perish!" But he forgot about the key.

Indeed, it was too bad that Nechypir made a fool of himself, for the entire village had been glad that Khvedir had been robbed.

On the very day that the father-in-law and son-in-law were in court, and the mother-in-law was serving as a witness, Marta— pardon me for saying this—gave birth.

No one was happy to see that infant. Khvedir did not like babies, and clearly he would not like the child of the man who had robbed him. Kharytyna, angry with Marta that her husband had turned out to be the way he was, and that Marta was fussing with the child of this "thief" "like a fool with an embroidered bag," often said impatiently to her: "Well come on, leave it alone!" Or: "How long are you going to be fussing with that *Moroka [bother]*?" This was how she referred to Marusya, Marta's little daughter. And as soon as Marta turned to the baby, she found her something else to do.

Marta herself was not happy with her baby—she did not know how to take care of it. At first she was even a bit afraid of it, because it was so small and limp—it flopped here and bent there, its head hung like a cucumber on a stem, and it could not sit. She could not stand its constant screaming, but did not know how to quiet it. It seemed ugly, and unclean, and her mother kept nagging her, reproaching her with Nechypir: "He's like this, and like that, and you, you damned creature, you're always defending him!"

Marta, by now unable to remember that she had ever defended him, retorted: "Leave me alone! When did I ever stand up for him? Let him go to the devil! May he go berserk!"

The anger that Kharytyna had felt against her daughter when Marta was an unwed mother was nothing compared to what she felt towards her now that her husband had turned out to be a thief—it was almost as if Marta herself had robbed her parents. They even ended up accusing Marta of assisting Nechypir in the robbery, saying that he himself had said so during the trial. Life became so unbearable for Marta that she could not live at home. On the one hand, there were all the reproaches, and on the other hand, she was still young, and wanted more from life.

And so, Marta decided to run away. She had spent her entire life with her parents, like a bird in a cage—they led their lives, and she led hers. It was only when she had worked as a servant that she had seen a bit of the world and had begun to think about gaining her freedom; but, trouble had caught up with her and crushed her like a hailstorm.

Then there was the hasty marriage. She too had thought that she should get married to hide "her shame," but now her parents were oppressing her like a heavy dark cloud, like a fog—she found it hard to breathe—and her thoughts turned to running away. She did not feel overly sorry for her child—she was not attached to the infant; she might have felt differently if she had been alone with it, but her parents kept grinding away at her like a grindstone. Moreover, her father and mother had not been overly tender and kind towards Marta when she was little, and so she, in turn, did not know how to be loving towards anyone.

Recently, Marta had struck up a friendship with a young neighbour woman called Maryna. Previously, Marta had never had any friends—she had rebuffed everyone—but she took a great liking to Maryna. This neighbour had happened to run by Marta's window when the baby was being born, heard her screaming, and dashed in to serve as a midwife.

Maryna was married and lived with a large, quarrelsome family. They had taken her in as a daughter-in-law when she was still very young, and ever since, had tormented her, mocked her, beat her, and vented their anger on her. And there was a lot of anger in that family—it was large, but there was not much land or grain, and so they constantly attacked each other. Mostly, however, they picked on Maryna, saying that she was inept and lazy. Every day she was assailed by her father-in-law, mother-in-law, brothers-in-law, sisters-in-law, all their children, and even her own husband. Moreover, Maryna's children, who came along every year, only to die an early death, had exhausted her.

And so she became vicious, like a mad dog that wants to rip everyone to pieces, and she found no greater pleasure in life than to hurt someone in her family—either by sticking a needle into a bench, or pouring salt into the honey. It was only at those times that she was happy, but she kept that happiness to herself; at all other times, she walked around glum and angry. Her eyes blazed so fiercely that, if it had been possible, she would have set fire to all four corners of the earth.

As a girl, she had been attractive, but now she was scrawny—just skin and bones—with sunken cheeks. Dark and gaunt, only her teeth gleamed, so whitely that they seemed almost blue. Her face became very animated when she talked, she waved her arms around like the wings of a windmill, and there were not many people who could curse like she could. Her one thought, her one hope, was to break free from the hell into which she had been cast, and so she began to urge Marta to run away with her to the distant city, saying that Marta could leave her infant with someone in the village and hire herself out as a wet nurse.

Terribly unhappy and bored, Marta truly wanted to see the city, the people, the world; it seemed to her that she had not yet experienced life. She thought and thought about it, and then something quite unexpected happened.

Losing her patience one day, she said that it was a good thing that Nechypir had stolen the money, because there was no other way of prying it loose—that they would never give any money to anyone, and that they were like that dog in the manger who, not having any use for the straw himself, did not let anyone else have it either. And her father, who never looked at his daughter or spoke to her anymore, yelled at her, as if he were speaking to a log: "Oh, you damned creature! So you're against me as well? Get out of my house! Go where your worthless dolt has gone!"

And he threw her out of the house.

And Marta was glad. She thought she would leave for at least a little while, and then, perhaps, come back; but she never returned.

One night, she and Maryna got their things together and left. When the families rushed out to find them the next day, they did not know where to start looking. They questioned the woman with whom Marta had left her baby, but she did not know anything.

The young women were gone and were nowhere to be found.

Before long, Ivan, Maryna's husband, did find his wife and, after beating her severely, brought her back home. But Marta remained in the city as a servant in the home of the police commissary where she did not need a passport to work; the family took a liking to her and would not let her leave. Moreover, her father and mother were not overly anxious to have her come back.

Marta enjoyed living in the city—it suited her perfectly; everything was brilliant, cheerful, opulent. She regained her good looks, and her strength renewed itself like grass in the springtime. She never sent any news back home about how she was getting along, and it seemed as if she had forgotten that she had a home. Every year, however, she did send two rubles and a gift to the woman who was taking care of her little Marusya.

After serving his time in jail, Nechypir wandered about aimlessly, moving from factory to factory, drinking and carousing. When he found out where Marta worked, he took her money, but did not take her away with him, and she was glad of that.

To tell the truth, Khvedir was happy when he was left alone once again with Kharytyna. It was so quiet now in their home, so splendid. He did his work and always tried to do his best, looking at things first from one side, and then from the other, squinting and munching as he worked. Kharytyna also did her work wonderfully well—the house was neat as a pin, and there was no screaming child in it.

Khvedir simply could not understand how people could live together in one big nest where children, crawling around like cockroaches, continually raised a ruckus on the benches; he was even repulsed when he saw that there were a lot of children in a house—as if their parents were as fertile as pigs or dogs.

He did not understand that a man lives in order to have children, and to see the children of his children, and so on; he lived for himself alone, and he rejoiced in knowing that he was doing everything for himself—raising his own barn, building a mill, crafting a sleigh, digging a well so that he would not have to go to the neighbour's home for water, and . . .

Well, had he not done a lot? But still, there did not appear to be an end to his work; it seemed to him that he would not finish all that he had to be before he died. He wanted to have more and more land. First, he bought a small plot and then took legal action against Motrya, Andriy's wife, to take away her garden.

Andriy had died a drunkard's death out in the street and, even though their father had divided his land between the two of them, Khvedir thought that he had the right to take away Motrya's patch of land and her stable. Motrya, of course, was a woman—a fool—who did not know how to deal with the matter and, just as it is impossible to forge cold iron, so tears had never moved Khvedir.

She kept wailing. "Take pity on me, in-law, and you too," she said to Kharytyna, "don't abuse me and my little children!"

But Khvedir insisted: "It's mine, and that's that!"

When Motrya bowed low before them, Kharytyna said: "It isn't a pound of your white flesh that we want—we just want the land that rightfully belongs to us. Go away, and don't worry."

Khvedir succeeded in taking away the garden patch from Motrya shortly before she remarried. And her second husband could not do anything about it.

Everything seemed to be going Khvedir's way now—he had a bumper crop, almost all the trees he had grafted were doing well, and he had raised two splendid one-year old colts and was already beginning to drive them. He loved horses, especially if they had long manes and tails, and could race like the wind.

While everything was going very well indeed for Khvedir, things were not going so well for Kharytyna. It could not be said that she missed her daughter, because she did not love her, certainly not the way she loved her own finger, which hurt if she cut it. Besides, she heard from others that her daughter was doing well, that she had regained her good looks and was happy; so, everything was fine, everything was good!

But all the same, Kharytyna began to have some second thoughts and to ask herself why they were living like this, just for themselves, not going anywhere, and having no one visit them. Did anyone else live like that? It was true that it was better to live without quarrelling and shouting, but all the same, when there were people around, the work seemed to get done faster, and they might help with this or that.

And so she concluded: "Oh, if only we could live for at least a little while as other people live."

"Uh oh," the people thought, "Kharytyna must be getting old, because she never needed anyone before, or maybe it's just a case of not appreciating what you have until it's gone."

Who knows? Who could figure it out? Kharytyna was like deep, dark water—no one could fathom her, and she did not say anything to anyone. But she began to grow despondent and to look closely at little Marusya—or Moroka, as she still called her. She started taking the little girl treats to win her over, and then, when Marusya was three years old, she brought her home.

Khvedir asked: "What's all this about?"

"Let's take her to live with us," Kharytyna replied hesitantly. "She won't eat much."

Khvedir responded: "The old woman didn't have enough trouble, so she bought herself a piglet."

But Kharytyna did not give up: "She's so quiet, so very quiet! And you know what, Khvedir, I'll have the village scribe write to Marta and ask her send us the two rubles that she's paying for her little girl; so it will be worth our while to keep her."

"Oh, I've said it before: 'Women—they're just fools!'" Khvedir shrugged his shoulders and walked out of the house.

And so Moroka remained in her grandparents' home.

She was already accustomed to Kharytyna—in addition to treating her to sweets, her grandmother had sewn her little jerkins out of scraps of fabric—and she called her "mother," something that made the old woman very happy.

But she was afraid of her grandfather, and ran away from him. For a long time, he did not pay any attention to her, as if she were a grasshopper scarcely visible in the green grass. He would glance at her occasionally, thinking: "And why is it that they're prettiest when they're young? No matter what it is, everything that's younger is prettier—trees, animals, people. It's only later that things turn ugly. But still, why does everyone fuss so much over children? Why can't they take their eyes off them? What's there to see—a child crawls around, doesn't have any sense, and doesn't do anything. And Kharytyna is no better than the rest of them!"

Khvedir just shrugged his shoulders.

One day Khvedir became ill. It was the first time that this had happened as far back as he could remember; he became bored with lying idle about the house, not able to lift his head or raise himself;

and, because he was not accustomed to being sick, he thought that death had come for him.

One morning, he was lying alone in the house, feeling sick and gloomy. Kharytyna had gone to the river to wash clothes, and little Moroka was playing with her doll by the clay oven. Suddenly, something occurred to the little girl and, hesitantly approaching her grandfather, she asked: "Do you want me to tell you a fairy tale, grandpa? It's a lovely, really lovely, story," she continued. "A magpie was cooking her children some gruel . . . I'll give some to this one . . . and to this one . . . Oh no, that's not right." And she started again, making even more mistakes as she counted on her tiny fingers with their sharp little nails,

The grandfather turned numb with astonishment; he looked at the child as if he were seeing her for the first time, thinking: "What's she like? Like a ripe strawberry . . . She's cute . . . Small . . . And her tiny nails . . . But why are they so tiny? What is it that she's buzzing in my ear like a little mosquito?"

He began to listen and to look more closely at "Moroka," but he must have appeared terrifying to her, for she stepped back from him and flung herself at her grandmother who was just coming into the house.

"What is it? What is it?" Kharytyna asked, seeing the little girl's terrified eyes. Moroka did not reply; she just snuggled as closely as she could to her grandmother.

Khvedir wiped his face with his hand—and it came away damp: "Children! Do they bring happiness?"

Kharytyna, thinking that he had fallen asleep, moved quietly about the house.

"Oh, what nonsense!" Khvedir angrily continued thinking. "Children just shorten our lives; every year that they grow bigger, we get older. It's some joy that we get out of them!"

From that day on, little Moroka led a very good life with her grandparents. Her grandmother continued to spoil her and, even though her grandfather did not learn to pet her, from time to time he would smile as he looked at her and then shove an apple into her hand—or a pear, or some berries, or a fistful of raspberries—and say: "Well, run along now! Go ahead and play!"

She Just Won't Die
(1903)

Spring is beautiful! No matter how many times you have seen it, you never tire of its wonders. But why attend to it at all? It arrives every year, and it disappears every year; everyone is accustomed to it, and everyone is familiar with it—so why pay attention to it, and why sigh?

And yet, one bright spring day, you leave the house, go outdoors, and glance up at the sky—with its little white clouds that look so soft, so very, very soft, like tufts of down—and it seems so close to you, ever so close, right next to your chest. And then you gaze out at the steppe that stretches green and even all around you, and at the flowers, every one of which is attired like a bride on her way to church.

And when you look at the grainfields on which long green blades are now unfurling on both sides of the reddish, firm, bristles that have been jutting out since the fall, and when you listen to the meadowlark, whose happy little song cascades from the heights—your heart begins to melt like wax in a flame.

This is what the old woman Kononykha was thinking as she lay wrapped in an old sheepskin coat on the clay bed atop the oven; she was so emaciated, and her skin was so sallow, that one would have thought there was only a sheepskin coat lying on the bed. The illness had completely wasted her away—her cheeks, mouth and eyes were sunken, and her nose, chin, and forehead jutted out like yellowed parchment.

She was lying down, but not sleeping; she wanted to make her way out of the house into the street, but could not get down from the bed by herself, and her daughter-in-law would not come of her own accord to assist her—*that one* did not give a care!

"Where has she gone off to, that Varka, that devil of a woman!" The mother-in-law was becoming enraged. "May she live to be like I am now; may this happen to her!"

But Varka, her daughter-in-law, was not far away. She was sitting—the way women, having come home from church, like to sit on a Sunday—with a few other women on the earthen embankment abutting the house. They were shelling sunflower seeds and talking.

"So your mother-in-law's still alive?" one of them asked Varka.

"She sure is!" Varka replied. Her bottom lip protruded in a pout, and her eyes narrowed.

"She's sent for the priest ever so often and received Holy Communion many times, and she keeps saying that she's getting ready to die—but she's still alive! It's quite a messy way of doing things!" said Mariya Zubkova with a bitter smile on her thin lips. She was a skinny, stern young woman, wearing a black headdress that nearly covered her eyes.

"It sure is!" Varka replied sulkily.

Haptsya, a small, goggle-eyed woman with eyebrows that were black as wagon-grease and rounded like little wheels, piped up: "See what she's like! She's enjoying life at someone else's expense! She should just go ahead and die!"

The youthful and dark-haired Kateryna sighed: "But when I stop to think that I too have to die . . . Well, may God protect me—I get ever so scared!"

Mariya—the thin woman with the black headdress down to her eyes—scolded her: "You're foolish! Are you about to die? You're far from dying! This is the way things are: you're young—so go ahead and live, but something old should just die, and that's that! No one has yet found a way to escape from death—no one!"

Kateryna spoke up: "But when I stop to think that I was here, and now I'm gone—it's just too terrible! I'm terrified, simply terrified!"

"But did you hear, my dear sisters," Haptsya interrupted Kateryna, "how old man Chaban died? He ate a lot of salted pork for Easter, and his stomach began to ache. He lay down on one side—oh, it was ever so painful! And then he tried the other side—and it was just as painful! Then he said: 'My dear children, my death has come for me! Get the coffin ready, my dear ones, for I'm about to die . . .'

"Quite by chance, the doctor came by; he went into the house, looked at him and said: 'Do you want me to help you get rid of this pain, old man?' It seems he wanted to put some kind of a little tube in his stomach, but old man Chaban said: 'No, thank you, kind sir; don't touch me, for I'm going to die anyway. I can feel it—my death is approaching. Let the children live by themselves under God's protection!' Then he crossed his arms on his chest, asked them to place a candle in his hands, and died.

"And he did the right thing, yes he did! Not like that self-indulgent mother-in-law of yours."

Just then something rattled at the window from inside the cottage. The women turned around and saw the bony figure of Kononykha standing at the window, clutching at its frame with one hand.

She was repeating hoarsely: "Varka, Varka, Varka!"

Varka rushed into the house, muttering: "May you . . .!"

Some of the young women trailed in after her.

The old woman immediately attacked her daughter-in-law. "Oh, you damned stinking scurvy woman, what are you doing to me? Just what is that you're doing to me?"

She began pointing her finger all around the house: at the table, strewn with leftovers—a crust of bread, a potato, and some spilled water, at the bench on which smelly and torn rags were lying, at the floor that had neither been swept nor smoothed over with fresh paste, and at the chipped clay hearth.

"What is all this? What is it? I told you—put a fresh coat of clay on the oven! I ordered you to patch the floor! Oh, o-o-o-h, oh, but it hurts! Why didn't you wash the dishcloths before the holiday?"

Kononykha's voice was growing stronger and angrier by the minute. A moment ago it had looked as if she were about to collapse from her illness, but now it seemed that she was completely healthy—even her cheeks were flaming. She was breathing heavily, however, as she continued shouting in a shrill voice that sounded like a cracked violin.

"Where are your eyes? Where are you hands? Have you gone blind? Have your eyes crawled out of your head that you're making such a horrible mess in here? Do you think that I'm . . . that is . . . No, just you wait! I can still show you! You-you-you-you . . .!" She raised her yellow, bony fist high in the air and gestured threateningly.

Varka, in the meantime, kept rubbing the same spot on the bench with her apron while observing her mother-in-law fiercely out of the corner of her eye and muttering in a low voice: "Oh, just stay in bed, why don't you!"

It was then that the foolish Haptsya came to Varka's defence. She began rattling away: "Listen, old woman, why are you always jeering at Varka like this? What's going on here? Haven't you died yet? And here I thought . . ."

Before Haptsya could finish speaking, Kononykha groaned and began to slide to the floor like a sheaf of straw. If the women had not caught her and held her up, her whole body would have been bruised.

Now the old woman turned as white as chalk and immediately became so weak that it was scarcely possible to hear what she was saying: "Oh, this is terrible! Save me! Let me breathe! Air! I need air . . ."

She was breathing shallowly and quickly, like a fish out of water.

Varka rushed up to her in alarm. "What is it, mother? What is it? Here, I'll help you up, I'll help you up."

Kononykha still mustered enough strength to give her a shove. "Get away from me!" she whispered hoarsely.

Varka pouted, turned around, and said angrily: "Fine with me! See, what she's like . . ."

She was so upset that she did not finish what she was saying.

The women grasped Kononykha under the arms and slowly dragged her out of the house into the yard. They placed her on the ground under an old birch tree by the fence, and she gradually revived.

At first she just lay there for a while with closed eyes, and then she sighed deeply a few times and smiled silently.

Varka remained in the house, and the women once again went out into the street to enjoy themselves.

Only one small, shrivelled, round-faced old woman with very shiny dark eyes and short bushy eyebrows remained with Kononykha. Her nature was such that she always smiled gently— both when she was silent, and when she was speaking . . .

And so now she smiled cheerfully and said: "God be with you, my dear sister, why did you get so scared? Because someone mentioned death? Well, what of it? After all, the time has come for you and me to die—we've had our fill of living!"

"Oh, don't say that, don't say that to me! Oh, my God, my Lord, I'm afraid, I'm so afraid . . ." Kononykha shuddered as if someone had splashed her with cold water, and closed her eyes.

"Well, as for me, I'm not the least bit afraid. I'm always imploring God: 'Oh, take me to you, O God, take me to your stars, accept my soul as soon as possible! I've had my share of prancing about in this lifetime!"

Kononykha, in the meantime, glanced up at the sky—and it became fixed in her heart; she glanced at the birch tree—and every tender young leaf, shining in the sunlight as if it were made of gold, clung to her heart.

"Oh, I can't, I can't die!" she groaned.

"Well, for heaven's sake! As if you had someone to leave behind, or something! One of your sons is in the army, the other is somewhere in Tomsk, and you don't have any grandchildren. Can it be your daughter-in-law you're sorry for?" Makarykha smiled lightly again.

"She'll never live to see the day!" Kononykha growled, and then she fell silent.

She began to examine every blade of grass that was near her nose and to breathe in the damp odour of the earth. It seemed that she no longer heard Makarykha, who continued talking about death.

"Well, as for me, I wouldn't mind lying down . . . lying down and dying . . . right now . . . To fold my arms on my chest and to fall asleep forever . . . Oh, my dear God—it would be so quiet and wonderful! Because everything, absolutely everything in the world dies, and that's good, because there's a time for everything."

She smiled ever so sweetly once again, and her eyebrows quivered, and her dark eyes glistened—just as if she were relating a pleasant tale.

"For heaven's sake, what are you saying?" Kononykha finally became incensed. "Do you find it so hard to live that you're invoking death?"

"Oh no, my dear; no, my little darling; it's not hard at all!" Makarykha replied with a smile. "Am I even hinting at something like that? Not at all! There's enough bread to eat, and enough of everything to eat with it . . . My old man may be a trifle stingy and somewhat flinty, but he's not a bad man; oh, no, he's not bad! And my sons are good too—they care about me . . . And my daughters-in-law—thank God—are also kind!"

"You certainly do indulge those daughters-in-law of yours!" Kononykha grumbled.

"Well, not really! As I was saying. . . everything's just fine, I tell you, everything's just fine. But . . . over there— 'that' seems so azure to me, so very azure, and it enfolds you and shrouds you like the finest muslin . . . Oh, if it were only possible to lie down quietly just like this, and . . . It's only the grandchildren that I would hate to leave. At times they cling to my neck like strings of coral beads, pleading: 'Oh, don't die, granny, granny, little grandma—they give me all sorts of pet names—we won't let you go!' Yes, that's how it is . . ."

She gestured resignedly with her little hand and fell silent.

"There, you see," Kononykha added.

"Well, fine, that's—me, but I'm surprised at you, my dear little dove, I'm really surprised! It seems that you've never known any good fortune. Your first husband died in the army, your second one was a drunkard who gave you quite a bad time before he died, and yet you cling to life like a hop vine clings to a willow—for some reason, you're sorry to leave it!"

"Yes, he was a drunkard," Kononykha seized upon her words and began to recall how things were. "Do you remember what a beating he gave me because I didn't hand him his sheepskin coat quickly enough when he was getting ready to travel with the wagons? My whole body was black and blue then! And then he said: 'Well, are you satisfied? Will you now know how to please a husband?' 'May you drop dead,' I thought!

"But I spoke sweetly to him: 'Oh, my dear husband, now I'll love you even more since you've given me such a beating!' But I thought to myself: 'Just you wait, you son of a devil, I won't die to please you, no matter what!' And I didn't die, and I even outlived him, so there!"

"I wouldn't want to experience anything like that, my dear! My old man may be flinty, and he does use his fists at times, but only when there's a reason for it, and not just for anything at all! Of course, everyone knows that it's our fate as women to bow down and submit from the cradle to the grave!

"Well, what's to be done—that's the way it is! But to spin out that thread so that there's never an end to it—that's too much! You're saying that life is beautiful, but I'm saying that death is beautiful as well! It's as if all the yarn has been spun . . . The suffering has ended . . . No more quarrelling, nor pain—there's no more of any of that!"

"Oh sure, that's what you say! You're so smart, but you're babbling God knows what! What do you mean there's no more pain? It's through pain that people go to meet their death, and no other way . . . And then . . . Then, in that very last moment . . . O-o-o-oh!"

Kononykha clenched her teeth, and her eyes widened. "How can it be that I existed, and then I no longer am? Like a lump of salt dissolving in water. Oh, Lord! I won't see anything anymore, I won't hear anything, I won't touch anything with my hand! The grainfields will blossom, but I won't be here! The grain will begin to fill out, but I won't know it! My daughter-in-law will fritter everything away, but I won't be able to say a word about it . . . O-o-o-o-o-h!"

Exhausted, she remained silent for a while, stretched her back out on the ground, and then once again began looking at the sky through the branches of the birch tree. The green leaves appeared to take on a yellowish hue against the azure background of the sky; on the old birch, the white, cracked bark with its black streaks and reddish specks, gleamed and shone like silver; and the cottage—her tumble-down cottage with its blackened thatch—was reflected upside down in a puddle in the middle of the yard.

All this seemed very dear to Kononykha, and she did not want to part with it, because, even though it did not amount to much, it was her own—it was familiar, real, unchanging, and, because of this, appealing.

"Moreover," Kononykha once again began to whisper, "when I think of it, when I remember about it, I feel dizzy and I faint, I faint, and, and . . . I just don't feel right . . . These thoughts come to me mainly at night.

"When I think how the w-w-w-w-worms are going to gnaw at me . . . in the grave . . . How they'll crawl . . . They'll crawl right into my heart . . . Oh, it's horrible! Oh, I can feel them on me, I can feel them!"

Her eyes bulged in terror, her mouth gaped, and her arms made grasping movements on either side of her.

"Well, what of it? You know very well that your soul will go directly to the golden throne," Makarykha stated calmly.

"Oh sure, and what about my sins? I only hope I don't end up in hell!" Kononykha laughed, her voice strange and hoarse.

"Holy, holy, holy!" Makarykha said softly, and once again she smiled gently. "Do you really think that you and I have any sins? Did we kill anyone? Did we ever work on Good Friday? It's the lords who have sins—they're the ones who will burn in hell. But why should we?"

"No, wait a moment, my friend, wait a moment!" Kononykha grabbed her by the sleeve. "When I think that the w-w-w-worms . . . That they're going to bore holes through me, like through a head of cabbage . . . I can feel them on me, and I can feel the holes . . . One hole next to the other . . . No, I can't stand it!"

She raised herself and then once again sank back heavily.

"Well, that's enough talk about that!" Makarykha said, for her heart was also beginning to turn cold at the thought of the worms.

She rose to her feet, went to the house, brought out some water, gave Kononykha a drink, and then said: "Well, farewell, my little dove; it's time for me to go and milk the cows, prepare some gruel for the children's supper, and help my daughters-in-law; there's still a lot to be done. I'll come to see you again tomorrow." And, like a little sparrow, she pattered away to her own house.

Kononykha fell asleep from exhaustion. It was quite late already, towards evening, when Varka brought her back into the house—which, in the meantime, she had tidied up a bit.

II

Kononykha did not want to die, and she did not die. She managed to get through the spring, and by summer she had recovered so well that she packed her daughter-in-law off to go and hire herself out as a servant.

"Go on, go and serve!" she kept saying. "Of what use are you to me here?"

The daughter-in-law was reluctant to become a servant—after all, who wants to place a yoke on one's shoulders? At home there was more freedom. Despite the presence of a mother-in-law, you could occasionally get away for a short time, take off someplace even during the working day, hear some gossip, and talk for a while; or you could simply sit with folded arms for a few minutes. Once you were in service, however, all you heard was—hurry, hurry, hurry!

This is why she tried to get out of it: "I swear to God, it doesn't seem right . . . For some reason I don't feel like serving."

"You're lazy, you lazybones, you devil of a woman!" the mother-in-law began to swear at her.

Varka pouted and mumbled: "So . . . so . . . I'm a lazybones, am I? And who does all your work for you? Well, it's all the same to me—may your misery devour you here. I'm going!"

"So much the better—I'll get along just fine without you! Are you the one who tenderly reared me, or what? I've lived my whole life without you—and I certainly don't need anyone to take care of me now!"

Varka did hire herself out to a landlord not too far away, and the old woman Kononykha was left alone at home. At first, when she went to feed the pigs or weed the garden, she walked very slowly, barely moving her feet and cursing the whole time. Then, she gradually started growing stronger and stronger. And she became happier, because she had fought off death.

Whenever she began to feel ill again, she would drag herself outdoors and lie down; as she rested, she would gaze at the blazing sky and listen to the insects chirping in the grass.

When Kononykha was not ill, she liked to get everything done, so that she could brag when her daughter-in-law came home on Sunday.

"There you are—you thought I couldn't do this or that without you, but just take a look around!"

And she would lead her out to show her the small patch of wheat—the whole piece was completely cleared of weeds.

The daughter-in-law would just mumble: "M . . . m . . ."

"That's how it's done!" the mother-in-law would say.

Kononykha sat quite often now with old Makarykha, but they no longer talked about death. They had other things to talk about—all the latest news in their own village and in the neighbouring one.

Makarykha spoke about these things without any enthusiasm, as if she had already withdrawn from it all. Kononykha, however, was completely caught up in all of it. Waving her hands rapidly, like a fish undulating its tail, and wagging her head from side to side, she rattled on and on, trying to find out about everything. She was interested most of all in weddings and births. For the last while she had not liked talking at all about funerals, saying only: "Oh, let them die, as long as we don't!" And she did not attend any funerals.

There was something else that Kononykha liked to do when she was not ill—she liked to go to church. But she thought very little about God there, unless it was the odd time that she happened to be praying. "Oh, my dear God, Jesus Christ, and my good St. Nicholas, do something so that my head doesn't hurt and my heart doesn't faint—in the name of the Father, the Son, and the Holy Spirit, amen!"

More often, however, as she crossed herself repeatedly and fastidiously, she kept looking all around to see who had a new sheepskin coat, and how it had been trimmed. Envious of everyone, it seemed to her that her own sheepskin was becoming too tight, and she thought: "There, you see, (it is true that when she was in church she did not swear, not even in her thoughts), well, how are they able to sew and buy themselves something new all the time? I can't afford even a new jerkin, and here they are— all decked out in new white sheepskins already! And why wear a sheepskin coat to church in the summer—isn't it hot in it? They're doing it just to show off and upset me!

"But just you wait! Just you wait and see. As soon as Varka gets her pay for the month, I'll immediately buy myself a jerkin—a green one, green like peas, and with red dots like poppies, so there!"

And truly, when the first pay period arrived, she took all her daughter-in-law's money from her on the pretext that she had to pay the taxes on the land. Then she furtively bought herself a jerkin.

When Varka saw the jerkin she burst into tears and started shrieking: "What have you done, mother? Honest to God! I slave away as a servant, and you spend my money on a jerkin for yourself? E-e-e-e-! A-a-a-a!"

"Oh, my daughter, you'll still earn more money—you're young! When I was your age, I never worried, and I really knew how to work—I did as well as any nimble lad! As long as one has hands and arms, one is sure to earn money!"

And she began to brag about what she used to be like, and she said it all in such a good-natured way, without any swearing, that Varka only shrugged and pouted. She did not take the matter to court or anything like that, for her conscience did not let her do it—it just did not seem to be the right thing to do! She knew that her mother-in-law would take away her money the next time as well, be it in a kindly manner, or with swearing, with curses, and with reminders about her soldier son, saying that she would write to tell him how "the devil's daughter respected his mother."

"I used to take care of your child for you during harvest! I bleached your linen cloth for you when you hired yourself out as a servant! I weeded the wheat for you. I weeded and hilled the potatoes!"

This is what the mother-in-law usually said to Varka, as if it cost her a great deal to care for her, and as if the wheat and the potatoes were not hers, but Varka's.

"Oh, the heck with your potatoes and all the rest of it!" Varka would reply and walk away.

But she did not abandon her mother-in-law; she kept returning to her and handing over her money and, when the older woman became ill, she fussed over her. But why? She herself did not know why. It was as if someone had bound her with a strong rope to her mother-in-law, and she could not untie herself. And she would silently curse her: "I wish you'd drop dead!" And she would criticize her: "All you know is how to pick on me!"

And she would complain to the neighbours: "Well, I sure have a cantankerous mother-in-law!"

And she grumbled, and hurled whatever happened to be handy, and slammed the door. But nevertheless, she did things the way her mother-in-law liked them done, and she obeyed her—she was like that by nature.

It could be said that she was good—but no, if she were good, she would not swear. It could be said that she was foolish—but no, she obeyed without arguing, and more often than not, she did things as her mother-in-law wanted her to do them.

When her mother-in-law began to complain that she was ill and that Varka would drive her into her grave, she would listen, even though she knew full well that her mother-in-law was a long ways off from dying—the old woman seldom mentioned or thought about death now—and even though at that very moment she was thinking: "Would to God that you don't live to see the evening!"

Perhaps she was "half-good," because there are people like that—and quite a lot of them at that!

III

Autumn was approaching, and Kononykha began to ail again—she kept getting sicker and sicker. Earlier, when something hurt, she had got into the habit of saying: "Who cares! We're going to go on living yet!" Or "Let others die!" And she would stretch out her scrawny, veined arms as if she were hanging on tightly to imaginary reins.

However, after the Feast of St. Mary the Protectress, she took to her bed—she lay down on it just like reed-grass is blown down by the wind into the swamp, never to rise again. But when the sheaves were being hauled from the fields, and when the rain began to weave its coverings, and when the earth began to be saturated with water so that it resembled glutinous bread dough, and when the leaves began to fall thickly from the trees and to rot on the grass so that walking became hazardous, and when stacks of grain were placed in the yard, and windmills began to turn as if they had gone mad, and when the steppe was half torn up by ploughs—that was when Kononykha truly became ill. She even lowered her arms, like the branches on a weeping birch.

She no longer went to weddings and birthdays, and she did not sit out in the street—nothing made her feel happy any more. Even work became repugnant to her, and she found it distressing to be alone in the house.

She would send for Varka and, groaning every minute, would curse her from her clay bed on top of the oven: "Why have you . . . O-o-o-oh . . . hired yourself out, you slut? Oh, o-o-o-oh, oh! What devil pushed you to go there? Oh, dear me! You should stay at home! There's work here . . . Nothing . . . nothing is getting done . . . Oh, o-o-o-oh, oh, oh!"

"But it was you who packed me off there!" Varka would answer angrily, and, by God, she really would have been happy to beat up her mother-in-law.

Instead, she crawled up to the bed and rubbed the old woman's spine with hot tallow, thinking all the while: "May the devil take you! Oh, my God! Have I gone mad? But then, how long is this abuse going to continue? You've got what you deserve, exactly what you deserve!"

And all the while, she continued to rub her mother-in-law's spine harder and harder, until the old woman began to groan, and then to cry: "Ouch, ouch, ouch! It hurts! Be gentler! Do you want to break my bones, you daughter-of-a-bitch, or what? Go to the devil! Oh, ouch, ouch, oh, oh, oh! Don't stop, rub some more! Where in the devil have you gone off to? You see, she's happy! Oh-ouch! Rub me! Do it harder! More! More! Why are you touching me like a cat with its paw? Where are you rubbing? Not there . . . Not here! Not like that! What? Oh-ouch! Rub briskly, because it seems to be getting better . . ."

When Kononykha began to feel some relief, she began admonishing her daughter-in-law: "Stop working right away, even if it means that you lose some money . . . But don't forget one thing—get me some kind of medicine from that landlord of yours, and make sure it's strong! Yes, and stop working for him immediately. Can you imagine? There's work piling up at home, and she's come up with the idea of serving! And just who is supposed to strip the hemp? Not me, that's for sure! Even if I get well again, I'm not going to do anything like that anymore. God forbid that I should call down more trouble on myself . . ."

The daughter-in-law, however, did not give up her job, and the mother-in-law was happy about that, for she once again rose from her bed and began to wander about like a shadow. She began to live like a worm that continues to live even after it has been cut in half.

Her health improved, but she was now afraid to sleep alone in the house at night; she kept imagining all sorts of things. At times it sounded to her as if someone were playing with human bones: click, click, click! Then it seemed that the scythe did not stop ringing right by her ear. Then it seemed that cold, heavy clods of earth were falling on her and clinging to her chest and hands, and there were so many of them in her hair that it all stuck together like a piece of black velveteen, and it was impossible to turn her head. Then it seemed that something was pulling at her and stretching her out more and more, like thread from a spindle, and she could not be pulled through, and this was very hard on her.

And so Kononykha called a lot of women into her home to make it less scary. The women sat around, talked, and then fell asleep wherever they were lying down, and she too fell asleep as they were talking.

She did not bother her daughter-in-law about leaving her place of work, for she once again had thought it over. She was sorry to lose the money, and she even ordered her daughter-in-law to convince the lords to give her—that is, the mother-in-law—a skirt, as if it were "for her deathbed," but she planned to wear it out while she was still alive.

When the rainy season ended, and the frosts started to set in, the old woman fell ill again, and she was so stricken that there was no end to her cursing, groaning, weeping, complaining, and grieving. Every day, every minute, she called for her daughter-in-law, but the latter began to look at her more and more angrily.

"Am I your guardian, or what? Lie there and be done with it!" This was her usual reply, but one time she let loose a string of abuse: "God damn you, but you've become loathsome to me! You're going to live another hundred years yet, and I have to sit here with you! Don't be afraid—you won't die. Oh no! Misfortune doesn't die!"

As time went by, Varka became angrier with her mother-in-law and, towards the end, all she did was swear at her. She cursed the old woman for not giving her time to breathe, for working her to death—for sending her to fetch the doctor, or to go, like a beggar, to the lord to get some apples, or some cucumbers, or a fermented drink, or some bread, sugar, milk, or whatever else she got a yen for.

And the mother-in-law wanted her to rub her down with this, or with that, or to turn her over from one side to the other, or to cover her, while complaining all the while: "It's cold right here, right here! The big toe on my right foot is frozen—cover it!"

And the old woman became angry, and almost scratched her eyes out, screaming all the while: "Oh, you lazybones, oh, you tramp! Where are you going? Even the devil's father doesn't know what you're doing!"

And then there were those times when she had to help the old woman sit down on a chamber pot—Varka's head swam from the heavy stench . . . But the worst was that her mother-in-law froze her soul with her terrible fear of dying, her closeness to death, and the fact that she absolutely refused to submit to it . . .

Once her mother-in-law told her: "This is what the fortune-teller from Yablunivka said to me: 'If you get through this Friday, you'll live a long, long time. Who can say, how long . . .' But Friday has passed already, and I'm not feeling any better! And as for you, get away from me, you snake! I can't stand to look at you, because you're waiting for me to die!"

But Varka had hardly made it to the door when the old woman started up again: "Oh, o-o-o-oh, oh, oh . . ."

"What's wrong, mother, what is it?" Varka rushed up to her.

What frightened her most of all was the fact that the old woman could no longer utter a word; she only shrieked her "o-o-o-h," stretched herself out full length and then crumpled again, pressed her head against her knees, and began crying out in pain once more . . .

When the pain subsided a bit, the mother-in-law took a deep breath and asked Varka to rub her: "Rub, rub, sweetheart, faster, sweetheart, more quickly, sweetheart, rub, rub!" Now she spoke softly and rapidly, like grain kernels dropping on a table.

Varka began to rub her as hard as she could and, perhaps for the first time, she truly felt sorry for her mother-in-law. Tears filled her eyes; she wiped them furtively and decided not to return to the landlord's that evening.

"Oh, you see, she's crying!" The old woman had noticed, because she always noticed everything. "But why?" And she smiled, and then she herself began to cry so hard that her dull, gray eyes began to shine from her tears, as glass shines in the sun. She pressed her head close to Varka's, and it was very pleasant for both of them—as if a flower had come into bloom before their very eyes.

But during the night, Varka again cursed her mother-in-law more than once, because the latter did not fall asleep for even a moment, and she did not want Varka to sleep either. The young woman, however, was drowsy, and her head kept dropping to the table as if it were a flail threshing wheat.

As soon as the old woman, from her perch on the oven bed, saw that the shadow from Varka's head was beginning to disappear, to move downwards along the wall, she would begin to shout in an inhuman voice: "Oh, don't sleep! Oh, Varka, don't sleep! What are you doing to me?"

Varka would wake up with a start, jump to her feet, and stand for a moment with blankly staring eyes, without understanding what was happening. When she finally got her wits about her, she would mutter quietly to herself: "Well, when are you actually going to die at last? There's no peace with you around!"

But then she would become frightened at her own words, and she would speak kindly, out loud: "What do you want, mother? Something to drink, perhaps? Or maybe you'd like to have your pillow straightened?"

Kononykha became most terrified when, be it during the day or night, her legs or arms became so numb that she could scarcely feel them, as if they were no longer there, as if she had died.

She was so unbearably terrified of dying limb by limb, that she would scream at the top of her lungs—she was prepared to scream, so that the whole world could hear: "Oh, where is my arm? Why has my leg gone dead?"

And after Varka had rubbed her arm or her leg, and the blood began to prickle her like tiny needles, she would become so happy that she was ready to be kind and to pity everyone on earth.

But God forbid when, as she said, "her heart stopped." Then it seemed that she could no longer speak; her eyes bulged incredibly and, lying in one spot, she flailed her arms and legs in all directions like a tethered bird, gasping and panting like a fish out of water.

This was how the old woman Kononykha was dying, but she had not died yet—she just no longer climbed down from her clay bed on the oven. In the meantime, however, some of her friends in the village had already passed on. Makarykha was among them. They say that when she was dying, it seemed as if she were going to a wedding. She kissed her grandchildren for the last time and said: "Well, my dear little children, I'm going to leave you now." And she gave her soul back to God.

Varka, who should have known better, told her mother-in-law that Makarykha had died. Upon hearing this, Kononykha began to wail and shout: "I don't want that to happen to me! I don't want it to!" And afterwards, she had an attack in her chest from which she barely recovered.

It was as if the passing of Makarykha—they were of the same age, had spent their girlhood together, and had been godmothers for each other's children—made her fear that death had grazed her with its wing as well, and had placed a mark on her forehead. It was as if the circle that had been drawn around her had become still smaller, still narrower; before this, death had been a little farther away, but now it was drawing nearer and nearer! Death! Oh, what a terrible misfortune!

"But why is she hanging on to life like this?" Varka thought. "She has no kin, no descendants. Her son is far away, and he rarely even thinks about her! If she were young—but she's such an old thing; and yet she's hanging on to life so hard that, honest to God, it's embarrassing in front of others. She just won't die as she's supposed to— quietly, like an ordinary human being! Will I too, someday, try to wriggle out of death's way like a snake?"

Chills ran through Varka at the thought of this, and she shuddered. She also had a great love of life: "No matter how one lives, as long as one lives!"

And so Kononykha clung to life, like a harrow clings to the grass! She clung to it in the hope that she would rise every day before sunrise when dew still covers the fields like tears, eat dark rye bread with salt and, afterwards, weed the garden until her knees fainted, or tie sheaves in the burning heat with her spine bent over like a bow so that later, like a bound willow, she could not unbend; or that she would strip hemp until sweat ran down her face, or spin until her fingertips were swollen, and then, dine on soup with a tablespoon of oil in it, or a piece of fat that's bigger than your fingertip; and that, afterwards, she would work in the same way until evening, and then, having eaten some bread and salt, she would lie down to sleep, and that was it!

She hoped that, on a holiday, she would go to church, talk with the other old women, and recall her youthful years. Even back then, there had been nothing very special about them, nothing but working in the tobacco fields and joking with the young men. Then, there had been her own wedding—actually, two of them—and then the children that she had found so hard to carry, and all of them—except for two sons—had died.

And, after this, there had been her husband's blows and more hard work; the deaths of her first and second husbands; the marriages of her sons; seeing one of them off to Tomsk, and the other into the army; the birth and death of her grandson. And then there had been the other people's weddings, other people's births, other people's funerals—and that was it. That was it!

But she still clung to that life, like a dog hangs on to a gnawed bone! Now she was terrified of the least little thing. If she got a boil on her finger, or if her tooth began to ache, she would immediately call out: "Oh, dear mother of mine! Oh, my dear God! What am I to do?" And she would begin to weep.

"Just put something on it—a carrot, or a baked beet, and that's all!" one of the old women would advise her.

But she did not want to listen to them! She would immediately instruct her daughter-in-law to fetch a woman healer, and if that woman was not able to help, she would send her off to find another one.

And all the while she continued wailing, hugging her knees with her arms, and rocking back and forth: "Oh my dearest ones, what is going to happen to me? Where will this lead me? Will the woman-healers help me? That one appears to be good, but does she know what to do for me? Oh, what am I to do? I'm so afraid; I hope no misfortune befalls me! What is this? I've never had anything like it, and now—here it is! Is it death that is revealing itself? Oh, o-o-o-h, oh! May the power of God protect me!"

And there were times when she would send for a priest, and she would confess and receive Holy Communion in the hope of getting better. And she would improve a bit, and then she would once again be like green wood that does not burn, but only smoulders.

IV

Winter came. It spread its white tablecloths on the fields, adorned houses and trees with white linen towels and headdresses, and draped kerchiefs and linen cloths on fences. Everything was so white that it blinded the eyes, and it was all so dreamy that when you gazed at it you felt drowsy with a silvery sleep in which you dreamed about golden stars, an azure sky, and sparks that continually scattered like those from a flint when you strike it with iron; and it was hard to tell if these sparks were coming from the snow or from the glittering stars.

At times like this, every blade of grass, slender as a hair, every rough spot on the bark of the birch tree, every ridge, every bump, every carbuncle, is iced with frosty needles and looks as if it has a wreath on it. Everything becomes wondrous and beautiful—the trees appear wider in that attire, and everything all around, tightly wrapped in white, seems to be approaching and drawing closer, huddling together, astonished by its own beauty, and casting a bluish colour, like steel, or a pinkish one, like a rose; and nothing stirs, as if it were all congealed, and it stands softly-softly, until the cold passes and life returns, or anther cold spell rushes in with the wind and drives away that beauty, like feathers, in all directions and raises a snowstorm, tears off the trees' attire—like a father, in a fit of passion, rips the clothes from his overly elegant daughters—and begins to swirl in white eddies from the ground upwards.

Or suddenly the rains come, and the snow begins to melt; it rises on top of the water, freezes, and ice is formed, and you can't walk on it or drive on it; all that remains of beauty then are the icy beads—above the windows, on the roof, on the door—that blaze in the sun, growing continually longer and slimmer, clear as tears, and dense as a cluster of blossoms. The wind rages, the wind reigns supreme. It crawls through every crack and, no matter how you heat the house, how you pack it in with manure, you cannot heat it, because the wind cuts through it without a knife, slips in without the aid of soap, and cools it off.

It was on such a cold and windy winter day that old Kononykha died.

She had complained for a long time that she was cold, and had fussed for a long time, asking that her daughter-in-law cover her, because the cold was moving over her body in "patches." First it would take hold of her here, and then seize her over there, but it was her feet that froze the most, for they had almost no life left in them—they were yellowish-white in colour, swollen, hard, and heavy.

Then she began to weep and wail: "Oh, how will 'that' be like? Oh, how will this world get along without me, and I without it? Oh, God, God, God!"

And she parted from life like a thread from a spindle—she stretched out first one arm and then the other one until her bones made a crackling sound, then she stretched out one foot after the other, and then she sat straight up, as if someone had lifted her. She wanted to straighten out, to feel herself, her arms, her legs, where they were. Then she drowsed for a while.

She awoke looking as if she were completely healthy, raised herself on her elbows, asked Varka to give her a pancake with some cheese and cream and, after eating it, asked that Varka kill some of the lice in her hair.

The daughter-in-law placed the mother-in-law's head on her knees, took off the old woman's cap, and slowly started to pick through the thick, long, grey hair with her fingers.

For some reason, Kononykha remembered her sons, and she started talking about them in a quiet voice: "If only I could see them! At least one of them—Mykola! I suddenly have such a strong desire to see them. If you only knew, my daughter, how I long to see them!"

Then, she suddenly let out a scream—one that sent chills down Varka's spine.

Varka thought she had unintentionally pulled at a hair, but then the old woman shouted: "Oh, where are my eyes? Oh, what is happening? Am I blind? Is it a fog of some kind? Have you slipped me something? What is this? It's like fire! Oh, save me, save me! Now it's all turning dark, dark! A. . . a. . . a . . .!"

The daughter-in-law rushed as fast as she could to fetch some people and, in the meantime, Kononykha's voice grew softer, and then she began to wheeze. She sighed deeply one more time, stretched herself tautly liked a string on an instrument and, when Varka returned with the old women, her soul was no longer in her body; only her corpse remained—cold, heavy, with rigid legs and arms, as if she wanted to run somewhere, to flee, to get away from someone, to defeat someone, so much so that her nails had sunk into the sheepskin coat and stiffened there.

They could hardly pull them away from the coat when it was time to wash her—so strongly had Kononykha struggled with death . . . In her eyes, those unseeing eyes, terror was reflected, or curiosity, or uncomprehension—who knows? When they drew her eyelids shut, her countenance took on a completely calm appearance, and it was only then they noticed that she had a gentle smile on her lips . . .

When she had been dressed and laid out on the bench, she looked nicer than she had ever looked in life. Her face seemed to be refined, or very delicately chiselled, and her wrinkles dissolved, because her skin was stretched over her bones. She appeared to be the thinnest around her eyes; they now peered like dark berries from under healthy, yellowish eyelids that were not completely closed—and the dark circlets of her eyes, covered with long eyelashes, could be seen from below.

Never before had anyone noticed that Kononykha had such long eyelashes . . .

The blizzard had calmed down, and the sun peeked through the clouds and glanced in through the window. It fell on the head of the deceased Kononykha, and her face shone like a honeycomb filled with honey, and the white wreath with the little gold icons lying on her forehead glowed and made her look still more beautiful. It was all very pleasant, and very quiet, and not at all terrifying, mainly because it was so quiet, so very quiet; however, it did seem strange, amazing, that she was just lying here and was no longer getting up or speaking.

"If only she would curse, or something," Varka thought as she looked back at her over her shoulder, in fright and with pity, from the oven into which she was placing loaves of bread for the funeral meal. "No, she won't ever get up again; she won't speak!"

It was Varka who was frightened, but not the neighbours who came to help her. They looked upon all this as if it could not be otherwise, as if Kononykha truly were no longer there. They bustled around the stove, tidied up and swept the house, and picked through Konkonykha's goods as if she could no longer see them doing this, referring to her only occasionally as someone who had been "immortal."

In the main, however, they carried on their own conversations, opened and closed the door with a creaking sound as they entered the house and walked out of it, and walked around the bench on which she was lying as if she were not a human being, but wooden, like the bench itself.

Outside, some men were constructing a coffin from boards that had formerly been part of the floor—that was the reason why the house had an even more abandoned appearance now. The scent of pine shavings was in the air, and only the monotonous thumping of nails being hammered and the scraping of the plane could be heard.

These men were not talking—what was there to talk about? It was only once that someone said: "Well, the old one finally died!" It sounded as if he were happy, but he had no reason to rejoice, because Kononykha had meant nothing to him.

Varka was terribly frightened. She did not know what to do now that the old woman was gone, truly gone! She had been so sure that her mother-in-law would outlive her, and she had cursed her, and wished death upon her, but then—wouldn't you know it!— she really had died.

And now Varka felt confused, and she lamented a long time over her mother-in-law: "Oh, my dear mother, oh, my darling little dove, why have you gone away and left me all alone? My dear little sun, you should have lived for a long time yet, and shone for a long time, and worked for a long time, but you have left the hard work to me, to me—with my poor little mind. You have gone to serve God, to guard his golden apples! Oh, my dear God! Oh God!"

Varka grieved for her mother-in-law for a long, long time, and the more time that passed, the more pleasant and loyal her mother-in-law seemed to her—she was already forgetting how the old woman had sworn at her, but she remembered that she had instructed her for her own good how to behave in service, how to do things so that she could live a better life.

"Do everything quietly, my daughter, furtively, and don't brag to anyone; wipe you footprints like a vixen with her tail and, when necessary, snarl and bare your teeth."

Varka also recalled how her mother-in-law had stood up for her at times. When they were alone, she would abuse her, but if any of the other old women said that Varka was slovenly, or denigrated her in some other way, the mother-in-law immediately rose to her defence: "Oh, no, don't say that! My daughter-in-law isn't like that."

And she had been so kind to Mykhalchyk, Varka's little boy. How she had doted on him—she had been a true grandmother!

"No, she was good, a good mother! And why did she have to die so young?" Varka kept repeating with a sigh.

She also recalled that just two days before she had died, she had given her a gift: "Varka, take that skirt, because I'm no longer going to wear it, unless . . . Well, I'll see how it will all be when I'm there . . . If you will dress me in it when . . . And take a few rolls of cloth—it's all yours . . . Oh, Varka, Varka, I used to spin once, and I used to weave, and who will wear it all now?"

"Varka, Varka!" Varka now seemed to hear this quite often at night. She would wake up and expect to hear what usually followed: "Rub my back for me."

And when she remembered that her mother-in-law "was gone," she would become ever so frightened.

This happened to her not only at night or when she was alone, but even during the day, when she was among other people.

She would be laughing loudly, and then she would suddenly think: "Was it mother who was calling me?" And she would turn cold.

And she would think: "Why didn't I listen then? Why didn't I pull out the onions and hang them in the chimney? Oh!"

Exactly when her mother-in-law had told her to do this, Varka did not recall; she only remembered that she had not done what her mother-in-law had told her to do, and this gnawed at her like rust eats away at iron, all the more so because it was not possible to go back in time, to do the impossible.

Varka was troubled most of all by the fact that she had not given her mother-in-law an apple when the latter had asked for it before she died. "Why didn't I give it to her? Why? Why didn't I do it, damned scurvy woman that I am!" She could not rid herself of this thought.

And then she would once again hear in her ear: "Varka Varka!" The sound was coming from up ahead, from behind, from down below, from up above, and from all sides.

Varka would turn white and cross herself, and Haptsya would begin making fun of her: "Why are you walking around like a fool? You should be happy that you're free now, but you're walking around all sad and gloomy—ugh!"

"Oh, yes! I should rejoice!" Varka would say, "when 'she' — she always referred to her mother-in-law now as 'she'—is always here, right here! Perhaps this means that I'll die soon?"

"What a thing to say! You're being foolish—your time has not come!" the stern Mariya spoke up.

"She really abused you when she was alive!" Haptsya roared with laughter. "Wasn't it enough for you?"

"That never happened!" Varka cut her off by denying the truth and what she herself thought, and she glanced down at the skirt that had belonged to her mother-in-law. "Why didn't I try to please her?"

Varka continued her thought out loud. "If only I had known that the end would come so soon—I would have done everything, listened to everything . . . If only I could see her once more, bid her farewell!"

"You see, she was knitting the net for so long that she knit you into it!" Haptsya observed.

Yes, indeed, death truly had nicked Varka as well, just as if it had started slicing a loaf of bread with a knife.

She began to mention death quite often.

"Will we also die soon? Which one of us will die first?" she kept asking her companions.

"It would be just as well if I did die!" she said once. "Because I'm always alone, all alone!"

But, of course, Varka did not die soon—for death is not granted to those who want it, but to those who do not seek it . . .

Why, Oh Why . . .?

(1901)

"Why didn't you come yesterday?" she asked, observing him intently.

"Just because," he answered quietly and weakly, as he always did.

They were standing under a willow in the damp shadows cast by the tree and the cottage that stood beyond it. The silver light of the moon lay all around them, but they appeared to be cut off from it by shadows—the large, long one cast by the cottage, and the willow's small, round one.

"Why, just because?" the girl flew into a rage. Her round eyes widened, her full, rosy face flamed, and her crimson lips drew taut in anger. She asked the question and fell silent, her lips tightly clamped together.

"Because my head ached," he replied and, leaning against the willow, lost his balance and slid down, like a leaf during a drought.

"My poor little Ivan," Marta said quietly, but with a smile, as if these words made her feel embarrassed, both for herself and for him. At the same time, she threw her strong arms around his neck and pressed her lips—damp like flowers at night, and trembling like butterflies—against his cheek. And she herself was fluttering, like a candle in church before God.

But Ivan did not respond with ardour. He moved away a bit and sighed: "O-o-o-oh!"

His lovely, remote eyes were melancholy, and they stared straight ahead as if they did not see anything.

"If you only knew how badly it hurt, oh my dear God!" he said.

Seizing his dark head in his hands, he shook it a few times: "If you only knew! It's as if something was all stirred up in it, like a yolk with the white in a spoiled, unhatched egg, or . . ."

"Oh, you poor dear, you poor dear," Marta cooed like an oriole, nestling still closer to him, so that her round, firm breasts, whose warmth could be felt through her shirt, were crushed and pushed apart to both sides.

"And when . . ." he continued, "someone . . . say, my mother scrapes a pot on the stove, or my father strikes a hammer on a boot as he pounds in a nail, then . . . there's such a sharp pain, and my whole being aches . . . There's a pounding in my head— thump, thump, thump—and it goes on incessantly . . . Oh!" Terror was reflected in his eyes the way fire is reflected on glass. "I almost go mad . . . Something pu-u-ulls, pu-u-u-lls and pu-u-ulls me upwards as if I were hanging on the gallows, or something like that . . . Oh!"

He collapsed completely and sat down on the ground, folding himself up as a scythe is folded, despite the fact that he was very tall . . .

"Oh, my God, how handsome you are," Marta exclaimed as she sat down beside him.

Her breath was warm—like steam rising from hot borshch. She breathed into his ear, and then once again wound herself around him like a vine.

He leaned back and his passion, like a green tree that smoulders for a long time, finally flared.

She burst into flames like a dry pine.

***

"Why didn't you come yesterday?" Marta once again asked Ivan at night under the willow tree.

"Just because," he said.

He lay down; there was no moon, and his figure immediately stretched out into a long, white streak on the dark ground.

"Was your head hurting again?" the girl asked.

She sat down beside him, tucked up her legs, placed her hand on his head, and gazed fixedly at his long, pale face that gleamed like snow in the darkness.

"No," he replied. And he dragged out his words slowly, the way a harrow is dragged through wet soil. "I didn't come . . . because . . . you know . . . I felt . . . a bit . . . lazy."

"What's this?" Marta said in surprise, not quite understanding what he had said.

"Well . . . that is . . . yes, indeed . . . you know . . . at times, something comes over me . . ." He sighed heavily and deeply. "Something comes over me . . . yes, indeed . . . and I don't want to do anything . . . and that's that! Nothing at all!"

"How can that be?" Marta shrugged her shoulders and, unable to restrain herself, kissed his beautiful eyes.

He sighed once again: "Take yesterday . . . I lay down . . . and I thought . . . should I go . . .? She's sure to be waiting for me . . . Yes, indeed . . . But after I had lain down . . . I couldn't get up . . . from that spot . . . and that was that! Neither my foot, nor my hand . . . would move . . . It was as if . . . they had gone numb . . ." What he had just said brought a smile to his lips.

"What is this? What will you be like when you become the master of your own household? Who will do the work after we get married?" Marta peppered him with questions. She was becoming alarmed, and she was cross, both with him and herself.

"I don't know," he responded quite simply and directly, and he locked his hands behind his head.

"Well, this is nothing. It will pass," she threw her head back unconcernedly and once again leaned over him.

Cuddling up to him, she placed her heart next to his, so that they would beat evenly together. He still felt a bit weary, and he did not feel like doing anything, but he raised his hand and began to touch her round neck—as sturdy as a cornstalk—her burning little ears, and the thick braids on her head; then he passed his hand over her face which was as tender as young leaves on a birch tree . . .

She pulled his hand into the bosom of her shirt, and they embraced and fell silent as they gazed up at the stars.

The night was warm, as warm as freshly drawn milk, and it was dark, so dark that almost nothing could be seen.

***

"Well, why didn't you come yesterday either?" Marta greeted Ivan angrily.

He was silent and approached her with a heavy tread.

"Can't you hear, or what?" she snapped sharply, and she could feel herself turn pale.

"I didn't want to," he retorted just as cuttingly and sharply.

"Ha!" the young woman screeched strangely, and her teeth made a grating sound. "Why's that? Are you courting another girl? Don't you love me anymore? Are you going to abandon me? You must be happy you're so handsome!"

"No," he responded quietly, as quietly as the rustling of reeds. "Don't curse, don't cry . . . it's not that . . it's . . ."

He fell silent and dropped his head down low.

"Well?" she inquired once again, full of hope and curiosity, like a well-filled ear of wheat.

"Everything has become repugnant to me," he spoke in a muffled voice like a broken bell, and he flung his hands far above his head and cracked his knuckles. Then, suddenly becoming talkative, he continued: "I dislike myself, and I've taken a dislike to people, to my father, my mother . . . Oh, it's a great sin!"

He moaned like a dove.

"And work has become repugnant to me . . . Why do it? What for? For whom? Everything, absolutely everything, has become repugnant to me . . . It's as if death were stalking me, even though I am strong and healthy."

He bent his sinewy hand and firmly clenched his fist.

"I have absolutely no desire to live . . . Mother wants to set me up with Mokryna, and I don't seem to care—after all, isn't it all the same? It's all repugnant. . ."

His lips dropped, and he lowered his head.

"Shame on you! Ugh!" This was all that Marta spit out, and, turning around so abruptly that her skirt wound itself about her legs, she stormed off.

He wanted to rush after her, to catch up to her, to turn her back, to kiss her, but . . . he did not. He just gestured hopelessly with his hand and remained standing in the same spot in the darkness—a darkness black as tar, which encompassed everything.

On this night there were no stars—they had hidden themselves behind the clouds . . .

Sketches
(1907)

"Homo homini lupus [est]."
[Men are wolves to one another.]

I

The season known in the village as "the dog days of summer" has arrived. It seems that something is continuously burning somewhere, spreading an unbearable heat over the earth; one can even smell the remains of a conflagration. The incessant heat is fatiguing, and it feels as if something is smouldering inside you. The overheated sea of grain, stretching in all directions, appears to be on fire. Everything is silent and motionless . . .

Under a stack of mown grain, three people lie sleeping—a man and two women. Their sunburned faces, over which flies are calmly crawling, are breaking out in a dewy sweat, and the sun's rays scorch them with kisses.

The man wakes up, stretches, yawns, and eagerly presses his hot, parched lips to the keg of water lying nearby. For a long time, the only sound that can be heard is the rush of water from the keg into the man's throat; it seems that it will never end, and that he will never find the strength to pull himself away from the keg—just as a bloodsucker has to be forcibly removed once it has attached itself to a body.

After a while, however, the man regretfully pushes the keg away and rises to his feet.

"That's it! Get up! It's time to work!" Speaking loudly, he turns to the two women who are sleeping side by side, and they awake with a start.

One of them is young and strong, while the other is old. The work begins—straw rustles under the scythe, and hands flash. The old woman is getting left behind; she finds it hard to lift a sheaf and twist a straw band to bind it. Her hands are growing weaker, and her head is spinning.

"Look, Dmytro! Before long, our 'granny' won't go harvesting at all. She's just like a small child—she can't stack even half a rick!" The young woman laughs irritably as she speaks to her husband who has forged ahead with a scythe.

"Yes, I know! Maybe the food she eats should also be cut in half," he replies in a mocking tone.

This mocking comment reverberates in the old woman's heart and, along with it, a salty tear rolls down her wrinkled cheek and falls on a golden sheaf.

When they return home from the field and sit down to eat, the old woman cannot swallow the food . . .

"Well, go ahead and eat, mother, or whatever!" Marusya says.

"No, sweetheart, for some reason I don't feel like it," the old woman answers, and she falls silent as a bitter thought creeps into her mind.

She remembers how long ago, when she was still young and strong, she too had felt burdened by her weak, ailing mother—at that time it also had seemed to her that her mother did very little, but ate a lot . . .

III

The apartment of a well-known doctor. A sign, posted on the front door, announces: "Patients are seen from 4:00 to 6:00."

In the dining room, a massive bronze clock with a gilded exterior is striking three o'clock. The doctor's family is having dinner.

His wife, who has large dark eyes, is ladling soup into the bowls and, with a gentle smile on her face, is speaking to her husband, who is sitting next to her. Close by, sit two little girls—like two white cloudlets in their white dresses and bare arms and necks—and a little boy in a velvet blazer, with long curls framing his eyes. Farther down is the governess, who sits stiffly, staring fixedly at her three charges.

A footman enters the room. The mistress immediately guesses what is happening.

"It's starting already," she says. And her amiable expression disappears as she knits her sable brows.

"Oh, the devil take it!" the doctor mutters through his teeth. "They won't even give me a chance to eat! Don't they know yet that patients are received from four o'clock? Who's out there?"

"It's a woman, a common person . . . with a sick child," the footman says, smirking.

"Well then . . . let her wait a bit; after all, it's no one important!"

The footman walks out.

In the anteroom that leads into the living room—filled with velvet, bronze, paintings, and mirrors—a woman sits diffidently on the very edge of a chair. She has a kerchief on her head, and in her arms she holds an infant. From time to time, she sighs. Not far from her stands a chambermaid, dressed in a well-starched pink uniform, her arrogance and indifference reflected in her face.

The infant whimpers, then it makes a slight rasping noise and, sounding as if it has choked on something, abruptly falls silent. The mother bends over it; there is nothing but exhaustion reflected in her face . . .

The stance of the chambermaid changes, and a pale ray of empathy flickers over her face. She draws nearer to the woman, saying: "Oh, my God! It seems to be dying right in your arms! Should I call the master, or what? Wait here, I'll run to him right now . . ."

The girl rushes off, rustling her starched petticoats. But Petrushka, the footman, intercepts her. They stand there, giggling and gossiping . . .

The dinner is drawing to a close, and the doctor, after kissing his wife's hand, contentedly begins to smoke an expensive cigar.

Meanwhile, the sick infant in the porch is contorting its tiny body and jerking spasmodically on its mother's lap. Suddenly it opens its eyes very wide—too wide—and . . . they become fixed in their eternal peace . . .

A Juxtaposition

(1907)

One fine autumnal morning, the sun awoke and began to weave lace and rosy flower-wreaths, to caress as a woman's heart caresses—to fondle, to pet, and to kiss gently, but not fervently as yet—the bluish mist that was rising upwards like a fairy's sky-blue veil, revealing a large city which also had to awaken soon to meet the sun, to meet joyous good fortune . . .

The tall crosses on the churches glittered in the azure expanse, and the tin-plated roofs gleamed like silver, and a penetrating, vibrant, all-encompassing warmth floated on high, while a light, soft coolness—which made it possible to breathe deeply—wafted gently down below . . .

Grey smoke from countless chimneys wound its way into the sky in delightful curls, looking like blessed souls and half suggesting slender human figures . . .

And the dew began to dry on pavement kissed by the sun—a sun that loved and pitied everyone, from the smallest to the greatest . . .

All of this—the sun, the translucent mist, the delicate dew, the cool breeze on the street below, the drowsy trees that stood and stretched their green arms into the air, the smoke, the dissipating curly billows, and the buildings, those creations of human talent and high art which seemed so beautiful in their light covering of dew and which, like young ladies, were fussing over their appearance in their multicoloured clothing, and, in the marketplace, a green sea of cabbages, watermelons, a riot of plants and vegetables, a red sea of eggplant and apples, and a rather small group of people who had just awakened, were freshly washed, and had not yet begun to sin—all of this blended into a wonderful harmony; all were the offspring of one father and mother, of one sun, of one sky, of one love . . .

It seemed that God did exist, and that He was indeed merciful.

But then, two people rounded a corner and marched by with clattering footsteps. Both were slender and of the same height; both were equally young and astonishingly handsome. Their powerful young bodies moved with the same graceful suppleness, and the faces of both of them were inspired with life—two pearls of humanity . . .

Except . . . What is this? One is armed, the other is walking empty-handed, and the first one has the right to beat, to kill the other one—his brother, his twin—to kill him on the spot without any penalty if this other one so much as moves the tip of his finger towards him. And his blue eyes become inflamed with anger, and he does not take them off his prisoner, and malice flickers across his face as if a snake were crawling over it . . .

And this other one—his God-given brother—is helpless; he can do nothing; he is being led, and he walks along, swallowing his tears and his malice, and his blue eyes are staring, but they do not see, and anger darts like a lizard across his tender face . . .

What kind of a curse is this? Who has made one man another man's prey? Who spills forth clouds of poisonous gas among his fellow men, so that one begins to hate another, so that his heart becomes inflamed, so that he desires the blood of the other, just as if the sun did not shine equally for all, as if there were no God either on earth, or in heaven . . .

They call this their right!

* * *

In the middle of the city there is a huge building; yellow and tall, it stands with barred windows alongside other homes, and because it ended up here in a residential district and not farther out—way out there in a deserted spot—it has painstakingly adorned itself. Its clothing, pale yellow in colour, is clean and new, and even though spots of sweat and blood can be sensed beneath the fresh paint, they cannot be seen.

In general, it does not want to differ from its companions on either side of it—the varicoloured, tall, slender buildings—especially from the one right next to it: a delicate white structure with little stone turrets and many balconies, where exquisite, fragrant flowers bloom in profusion. They are blooming—well, why should they not bloom here? They have no minds, no power of comprehension!

Through an open window, music—enchanting music—can be heard . . . Why should it not be enchanting? Clusters of sounds converge and then disperse from under delicate white hands; they gather together like a flock of trembling butterflies, like a school of golden fish, like the silver droplets of a waterfall, like human winged thoughts and dreams that cannot be stopped—and transform everything into diamonds . . .

The young lady stopped playing and walked out on the balcony. What a wondrous beauty she was, and what an aesthetically pleasing picture she made—her light, silk dress rose and fell with her every breath; her neck that appeared to be hewn from warm marble; her slippers, ever so fine, delicate, and brown, with long pointed toes; her black curls that the breeze gently ruffled as it flitted by; and the gilded combs adorning her tresses. . .

Everything was also harmoniously arranged in the room from which she had just walked out—the rugs that were spread over the entire floor so the ear would not be offended by a jarring sound; the electric lamp clad in silk paper; and the countless valuable paintings and costly figurines . . .

She stepped out on the balcony, breathed in the fragrant scent of the flowers, and glanced down at the street below—the one she stood so high above . . .

Two men were approaching the yellow building; both were young, both were handsome, strong, and healthy, and, on both of them, buttons glittered in the sunlight—yellow buttons on the first one, and white ones on the other.

That petite young bird standing amid the fragrant flowers on the balcony almost screamed—it was the first time she had seen anything like this. Formerly, only grey, nondescript men—disgusting, like lice—had been led there, and she had never paid any attention to them, because they were "they," and she was "she."

But now. . . . Oh, my God!

She returned to her music, and the notes began to weep and groan as if every one of them had turned into a tear.

But . . . not for long!

From Heart to Heart

(Excerpts from the diary of a literary man)
(1909)

(February, 19—)

Enough! I no longer want to write as I used to write, as I always wrote, as everyone always writes—with a plot, a beginning, an ending, a prologue, an epilogue, and with the action unfolding slowly and harmoniously as if it were "driven by an inner compulsion" as Count Tolstoy used to say; with the heroes all falling into place—either getting married or being hanged—and with the characters and all the peripeteia being detailed with an almost mathematical precision . . .

And all this is done to enable the dear readers to digest the works properly or to satisfy the egoism of the author who takes great joy in demonstrating, as it were, how ingeniously he was able to design his "puzzle."

No, enough is enough! I no longer want to go about it in this way! I will closely observe life itself; I will cut away living, quivering slices from it and record them meticulously in my album and . . . nothing else! And the pages of my album will grow taut and begin to tremble and come to life; and every letter will be filled with life-giving blood, and they will all live, sing, laugh, cry, and this will be life itself—not an apparition, nor a "vision," nor a splinter of life—but life itself, and it will speak on its own behalf! And it will attract people's souls, and give them peace, true peace, and perhaps the strength or the inspiration to go on living . . .

Life itself is the goal, the task, the blessing of all of us—poets, musicians, artists—who wander about irrepressibly like will-o'-the-wisps over graves, and who bear on our banner the words: "from heart to heart" . . .

It is real life that is the goal—not the creation of stories, novels, dramas and the like that are churned out one after the other as if by some automatic apparatus which ensures that the slipknots are tightly joined so that the mesh being woven about life has no holes in it—holes that might be noticed by the *vulgus profanum [the ignorant masses]* . . . This kind of creating is not worth the effort, especially as it ends in shameful lies!

Life is not like that! It is composed of fragments, of stripes, and these are not always equally bright or equally dark. There are some lives in which the end is so far removed that it appears not to exist or, at least, not to be noticeable. And sometimes it happens that a single bright, passionate stripe appears in the life of an undistinguished person . . . and it is this stripe that endows that life—and the world—with value!

But why do our gentlemen-poets, who become enraptured by such a "special moment" in a person's life, conjure up a complete, symmetrical life for this person? Why do they, having taken the body of one man, attach another person's head to it and proceed to pair mismatched arms and legs, eyes and ears? They do it to create a "harmonious picture," not only for the sake of ideal beauty, but for the sake of realism itself . . . It is absurd, absurd, absurd!

Life and nature encompass more than the greatest talent can portray, and anyone who has strolled down a wide street and glanced in through someone else's window knows this . . .

There was nothing remarkable to be seen—from the ceiling, a white lamp was suspended like some fabled white bird that had widely spread its transparent white wings. A round table was standing in the centre of the room; a yellow samovar was steaming on it, and someone's slender white hand was unscrewing the stopper. Around the table could be seen the charming faces of little children waiting for their tea or milk. This was all there was . . .

Is there any great artistry in this? Is it worth anything? But I stood for several minutes by that window—for this was a slice of life, of life itself, not something that was painted or printed. It clung to my heart, and something within me softened, melted and glowed dimly, like the red light of a votive lamp . . .

Or when, for example, I hear someone call out from afar in the frosty air of the night's darkness nothing more than: "Cabby!"

And shortly afterwards: "Let's go-o-o-o-o!" And once again my heart trembles, and I listen with pleasure to this "o-o-o-o!"

And I revel in this pleasure as the air chases it, and swallows it . . . swallows it . . .

At times, the very sound of a drunken voice is pleasing to me, for it is real and warm, not like "our" contrived, theatrical, artistic voice that is like the brilliant, silvery image of a live person reflected in a mirror . . . No, with such an overly brilliant "image" it is impossible to fool anyone, to convince anyone, or even to satisfy or find "justification" for oneself . . .

Enough! It is necessary to break the golden chains of art! Life, life, and only life! It is pressing in on all sides of us, it is begging to be caught, just like the rain that falls and fills, to the brim, all the valleys, the ditches, and the troughs that fine art purposefully sets out for it.

***

So, today I shall go out into the street. What will it show me?

I take a seat on the urban train and glance up. A young girl with an infant in her arms is sitting across from me. She is very young, very fresh, and her colouring is beautiful—thick, pitch-black eyebrows, hair as black as a raven's wing, lips as red as blood, and her cheeks . . . Why are they growing redder by the moment?

The conductor comes up; she gives him her ticket and, blushing like a rose, casts a glance at two men sitting side by side who appear to have been placed directly opposite to her by fate itself. They are old and ugly, with ruddy countenances; their obese faces are distorted by malice—the malice of hypocrites and Pharisees, the assiduous watchdogs of people's morality.

She glances at them, and her face turns crimson, like a poppy. She looks over at me and . . . her face blazes like flames in a fireplace.

Oh, have no fear of me, my dear girl! I have known your dark secret, your unending grief for a long time; I know it, and I will always know it . . . I have divined it, as if our souls had come into contact with one another, as if we were two fish swimming along together; I have guessed your deep secret, and I will not reveal it to anyone . . .

Gently, so as not to hurt her, I look at the child and immediately surmise who its father was, and what he was like.

The tiny infant that she holds awkwardly—as if it were a lump of clay—is so small that its unformed dough-white face should be devoid of expression; but, as a result of some cunning jest of nature, it already has—with its pouting little lips and its tiny wrinkled nose—an expression of such arrogant disdain for people, of such intense egoism, that I am able to guess at once who its father was, and what he was like.

A terrible grief envelops me, and I want to fall to my knees and express my sympathy to her; I want to swear to her that not all people are like "that one," for I know that now she is certain that this is the case, and that I . . .

I draw nearer to her so that she might know that she has no need to fear me, for I am a poet—and the goal of poets, their calling, is to increase joy, to lighten people's grief; it is not without reason that we have the capacity for metempsychosis. I want to show her that my heart is filled to the brim with her, that today her precious little heart, formerly pink, but now turned dark like a gloomy cloud, is throbbing audibly within me, within my own body . . .

I draw nearer and . . . just think! She leaps up like a deer startled by a hunter, shudders, and jumps—Did she have to do this? Did she really have to?—from the car, almost catching the child in the door . . .

This is a fragment of life, a slice of life, without a beginning, without an ending, that exists *und für sich [of and for itself]*. And it is not necessary to beat it into the chains of creativity, into the chains of a story, a novella, a novel about a poor comely dressmaker with the little son that she bore a general . . . What for?

This life evokes sympathy *co ipso [just as it is]*; it awakens the slumbering or satiated mind of the onlooker like a storm at sea, like a hurricane in the desert; this life requires assistance—precisely because it has not been prettied up, painted, placed in a gilded artistic frame, and given the theatrical ending of suicide. Sometimes, the frame attracts all of our attention, while life itself screams out about the urgency of altering our two-faced morality, about the absolute need for purity, for changes in many of our social relations, for the equality of women! This is all that is needed; it is this that should be our highest goal—except for an insightful figurativeness—the end goal of every conscientious artist, if he does not pursue only his own glory, but wants to serve all humanity with his talent

***

Well, let us continue . . .

When I walked out to the platform of the car to have a smoke, there were two young school boys standing there. Their rosy faces, with their bright eyes and chubby cheeks, immediately caught my attention. I was especially touched by their little ears that stuck out like those of baby bats from under their neatly shaped ball caps; these ears were illuminated with rosy blood and sparkled in the sun like ripened pink cherries or delicate, transparent sea shells . . .

The boys were still at an age when they nestled up to warmth and to kindness like girls, and voluntarily offered their tender cheeks for a mother's kiss; they were still like saplings without any bark—they had not yet grown tough or hard like a tree trunk; they had not yet become filled with masculine self-reliance and the significant doses of contempt for human frailties that usually overtakes them in the upper grades. At the same time, even though their little faces were tenderly childish, they were serious in appearance—with furrowed foreheads and frowning eyebrows— for they were earnestly pondering a scientific problem: why do sparks fly out from under the wheels intermittently, instead of continually?

One of them pointed out that he had used a comb to create an electrical device that made the paper dolls of his little sister, Marusya, dance, and now she thought that he was a magician because he could do this. These young boys captivated me more and more, for they were the springs of pure life that perhaps one day would become turbulent, muddied torrents, and I greedily drank the healing water and could not get my fill of it; I could not look enough or hear enough . . .

I drew nearer to them and wanted to help them in the resolution of their problem. I wanted to become a part of their small group. But the children became frightened, turned red, fell silent, and then darted away like sparrows that allow a human being to come near to them, but not too near.

***

I also disembarked from the car . . .
I got off and walked down the street . . .
"Right, left . . ."
Two men who were quite tipsy were walking in front of me. They were supporting one another, and one of them was telling the other one how he was going home the day before with a friend, and when he arrived there he did not recognize where he was: "Was this my house or wasn't it? And you know, my brother, I just didn't know . . . I didn't know.. . ."

He must have been in the same condition yesterday as today, I thought.

"Well, you know, my brother, Senka says to me: 'Give me your accordion!' Take it, my brother, go ahead and take it . . . And Senka says to me: 'Give me your galoshes!' Take them, my brother, take them . . . I won't begrudge them . . ."

And his friend, stopping for a moment on the sidewalk with his legs far apart like the forked branches of a tree, and swaying and grabbing on to the coat-tails of the other, began to speak: "I really like you, Maksym, I really do! No one knows how much I like you!"

I also took a liking to this Maksym. I liked them both for their sincerity, for this inebriation, this moment of oblivion, this abyss of tenderness and love, for these gentle words, for the softness in their voices that were accustomed to quarrelling and cursing.

I myself do not drink alcohol. I detest it both in the tavern and in the theatre, and I am aware of all the harm done to people by this "devil's herb."

But I am not able to restrain my heart which, like a tuning fork, resounds together with the hearts of these tipsy men. It does not matter that it is alcohol that is eliciting the boundless tenderness within in them in lieu of their former enmity; for a moment, their souls, in all their ecstasy, have unfolded like flowers towards the sun . . .

It was one of the kaleidoscopic patterns of life . . . And I was ready to listen and listen, and to follow these two figures that swayed like stems of grain in a field—to go only heaven knows where. But they turned off into a wineshop and vanished from my eyes . . .

***

I began going uphill. It was very slippery that day, for sleet had fallen the day before, and a layer of bright, crystal ice had formed, and because of this, I was moving very slowly. Moreover, my thoughts about creativity, about life, and about the responsibilities of art prevented me from walking quickly.

All of a sudden, I heard a shrill, hoarse, and angry voice behind me: "Well, what am I to do with you? What am I to do? Well, go by yourself, go! I'm tired as it is! And how am I to go back home at night all by myself? How? And at night? I really don't know! No, go on, go by yourself . . . by yourself!"

Hearing this voice, I turned around . . .

Two grey female figures were crawling along right in the middle of the street. One of them, the older one, was puffing heavily, like a blacksmith's bellows; she was leaning with all her strength on her umbrella and continually grabbing on to the other one, silently doing her utmost to conquer the treacherous slope.

The other one—the younger one whose voice I had heard—kept repeating the same words over and over again in that shrill, harsh voice that tore at one like thorns and clamoured stridently in one's ears: "Well, what am I to do with you . . . Go by yourself, by yourself . . ." and so on.

I was dumbfounded. What was all this about? What was going on here?

The old woman was bundled into a very heavy winter shawl that probably added greatly to her weight and turned her into a ponderous "sack of sugar." The young woman was wearing a hat, and I noticed that even though she was dressed poorly, her clothing was rather flashy . . .

I rushed up to help them . . .

They both immediately came to a stop on the slope—the older one possibly to catch her breath, the younger one in order to tell me her story.

"You see," she began, "I'm taking her to see the Governor . . . But where does he live?" She said the latter sentence to herself. "Let him put her wherever he wants to, either in an insane asylum or wherever . . . because . . . I don't have the strength to look after her! She's my mother . . . only she's completely mad, while I . . . (She tossed her reddish curls that protruded from under her little hat.) . . . while I still have my wits about me as yet . . ." She smiled happily and a little slyly . . .

I glanced at her and then looked at her mother, who was standing without speaking, panting and gaping at me with her bulging, fishlike eyes, and . . .

My God, I was seized with fear—an octopus-like fear that had monstrous tentacles!

Insanity—a terrifying, undeniable insanity—was staring right at me with four eyes, stretching towards me with four arms, approaching me on four legs! Those eyes! Whoever sees them once will never forget them—clouded over, stupefied, without any glimmer of light!

What was I to do? How could I help? My heart ached in my chest, and I myself felt half insane, ready to go completely mad. I wanted to use all the power of my soul to free the women from the embrace of this fierce enemy of all of humanity, from this werewolf; I wanted to save them . . . But how?

First of all, I decided to take them home, and once there, after finding out all about them from someone and after considering everything carefully, to come up with a plan of action . . .

But when I requested their permission to take them home, the older one only groaned and smacked her lips noisily, while the younger one began to argue with me.

She said it was necessary for her to see the Governor as soon as possible, for she did not know how she would get home that night.

It was noon when we met.

Her "train of thought" was somewhat murky, but I decided that perhaps her idea was better than mine. I hired a cabby, gave him the address, paid the fare, and settled them in the carriage.

I had planned to follow them, but when I was helping the younger one into the carriage, the scent of cheap powder engulfed me as she whispered in my ear: "Come to see me in the evening, come without fail! It's not at all expensive . . ."

She did not finish what she was saying, but there was no need to, for her intrusive, matter-of-course, and shameless smile said it all for her.

Jumping back as if I had been slapped, I remained standing in the middle of the road for several moments . . .

***

Oh, you damned liar! You rotten, worthless, spineless person! So this is what your sympathy for people is really like? You are afraid?

You are afraid of real misery, of the ugliness of reality, of genuine lunacy!

You are afraid of life—you, with your artist's sense of order, your famous sensitivity, akin to the sensitivity of a mimosa leaf—you are good only for slowly entangling the ephemeral, delicate cobweb of a literary work, pretending to be writing with "the blood of your heart," seeming to be fainting over your heroes, as if you were truly tasting the poison on your tongue, on your palate, in your throat, when they, of their own free will, end up committing suicide; going mad, when they go mad, knowing incontrovertibly that you are truly losing your own mind, as if a screw in your brain has come loose, a hook has sprung free—and there you have it! You too are done for; you are insane!

But no! Stop it! You are not going mad, you will not die, you will not bleed to death, for . . . all this is a lie, it is only "the irritation of decaying thoughts" . . .

And that great sympathy for the people about which you bragged—it is also a lie; for when you met up with real life, with actual wretchedness, with actual insanity—you stepped back and were afraid . . .

And I felt awful, ashamed, because of the fact that we are only ugly buffoons who fool people, evoking "noble feelings" in them with our treacherous dissembling, without having any such feelings ourselves, or we rouse them for only a moment within ourselves as we chase after chimerical glory, seeking to please our insatiable egoism . . .

For sometimes it also happens that we take our radiometric sensitivity that responds to the slightest ray of the sun—our talent to be set afire by another person's passion, to weep with another person's tears, to think the thoughts of others, to ache with another's pain, to live the life of another person—and we use it to combine various pebbles into interesting figures, shaking our kaleidoscope every second to make them ever more enchanting, in order to continue creating endlessly, boundlessly . . . To what end? As a game! And it sometimes happens that to some extent we take advantage of people's grief as we search for themes, as we chase down—as on a hunt—fire, death, betrayal . . . And we do this instead of consoling, comforting, easing, and saving life!

And so I called a cabby, sat down and drove to the Governor's home. But I did not find them there; and even though she had invited me to her place, she had forgotten to give me her address, and so I lost them forever!

***

(A year later, February 20, 19—)

But there must be someone who has need of me, who yearns for my reassurance, my comforting words, my unreserved sympathy—"from heart to heart"; someone who is aflame for me, who desires me, who longs for me, someone who is a stranger among strangers, who in the midst of his kin and in the circle of his dearest friends feels alone; for even though we may be wreathed by a love that encircles us like a garland of fragrant flowers, we all have our own, our solitary pain.

We are all alone, for there is no one, no one in the world who can fully understand—drop by drop—our suffering, the full measure of our pain. As a result of the physical inability of others to understand our pain, they will either decrease it or increase it; but this is not at all what is needed, not at all, not at all!

. . . We are all alone, for no matter how wide our circle of friends, the circle of strangers is still greater—there are millions of them, hordes of them, and these hordes turn life into a desert peopled by multitudes who do not want to know one another, who do not speak to one another "with a kind, gentle word," and who never turn to one another if they are not related through blood or marriage, if they are not in obligatory relationships with one another; but they live close by one another, beyond the wall from one another, next door to one another, across the window from one another . . .

Why, just over there, in that house that is across from me, a young woman lives on the first floor . . .

Through the tiny window one can see the small room that is lit by a lamp. A young woman sits by the table and sews endlessly, while salty tears, pouring down on her hands, blind her eyes and dampen the fabric she is sewing. And she relates her woe to her sister, who is admiring her own beauty as she combs her long hair in front of a crooked mirror. And it seems to the young woman that a vast number of plucked roses covers the entire floor of her happiness, for they are dying, just as she is dying with every word that escapes from her pale lips—for he no longer loves her.

Her sister, with her hair half unplaited, flings herself at her, kisses her, pities her, and even cries with her, but this does not ease her pain, for icy death is lodged in her breast; and her young sister, who herself still loves and whom others still love, finishes braiding her hair and departs . . .

Do not weep, my darling; do not grieve, my precious, for I am here; I am the one who knows all your sorrow, even though I do not know you. And I will not leave you, and you will not know who I am, and I will not speak to you, so as not to startle the butterfly that you are; but you should know that I am here, that my soul, like a chalice, is filled to the brim with your tears . . . even though I am neither your brother, nor your lover . . .

***

And on the second floor of that building lives—or, I should say, is dying—a sick, very sick father; by his bed, which he has not left for a long time now, and by the little table on which stand fragrant medicines and a green night lamp, flutters the slender figure of his daughter.

She loves her father and feels sorry for him, but he has been ill for a long time now and, despite herself, she is beginning to feel the weight of her sacrifice; she feels—even though she fears this more than anything in the world—that this sacrifice is great, the sacrifice that she is constantly making for her father, day and night at the cost of her beauty, her youthfulness.

He also feels this, and he wants to die to free her more quickly; but he also wants to live regardless of everything else—this is the imperative of life itself! He is angry, and so he torments her, forcing her to sit at his bedside. And then he feels more sorry for her than for himself and chases her away to enjoy the pleasures of life. He forces her to go to them, while he lies dying . . .

Enough, enough! Do not impose on your child, old man! I will share your illness with you . . . And believe me—every part of your body that aches will also pain me, for I want to suffer with you. And you should know that I can already feel it clearly—my legs are filling with water just like yours, and I do not have enough air to breathe, and my head is spinning, because . . . I am filled with your illness . . .

***

And on the third floor, closer to the sky, a young poet sits in the darkness in an unheated room. He is dreaming, while gazing through the window at the stars, and there is no end to his suffering, for he is unable to conquer the rhythms, and his thoughts are not arranging themselves to conform with the metre of the verse. It seems to him that there are no sharp golden words to express that which is transpiring in his soul, and he wants to create something exceptional, something great, so that the world might shudder upon hearing it.

He unfolds his wings and, with the wide wingspan of an eagle, is prepared to soar upwards in a sweeping movement towards the sun—but instead, he twists on the ground like a snake whose head has been trampled . . . And he sees the stars, and every one of them penetrates his soul with its light and, teaching him unknown words, lifts him upwards . . .

But once again doubt and despair overcome him, and he wrings his hands in agony and groans . . .

"Well, then," the deep, good-natured voice of his friend resounds suddenly from the bed. "Are you still dreaming? 'Creating?' 'Pondering?' 'Oh, you poor toiler of the arts!' You would be better off to go to sleep, ha-ha-ha-ha!"

No, "do not let your spirits droop, my friend, do not let them droop!" Oh how well I understand you, for you are—me . . .

Just a little more, just one more effort, just one more wave of your wings and you will be . . . in the unattainable heights! And then let them curse you down below, let them laugh at you, let them be envious, or let them bow down to you—it is all the same to you, just as it is to a god!

I am following your every step; I live because of your music, your happiness, my brother, my dear friend, for we are tainted with the same poison. Come to me, into my magic "palace" that I have built for you out of inspiration, out of the sun's rays . . .

Come to me, all of you—all of you who have wept, who have felt pain, who have suffered—for you are my children, for I have created all of you myself. For none of you have ever existed in the building across the way from me—not you, my sweet sister with your broken heart; nor you, old man, facing death; nor you, my indigent poet. It is my spirit that has given birth to you, because all I can do is create, just like nature itself. For I do not live, I only create . . . create . . .

And if my beloved were lying dead right here beside me, then in one half of my heart I would be weeping and wailing, groaning and agonizing, while in the other half—the grief and the excruciating pain would be growing into a story . . .

And this is our curse, our happiness, our poison, and our calling!

The Engine Driver
(circa 1910)

A train . . . In a third class car sat two youths who did not distinguish themselves in any way from the rest of the passengers. They could have been tradesmen, or poor students without uniforms, or salesmen from a second-rate store; in a word, they belonged to the "proletariat." Both were dressed in well-worn jackets of an uncertain colour, cotton shirts—one blue, the other red—and pants that hung loosely over their boots.

The young man in the blue shirt was wearing a hard-hat. Small, blond, scrawny, and pale, he had faded eyes, a short bristly moustache, and trembling lips that he bit nervously while staring intently out the window. It was obvious that he was not looking at the fields and forests that stretched alongside the railroad track, because he kept his eyes turned in one direction, and his gaze did not shift. His hands, slender and heavily lined with taut blue veins, had a slight tremor, and his curved fingers kept opening and closing like the claws of a cat about to pounce on a mouse.

His companion, who wore a peaked cap without any markings, was quite different in appearance. Sitting upright, and looking healthier and more animated, he had broad shoulders, big grimy fists, strong jaws, and a round swarthy face that was beardless and seemed to be lightly sprinkled with soot. There was an amiable and candid expression in his large grey eyes, and he did not appear to be thinking about anything; instead, he kept himself amused by swinging his foot and making his boot creak softly.

When the conductor came through to check the tickets, this young man gave him a toothy grin and said: "Well, you know, there's no need to bother us—we're 'one of the family,' you know."

The blond man just waved his hand irritably without even raising his eyes, and the conductor walked past both of them.

One of the passengers was curious to know why the two youths were not asked to show their tickets.

"Well, we, you know, live not far from here," the youth with the sanguine temperament responded. "They know us, you know, on this particular run. We're engine drivers, you know. That is, he's an engine driver," he nodded his head at his blond comrade, "and I'm his assistant."

Everyone involuntarily turned to look with curiosity and respect at the blond youth. He was the kind of man who never attracted the attention of others, remaining unnoticed, just as the inner workings of a clock are not seen when you look at its face. Everyone knows and feels that within the clock everything is moving ahead, but who is in control of that movement? Is it the All-Seeing Eye in the halo of a triangle? Or is it just a diminutive man like this one who sits somewhere at the front of the steam locomotive between the unbearable heat on one side and the icy cold on the other, and on whose will, ability, and watchfulness depend the lives of thousands of people? Is he the one who bears a greater responsibility, perhaps, than a chieftain who leads thousands into battle, all the while either performing great deeds of bravery without realising it, or committing grave mistakes because of his seemingly insignificant rash acts?

"So then, you're an engine driver?" a passenger turned to the blond young man. "Tell us about it. Do tell us; it sounds very interesting."

"What's there to tell? Really, it's nothing," the youth responded, grimacing and speaking with a pronounced Polish accent.

"Well, how do you go about it? What do you do? How much are you paid—well, all the same . . ."

"Between forty and sixty *karbovantsi [dollars]* a month," the blond youth said, drumming his fingers on the bench.

"Where did you study to become an engine driver? You did have to study, didn't you? Really, what is it that you do? We don't know anything about it. Tell us, please." Everyone was interested now, and the passengers, smiling bashfully because of their ignorance and intrusiveness, crowded around the two young men.

"There are special railroad schools. Didn't you know that?" And the small man gave a short laugh.

The bigger youth laughed merrily.

Someone from the crowd said: "Yes, yes indeed, but what kind of a course is it? What kind of qualifications do you need? Do you need a general education as well?"

"What kind of morals?" a grey-headed man in an attractive overcoat inquired completely out of context. "That's what's interesting."

They were all staring at the two youths as one observes animals in a cage, with curiosity and a degree of uncertainty.

"As for me," the blond youth said, "I went to an applied science school until the sixth grade, and then I voluntarily left it and transferred here . . . It was the railroad that always fascinated me," he added.

"As for me," the swarthy youth guffawed, "I was just a simple stoker. I've had a scorched little head all my life."

"This is the second year that I've been driving a steam locomotive," the engine driver stated proudly, without waiting to be asked any more questions. He was obviously warming up to the conversation. "I already have a locomotive of my own. And now I'm on my way," his voice quivered like that of someone in love, "to look at a new steam locomotive that will be placed under my full control. It was assembled over there, in the station workshop, because, of course, many of the parts come from abroad—the wheels, the armature, the manometer, the regulator, and so on. Whatever it's called . . ." Without finishing what he was saying, he turned to stare out the window again; his eyelids were trembling, and a furrow appeared between his eyebrows.

"Well, is your work very tiring?" the passengers directed their question to the assistant; it appeared they did not want to trouble the engine driver.

"It all depends, you know . . . At times, of course, it's, you know, tedious . . ." This young man was not an orator. "They pile the work on you, you know, and sometimes you can't sleep for twenty-four hours at a stretch; then, you know, there's a fog in your eyes, red circles, and you shake all over . . . No! Enough's enough! But, you know, you get the urge to go on without sleeping or resting, because you're paid a special rate for every kilometre, and so you run up as many kilometres as you can." He stopped talking for a short while and then continued: "In the winter it's difficult to travel, you know—the cold pierces you on one side, while the fire, you know, tries to creep up to kiss you on the other side . . . Well, the devil take it! Ha-ha-ha!" He laughed loudly and merrily.

"Have you ever had an accident of any kind?"

"No," the swarthy youth replied curtly.

But the engine driver whispered softly, as if in a confessional, so that only those who were close to him could hear him. "Only once . . . There was a man . . . I drove over him. . . I saw him, but I drove over him . . . I couldn't stop." A spasm convulsed his face and a singular sorrow filled his eyes.

When the passengers heard about the murder that no one could call a crime, they all fell silent.

The silence lasted until the train began its approach to the station. On its way there, it had to go past some huge red brick buildings with black roofs and large windows covered with grates, behind which you could see the locomotives that were kept there. The entrances to some of the roundhouses were opened wide, and the locomotives, their copper parts shining resplendently, sailed quietly out of them over the rails. It was here that they were manoeuvred back and forth.

The engine driver pressed the hand of his comrade, and both of them moved closer to the window.

"There she is, my 'Ophelia,'" the engine driver said excitedly. There was a note of eagerness in his voice, and he referred to his new locomotive by name instead of using the number assigned to it.

"Where?" his assistant asked him.

"Well, can't you . . . Oh, the devil take it . . . Over there, the one with the wide head."

Annoyed, the engine driver did not respond to any more of his assistant's questions. He was all eyes now; he stared and stared, but could not get his fill of looking at this new locomotive which seemed to be, without doubt, the dearest thing in the world to him.

"She's beautiful, very beautiful . . . Well, we'll give her a try." This was all he said as he cracked his knuckles.

The locomotive was truly splendid. The only one with a wide funnel smokestack, it stood out among the others that had narrower smokestacks built in the newer fashion. Enveloped in clouds of steam like a bride in muslin, it flashed its copper components like a woman wearing a gold headdress, pierced the eye of the beholder, like a village beauty, with the red spokes of its wheels and the bright green of its tenders, and flaunted its comely black head perched on a thin neck and wreathed in curls of black smoke. It was moving ahead slowly, gracefully, with a light rustle as if it were wearing a silk skirt, and then, when the engine driver who was steering it increased its speed, it made a knocking sound, rapidly spun its wheels like a stroboscope, and disappeared. The blond engine driver seated in the car and the one driving the locomotive scarcely managed to exchange greetings during the brief moment when the locomotive engulfed the approaching train with its hot breath and blew its terrifying whistle as a greeting to its future lord and master.

"Hoity-toity! Just look at the airs she's putting on!" the assistant laughed. "She doesn't even want to look at us . . . the beauty!"

"That's fine, we'll tame her; she'll obey us," the engine driver smiled contentedly.

They talked about the locomotive as if it were a living being, a real person. And it would have been difficult to do otherwise— it quivered and was so full of life and power, that you did not want to believe that it was not moving of its own accord, pushing onwards, ever onwards, conquering and subduing everything in its path, and announcing, with its presence, the progress of mankind that demands so many sacrifices as it leads us into unknown and wonderful countries, while distancing us from those times when people were not aware of the power of steam and had not experienced rapid motion—when they still envied the speed of a horse's gallop.

The Artful Man
(circa 1910)

On a corner bench of a stuffy, third-class railway car packed with passengers, sat a thin, sad-looking young woman, dressed in an old dark coat and an outmoded hat. Probably a teacher or a governess on her way to her first interview about a position advertised in a newspaper, she did not suspect that fate might cast her into a dark kingdom of evil and human injustice from which there could be no return . . .

It was difficult to breathe, for it seemed that there was absolutely no air in the coach—it had been replaced by the smoke that drifted in thick clouds under the ceiling, the pungent odour of garlic, and the breathing of several dozen people crowded together. To make matters even worse, the windows could not be opened to let in fresh air; the double-hung windows were tightly sealed.

With the exception of the young woman and an artful man who was sitting across from her with his two children, all the passengers in the coach were Jews. Some of them, having donned their multicoloured prayer shawls and fastened their forelocks on their temples, mumbled their prayers; assiduously licking the index fingers of their right hands as they turned the pages of their soiled prayer books, they continually raked their thick beards with their left hands. Others were eating a greyish mixture; they kneaded it with their fingers and, after every mouthful, took a bite of bread. Still others were smoking and conversing among themselves, and the distinctive guttural sounds of their language prevailed in the coach.

"So, we've buried their mother, and now we're travelling," the artful man unexpectedly addressed his vis-à-vis. And he nodded at the two children squirming beside him.

One of them—a boy of about seven, in a pink shirt and a felt cap—was standing beside the window. Pressing his forehead to the cool pane, he did not step away from it for a second.

The second one, a two-year-old child with a broad, pasty face, and dressed in a shirt cuffed up to its armpits, was lying on the floor among the cigarette butts.

"Well, what am I to do with them—with these children? Where am I to go with them? It's a great misfortune! Their mother has died—yes, yes, she's died!" the artful man lamented once more after a short pause.

And he leaned over towards his neighbour.

The young woman looked at the man with a mixture of anxiety and sympathy, but did not say anything.

"Hey, Vanka." The man, having received no response from her, turned to the smaller of his two sons, who was chewing a piece of bread he had found on the floor. "Do you want a little bun? Do you?"

The child crawled towards him.

"Oh, just you wait and see; when we come to a station—I'll buy you a little bun . . . Oh, alas and alack—the grim reality of being an orphan! O my po-o-o-or little o-o-orphans!" he drawled. "Oh, it's quite obvious, my dear young lady—yes, it is—that you're probably an o-o-orphan too, my lady . . ."

And he lurched, seemingly accidentally, in the direction of the young woman.

She shuddered and turned pale, but remained silent. A feeling of revulsion for this man and his grief swept over her.

They pulled into a station.

An announcement was heard beyond the window: "The train departs in ten minutes."

The artful man got off the train.

When he returned after the second bell, he was unsteady on his feet and staggered from one side of the car to the other.

Vanka, catching sight of his father, stretched out his little hands to him and wailed: "Daddy! Daddy!"

"There's no bun for you, my little fellow, none at all!" the man said.

The child began howling.

"Now, now, what's wrong with you? A b-b-bun," the father, speaking with difficulty, picked the child up in his arms. Then, lying down on the bench, he placed him on his chest.

Vanka began yanking his father's beard and mussing his hair; forgetting all about the bun, he was now laughing uproariously. The artful man, smiling a gentle, drunken smile, was loudly slapping the little boy's bare back. And then he suddenly fell asleep and began to snore.

The child once again crawled down to the floor.

"The poor children! What unfortunate children!" the young woman thought. "Their mother has died, and their father is a drunkard."

She felt pity for them, but when Vanka crawled up to her and clutched at the hem of her skirt—probably in an effort to stand up— she gently freed it and moved away . . .

The Little Nun
(circa 1910)

Very early one morning, not far from the station of Narva on the Baltic rail line, two nuns entered our coach. They emerged from a group of nuns who, with their incessant buzzing, their bustling about, and their black garments, called to mind flies crowded together in a glass.

When the first bell sounded, they all gave the same startled jump and then quickly began to make the sign of the cross, blessing themselves and each other. A chorus of diverse voices could be heard: "Christ be with you!"

Then the two nuns who were travelling began to ascend the steps leading up to the coach, while those who were seeing them off moved in closer to the train, craning their necks to find the window through which they could see their friends. Upon entering the coach, the two nuns scrambled to find seats and, in their haste, overlooked a number that were empty.

I moved a little closer to the window, leaving them the end of my bench.

One of them, a nun advanced in years and with a full face that resembled a waxed golden apple—completely white but tinged with yellow—greeted me politely, softly murmuring: "Christ be with you."

Then, instead of sitting down, she asked me if I would let them by to the window to have a look. I moved to one side to give them passage, and both of them, flattening themselves like Egyptian statues with their bodies *en face* and their heads and feet in profile, pressed themselves against the window and continued their conversation with the nuns who were standing down below by the coach.

I did not pay much attention to what was being said. Only an occasional, uninteresting snippet of conversation reached me: "In the second yard, to the left . . . Don't forget to take a kerchief!

The book is over there . . . If the Lord is willing . . . It will be a good hour or so . . . Well, Godspeed! Godspeed! We'll wait, if the Lord will be so kind . . . Make sure you don't tarry there too long, for without you we simply can't . . . So pick more, don't be lazy! The Lord will not forsake you; Christ is our Saviour!"

The second bell rang and, finally, the third, and the train, swaying slightly and clacking rhythmically over the joints in the rails, began to pull away.

The shrieking voices of the nuns could be heard in the distance: "Christ be with you! Mother of God, our Protectress!"

But as the rumbling and the distance increased, it became impossible to distinguish the words.

My nuns were still standing at the window, and the one who had her back turned to me was chortling and speaking energetically: "Oh, that Sister Marekhva! Wouldn't you know it— she even begrudged us a little teapot for the road. I swear to God, it's true!"

"Well, and as for Mother Mytrokhvaniya—wouldn't you know it—she almost burst with anger that she wasn't chosen to go and do the picking," said the other nun, the one for whom I had made room beside me. There was no laughter in her voice, however, only overtones of anger and triumph.

"Well, it's too bad! Let them sit in the cloister for a while. They can't always do all the travelling."

The first one laughed again, and then both of them turned around to settle down on the seats.

The older, heavy-set nun with the yellowish face I had observed earlier, but the other one . . .

How could I have failed to notice her? Probably, because I pay very little attention to nuns in general. But now, having glanced at this second, smaller nun, my heart was seized with anguish.

"Oh, God! Can it be possible?" I asked myself. "Such a pretty face, so fine, so delicate, without a single blemish—like the first white blossom of an anemone; such delightful dimples that flit across her cheeks and tiny chin, and then disappear once again; such wonderful eyes, cheerful, carefree, and clear; and such supple movements . . .

"And then—there's the black clothing, the renunciation, the oblivion, a living death!

"No! It cannot be! It's as if a butterfly with brightly coloured, variegated wings has fallen into pitch-black ink!"

I immediately invited her to sit beside me. I wanted to strike up a conversation with her and uncover her secret—for I was certain that she harboured some kind of secret.

Notwithstanding the older nun's whispered warning—"Move away. He's a man!"—the younger one casually and cheerfully sat down beside me.

I started speaking: "You're so young." She appeared to be about eighteen. "How did you end up—how could you end up in a convent?"

She did not seem to understand, not so much my question, as the astonishment, the alarm that resonated in it.

"What do you mean 'young'? Why, there are many young ones like me—an entire aviary! Anyway, I've been in the cloister since I was little. My mother made a vow, because for many years God had not given her any children. So, when she was carrying me, she promised me to God and, after I was born, the Lord sent her three more children to gladden her heart."

She said all this very calmly and evenly, the way a clear stream flows, without any resentment or ill-will towards her mother who, without asking her, had locked her up forever in a cage, removed her from life, from the world.

"But aren't you bored in the convent?"

"Bo-o-ored?" she drawled. "Why? No, how could one be? We're always embroidering, or stitching quilts. Everything we make is very beautiful."

And the word "beautiful" was drawn out in the most delightful way as she pursed her dainty little mouth.

"Quite recently we embroidered a bride's trousseau for the daughter of a wealthy merchant. I tell you, the batiste was as fine as a cobweb . . . It was all done in white embroidery. We embroidered rosebuds and forget-me-nots . . .

"And, O Mother, Most Holy Mother of God! You should see how we embroider the chalice cloths and the icons. They're all gold—and so beautiful! There are times when we embroider so much with gold that our eyes sparkle with it. You simply can't leave it; you're at it from dawn to dusk, but you can't stop working at it! And when the face of the Holy Mother, and her hair, and all the rest of it is turned out by your hands, and it all appears alive, only the lips can't talk . . . Oh! It's wonderful!"

She sighed, smiled, and clapped her hands, which peeked out from narrow sleeves buttoned at the wrist. These small hands were exceptionally fine, and her fingers ended in narrow, pink tips that resembled tiny grapes.

I also sighed, but for another reason.

She continued talking, but in a more reserved and solemn tone. "I haven't taken my final vows yet . . . But soon, quite soon, I will accept God's blessing . . . I will finally be worthy of it . . . Mother Svydonya," she added, pointing at the older nun, "has promised me . . ."

She did not complete what she was saying, as if she had run out of breath. Her eyes became wider and even more beautiful, and just a bit hazy, as if they had been overcast by a light dust-cloud.

I wanted—I was ready—to scream and wail, just as I would scream if I saw someone being cut down, murdered in the street in broad daylight . . .

She was speaking in a voice that was becoming increasingly distant and quiet: "How beautiful it is in our church! O my God, my Lord! You should see it! The icons are ancient and dark; only the eyes are visible, and the gold gleams . . . The windows are narrow and way up high, wa-a-ay, wa-a-a-ay up high over your head . . .

"And when our sisters sing, well, you have to hear it! When they sing, it's as if God's angels were flying above you, touching you with their divine fingers . . . Oh!"

She fell into deep thought.

"Blessed are they who believe," I reflected.

At that moment, the train was passing through Narva. All the passengers who were not sleeping rushed to the windows.

From the railway embankment, only one end of the waterfall could be seen. But even though it did not reveal itself in all its beauty, the part that was visible was exceptionally brilliant!

Imagine some latticework, a most delicate veil with a whole host of water droplets as fine as a cloud of dust. The droplets rise into the air and then drop down again. Entire tapestries of water lift themselves upwards, remain suspended for a moment in a strangely heightened state of tension, and then, once again, tumble downwards. Add to all of this the pink rays of the sun in the east that permeate the water and turn it rosy, trimming it at the edges with a searing gold, and . . . you will understand how beautiful all this was . . .

Even I, a vigorous champion of the arts, was moved by the sight; I, a person who values art more than nature. For what is there to be said about nature, when even the best musicians are able to find only two basic melodies in nature: the warbling of the nightingale, and the rumbling of thunder . . .

Or take the field of industry. What is there in nature that can compare to those wonderful silk veils, tulle, and gauze that factory workers provide in endless quantities for women's clothing? It is true—nature has given multicoloured wings to butterflies, and white petals to lilies, but how little there is, after all, that can be valued more than art! But still, even I, an ardent admirer of art, was enraptured for a moment by this sight, and my little nun was even more enthralled—she became ecstatic.

"O the wonders of the Lord!" she could only whisper as she crossed herself.

Forgetting that I was a man, she tugged at my sleeve to make me look at the view.

Then she ran up to a little curly-haired boy who was shouting: "Mummy, mummy, look! Why is it leaping? Who is lifting it up?"

The little nun hugged him, kissed him impetuously, and said: "My dear child, it's one of God's wonders!"

Reskin says that the ability to experience ecstasy is the greatest talent of all. In it is found joy, the power of life, and the mystery, the promise, and the guarantee of happiness. Yes, if it can develop freely, but in this case . . .

In Narva, both nuns got off the train.

The young one swiftly and nimbly gathered together some bundles wrapped in store-bought kerchiefs and said her goodbyes to me: "Christ be with you!"

As she ran out of the coach, she urged the older nun to hurry. Glancing at her impishly and animatedly with her cheerful dark eyes, she said: "Well, now we'll have some tea, my dear mother

. . . Oh yes we will! With some consecrated bread, and it's fresh bread at that! Sister Marekhva tried to pass off some stale bread on us, but I'm no dummy . . . Ha-ha-ha! I swapped it!"

Following them with my eyes, I was left with my own thoughts, with my own questions.

"Will she be able to endure it? Won't this end in a catastrophe?

"What will happen when she withers like a flower that is placed between the pages of a book, when she loses her spirit, when her fate becomes that of a precious ring cast senselessly into the sea?

"It's sheer madness and savagery!"

A Brief Moment
(circa 1910)

At a table in the tavern of Moshka the Jew sat a couple of old in-laws who found it more convenient to drink there than at home. Between them stood a half-empty bottle of whiskey and, on a plate next to it, lay some salted cucumbers and a crust of bread. In the corner above the men burned a small metal lamp that flickered like a distant star.

As they sat at the narrow, grubby table, the two in-laws cut a comical figure; leaning their elbows heavily on the table, they propped up their heads on their hands and, facing each other, drew so closely together that their noses almost touched . . . The plates, the bottles, the bread, and the shot glasses stood on either side of them, to the left and to the right, and, with every passing moment, they proposed a drink to each other.

"Well, then! Well, old buddy, let's have one more glass, another small glass, another fine glass . . ."

And their words were so tender and so sweet, and their smiles so amicable, one would have thought there were no people happier than they . . .

Suddenly, a small Jewish child ran through the room shouting: "Hey, you drunkards! Get out of here! Daddy says it's late; the New Year has arrived."

And truly, something on the wall in the adjoining room crackled furiously, like fat sputtering in a frying pan, and then clacked noisily twelve times.

"Right away, my little one, right away," responded Khoma, one of the in-laws. He was an ugly, flabby-faced, beardless man with a long moustache, and his head, covered with closely cropped hair like that of a soldier, was so grey that it looked almost silver.

Continuing to speak in a most amiable voice, he turned once again to his companion: "Yes indeed, Akhvanasiy, old buddy, they're saying that the New Year has arrived. Will you have another drink?"

"Why, of course," the other old man said in some surprise. Akhvanasiy, a small lean man, devoured by life as a scythe is eaten away by rust, had a head that was covered with curls, and both his hair and his beard had remnants of straw and feathers stuck in them, like wool flaked with bits of straw.

"Well, then, I salute you with the New Year!" Khoma said animatedly.

He poured both of them a drink and leaned forward to exchange kisses with his buddy.

"It doesn't much matter if it's a new one, or an old one," Akhvanasiy said.

They exchanged kisses, downed their whiskey with palpable pleasure, and took a good bite of the salted cucumbers. Then they hiccoughed . . . and fell silent.

Khoma fell into thought.

"I remember," he said, "when I served as a colonel's orderly, yes indeed . . . They were celebrating the New Year . . . Oh, dear mother of mine, what a ball that was! There were ever so many guests—crowds of guests! They were drinking wine—the one that foams, that sparkles . . . They were ever so happy, you see, that the New Year had arrived; they greeted one another with the New Year, and with new happiness in the New Year . . ."

"It doesn't mean a thing! Even if it is new—so what?" Akhvanasiy did not seem to understand. "But let's have another drink!"

And they had another drink.

"How strange you are," Khoma said.

And he began to explain to his in-law, gently and in great detail, that what was new was not old, and that what was old, was not new!

"So what?"

"So, you see, it means that what is new, is better."

"Better? What do you mean?"

"Well, it means that the New Year will be better than the one that has just ended. You see, that's the hope that everyone has, and that's why they all rejoice and salute everyone!"

"Salute them with what?"

"What do you mean, with what? With the New Year, of course!"

"Come on, Khoma, pour us another glass."

They downed another drink.

Akhvanasiy's tongue did not want to obey him, or perhaps the whiskey prevented him from thinking and speaking as quickly as Khoma could, and that was why he began to speak slowly, mewing softly like a crane.

"Yes, yes . . . It's the New Year. How can it be any better than the one that has just ended . . . The old people grow older, while the children grow bigger and demand more food . . . But the soil produces less every year and . . . it is divided into smaller and smaller parcels . . . Why, take even me, for example . . . Our father had a strip of land that was about twenty yards wide, and there were four of us . . . So, how much land did each of us get? Five yards, right? Now I too have four sons, so . . . How much will they get now?"

Akhvanasiy was no longer capable of figuring this out by himself, and his in-law Khoma was immersed in his own thoughts. More than likely he was thinking about the colonel who once thrashed him right on New Year's Eve for supposedly not shining his boots properly, and all the guests had already assembled for supper, and the room was aflame with candles . . .

Akhvanasiy continued mewing slowly: "It's fine for you, old buddy; you're a vagabond."

"Yes, yes indeed—I'm all alone in this world," Khoma said gloomily.

"You have no land, and you have no family—all your kin died while you served in the army. And so when you drink, no one says a word to you . . . That's good . . . But as for me . . . Oh, how she rails at me! Oh, she really lets me have it for drinking. But how am I not to drink? What am I to do now? All of our older children have died off, and only the little ones are left . . . But will I be able to give those hungry children as much food as they want? Am I to produce some land out of nowhere for them?" The old man hung his head dejectedly. "It doesn't matter at all if it's the Old Year or the New Year, I'm still caught in the same predicament. What the devil do I need this New Year for? Oh, yes, that's how it is, my dear little whiskey!"

And weeping, they washed their faces with their drunken tears.

And weeping, they embraced and exchanged kisses.

One Night

(circa 1910)

They were sitting in the darkest corner of the railroad car, partially screened by the overhanging top berth. The light from the lantern positioned above them did not reach them. Their figures, dimly lit by another lantern that hung at the end of the coach over the opposite door, were barely discernible; their faces appeared to be almost as dark as their clothing.

She was weeping bitterly and unceasingly, and he was not able to console her.

The corpulent conductor walked past them frequently, and, every time, he aimed the greenish, flickering light of his lantern at them. Gazing intently at their faces in the darkness, he wore the sympathetic but slightly bemused smile with which one smiles at lovers.

"The dear ones aren't quarrelling; they're only entertaining themselves," he thought. And he walked on through the car, keeping an eye on them, and waiting to see the end of this comedy of love.

But . . . this was not what he imagined—not at all . . . Oh no, not at all.

She was not weeping because of him, nor for him. She was weeping for her deceased husband. Tears were coursing down her face involuntarily, endlessly. Her shoulders trembled, her breathing was ragged, and her handkerchief was soaked.

"It's only today that I'm crying like this," she finally said shamefacedly through her tears. "Ordinarily, I seldom cry. Today I was there—among the fir trees in the valley . . . On the crest, the rosy evening sun lit the fir tees . . . Every needle on their tips was golden, but down below, they were dark, very dark, almost black . . . We used to sit there. How he loved those trees, and how he loved that spot! He was . . . Yes, he was, was, was, was!"

She repeated this word several times in the same tone of voice. Her sobs became even more distressing and, exhausted by her weeping, she unthinkingly leaned her wet cheek against his bowed one. Her burning tears seeped into his eye, and his eyes also filled, but he did not say a word—he remained silent, listening, and did not attempt to quell her distress.

"How could this have happened? How can this be? I'm still waiting for him. How can this be?" she asked in despair and, numb with weariness, reached out her hand to find his.

At first he did not realize what she wanted, and it was only after a moment that he gave her his hand.

She squeezed it lightly and let go of it immediately. Drawing back, she sat up straight, calmed down, and gazed in the other direction with unseeing eyes. After a moment, she ceased her sobbing, as if she had found some inner strength—the capability of showing fortitude and endurance, and of remaining silent and bowing to fate . . .

"Yes, my poor friend, my dear companion, he is unforgettable! I too am unable to understand how this could have happened! Why, for what reason, is he no longer with us? I can't believe it, and no one will believe it," he murmured, sighing heavily.

At this moment, the song of a tipsy labourer could be heard from the adjoining compartment.

> "Oh, when I wa-a-a-as a footloose boy,
> The playmate of the see-ee-eedling tree-ee-ees . . ."

Her entire body shuddered like a tree being felled, and she whispered timidly: "Oh, there are so many memories! Everything . . . everything reminds me of him . . . He's everywhere . . . absolutely everywhere. He . . . O my dear one!"

These last words she uttered somewhat bashfully, but with a great tenderness. "This song—it also reminds me of him! He had a talent for comedy; he could mimic everybody, and he knew so many of these silly, popular songs."

She shuddered, and he embraced her shoulder, placing his arm over the heavy warm shawl in which she had bundled herself.

She started to cry once again, but controlled herself almost immediately.

Then she glanced at a young woman who was sleeping on the bench across from them, and a thought suddenly struck her: "If this woman were not sleeping, he would not have embraced me; if this woman were not sleeping, I would not permit it . . . But then, why not?"

She sat quietly, supported by his arm; huddling and nestling up to him, she sighed deeply, as she silently recalled her dear departed husband and his love for her: "He was so tender! So loving! No one else could love like that . . . I meant to say . . . could love me like that . . . No, no! No one! Never!"

"No, my precious darling, someone can, someone can!" he thought. But he kept these words to himself—for he could never have spoken them, not even on pain of death.

She wanted to talk endlessly about "him," to talk about his beauty, his love, her grief, and their love—something she had never spoken of to another living soul. Her bashfulness melted like the snow, and she talked, and talked, and talked.

This was the first time he had ever heard her openly express her feelings and bare her soul. Formerly, he had seen her as a proud, cold, distant, and sarcastic woman—now he saw her as a grieving one.

"He was so loving, so tender, but I was so cold—at times I seemed to be made of marble. Oh yes, I was so cruel! In all the time we lived together, I did not tell him even once how handsome he was!" She flushed, and shame flooded her face.

"But then . . . I . . . You know? I do not like 'love' . . . I want . . . I wanted friendship, but it turned out differently! We were friends, just like you and I are . . . But suddenly, unexpectedly—it was 'love' . . . I don't know . . . This disturbed me . . ."

She wanted to free herself from his embrace, but she did not know how to do this without offending him.

The conductor, walking past them with his lantern once again, gave them another look, as if he understood everything.

After he disappeared from view, she said: "Who does he take us for? You know, he's getting the wrong idea about us."

"Yes, yes, I know," he answered calmly.

"So what should we do about it?"

"Nothing at all," he responded, still more calmly.

"I find it offensive," she said, jerking her shoulders. "He's interpreting our situation incorrectly. He thinks that . . . that there's something between us . . . and everyone is thinking that! This is quite impossible!"

"Well, let them! And there is something to it," he said quietly, reverently, in the way in which believers say their prayers. And then he added passionately: "But you go on talking—talk, talk some more."

Yes, it was possible. But only here—at night, in a railroad car, without people, without solid ground, as if they were in the chalice of a huge flower that protected them from everything with its petals, its fragrance.

She disengaged herself carefully from his arm, rose to her feet, and pressed herself closely to the cold, misty window.

Dawn was breaking. The fading stars were disappearing, one after the other, in the pale sky. An opalescent fog was rising, taking on the outlines of fantastic, nimble figures that flew in a frenzied, joyful dance, scarcely touching the ground with their feet. Their garments were gradually turning rosy in the light of the morning star, but they continued to emerge and rise upwards in a never-ending dance. Grief gives birth to joy. Tears give rise to smiles. And, in the same way, the fog brings forth these floating visions.

"Nevertheless, it's time for us to go to sleep!" she said, turning towards him with a light smile.

"I don't want to sleep," he replied. "How about you? It would be best if we didn't go to sleep tonight, for it's pointless to sleep. Isn't that true, my friend?" He smiled kindly.

"Yes, indeed! But I want to lie down for a while, and so should you."

She began to prepare a bed for herself on the upper berth.

He wanted to help her climb into it, but she abruptly dissuaded him: "No, no! Why are you doing this? I'm not going to help you! I can manage quite nicely by myself."

And she scrambled up spryly into the top berth.

He also made himself comfortable in the upper berth above the young woman who was sleeping on the lower one. For a long time, they remained silent. They were lying side by side, like Tristan and Isolde. But there was no sword between them, and there was no love between them . . .

He felt infinitely fortunate, fortunate to be experiencing a night that millions of people never have the chance to experience—a pure night, a holy night. He was fortunate to be able to share her grief, to have her place her trust in him, as in a friend, a brother. He was fortunate that, for the very first time, he did not see the woman in this woman. He did not love her, but all the same, he would have renounced everything—his family and his children whom he loved more than life itself—for her, for her friendship. He would have disowned them and followed her to the ends of the earth, to death . . . He felt fortunate that he was human . . .

This night was the first time that she stopped thinking about suicide, about death, and she wished—so hard that it hurt—that her dearest and most wonderful one who was no longer with her on this earth could see her with their friend and rejoice along with her, for she had found someone who understood her . . .

If she had tried to express what they were feeling, she would not have been able to find the words, for there are no words that are gentle like a shadow, swift as light, beautiful as the stars— words capable of capturing the feeling of kindness, the feeling of truth, the feeling of freedom that filled her heart on this night.

They lay there for a long time with closed eyes. It seemed to her that he had fallen asleep.

She quietly slid down, wrapped herself tightly in her warm shawl, and walked towards the door on the right.

He quickly raised himself and said: "Don't go that way!"

She silently turned around and went to the left. When she returned to her place, he seemed to be sleeping.

But how deeply his solicitude had touched her! Who knew what he had been concerned about—the drunk man in the next coach, or the filthy conditions there. But he had been afraid for her, for whatever reason, and he had revealed his concern so simply, so "soberly," and at the same time, so naively, that she smiled to herself.

She lay down and closed her eyes, but could not fall asleep. Glittering cushions sparkled in the air before her eyes. Her entire field of vision was a web of reddish-gold, and a floating pattern of blue flowers emerged on it. Finally, against this backdrop, the head of a little girl appeared, the daughter of the man who was lying in the berth next to hers—a girl with charming blue eyes, half-opened rosy lips, and two attractive, tightly woven braids hanging down her back. She recalled the unexpected and touching love that this child had shown her, a love she had done nothing to elicit, and which, perhaps, was extended to her simply because she was her father's daughter . . .

"You aren't sleeping, are you?" he suddenly asked her. "I can sense it . . ."

Instead of replying, she began to recite a poem without opening her eyes:

> "Flowers sparkle down below,
> Stars twinkle up above;
> My dreams, pure and golden,
> Fly swiftly, ever so swiftly,
> From the flowers below to the stars,
> From below to above, and back again —
> From the stars up above to the flowers . . ."

"Whose is this?" he raised himself on his elbow, listening as if he were spellbound.

"It's one of mine!" she said. "But you know, I wrote verses only once in my life, at the time that we were . . . engaged . . . Not before that, and not afterwards . . . And now I don't understand, and I can't understand . . . not a single verse. Isn't this strange?"

"Yes indeed!"

"Here's another one:

> A train . . . to the winterless south of impulse . . .
> Clouds of smoke . . .
> A train . . . superfluous scrutiny . . .
> Thin streaks of steam.
> A train . . . where a beloved's profile is . . .
> O absurd inquisitiveness!
> O you dreams, dreams—without end!
> She is in mourning. In her eyes is a heartfelt grief.

Fate, it seems, has not granted her good fortune . . .
And next to her, a little girl is laughing . . .
Droves of yellow and blue railroad cars . . .
Once again a wondrous, beautiful picture . . .
Who, where? Thoughts flow like water.
Where are you from, my bright angel?
Next to me is a bridegroom with a black moustache . . .
A wedding ring gleams on his finger."

He was looking at her, and he could not say if she was beautiful or not, but to him she appeared to be out of the ordinary.

"Of course, a ring!" she repeated, gazing thoughtfully at her hand on which there were two wedding rings—on her second and fourth fingers. "Do you know how I came to own this ring?"

"Tell me! I noticed quite some time ago that you had it, but how did you get it? It ought to be too big for you . . . Tell me, tell me!"

He laughed, or rather, he did not laugh, but she seemed to hear laughter in his voice and . . . this was enough for her.

"He had very small hands," she replied coolly, and, glancing at his large hand, she fell silent.

He did not dare to pursue the matter.

Eventually, he fell asleep, exhausted but happy. She did not sleep at all.

In the morning, they arrived at the station where they were to part. She was supposed to go on—he had to remain behind.

When the hour of parting came, she quickly dashed about the platform holding her hand to her chest and breathing heavily: "Oh my heart, it's begun bothering me since the time that . . ." she did not finish what she was saying.

Turning around abruptly, she extended her hand to him: "Farewell! Thank you!"

He feverishly began kissing her hand and would not let it go.

Trembling like a butterfly, she gently touched his forehead with her lips.

"Allow me to kiss you," he said, and he kissed her tenderly and fearfully on the lips.

She stood, cold and unmoving, like a marble statue and, tightly pressing her lips together, accepted this kiss, for she trusted him; she believed in him, believed in his friendship.

Afterwards, she moved away and, without a backward glance, began walking towards the coach.

He ran after her, embraced her, and kissed her again—this time with hot, damp lips.

She shuddered, recoiled, and rushed headlong to the coach. Leaping up to the wooden platform, she gripped the steel railings convulsively and unthinkingly, her distraught eyes staring into the distance.

She did not see that her friend was following the train as it departed from the station.

He was walking swiftly, waving his hat incessantly, high above his head.

Why Do They Laugh at Him?
(1914)

But they do laugh at him, they really do!

They began to laugh at him when he was little, and even now, after he has turned grey—they still laugh at him.

But why? It is true that his round head is perched on a scrawny neck like a good-sized head of cabbage, or a pumpkin, or a big bowl; and it is true that he is small, frail, and short—but so what? Is that not how it is sometimes? It is true that his ears stick out on both sides of his head "like the wings of a little bat," as granny used to say, but so what? There are lots of cases like that!

Is it because the hair on his head is all matted like wool? Well, no, it is not because of that . . . Or because his round eyes bulge comically? More often than not, he lowers them when he needs to figure something out, and he stands like that for a long, long time, hanging his head and scratching the nape of his neck.

When he finally does figure things out, he raises his eyes, and a charming smile—a strange, bashful, artless smile, that is seen only on children's faces, but which he retains even in his old age—flits across his countenance. At such times his face, even though it is quite homely—just a simple peasant's face, grey, blotched, and infrequently shaved—becomes most beautiful for a moment, as if an exotic flower had come into bloom.

And then he usually says: "Uh-huh, that's it . . . How's that again?"

Perhaps they laugh at him because he is dimwitted? Well, he is not completely dimwitted, because he is good at all sorts of manual trades.

No one taught him how to thatch roofs—but he thatched the roof on his house; and no one taught him how to build fences—but he builds them. And he constructed a shed for himself without the help of any carpenters. It is true that he built it clumsily, sluggishly, slowly. He either bustled about—scraping away busily like a chicken with its claw—without actually accomplishing anything, or he simply stood and scratched the back of his head until he hit upon what he should do next. Then he would say: "Uh . . . uh . . . uh . . . I should have . . ."

And he would redo things ten times over. But he worked diligently, without stopping—from morning to evening, and from evening until morning, like a bee or an ant that drags a burden much heavier than its own weight.

He was not lazy; nor was he timid. Do you think anyone in the village would climb up the tall poplars when nests—at a *kopiyka [penny]* per nest—were being torn down in the lord's orchard? But he clambered up a tree that was so tall that the cap fell off your head when you looked up at it—and the tree was as brittle as crispy pastry.

When the neighbours saw what he was doing, they shouted: "Hey, Martin! You're going to orphan your children!"

But he kept climbing upwards, not the least bit afraid. And when the lord dug a deep well out in the steppe—he wanted water that was crystal clear and as cold as an ice floe—would anyone else have descended to clean the bottom of it?

He worked like this wherever he went, and he never refused to do anything. He did his own work and that of others; he did whatever he was asked to do, without question. He worked, because work was his whole life.

He worked, but did not grow rich, because he was so clumsy, so retiring, so small, with such a big head and bulging eyes. He had been that way as a child, and he remained that way when he grew old . . . And they laughed at him!

During his childhood, the boys laughed at him when he grazed horses with them in the steppe at night. For in the spring—when the steppe reels with the fragrance of its white and yellow and red flowers; when the nightingale trills its sweet, enchanting songs; and when the moon generously scatters its silvery rays on the earth—he would lie on his stomach and, cradling his round, matted head in his hands, gaze goggle-eyed for hours on end into the distance.

And he would listen for hours on end, cocking his tiny batlike ears. Sometimes it was even difficult to snap him out of his trance; but the boys chattered, shouted, and roared with laughter, and finally one of them would poke him in the side and yell right in his ear: "Martin, are you deaf?"

"Huh?" he would say, as he came out of his trance.

He always stared like that, as if he saw something that others could not see; and he listened, as if he could hear something others could not hear . . .

It seemed that he was not looking at the moon, but through it—at something far beyond it; and he was not listening to the nightingale's songs, but to voices that were a long way off in the distance . . .

But he never boasted to any of the boys about what he saw or heard beyond what they could see with their own eyes and hear with their own ears.

Occasionally, one of the boys would ask him: "Well, why are you staring like that, all pop-eyed, at something that can't be seen?" Or: "What do you see out there?"

"I'm just looking," he would say, blushing furiously. Or: "You see, it's this . . ."

But what "this" was—he would never say. But his usual charming smile would light up his entire face, and his countenance would appear to bloom . . .

He could not say what "this" was, but he could feel it all around him—and even within him. It was something big, most beautiful, and—like the dew on a flower, like honey in a honeycomb—it filled his entire soul; it filled his soul to the brim, to the very brim!

Some days, Martin would rise before dawn on a summer morning and take his sheep to join the flock. This is when everything—the grass and the trees, all damp and grey with the morning dew—is awakening from sleep; when everything underfoot is still misty, while in the sky, the stars—that rejoiced all night like young maidens at a dance—are beginning to fade, and the pink dawn gradually embraces everything from below, covering the subdued yellow and green streaks that were formerly there; and the pale blue background takes on a deeper hue, and finally . . . the sun lifts itself upwards, while the silvery clouds—like tiny, silver scales—cover half the sky . . .

At times like these, Martin would take off his cap, cross himself, and whisper softly: "Oh! This . . . O my God . . . O God!"

And the same thing happens in winter, when the earth is covered with the soft down of white swans; and the trees, muffled in delicate wool, bend to one another, nestle closely together, and bewitch and enchant one's eyes like a dream, like a fairy tale!

And in the autumn, when the summer attire of the trees changes to gold—from a soft honey gold to the copper gold of a coin—and the black branches of the leafless trees cut into the clear, cold, glassy blue sky and are etched upon it.

And in the spring—the beautiful spring in which everyone takes delight! How lovingly one's soul is caressed, as orchards, blooming with pinkish white blossoms, captivate the heart and make it faint!

And as Martin lay under a cherry tree on a spring Sunday—on that day he only tended to the livestock, because after all "it was a sin to work on a holy day"—and inhaled the sweetly scented air, he would think: "Is it really possible to quarrel, to fight, and to get drunk, when God gives all of us such . . . that . . . this . . . everything . . ."

His thought could go no further, but he could feel "this" deeply—ever so deeply—within himself, and his soul flamed before the Lord, like a votive lamp burning in front of an icon.

He also felt "this" in church, when young schoolboys, with their high-pitched, ringing voices, sang holy songs in the choir loft; and when the priest in gold—albeit old—vestments walked around the church and swung the censer so vigorously on its copper chains that the glowing coals were engulfed in a red circle, but did not fall out; and when the incense rose in clouds before the "gods," and the aroma spread throughout the church, mingling with the odour of wagon-grease and sheepskin coats; and when many hands, crossing themselves, quivered like the wings of birds flying in a wedge; and when the candles burned, flickering and fluttering like the tiny hearts of infants; and when the word of God resounded through the church and fell deeply into Martin's soul—like rye seeds into a soft furrow—even though he did not always fully comprehend it.

He was barely literate; a long time ago he had gone to school—for two winters—but he had not learned how to write. It was difficult for him to scrawl something that resembled his name, and he could read only "the Gospel," and no other book.

How this could be, I truly do not know, but I do know that he read the Gospel and knew it well. While serving in the army as a colonel's orderly, another conscript, also an orderly, but one who knew how to read and write better that he did, told him a lot about Jesus Christ—how He was born, how He lived, and how He died—and, when they parted, he even gave him his old Gospel book.

What impressed Martin most was the fact that Christ and His followers, the apostles, were ordinary people, plain simple folk "who were just like us."

And so Martin read the Gospel, or—who knows!—perhaps he recited it from memory—but how could he retain it all in his head?

He read and thought about what he was reading; he began to read wherever the book happened to open, and he always said: "I only know how to read the Gospel; I can't read anything else."

Everyone was amazed at this. How could this be? He apparently did not know how to read, but he truly could read the Gospel. His favourite parts were those that described Christ's suffering— how they had tortured Him, laughed at Him, roared with laughter, spat at Him, and beat Him, while crying out: "Guess who struck you!" And then, placing a wreath of thorns on His head, they had ridiculed Him and crucified Him.

He also liked some passages that he found difficult to understand, but which he knew contained profound, holy, and sublime words: "Blessed are the meek, for theirs is the Kingdom of Heaven . . ."

Martin had experienced "this" from his childhood years. When one of the boys offended him, he would just turn away silently and leave, and then he would hear the taunting laughter of the children and their shouts: "Lump of dough!" "God be with him!" These were his street nicknames, and everyone continued teasing him the same way when he grew old.

But, at the very moment that he was being teased, something warm would flood his soul, and it heartened him and filled him with a rosy light . . .

"Let them," Martin thought. "It doesn't matter; let them laugh. But as for me . . . I'll remain silent . . ."

It was in this manner that Martin's peers often laughed at him when they were all still children. And his brother Ivan—there were two brothers in their family, Martin and Ivan Horenko—laughed at him in the same way. Nimble, lively, alert, clever, good at everything, with an impudent smile on his thick, red lips—Ivan was the kind of person you did not fool around with. The girls liked him very much, but the boys feared him.

After he had grown up and completed his stint in the army, he returned home and, being well-educated, managed to wrap the entire community around his finger. He was put in the position of village secretary, and many bribes came his way. When he rented the lord's land for ten rubles per *hectare [2.5 acres]* he charged the villagers from fifteen to twenty rubles. He married a girl who was an only daughter, opened a shop in the village, and became very rich, whereas formerly he had been as poor as his brother Martin.

They each had inherited only two *hectares,* and with that you can feed only yourself and your family—nothing more! So Ivan not only laughed at Martin—he also scolded him; he scolded him soundly "as only he knew how." If Martin gave away something—whatever it was that he had, be it an apple, or a slice of bread, or whatever—to one of the other children, Ivan would become enraged: "Why did you give it away? You should have eaten it yourself, or at least given it to me, you stupid old cow!"

"Let it be," Martin would say. "You see, it's this way . . ."

"Oh sure, it's this way, and it's that way, you stupid, rotten, good-for-nothing. You don't have a clue as to what you're doing . . . You don't have any brains! If it were me, you wouldn't see me giving it away— no, you most certainly wouldn't!"

"But for me, it's like this . . . It's as if it were tastier this way," Martin would reply.

And then Ivan would roar with laughter like a madman, because even though he found his brother's stupidity and goodness annoying, he also found the idea funny—very funny indeed—that Martin, "without eating something," found it tastier than if he had eaten it . . .

But Ivan did not scold Martin—he only laughed at him—when he encroached on Martin's land while building himself a house. And Martin, disregarding the urging of his neighbours, just flung his hand out in a dismissive gesture and said: "Oh, God be with him! I don't want to sue him!" And after remaining silent for a short while, he added: "It is easier for a camel to pass through the eye of a needle than for a rich man to enter the Kingdom of Heaven . . ."

And Ivan, after hearing about this from others, generously gave Martin a stack of last year's straw—slightly rotten and gnawed by mice—to burn in his stove, because Martin had run out of fuel during the Lenten period.

In addition to his brother Ivan, Martin had a sister who never laughed at him, perhaps because she did not know how to laugh like other people, or perhaps because she was always laughing, laughing uproariously, screaming with laughter. She was known as "Crazy Natalka."

All one had to do was show Natalka a shiny necklace or a red ribbon, and she would begin to roar with laughter. Her wide mouth would stretch to her ears, her little grey eyes would leap with joy, her forehead would gather into tiny folds and, from her chest, a deep guffaw—"Ah haa . . . haa-haa-haa!"—would pour forth endlessly, boundlessly . . .

She had started to laugh like this as an infant. It did not matter if she happened to be staring at the stove where a fire was flaming and mutating into wonderful jagged stripes, all red at the bottom and white with blue edges on top, or if her mother handed her a greasy pancake. She would take the pancake and eat it, laughing so hard all the while, that the oil ran down her cheeks and chin. And her shirt and her hands got all greasy, but Natalka would continue to laugh until she finished eating the pancake . . .

Another time, she might cock her head and look at a bird that was flying in the sky; and once again there would be this unending, insane laughter . . . Everything shiny, red, or gold drove her into gales of laughter—poppies blooming in the field and illuminated by the sun; glass sparkling in windowpanes; a golden cross glittering on the bell tower; and the sun itself, all fiery in the sky.

And she laughed like this all her life, but she did not do anything, nor did she know how to do anything. And no one could ever teach her anything, even though she was not lazy.

She listened to what people said, but no matter what one tried to get her to do—she always did it backwards. When she spun, or weeded, or trimmed the tobacco plants—she did not do things the way others did them. She spun the thread in the opposite direction; pulled out, not the weeds, but the vegetables; and tore off the main leaves instead of the side shoots of the tobacco plants. She was scolded and beaten, and old women cast spells on her. All kinds of things were done to her—but nothing helped, because, as the saying goes: "She was born with a screw missing."

This was how she grew up, and even though she turned out to be a strapping young woman, she had to go begging. People gave her alms for Christ's sake, and they also gave her things because she sang in a way that touched their hearts. This was all that she knew how to do. It is true that she did not sing the songs that other girls sang, or those that beggars wail in the marketplace; she did not even sing with words.

It was not so much that she did not know how to talk, as the fact that she never talked with anyone; instead, she wailed—delightfully, exquisitely, like a flute, or an exotic bird. "Aaa . . . yu-it . . . ee-it" she would trill in a high-pitched, unnatural voice, and follow it with: "Oo . . . oo . . . oo . . . la . . . la . . . leet . . . krah . . . karrr . . ." in deep, low, unearthly tones.

If people did not see that it was a person who was singing, they listened attentively and wondered—fascinated by the strange sounds. Upon seeing that it was a young woman, they were struck dumb, but then would toss her a copper coin . . .

Martin liked his sister's singing more than anyone, and Natalka sang especially movingly for him in the dense thickets of the swamps. And he, in a shy, bashful way, would caress her warmly, patting her poor little head with its tangled, dishevelled hair. And at those times she cried—she wept, instead of laughing . . .

All the girls in the village also laughed at Martin when—as a youth—he worked alongside them during the harvest. They did not see him at their parties, because he never went to them. They laughed at him and teased him, calling him "an old boot," "a sack," "an idiot," "a wet rag," and the like.

One of the prettiest girls in the village also laughed at him—even though she was poor. Attractive and blond, she had milky white teeth and eyes that were opened as wide as the world. Her name was Motrya Kovalenko, and all the young men courted her, but every one of them met with a rebuttal. She laughed at Martin, but just the same, she presented him with her *rushnyky [embroidered linen ceremonial cloths]*. How did this happen? Why? It was like this. Martin never made passes at her, never hugged her tightly around the neck as if he wanted to cut off her head, as the other young men did; he only worked diligently. And he did Motrya's work for her as well; he did it out of the goodness of his heart.

Who knows how he managed to do both her work and his own, given his clumsy "rake-like" hands and the sluggishness of his overly large feet that, step by step, slowly, like curved runners on a sleigh, trudged back and forth. But he hurried along as best he could, and not once did Motrya have to carry a heavy sack filled with grain on her back, and not once did she have to rake up the straw left by the threshing machine . . .

And so, one spring day, having met Motrya unexpectedly beyond the garden plots—just when the tiny stars, igniting in the clear sky, seemed to be breathing with a living spirit, singing songs that could not be heard, and speaking a language that could not be understood, and when the moon, like a narrow silver boat swam out suddenly from behind a small cloud—Martin approached her shyly and, scarcely touching her, said: "If I, you know . . . kissed you . . . I would think I was in heaven."

"You're a fool," Motrya replied and burst out laughing.

He hung his head and scratched the back of his neck, but his face beamed with that wonderful, charming smile that made his entire countenance bloom.

"Send the matchmakers," Motrya flung out at him, as she disappeared.

And so he sent the matchmakers and won her hand in marriage, and they were wed. After it was all over, even Motrya could not understand how it had happened that she had fallen in love with such "an oaf," "a clod," "a blockhead," "a slob."

But when her former friends were not laughing at her, she did not feel unfortunate, for Martin not only did not beat or scold her—he was completely incapable of anything like that—but he listened to her with both ears and did everything according to her instructions. If she told him to sell a horse—it was sold; or to trade it for a cow—it was traded; or to hire himself out to the lord—he did it; or to send his daughters to work in the Jew's tobacco fields—it was done. And Motrya did exactly as she pleased, much to the annoyance of the neighbouring women, whose husbands ruled high-handedly over everything, got drunk on a regular basis, quarrelled with them, and beat them up.

As for Martin, he neither drank nor smoked. And Motrya, knowing her husband's pliable nature, served as his mouthpiece with other people; she quarrelled, shouted, defended her property whenever it was necessary to do so, and fought for "her rights" everywhere.

If the tax-collectors wanted to claim a hog for outstanding taxes, Motrya would chase them out after receiving an extension. Or if a neighbour sold a cow that he claimed gave a pail of milk, whereas it only produced two cupfuls, Motrya would demand that the neighbour lower the price of the cow, even though Martin did not think it necessary and never would have done so himself. He just would have said: "Let it be! God be with him!"

Thus it was that Motrya lived with her husband, without experiencing the woes that other women came to know. But she had her own grief—her sons did not live long.

She gave birth to many children—seven in all—but only three girls survived, while all four boys died in childhood, The doctor said it was the father's fault because he was sickly—he had tuberculosis, or something like that—but how sickly could he be when he never stopped working and could lift things weighing a hundred kilograms? It had to be a lie, but, O God, how pitifully the children died.

Each little tyke, in turn, would reach the age of six or seven, apparently healthy and growing, with round, rosy cheeks like puff pastry, and eyes that protruded "just a mite, like the stars," the mother said. And each "lively little fellow" was talkative, and tried to do everything, chopping with an axe like his father, raking the hay and then . . .

And then one day he would quite suddenly begin vomiting—so hard, that it seemed his soul was leaving his body; his eyes would roll wildly to one side, and he would open his mouth like a fish out of water, become breathless, and yell during the night—

Lord save us!—so plaintively and painfully, like a seagull in the marshes; then he would begin to toss around, and his arms and legs would cramp as if he were being stitched together with a needle, and his face would pucker as if it were being pulled on a drawstring, and then . . . he would become unconscious, and lie still, ever so still, and slowly fade away; he would fade away just as a flower silently withers . . . And, after three or four days, he would be gone . . .

Dear God, how the mother wept for her unfortunate children, lamenting that the Lord had not allowed her to have her fill of gazing upon them, of delighting in them, of loving them!

But no one saw how bitterly Martin cried, for he was always busy working. And when he was bending over an axe, or a hoe, or a scythe, no one could see the salty tears that fell on the cold steel, on the silent wood, on his callused hands, and on the black earth . . .

So, only three daughters remained. One was just seven years old, but the other two were grown-up girls who worked as maidservants.

Martin was very kind to all his children.

When they were little—and whenever there was no work to be done, or if it was a holiday—he hovered over them so lovingly that there was no need for them to have a mother. When the daughters grew up, however, he became shy with them—as he was with all people—and he never said much to them, although he probably loved them just as he always had.

They, like all the other people, laughed at him because he was strange, but they would have scratched out the other children's eyes if any one of them had dared to say anything against their father.

And they stated everywhere: "Our father isn't like other fathers who take away from their daughters all the money that they've earned!"

And truly, Martin—God forbid!—never took away the money that his children earned through their backbreaking work as servants.

It was only when his debts were really pressing that he would say to one or the other of his daughters: "Perhaps, my daughter, you could . . . that is . . . could you . . . could you lend me a bit of your money?"

And the daughter would invariably give it to him. The older one, Kharytyna, who resembled her father—she was homely, but good-natured—would even add: "Go ahead and take it, father, take it. Of course you need it, and where else are you to get it?"

The middle one, Mavra, who took after her mother and was just as pretty, would frown a bit—she did not like to part with her money—but, nevertheless, she did give it to him.

And it was always like this—it really was strange! They listened to their father even though he did not beat them, or scold them, or yell at them. He would only scratch the nape of his neck, look up diffidently, and say: "My daughter, you know, perhaps . . . you should not go to so many parties . . . because there will be gossip . . . Yes indeed."

And the daughter would not go out anymore. Kharytyna would remain at home without saying anything, but Mavra would say something like "Stay at home yourself!" Nevertheless, she too would remain at home, and even when she did go out, she was as cautious with the fellows as she was with fire, so that—God forbid!—there would be no cause for shame, and her father would not be offended or defamed. She knew what he was alluding to, what he feared might happen to her or her sister, and she knew that her father always thought about her and her sister, and wanted what was best for them . . .

And truly, even though Martin considered all fine clothing—a velveteen jerkin, a fancy gold necklace, or things like that—as sheer frippery, as whims, saying: "It's just foolishness," he did not forbid his daughters to dress attractively.

He himself walked around in tattered, ragged clothing—he wore a clean shirt only on Sunday—but he took delight in gazing at his daughters when they got all prettied up and strolled together through the village in their necklaces, crimson skirts, and gleaming black velveteen jerkins, adorned with multicoloured ribbons that streamed down their backs and floated behind them in the wind. And because their father felt this way, and because he tried to earn as much as he could by hiring himself out as a watchman for the winter to ensure he would have enough money to pay the taxes without touching his children's earnings, his daughters had so much clothing tucked away in their trunks and dressed so well, that at times they were attired better than the daughters of rich parents . . .

The people laughed at Martin for pampering his daughters, and they laughed at him for a lot of other things too! There was, for example, ever so much laughter when Martin built himself a new house!

He saved money for that house for a long time, serving as a night watchman for three years, and doing day labour. In the summer he worked in the hay fields and harvested the rye for one-tenth of the yield, and in the fall he threshed the rye in exchange for bullets. No matter what kind of work turned up, he would take it on. A sizeable portion of the girls' wages went into the house as well, for it cost more than two hundred *karbovantsi [dollars]* to build it.

It took Martin a long time to complete the house, a very long time—as much as three or four summers. The first summer, he put up the posts that hold up the roof, laid down the rafters, wattled the walls, and covered them temporarily with straw for the winter. The next summer and fall, his wife coated the walls with clay mixed with manure—and they turned out to be as warm as pillows. It was only during the third summer that he saved enough money to make the doors and the openings for the windows, build the oven, and put the chimney flues in place; and then Martin thatched the roof, while his wife packed the floor.

During the fourth summer, or rather, in the fall, they whitewashed all the walls and left the lord's manor to live in their new home. They moved into it, and even though they had taken much pleasure in it while they were still building it, they could not stop admiring it, extolling its virtues, and swooning over it with delight. Martin would gaze at it from one side and then from the other, and everything looked so nice, and it was all so pleasing.

And best of all was the fact that five windows had been cut in the walls, and you could look out on all sides from it—to the east, the west, and the south. And Martin was happy that the sun would peek in on them—the soft, pink light of the east; the red, waning glow of the west; and the blazing sun of the south, so fiery that the eye could not tolerate it . . .

The people laughed and said: "The fool! He's poked so many windows in the house that it looks like a sieve—it will be good and cold in there in the winter."

But that did not bother him at all! With all the light, it would be bright and cheerful, and the view was splendid. It was true that one window looked out directly at the neighbour's livestock pen and a pile of manure, but that did not matter. It pleased Martin and Motrya to look out in all directions from a house that was their own.

The other nice thing about it was that the main beam was not whitewashed, but painted with genuine, gleaming oil paint. That is how it was! And afterwards, whenever Martin worked in the house, he would glance up at least once at the beam from which a good-sized lamp hung and think to himself: "Well done!"

But the nicest thing in the house was the metal plate—a steel plate marked off into quarters—that was attached to one side of the oven. Yes, a metal plate with no apparent purpose. Yes indeed, what was it for? Martin could not say what it was for; it was big enough for only one samovar stand, and it was attached so crookedly that no fire from the oven could ever have reached it. All the same, it was good; yes sir, it was good. As Motrya said, it really did look as if it belonged to a lord, and even though the people laughed, it did not bother her at all!

And did they not laugh at the tiled flues on the roof that looked like enamelled pots? Martin, however, like the wren that diligently weaves one hair after another into its nest, rejoiced in his home. He took delight in it, and it meant the world to him. He always had been a "fanatic about neatness," but now he gathered up the smallest splinters and laid them carefully in a pile. For her part, Motrya continually smoothed down the earthen floor, and yelled at the children not to litter it.

And did not the people laugh when Martin hired himself out to the lord as a watchman? The lord would go away for the winter and leave Martin in charge of his property—his house and his orchard—and Martin would not take so much as a dry branch from that orchard for firewood; instead, he used dung to warm his house.

"What a fool!" the people said both behind his back and to his face. "There's all that firewood there, and he's heating his home with dung! You ought to chop down enough for yourself and for your neighbours; the lord won't be any poorer for it."

"Oh, no," Martin said. "I can't, you know . . . on my own . . . that is . . . I can't."

"But it belongs to the lord, not to the people," the people explained to him. "What are you—a child or something, that you can't understand that?"

"Uh-huh, you see," he said, scratching the nape of his neck, "but isn't it all the same?"

"Well, who has ever heard of such a thing—to stand up for what belongs to the lord as if it were your own?"

Martin had behaved the same way when he served as an orderly in the army. He had rushed about and done his best for the colonel, just as if he were working for his own father. And how did the colonel reward him?

"You fool, you blockhead, get away from here!" This was all that Martin ever heard from him.

But Martin always replied with the same words: "I'm listening." Or: "That's exactly right."

And he took such a fancy to the lord's little daughter, the tiny blond Musya with her lively dark eyes, that he doted on her almost as much as on his own daughters. He carried her around in his arms, and she was so soft, so delicate, so pretty—just like a flower bud. In the winter, she was like a fluffy snowflake in her white fur coat; and in the summer, she was like a fleecy little cloud with her white, muslin clothing and her dimpled arms and knees. And she liked him and stroked his dirty, bristly cheeks with her little hand saying: "My Tin, My Tin."

They both cried when they parted . . .

The people found this amusing. After all, was he a woman that he served as a nanny?

And did they not laugh because Martin could not imagine a theft or a murder? He knew very well that there were thieves and murderers who kill, rob, and do away with people, but he could not believe it, and he did not believe it, saying: "How can that be . . . a human soul . . . that is . . . to kill it? No . . . that just can't be!"

"But you heard what happened, didn't you?" they said to him.

"Well, that is . . . I don't know . . ."

And so he did not believe that it was possible to kill a human being, nor would he have believed it even if he had seen it with his own eyes . . .

And did they not laugh when Martin sat at the very back at meetings and listened while they all argued about matters such as debts and collecting money? And they all interrupted one another, shouting in outrage that the secretary was deceiving the community—he worked the abacus too swiftly; "the shouters" got their way. Some swayed the people with liquor . . .

Martin listened and listened—but he did not understand anything . . .

"Well, what about you, brother Martin?" one of the men would turn to him jokingly. "What do you say?"

Martin would scratch his neck, hang his head, and blush bashfully: "Well, what if we . . . that is . . ." he would say, "did it without cursing, without quarrelling and according to the truth?"

Everyone would roar with laughter, but sometimes they felt a bit ashamed, because really, no matter whom they elected as the village chief, or as the secretary, or as the tax collector, or as the "empowered one," there immediately were excesses and cheating. The community's money was loaned out for the interest that it could earn the elected individual; land was purchased with the community's money, and houses were built with it—oh, would to God it were not true!

So the people thought and thought about it, and then they elected Martin Horenko as the collector—to gather money for the "bank's" land. Martin was illiterate, but that did not matter! Someone else could keep the records. He was not very agile— but so what? He would get things done more swiftly than an agile person. He was not overly clever—but so what? All the clever people in the village had robbed the entire community, but Martin would not take a *kopiyka* that belonged to someone else; everyone knew that . . .

Yes, they elected him as the collector, but do you suppose they stopped laughing at him? Not at all! He was the butt of everyone's jokes.

"Well, God be with them, let them laugh!" Martin said, and he went about his task solemnly and diligently.

It did not matter that he was illiterate—he developed a counting system of his own using crosses. He wrote down in a book who in the community had given money, and who had not, and he would get the money from the people before the deadline "without fail," because he went about it in the following fashion: he would come to a man's home and sit there for the whole day, and even for the whole night, until that man gave him the money or swore an oath that he would do so, because—strange as it may seem— even though they all could wrap Martin, like a fool, around their little fingers, very few people ever managed to cheat him.

But they laughed at him—they laughed at him and could not get their fill of laughing.

You Say There Is No Idealism Now . . .

(no date)

"You say there is no idealism now, that it is no longer encountered in its purest forms. But what about this?"

He was a fortunate man who had a large family with whom he lived in complete harmony; he had a good position in his department, where he was up to his ears in work.

On workdays, he had many acquaintances, friends, and co-workers—both subordinate to and independent of him—and many forms of entertainment.

On holidays, he would leave all these people and things that he loved and which reciprocated his love, and travel more than a thousand kilometres to visit her—an isignificant tiny grey bird who lived the confined, uneventful, cheerless, circumscribed life of an impoverished teacher in a girls' academy . . .

What was this?

You—a pitiful, unremarkable little grey bird with the soul of a nightingale—did not expect this.

You did not expect such kindness, because you had grown accustomed to being forgotten, you had grown accustomed to not being noticed, you had grown accustomed to loneliness—the kind of loneliness when your "I" chokes and sucks at you, sucks at you like a loathsome octopus that attaches itself to you and sticks fast with a thousand suckers . . .

And there is no help, there is no way out—except for suicide.

And the apparition lures you and pushes you towards an abyss, whispering all the while: "End it all!"

Who needs you? Probably not the girls, these self-assured, bantering butterflies who, as yet, do not "seek the human being" in people . . .

If you were to die—there would be hundreds, thousands, to take your place tomorrow, and, possibly, they would be better, for they are younger; they are neither weary, nor crushed, and they have a burning desire for life, and . . . These are exactly the kind that are needed!

And so he arrived . . .

He entered the room, kissed her like a brother, took her hand, and, gazing into her eyes, inquired: "Well, how are you doing, how are you? I've come to see you. How are things going for you?"

She crumpled into a little wad. She found it hard to breathe. She could not believe that all this had been done for her, that such a thing was possible.

Her soft cheeks, already lined with fine wrinkles under her eyes, flamed for a moment with the redness of a rose, and her silver-tinged, slightly greying hair came undone on one side from the startled, involuntary movement of her hand . . .

And even though her heart began to sing with happiness, she could not believe him, and so she asked: "You've come to see me? That's impossible . . ."

"But we've been friends since childhood," he said, gazing tenderly into her eyes once again.

"And so?"

"You're all alone!"

"And so?"

"Your soul is purer that the snow!"

"And so?" she kept repeating stubbornly. "You live so far away, you have a family, you're very busy, you have so many friends, so many relatives, so many blood ties—the ties that usually are the only ones to bind people, to bind them so that they need no others . . ."

"But all the same, I've come because of you, and for you," he said simply and, at the same time, elatedly . . .

It was then that the happiness born of friendship came alive for her.

Little by little, she poured her whole soul into his.

And all the minutiae of her drab, imperfect existence, all the insults that people were not stingy in heaping upon her, all her thoughts—gentle and hesitant, like evening butterflies—that tortured her in her desolate loneliness, found a response within him.

From time to time, she interrupted herself, brushed her hand over her eyes and, smiling a beautiful, bright smile in which her nightingale's soul could be seen, said: "No, this is a fairy tale, it's all just a fairy tale!"

The warm, pure, and starry spring night looked in on them through the window and whispered with its tender, damp leaves that were just unfurling: "A human being, a human being, a human being . . ."

And so a life was saved.

The Lonely Hero
(no date)

He, a full professor in the Department of Russian History, did not resemble a hero in the slightest. Short and skinny, he had hair that seemed to be plastered to his head, a face creased with wrinkles like a grey pillowslip on which someone had been sleeping for a long time, completely nondescript eyes that hid behind gold-rimmed eyeglasses, and a hoarse, muffled voice . . .

And yet, there was nothing in this world that he wanted as much as to be a hero—to have students listen to him with mouths agape like those of fish, with bulging froglike eyes, and with bated breath, so that silence reigned all around.

And he wanted the lecture-hall to be overflowing—like a church—with listeners, with students seated on windowsills, on the podium at his feet, and wherever else there was room to sit; to have the huge university convocation hall so crowded with students that they would be milling about in the street, that it would be difficult to breathe in that great crush of humanity, that the heads in the crowd would be lined up like earthenware mugs in a coffee shop—different but blending into one another.

He wanted these crowds to encircle the entire building, so that the power of his word, like a sorcerer's wand, would transform his listeners, raising them to the level of historical paragons, endowing them with a courageous spirit, a love for their people, for their native land, so that they would be prepared to go through fire and brimstone, so that . . .

But, alas, he had dreamt like this from the time he was a lowly university lecturer until now, when he was a full professor, but he had not been endowed with the requisite skills . . .

Students had stopped coming to his lectures long ago, and for quite some time now he had to be satisfied with having three or four of them in attendance. Receiving his professorial salary, he lectured day after day, year after year, but he lectured insipidly, and in such a boring manner, that he exhausted both himself and the students who happened to come his way.

And he took revenge on those students who did not attend his lectures by tripping them up on dates when he examined them. He himself had an exceptional memory—he remembered not only the year, but also the month and the exact day on which historical events had transpired.

Time moved on in this way. The years slipped by . . . and Bovkun's hair turned grey, and he grew old . . .

And he became weary without ever finding his audience, for even though he considered himself worthy of becoming a hero for them, he was a hero only in his dreams.

And then, it was unexpectedly suggested that he should lecture in courses that were organized for women. Rejoicing, he regained his spirits, for, my God, it was a new audience—and he would surely conquer it.

When he first laid eyes on this audience—on the array of azure, pink, and crimson garments, and the pretty eyes, grey, dark-brown, blue, and hazel which were, he thought, gazing kindly at him— he became intoxicated with joy at the attention and respect he was being accorded. And he started out with great enthusiasm—insofar as he could muster such enthusiasm—to lay out his favourite theory about the political wisdom of the Slavs, a wisdom that manifested itself at a very early stage in their history by the fact that they summoned the Varangians to rule their kingdom, and this was done precisely because they were foreign kings.

After this, in keeping with his usual method, he started in on his bibliography—citing the views of various authors who dealt with this controversial topic, and dates, and more dates, and still more dates . . . and the writings of these authors, and their translations, and so on, and so forth.

He felt his chest become inflamed and bright, as if it were filled with the dazzling splendour of the sun . . .

During all this time, those grey, hazel, and dark eyes were gazing at him wide-eyed, with interest, as if they were entranced—to the point that he began to think to himself with a slight smirk: "The dear sweet little fools, they probably don't understand it all!"

The lecture ended . . .

The second lecture and the third one followed the same pattern, with an almost full lecture-hall, and the professor rejoiced and said: "No, they really do understand, they do have feelings . . . They're not like those male students who begin criticizing before they've learned anything."

But, alas! Within a week, the lecture-hall was only half-full, and after still another week—only a quarter of it was filled.

The professor was angry, and he often made fun of "women's intellect," "the stupidity of women," "the absence in them of any lofty flights of thought," etc. But at the same time, his offended egoism gnawed at his heart day and night, like a mouse, and he tried to think of all sorts of ways to win back his audience.

He complained to the Dean that the students were not attending his lectures, and the Dean promised, with a sympathetic smile, that he would urge the students to make an effort . . .

It did not help at all! The usual number showed up.

The professor hinted that during the examinations he failed those who did not attend lectures, because if one did not attend lectures one could not know what the expectations of the professor were. It was no use! Perhaps an additional two or three more girls put in an appearance.

But wait! The professor had an idea!

He had heard that one of his colleagues who enjoyed great popularity had earned it mainly because he always ended up talking about the burning issues of the day. So he decided to do the same thing. One time he stated that history is like a teeter-totter—one end goes up, and the other one comes down; today Pureshkevych is down, while Milyukov is up, and the next day the reverse is true . . .

It did not help at all! One more student may have dropped in, but then again, she may have been one of the regulars—who could tell? Another time he tried introducing a romantic note—it is well-known that love is a woman's concern—by describing the romance of St. Volodymyr and Rohnida.

Things seemed to go a little better . . . More students began attending . . .

He breathed a sigh of relief. But then, without any rhyme or reason, the barometer fell and did not rise again . . . Nothing helped now, and, to make matters even worse, the faces in the audience were never the same—today, there would be one group of students, and the next day it would be another one.

"They must be taking turns," the professor realized. "The little idiots are learning from the male students how to make fun of the lectures," he thought. "But the latter, at least, are men, but these are . . . Well, everyone knows what women's minds are like."

And so he became an adversary, a derider of women's emancipation. He began to discredit it everywhere, whether it was to the point or not, basing his views on his experience in the women's courses.

As for his lectures, he read them so monotonously, so drowsily, and with such a lack of enthusiasm to five or six students, that he himself almost nodded off in the middle of a word, yawned about ten times a minute, threw his hands up in the air, constantly looked at his watch, and stretched until it looked as if he were standing on stilts—and all because of the nebulous boredom that settled all around on everything. It seemed that the walls, and the ceiling, and the floor were weary of listening to him, and that the flies were falling down in a stupor—as if they had nibbled on a toadstool.

The students became infected as well; some yawned discreetly, covering their mouths with their hands, while others yawned overtly, widely opening their mouths and distorting their attractive faces.

One day he came and found only two students present. And even though he was already white with anger, he turned even whiter.

He stood there for a while, and then, after saying in a trembling voice: "Well, '*tres collegium facinnt' [three people constitute an assemblage]*," he began lecturing.

And this time he lectured a little better and in a more lively fashion; he yawned less frequently, was less inclined to drag out his words like a saw scraping through iron, and it was all because he had come to a decision . . .

When the bell rang, he rose decisively to his feet, his face turned beet red, and he said to the students: "I am very grateful to you for your diligence, but I am not one of those professors who . . . Well, they say there was a professor who could lecture when only one student was present in the lecture-hall, and irrespective of this fact, he always began with the words: 'My dear gentlemen . . .' I am not able to do this . . . I will not lecture when there are only two students present . . . Do as you see fit."

And, flinging his head back proudly, like a true "hero," he stalked out of the room.

When he entered the lecture-hall the next day—unfortunately, it so happened that the university clerk did not manage to forewarn him in time—there was no one there! Not a single living soul!

The professor was struck dumb . . .

The walls, the ceiling, the windows, the floor, and the desks were standing and gazing at him attentively, but he . . .

Tears oozed from his nondescript eyes, misting his glasses . . .

His dreams of glory, of a huge audience—everything had perished . . .

Yes, he truly was a hero . . .

Lesya Ukrainka

1871-1913

Biographical Sketch

Lesya Ukrainka is the literary pseudonym of Larysa Kosach-Kvitka, who was born in 1871 to Olha Drahomanova-Kosach (literary pseudonym: Olena Pchilka), a writer/publisher in Eastern Ukraine, and Petro Kosach, a senior civil servant. An intelligent, well-educated man with non-Ukrainian roots, he was devoted to the advancement of Ukrainian culture and financially supported Ukrainian publishing ventures.

In the Kosach home the mother played the dominant role; only the Ukrainian language was used and, to avoid the schools, in which Russian was the language of instruction, the children had tutors with whom they studied Ukrainian history, literature, and culture. Emphasis was also placed on learning foreign languages and reading world literature in the original. In addition to her native Ukrainian, Larysa learned Russian, Polish, Bulgarian, Greek, Latin, French, Italian, German, and English.

A precocious child, who was privileged to live in a highly cultivated home, Larysa began writing poetry at the age of nine, and when she was thirteen saw her first poem published in a journal in L'viv under the name of Lesya Ukrainka, a literary pseudonym suggested by her mother. As a young girl, Larysa also showed signs of being a gifted pianist, but her musical studies came to an abrupt end when, at the age of twelve, she fell ill with tuberculosis of the bone, a painful and debilitating disease that she had to fight all her life.

Finding herself physically disabled, Larysa turned her attention to literature—reading widely, writing poetry, and translating. She shared these literary activities with her brother Mykhaylo (literary pseudonym: Mykhaylo Obachny), her closest friend until his death in 1903. When Larysa was seventeen, she and her brother organized a literary circle called *Pleyada (The Pleiades)* which was devoted to promoting the development of Ukrainian literature and translating classics from world literature into Ukrainian.

As a teenager, Larysa's intellectual development was further stimulated by her maternal uncle, Mykhaylo Drahomanov, the noted scholar, historian, and publicist. He encouraged her to collect folk songs and folkloric materials, to study history, and to peruse the Bible for its inspired poetry and eternal themes. She was also influenced by her family's close association with leading cultural figures, such as Mykola Lysenko, a renowned composer, and Mykhaylo Starytsky, a well-known dramatist and poet.

Lesya published her first collection of lyrical poetry, *Na krylakh pisen' (On Wings of Songs)*, in 1893, a year after her translations of Heine's poetry, *Knyha pisen' (The Book of Songs)* appeared. In the Russian Empire, Ukrainian publications were banned; therefore, both books were published in Western Ukraine and smuggled into Kyiv.

From the time that Lesya was a teenager, she often had to go abroad for surgery and various treatment regimens, and was advised to live in countries with a dry climate. Residing for extended periods of time in Germany, Austria, Italy, Bulgaria, Crimea, The Caucasus, and Egypt, she became familiar with other peoples and cultures, and incorporated her observations and impressions into her writings. An inveterate letter writer, she engaged in an extensive correspondence with the Western Ukrainian author Olha Kobylianska that led to an exchange of sketches both entitled "The Blind Man." (See Volume III of this series.)

In addition to her lyrical poetry, Ukrainka wrote epic poems, prose dramas, prose, several articles of literary criticism, and a number of socio-political essays. It was her dramatic poems, however, written in the form of pithy, philosophical dialogues, that were to be her greatest legacy to Ukrainian literature. Only one of Ukrainka's dramas, *Boyarynya (The Boyar's Wife)* refers directly to Ukrainian history, and another, an idealistic, symbolic play, *Lisova pisnya (Song of the Forest),* uses mythological beings from Ukrainian folklore. Her other dramatic poems issue from world history and the Bible. With their sophisticated psychological treatment of the themes of national freedom, dignity, and personal integrity, they are a clarion call to people the world over to throw off the yoke of oppression.

In 1901, Lesya suffered a great personal loss—the death of her soul mate, Serhiy Merzhynsky. She wrote the entire dramatic poem *Oderzhyma (The Possessed)* in one night at his deathbed. A few years later, in 1907, she married a good friend of the family, Klyment Kvitka, an ethnographer and musicologist. It was he who transcribed and published the many Ukrainian folk songs that she had learned as a young girl in her native province of Volyn.

Despite many prolonged periods in her life during which she was too ill to write, upon her death in 1913, at the relatively young age of forty-two, Ukrainka left behind a rich and diversified literary legacy. While it is the deep philosophical thought and the perfection of her poetic form that have assured her a place among the luminaries of world literature, her prose works, which she continued writing throughout her literary career, provide a fascinating insight into the inner life of this gifted, multifaceted writer, and reveal her perceptions of the multi-layered society in which she lived.

Christmas Eve
Vignettes
(1889)

I

The *kutya [boiled wheat and honey]* and *uzvar [stewed fruit]* are on the table, and the family is dining. The room is brightly lit, and the lamp flames festively, with a jubilant glow. Everyone speaks quietly, everyone tries to say something uplifting, everyone feels fortunate and full of hope, even though no one knows exactly what to expect or whether hopes will be fulfilled . . .

Joy, flying swiftly from face to face, twinkles in eyes like a star, rings in the clinking glasses, and resounds in the pealing laughter of children. There is talk and laughter, but not that boisterous, uncertain hubbub when people talk and laugh too loudly in an effort to deafen their grief and their tears; no, this joyous clamour is serene, even though it is hearty. How pleasantly, how reverently the familiar words echo: "It's Christmas Eve! May this holy evening bring us good health!"

2

The room is elegantly furnished; it is evident that wealthy people live here and, for the holidays, the room is decorated even more splendidly. The table is covered with a snow-white cloth and the choicest foods and drinks. It is bright and festive here as well, but the cheerfulness is not as genuine, as if the jovial words are being uttered on compulsion; and the smiles gracing the lips are somewhat stiff and forced.

At the edge of the table, in a soft, velvet armchair, sits a young boy; his handsome face, white as wax, contrasts starkly with his dark eyebrows; his lips are smiling, but the smile is tinged with apprehension—even though the boy strives to hide his concern, and the others pretend not to notice it . . .

From time to time, the boy stops speaking in the middle of a conversation, sinks his dark eyes far into the distance, and falls deep into thought. Oh, how jolly it was last year on this night! He had been so full of life, so full of hopes—but now . . . Now he has no strength left; he is ailing . . . Will he live to see another Christmas Eve? But what is this? Is it the same worry once again, the same grief? No, that's enough of that! Everyone is wishing him good health and good fortune so cheerfully—much too cheerfully! It is, after all, Christmas Eve!

3

A field, as white as white can be. The road, winding and vanishing in the nocturnal, freezing fog, is scarcely visible. A light sleigh flies swiftly, as swiftly as possible—but how slow the ride seems to the youthful traveller! A young schoolboy is on his way home from a distant school—and the poor lad is late. He peers anxiously into the fog—is there a light flickering anywhere?

Oh, the trip is such a long one! If only it were possible to travel more quickly, to come home in time for the Christmas Eve supper, to eat *kutya* with his brothers and sisters and join them in the ritual calling of the frost!

Out in the fields the frost is piercing, and the boy energetically rubs his hands and stamps his feet—it is so cold! But there is no time to bundle up more warmly—there, in the distance, he thinks he sees the gleam of his village!

Yes, there it is! Like will-o'-the-wisps, flaming lights emerge one after the other in the darkness, flicker cheerfully and, like children's twinkling eyes, greet the young boy: "It's Christmas Eve! It's Christmas Eve!

4

A tiny, crowded room. A girl is sitting at a table near a small lamp; her head is bent over her sewing—an elegant, white silk gown. It is a rush job! The needle flashes briskly in her swift hands. It is the last evening before the holidays, and the ball gown of the wealthy young lady is not yet finished! A large shop would not have taken on this task—there is enough sewing to be done there without this gown—and even if it had accepted the order, it would have cost the young lady dearly. But the poor seamstress did take it on—right before the holidays, and she even has to show gratitude for the pittance she is receiving for it.

It is quiet in the room, and all that can be heard from time to time is the penetrating rustle of the silk, and the sighs of the seamstress. How lonely this worker is now, and how quiet it is in her little room. But formerly? The work stops, her needle falls from her hands, and the gown slides to the floor. What is happening? Is this the time for sinking into reveries? It is the last evening! She must get on with her sewing!

Finally, the work is completed. The seamstress rises, straightens her bent back, walks up to the window, presses her forehead against the cold pane, and gazes with weary eyes out into the street. In a window of the neighbouring building she can discern movements—small figures in bright garments—probably the Christmas tree has been lit . . . And, in another dwelling, a bright light glows—the people there are probably dining . . . The seamstress looks intently at that window and the soft light within it, and tears tremble on her lashes . . . People are celebrating Christmas Eve! And what about her? Why, it is Christmas Eve for her as well!

The Moth

(1889)

In a dank, dark cellar, a pitiful grey moth clung to a barrel of sauerkraut. Dejected, he hung there, pressing his dark wings closely together. And he felt ever so lonely, even though he was not all alone; he did, after all, have a neighbour—a bat. But having this neighbour was of little consolation to him. The bat was gloomy and uncommunicative and, to make matters even worse, looked with contempt at the miserable moth, who, in his view, was not at all his equal.

The bat lived quietly in his corner, neither grieving for anything, nor longing for anything except, perhaps, for an even darker corner where he would be able to rest peacefully and never see the light—the light that he found so painful and irritating. It is true that he was not troubled very often by light in that cellar, but still, there was the odd time that someone came down with a candle and, occasionally, even leaned over the barrel while taking out some of the sauerkraut. The bat found this most unpleasant. If it had been within his power to do so, he would have extinguished that light forever with his wings.

In his brief life the moth had not yet seen any light, but he intuitively felt that there must be a better and brighter world than his native cellar. Occasionally, a tiny pale ray of light did fall through the small window in the cellar, but the moth could not comprehend fully what this faint light was, and what it really represented. In the dark corner, the ray was barely discernible— slender like a thread, and pale like an ailing child.

The moth often sat and sent his thoughts into that bright world— but where, exactly? Neither his mind nor his heart knew the answer, and he had no one to confer with, because where was this advice to come from? There was only the bat, but as you yourselves know, there was precious little advice to be gained from him! And the moth had neither the courage nor the strength to fly away in search of the source of that light.

Who knows, the moth might well have spent his entire brief life pining away in the solitary darkness but, as it was, a different fate awaited him.

One day, a maidservant, coming into the cellar to fetch some sauerkraut, placed a candle on the floor, right across from the moth.

God! How magnificent, brilliant, and alluring that light appeared to him. Mesmerized by the bewitching flame, he fluttered his wings and was ready to fling himself at it, but, at that very moment, the servant picked up the candle and began making her way out of the cellar.

Overcome by a desire to reach the enchanting light, the moth forgot about his ignorance, his helplessness.

"The light! The light!" he cried.

And he soared after it.

The bat whistled derisively in his wake and then crept even farther behind the barrel, where he once again fell asleep. He never had any dreams.

But the moth flew after the candle as swiftly as he could with his weak little wings.

And suddenly he found himself in a large room in which many people were seated at a table. And on this table stood a brilliantly shining lamp.

The little moth, awestruck by the dazzling rays, fluttered his wings and dropped helplessly to the table. Just as one of the guests was about to sweep him away, he quickly revived, flitted upwards once again, and began circling the lamp. He wanted to come as close as possible to the lamp that to him seemed like a sun.

Did he stop to think that he could lose his life there? But who can foresee death in such blazing splendour? It flames, sparkles, and flickers—and there is light there, and warmth, and life!

The moth flew ever nearer and nearer to the fatal light.

Oh, it would surely destroy him!

The people tried chase him away from the light, but in vain.

The moth flew into the heart of the flame.

There was a crackling sound!

And he perished.

The lamp flared momentarily and then began to gleam with the same brilliance as before.

"Such a foolish little creature," one of the company said. "Did someone tell him to fly into the flame? They tried to chase him away from it, but no, he persisted in going there! A foolish creature meets a foolish end!"

But would his death have been any more meaningful if he had slept forever in that dark cellar?

The flame had consumed him but . . . he had been eagerly rushing towards freedom . . .

He had been seeking the light!

Spring Songs
A Recollection
(1889)

It is winter, and snow has been covering the green rue for quite some time now, but my mind is brimming with memories of spring, with sonorous spring songs. Why this is so—I cannot say.

Who knows why a tear rolls down from an eye on a cheerful morning in summer, or why the breath of spring is recalled on a grim winter's evening.

Why?

Who knows?

I recall how, on quiet spring evenings, I used to sit alone in my cottage on the outskirts of a hamlet amid the Kharkiv steppes, thinking about my native Volyn and sending to it my melancholy thoughts. Oh, those evenings . . .

The sun is sinking in the west, and its fiery rays engulf the parched steppe in crimson flames. A dust-cloud, whipped up on the road by a herd of cattle, drifts across the setting sun and, like smoke rising from a blazing fire, appears to be tinged with ochre.

The villagers shout and rush about as they herd their cattle. Young boys cluster around a well, watering the horses.

Shrieks, clamouring . . .

Gradually, everything quiets down, except for subdued voices near my cottage. The villagers are assembling for their *kolodky* *[talkfests held while seated on logs]*. Every evening, they gather beneath my window and talk—sometimes, until quite late.

"If only God would send us some rain!" I hear an opening remark.

Their conversations always begin this way, and these words are not tinged in the least by the nonchalance that usually marks them in discussions about "the weather." No, along with these words, I hear heartfelt sighs; it is evident they are not being said "just for something to say."

"Yes, indeed, if only God would grant it! The way things are now, no one knows what to do. It looks like we might have to plough the fields again and start all over!" one farmer speaks up in a worried tone.

"It's too late to plough the fields a second time!" another farmer disagrees.

"But there's no other way out," a younger married woman interjects. "Our fields are ever so small as it is—almost as if we had stolen them—and if everything on them is scorched, what will we do then?"

"What will we do? We'll start raising the issue of our land again with the lady."

"With the lady? Start those discussions with her all over again? To have the same thing happen as happened last year—when we had to spend more trying to get our money from her than what we finally got?"

"What else are we to do?"

The general conversation comes to a halt, and all that can be heard now are fragments of interchanges between individuals who happen to be sitting beside each other.

From the other end of the village, the sound of singing starts drifting in. The young men and women are gathering for their *vulytsya [evening revelries]*.

A young manservant saunters down the street; he ambles along quietly and nonchalantly, his torn jacket draped casually over one shoulder. As he passes by my cottage, he suddenly raises his voice in song:

> "Hey, I grew up in bondage, in servitude,
> And never knew good fortune!
>   Oh, hey!"

He too is on his way to the dam, where the evening revelries of the young people are already underway on the logs beneath the willows.

On the logs below my window, there are only older people—with the exception of two younger women who, because they are married now, can only gaze yearningly at the other end of the village, where the willows rustle over the dam.

> "In the field there are two stars,
> They are my brother and sister! Hey!"

This new song resounds as if in response to the song of the servant. It is sung by a young soldier who has returned to the village on leave. Except for a small plot of land and an old cottage, he has nothing to come home to; he has no family and so, hearing the voice of his friend as he steps outside his cottage, he joins him in song. A short time later, the two men meet and trail off together to the dam. Their youthful voices echo from afar:

> "I have no kin, no family,
> No faithful wife! Hey!"

The conversation beneath my window resumes.

"Did you hear that we've been called to the district office tomorrow?"

"Why?"

"Well, they say that they're going to read us something about that summons for our property. Our lady isn't going to give up her land that easily!"

"Her land? If only it were hers! It's been ours from the time of our grandparents and great grandparents!"

"Sure! That's the way it was in our grandparents' day, but it's different now for the grandchildren! They're going to drag us through the courts for quite a while because of this inheritance of ours!"

"Yes, they will. They'll drag us all right—may the devil drag them!"

A loud hubbub ensues. It is not possible to follow the flow of the discussion. Only snatches of conversation can be picked out in the general commotion—when one of them shouts in a deep, determined voice: "No, that's enough! That will never be! What's mine is mine—it's not yours!"

All the while, more and more songs reverberate ever more loudly through the hamlet.

A comely girl walks by at a fast pace, her sturdy figure pleasantly defined in the light of the young moon that has just sailed out into the tranquil sky. A profusion of ribbons flutters on her wreath and, even in the twilight, her fine garments and bright coral beads glimmer from afar.

She is poor, but she has no one else to look after, and so she is always better dressed than the girls whose parents are householders with families; whatever she earns, she spends on herself. She is singing far too loudly and too brashly:

> "Oh, even though I'm poor —
> People will take me in.
> But as for you, O fiendish kozak,
> You'll never a partner win!"

Suddenly, the shrill voices of three girlfriends, who are racing swiftly down the street as if someone were chasing after them, ring out:

> "O God, grant us our wish—
> to say our marriage vows
> standing on *rushnyky.*"
> *[embroidered linen ceremonial cloths]*

The individual songs soon end and, from under the willows, the songs of two large groups—one made up of girls, and the other of young men—resound.

The singing of these impromptu choruses spreads over the hamlet and soars into the expansive steppe, far into the distance; the songs interrupt each other, blend together, and then die down once again.

Now, only the singing of the nightingales can be heard as they warble in the orchards. Before long, however, the clear, resonant trilling of the birds is once again drowned out by the even more vibrant singing of the young people.

But then the youths burst into another song:

"A dove perches on an oak,
    his mate on a cherry tree;
Tell me, sweetheart, tell me true,
    What do you think of me?"

They are interrupted by the girls' group:

"Advise me, fair maiden,
    as would my own mother,
Should I wait for you,
    or marry another? "

Then the singing of the two groups becomes confused and all jumbled together; and, instead of a song, ringing laughter pours forth.

The older group falls silent. Some are listening to the singing of the *vulytstya,* while others are pondering serious problems. Still others have drifted off home already, and only the two young married women are still conversing sorrowfully—probably sharing some domestic problems with each other.

The nightingales in the orchards are warbling clearly, loudly, and cheerfully, and their song soars and flows longingly, blending in with the singing of the young people. There is something similar in these songs.

Then, more serious sounds are heard—all the young people are singing together now:

"The recruits were called up on a Sunday morning . . ."

Oh, the heart of more than one old person must tremble when it hears this song . . .

After some time, there is no one left on the logs beneath my window. The crowd has gradually dispersed, one at a time.

The young people are still singing under the willows, but, finally, they too grow tired and begin to leave. In various corners of the hamlet, the girls' songs reverberate in gentle echoes as they wend their way home.

The moon is gleaming brightly in the dark sky, and the crowns of the willow trees on the dam darken in the distance. The nightingales gradually subside, and then fall silent. Everything and everyone is sleeping, except for one young man who continues singing as he rambles down the street:

> "Oh, I can't sleep, I can't lie abed,
>   And I don't feel sleepy at all!"

He sings lustily, and his song breaks the silence of the night and spreads over the hushed steppe. He walks on, gradually disappearing from view in the evening twilight until he is no longer visible. Only his song floats in from beyond the dam:

> "Shine, O moon, shine on,
>   and you too, bright star!
> Light the narrow pathway
>   to my sweetheart's yard."

It Is Late

(1893)

The clock struck once and stopped chiming . . .

The sound reverberated sadly in the heart of the woman sitting at a table before an open book. She had been sitting in the drawing room for a long time, but she was not reading; her eyes gazed unseeingly into the distance, and her gaunt face, tense with waiting, was marked by sorrow and resignation. Her black clothing and her smoothly combed hair—black with quite a bit of grey in it—gave her the appearance of a nun.

If anyone were to look at her now and at the large portrait that hung on the wall in this drawing room, it is doubtful that he would guess that the elegant beauty—in a ball gown, with a haughty smile on her crimson lips and thick curls on an alabaster forehead—and the worried, withered woman were one and the same person.

The woman herself had long ago become accustomed to viewing this portrait objectively, as if she were looking at a picture or a portrait of a stranger.

But she never could become accustomed to the tone her husband used when he asked guests: "What do you think? Whose portrait is this?" And then, delighted by their hesitation, he would state: "It's my wife! Ha-ha-ha!"

This brief laugh stung the woman's heart to the quick.

She recalled how her first husband had used almost the same words: "Just imagine! This is my wife!"

But he had said them in such a way that everyone could see how incomparably better the speaker thought the original was when compared to the portrait. Her poor first husband! How he had loved her—no he had hardly dared to love her—he had worshipped her.

Now, she often recalled the look on his face when, eyes and diamonds sparkling, she whirled around the dance floor. And it was only now that she understand the carefully concealed sorrow that occasionally surfaced in his deep eyes. Poor man! *C'est une bonne pâte! [He's a good fellow!]* This was the most generous compliment he had earned from his glittering wife.

She had permitted him to love her and felt that this was a great kindness on her part. When he died, she was still attractive—*une femme de trente ans [a woman of thirty]*—still beautiful enough to bewitch a young doctoral student, who was now her husband.

Oh, this one most certainly was not *une bonne pâte!* But then, his wife had not given him any nickname at all; she did not understand his nature.

At first, he had loved her—she was still beautiful. But later, he seemed to be determined to make her less attractive. He insisted that she sit and work with him on his political economics and do translations for him. She never could understand why he asked this of her, when there were so many translators available, all of whom were better than she was; but this was his wish.

He did not enjoy formal balls and dances, but he did not prevent her from attending them; but then again, he told others, as if it were a big joke, that his wife "shone" and "stood out" at these events. The tone and manner in which he said it, however, gave it a negative connotation.

Oh, that humour of his—for the sake of a good joke, he would not take pity even on his own mother. He did not watch her with sorrowful eyes while she danced away the night until dawn; no, he simply sat at home with a book, or went to a friend's home for some conversation. And then he greeted her with these words: "Ah! You're home already? Is it that late?"

"My wife is free to spend her time as she sees fit," he often said, and he applied the same principle quite liberally to himself.

His wife began returning home earlier from her elegant balls, and then she ceased going to them altogether. Gradually, she began wearing black clothes and combing her hair smoothly, just like her husband's sister, a young lady who, according to the husband, was an embodiment of the feminine ideal. But these changes simply made it impossible for the husband to see his wife in the large portrait that hung on the wall.

Her husband had a great deal of influence among young people. More than once, when he came home late, he said: "It's very late!

But it doesn't matter. It is necessary to enlighten the younger generation, and it doesn't matter at all that my throat aches from talking so much today. I'm sure my eloquence has not been wasted!"

As the wife of a professor—her husband had already attained the rank of full professor—she came up with the idea of holding a *jour fixe [an at home day]* for young people . . . But these only gave rise to witticisms on the part of the professor: "It was in those days when my lady was Aspasia *[an Athenian courtesan]*."

This meant, that it was during her *jour fixe* period. It has to be said that this idea did not last very long. Once, she asked her husband which books she should read in order to learn something about political economics.

He burst out laughing and said: "First of all, it helps if one does not limit one's reading to novels written by Gyp . . . but then, if you want to, go ahead and read Marx's *Kapital* in German . . ."

These words, and others similar to them, were spinning through the poor woman's mind as she sat over the open book. At the same time, her husband's face, with the faint, derisive smile on his lips and the pitiless humour in his metallic dark eyes, came alive before her . . .

The clock struck two, and then three, but her husband still did not come home. At last, when the hands of the clock were almost at four, the doorbell rang, and the wife, without waiting for the servant, ran quickly to open the door.

"Good God, it's so late," she said to her husband in a tenderly reproachful voice. "Well, really now, how can you ruin your health like this . . ." and she continued elaborating this theme for some time.

Her husband listened until she had finished, then yawned, and said: "All this has been said with great sensitivity, but it's not to the point. The first thing that you said, however, was very much to the point—it truly is late—and *ergo [therefore]* I am going to bed. Good night!"

And, bowing politely, the professor set off for his study.

The Only Son
A Fragment
(1894)

Today Ivan's home is filled with sorrow; every so often, the wailing of Ivanykha, Ivan's old wife, breaks the silence, and it is a heartbreaking sound. But then, it is not at all surprising that she is weeping—her only son has been called up to serve in the army, and has to leave shortly. So, there you have the reason for such a happy gathering!

"Sit down, my dear son! Sit down, my darling child! Let me look at you for one last time in your father's house! Oh, what a terribly dark hour this is!" And she once again burst into tears.

"Mother! That's enough! Why are you carrying on like this? We don't know anything yet, but you're already . . ." The son, sad and gloomy, spoke up from behind the table where he was seated. "Why are you worried? Maybe they won't accept me; after all, I'm your only son."

"Oh, my unfortunate fate! My only son! What about Petro? And Hrytsko?"

"Well, what about them? They're not really your sons."

"Not really my sons! Even if they're not really my sons, they're still family. I went to see the lord the other day, to ask him if they could take you away, seeing that you're my only son, and he said that if my husband has sons, and if we all live together, then we're all one family. I said: 'But I only have one son; those other two aren't mine!'

"And the lord said: 'Well, that doesn't matter; if your husband has sons . . . then . . . then . . . they can take yours!' Oh, this is terrible, just terrible!"

"Mother! For the love of God!"

"Oh, my dear son, my darling Korniy! I won't see you again. Why, oh why, did I marry again? It would have been better to remain a widow than to lose my son, my darling son . . ."

"Mother! Father's coming!"

Ivanykha wiped her eyes with her sleeve, sighed heavily and, looking half dead, began preparing breakfast.

Ivan walked into the house with his sons. Glancing sternly at his wife, then at Korniy, he seated himself at the table.

"Well, old woman? It's time to have breakfast, and then, God willing, he'll be on his way."

"Right away. What's the big hurry? There's time yet."

"The other young men are assembling already."

Ivanykha did not reply, because it was difficult for her to utter a word. She could not cry out loud in front of her husband—he did not like that. He had already reminded her once that she had not cried when his Petro had been called up.

She continued bustling around the stove, but her eyes were drawn to her beloved son, who was sitting with a grim, morose, and somewhat hostile look on his face.

"He's just like his father," Ivanykha thought. "My dear departed husband was just as silent and gloomy as Korniy. But even so, he is my own son and will be kinder to me than those two. It's a fact, that if they're not your own children, they won't like you—no matter what you do for them."

Her eyes filled with tears, and her hands were shaking so violently that she almost dropped the bowl of barley gruel as she carried it to the table. Quickly setting it down, she moved back and leaned against the wall, looking at her son and shaking her head in despair, while copious tears rolled down her cheeks.

"Sit down, mother," Korniy said softly.

"There's no time, my son, but I guess I will sit down for a bit." She sat down, scooped up a spoonful of gruel, and lifted it to her lips; but then she abruptly threw the spoon down on the table, fell on her son's shoulder, and began to weep.

Her son sat still, staring at the floor, his lips pressed tightly together. Petro and Hrytsko continued eating slowly, all the while casting oblique looks at their stepmother.

"Eech! What a foolish old woman!" Ivan spoke up. "Why carry on like that? How will it help you? If they're going to take him, then . . ."

"Then you'd be very happy!" Ivanykha shouted, leaping to her feet.

Her teary eyes blazed with unrestrained rage. "You're happy to get rid of my child! He's like salt in your eyes! So you say they're to take him? May you and your children not live to see the day! May the merciful God grant this!"

"Shut up, old woman!" Ivan said quietly, but emphatically.

"That's enough, mother," Korniy said, still more softly.

He stared fixedly into his stepfather's eyes, and the latter dropped his gaze to the floor.

No one said a word.

"Hello! God be with you!"

Everyone glanced at the door. An officer had come for Korniy.

"I wish you a good meal," he said, when he saw that they were having breakfast.

"Please join us," Ivanykha spoke up through her tears.

"Sit down and stay a while," Ivan added.

"There's no time to sit, my good people. I've come, or rather, the time has come . . ."

Alarmed, Ivanykha involuntarily stepped up closer to her son and peered at the officer through eyes brimming with tears.

"Because, you see, it's . . . uh . . . getting late," the officer continued, sounding as if something were troubling him. "Before, uh . . . Well, we should be on our way, so that we get to town before nightfall, or else . . . Anyway, get ready, young man!"

And, having said this, he walked out of the house.

Korniy rose to his feet and, without looking at his mother, moved away from the table.

"Oh, my dearest son!" His mother suddenly shouted in despair, embracing him convulsively.

"Mother! God be with you! Why are you worrying yourself to death? I'm only going to the recruiting office; they haven't drafted me yet; maybe they won't accept me," Korniy attempted to calm his mother. "You'd do better to get me some bread for the road and see me off . . ."

Ivanykha was still weeping and clinging to her son's shoulder; gradually, however, his calm words had a soothing effect on her, and she moved away from him and began putting together a few things for his trip. Working slowly, as if she was not aware of what she was doing, she continually wiped her eyes, already red and swollen from crying, with her sleeve. When her task was finished, she stood as if dumbstruck, her arms folded, and her eyes riveted on the bundle.

"Well, old woman? Is everything ready?" Ivan spoke up.

Korniy picked up his cap, and Ivanykha, as if snapping out of a trance, grabbed the bundle with both hands.

"I'm going with Korniy!" she cried abruptly and decisively.

"Where to?" the old man asked.

"To town. I'll go at least that far with my darling son."

"Oh, of course!—he simply can't do without you! Just don't think that I'll let you take the horses and tire them out."

"I don't need them! I don't need your horses! May those horses be used to haul you to the cemetery! May the wolves devour them before evening comes! I'll go with my precious son without your rotten horses. I'll go even if you beat me, even if you kill me!"

"Shut up, why don't you! You've really split your mouth wide open this time—from one ear to the other! Who the devil is going to kill you, you insolent old hag? For all I care, you can go to town, or you can go straight to hell—to the devil himself!" Ivan yelled furiously.

Ivanykha became frightened for her own safety—what had come over her? This was the first time that she had dared to speak so sharply to her husband—and with curses, at that. But then, he had really hurt her to the quick. And besides, on this day she did not care about anything . . . She threw on a homespun coat, tied a kerchief on her head, and walked out of the house.

Her son followed her, then, stopping in the doorway, turned around to his stepfather, and said: "Farewell, father."

"Why bother with these farewells? You'll be back," the stepfather said grimly.

Korniy glanced over at Hrytsko and Petro; but they were engaged in a conversation at the table and did not even look up at him. It seemed that he wanted to say something to them, but then, as if recognising the futility of such a gesture, shrugged his shoulders and followed his mother outside.

They passed through the gate. Out on the street, they came across a group of young men who were also on their way to the district office. These youths were being followed by a group of women— mothers who were seeing off their sons. Ivanykha joined them, while Korniy caught up with the young men, and they continued down the road to the district office. Young women's faces—some of them tear-stained—peered out at them from cottage windows.

A girl with a potsherd in her hands bolted out of a house, ostensibly to get some embers from a neighbour. Stopping at the gate, she stared intently at the passersby. Korniy glanced back at her, and she shaded her eyes with her hand, as if to protect them from the sun.

Before long, they arrived at the district office, and the young men went inside. Korniy was the last one to enter and, as he crossed the threshold, he hesitated for a moment and then looked back. The girl waved to him with her sleeve, and then, lowering her head, went quietly back into the house—without any embers.

II

In front of a large and dirty stone building in a narrow and disgusting yard that looked like a refuse dump stood a large crowd of people comprised of men and women, both young and old. They were the family members who had accompanied the young men to the government office. And, in this office, a matter of a somewhat dubious nature was in progress—the drawing of lots.

The young men were already inside. The first people to arrive tried to make their way into the porch; they wanted to peek through the glass door to see exactly how the lots were being drawn; however, they were not supposed to stand there and were chased away so that the entrance would not get crowded. Forced to remain in the yard, they gazed with sorrowful eyes at the windows on the second floor of the stone building, where the office was.

Even before knowing the outcome, some of the women were wiping away tears; others were still trying to keep up their own spirits, while consoling others: "Oh, my good woman, why are you crying? You'll have your share of crying; there will be plenty of time for that!"

An old woman in front of the gate was softly trying to persuade the lord's servant to do something for her. The girl was listening intently, and it seemed she was prepared to agree.

"Take me there, please take me there, Hannusya!" the woman was pleading. "I'll stand somewhere in a corner behind the young ladies. The mistress won't be annoyed; she's kind, and the young ladies know me . . ."

"There's nothing to fear from the mistress and the young ladies, but the master doesn't like it when people go into the official quarters."

"Oh, but the lord won't see, will he? He's sitting with the gentlemen behind some papers. I'll just stand in a corner."

"Well, what's to be done with you, Ivanykha? Go ahead, but watch out! If the master gets angry . . ."

"No, no, don't be afraid! Thank you, Hannusya, thank you. But if I could just ask you to lead me to the offices, my dear, because I don't know how to get there by myself."

Ivanykha spoke the last words as she was following the servant up the stairs. As she made her way up, she met young men who were already on their way down. Some were happy, while others were sad, depending on the lot they had drawn. Some were still arriving on the double, and these young men pushed past her as they rushed up the stairs.

When Ivanykha reached the official rooms, she saw that the lord's wife was standing by a table in the outer office, cutting something. Ivanykha softly tiptoed up to her, bent over, and kissed the hand in which the lady was holding the scissors.

The lady jumped and dropped the scissors.

"Goodness, how you startled me, Ivanykha! Why are you always kissing my hand? You know I don't like it," the lady said, somewhat confused and a trifle angry.

"But how could I not kiss it, my lady?" Ivanykha said. "Forgive me, my lady, for barging into this room, but I'm going to ask you if you'd let me stand for a little while in the lord's office, just to have a look. It's my son who's drawing a lot today."

"Well, why not? Of course you may, go ahead . . . The young ladies are there as well. Hannusya, take her there."

"Thank you, my lady," Ivanykha wanted to kiss her hand again, but the lady withdrew it and looked at her reproachfully.

The old woman began to move towards the threshold, but then stopped. She turned back to the lady and looked at her diffidently, with a question in her eyes.

The lady glanced up and stopped cutting. "What is it, Ivanykha? Do you want to ask me something?"

Ivanykha hurriedly walked up to the lady, bowed down low to her, seized her hand, kissed it, and spoke rapidly, her words punctuated by racking sobs: "Oh, my lady, my dearest lady! Save me; I'm so unfortunate! And I'm hoping that you at least will take pity on me. You have such a kind heart. You have children yourself, and so you know how a mother's heart aches for them. You see, I . . . I have just the one son . . . He's all I have. I'll be orphaned if he goes! O merciful God . . ."

"Ivanykha! God be with you! Why are you crying? He hasn't taken his turn yet . . . I've already told the lord, and well, if it's at all possible, they won't take him, but neither I nor the lord can do anything about it—the lord isn't the senior official, and they won't change the law for him."

"Oh, but still, perhaps they would listen to him if he put in a good word. My dear lady, my dearest lady . . ."

Ivanykha wiped her tears and looked at the lady as if she were waiting for something. Then she reached into her bosom and took out a few eggs and some nuts tied in a kerchief.

"Perhaps you'd be so kind as to not refuse . . ."

The lady flushed in confusion. "What are you doing? God be with you! What's this for? No, no, I don't want it! What's the reason for it? Take it back."

Ivanykha became confused as well—she did not know what to do. "Let the children eat them, my lady. Enjoy them in good health. After all, it's really nothing."

The lady finally accepted the nuts, but Ivanykha had to take the eggs back home. The awkward conversation was interrupted by the servant, who said that if they wasted time like this, all the young men would have finished drawing the lots in the other room before they got there.

Ivanykha walked quietly into the room where the young ladies and the children were standing in the office doorway. From there, she had a good view of the business at hand—the drawing of the lots. She could see a large table covered with red felt all splattered with ink; she could also see the gentlemen seated at it. Although clearly bored, they made every effort to retain a semblance of seriousness and dignity.

There was a "drum" in the middle of the table, and another one farther down, on the edge, alongside the "wheel" with the paper lots. A small, scrawny young gentleman with a nasal voice was calling up the young men. One after the other, the men walked up with measured footsteps and, with feigned indifference, reached for a lot as if they intended to light their pipes with it—as if they did not know that this paper was deciding their fate.

The young gentleman called out: "Ivan Bodnarchuk!"

A robust youth stepped forward, and a military man, sitting in the office, looked at him as if to say: "What a fine soldier he'd make!"

A number was read out: "Five!"

The young man, looking as if all this had nothing to do with him, took the piece of paper, turned around in a dignified manner, and walked into the corner of the room where his friends were.

"Well, what does it mean? Will he be drafted?" Ivanykha softly asked the servant.

"Of course! You just heard—number five; that means he'll be the fifth one to go. The one who draws a small number, gets drafted, and the one who draws a big one—might not be taken."

"God, what nerve that young man has!" one young lady whispered. "He didn't even blink!—as if it weren't he who was being conscripted. He's like a stone!"

"Oh, how bitter my grief is!" Ivanyhka sighed.

"Semen Vesely!" The roll call was continuing.

"Number 385!"

The young man walked away in the same manner as the previous one, without any hint of joy or relief on his face.

"Petro Viytyk!"

Viytyk was not there; he was sick and had not come to the recruiting office. The officer who was to draw his lot for him was a tall, stout man; walking on tiptoe, so as not to make a racket with his big boots, he teetered unsteadily, striking a comical figure.

The young ladies broke into giggles: "Oh, look! He's just like a bear!"

Gingerly, as if he were handling something very delicate, the officer drew a lot and gave it, just as carefully, to the lord, who called out: "390!"

"He won't go," the young ladies decided.

"See who gets all the luck, without needing it," Ivanykha said plaintively. "I know Viytyk; he's from our village. My God, you should see him! What kind of a soldier would he be? His arm has been withered from birth—he's a cripple, nothing more! See how God favours him!"

More and more young men, all in the prime of their youth, stepped up to the table. They walked towards it like a flock of sheep, as if they did not know where they were going, or why. One after another, the youthful faces appeared and disappeared—saddening the eyes, and wounding the heart.

The heavy air, reeking with smoke from the lord's tobacco, swirled around heads. The candles on the tables, glimmering dimly in the smoky haze, cast a feeble light on faces flushed from lack of air, on grey homespun coats, lambskin caps, pointed police berets, and the golden frames of the tsar's portrait. It was difficult to breathe, nauseous. All that could be heard in the room was the voice calling out the names and numbers, and the rustling of paper.

Ivanykha was trying to catch a glimpse of her son's face, but she could not see anything in the grey haze.

"Korniy Udovyn!"

That name reverberated painfully in the mother's heart.

Korniy walked up as decisively and in the same dignified manner as everyone else, and drew his lot just as casually. He stared at the floor, awaiting the verdict, and did not even glance at the door where his mother was standing.

"Three!"

"Oh, I'm done for!" The mother's shriek echoed unexpectedly.

There is no sound to which this anguished cry can be compared, but those who heard it would never forget it.

Korniy shuddered and looked up at the door, but his mother was no longer there. Calmly, without hurrying, he made his way out of the recruitment office. It was only when he reached the porch that he quickened his pace and, completely ignoring the remarks of his friends, their questions, and their pity, he rushed down the stairs and out into the yard.

His mother was waiting for him. She silently seized him in her arms and pressed him to her, as if she wanted to hide him, to protect him from an evil, mighty power. Korniy did not say anything—there was nothing to say.

"No, Korniy! Let's go, let's go! I know the lord. When he comes out, I'll fall down at his feet, and I'll beg him, I'll implore him—maybe he'll grant me this, maybe they'll free you."

"There's no need to do that, mother! The lord can't do anything about it. I don't want you to do this!"

"Well, let's go and ask someone to write a petition. You'll give it to them tomorrow, and maybe . . ."

"I don't want to, mother. And it's too late for a petition now—the draft is tomorrow."

"Tomorrow! Oh, it's tomorrow! Let's go, my dear son, let's go to the lord!" Ivanykha, drowning in tears, persevered.

Her son took her by the arm and led her out of the yard into the street. She went along without knowing where she was going, without resisting.

A light autumnal rain was falling. The sky was overcast—it was gloomy. On the street corner, a solitary lamp was reflected in a puddle, like a dull, yellow stain. The wind drove the rain into people's faces. It was damp, wet, depressing. The people were weeping, and so was the sky.

III

There were throngs of people massed in front of the government offices. And there was such a hubbub, such lamentation, such tears! Women were gathered in large groups in the yard, and crowds of them stood out in the street. Some were anxiously waiting for their sons to come out of the office, while others were already weeping and wailing as if their sons were being laid out in coffins. The Jewish mothers were taking it the hardest—they were fainting and collapsing on the ground.

Ivanykha had started crying early in the morning, and she was still weeping now as she waited for her son. Her neighbours were saying something to her in an attempt to lift her spirits, but she was no longer listening.

She had no hope left.

This morning, she had gone to see the lord, even though her son had tried to stop her. But it was true—the lord could not do anything to help; and he had even scolded both her and the servant who had let her in—that was the kind of heart he had! But then, what could you expect, when there were so many people who came to petition him in the course of a day.

She had only one hope left—that her son might prove to be unfit for service. Unfortunately, however, it turned out that Korniy—tall, strong, and broad shouldered—was a fine young man without any physical defects.

Have pity, O God, on a young man's comeliness!

"Oh, it would have been better if he'd been born a cripple!" Ivanykha lamented.

"Don't tempt God's wrath, my dear kinswoman," her neighbour began saying to her, but then she just waved her hand dejectedly—she had enough worries of her own.

The young men began filing out of the office—and there was more weeping. A few of the boys were crying in their mother's embrace, but most of them, trying hard to appear nonchalant, had assumed a carefree, or even cheerful look.

The recruits who had no kin gathered together and, singing boisterously, trailed off to the tavern. The married men were getting ready to go home, and the other young men went off in all directions. The din and confusion escalated, and the wailing of the women grew louder.

Ivanykha was exhausted from weeping. She was standing and gazing intently at the door out of which the young men were exiting. One youth was coming out now—he was accepted; then, another one appeared—a Jewish boy—and he too was accepted; and so it went, on and on, but Korniy was not among them.

Finally, he came out—pale, with furrowed brows, and eyes that stared intently, hopelessly.

His mother saw him, took a better look, clasped her hands, and fell lifelessly to the ground—without a word, without a sound—as if she had been cut down by a scythe. Her son lifted her up, placed her head on his shoulder, and gazed at the pale, old face, frozen in sorrow. They stood there, inert, like figures carved in stone—figures of mute grief.

"Korniy, for the love of God, bring your mother to our place! What's wrong with the two of you?" a small, dark woman, dressed like a townswoman, unexpectedly addressed them.

She had been watching the crowd through her window and, seeing Ivanykha faint, had run outside to help. As the wife of the watchman, she lived in the manor yard and, not having anything much to do, spent entire days sitting beside the window, observing everything that was happening out there, in the wider world. She knew Ivanykha from a long time ago and felt truly sorry for the old woman, who was taking it all so hard.

"Is it you, Yevdokiya? It's good to see you!" Korniy replied. "Thank you for your offer; if you'll help me, I'll take her to your home."

In the meantime, Ivanykha regained consciousness. At first, she looked at her son as if she were still in a daze, but then she suddenly remembered everything.

"Oh, I'm done for now! Oh, my son, my only son! Oh, there's no longer any reason for me to live! O-o-o-h, I no longer have my darling child!"

Korniy and Yevdokiya, supporting her under the arms, led her, still wailing, to the cottage where Yevdokiya lived. There, Ivanykha sat down on a chair, lowered her head to the table, and began lamenting so loudly that the watchman, hearing her voice, ran out of his office.

"My God! What's going on here? Oh, it's you, Ivanykha!" The watchman frowned and shook his head worriedly.

Just then, the office door squeaked, and the watchman, jumping in fright, said nervously: "Hush now, Ivanykha! Nothing will help now. And there are lords here . . . you know . . . Someone might come by unexpectedly, and then both you and I will be in trouble. That's enough now, that's enough. Oh, my God!"

Ivanykha seemed to calm down a little. But when she raised her head and saw her son, she began wailing again.

"Korniy," Yevdokiya spoke up. "Perhaps you should go outside for a while, so that you don't grieve your mother; and you yourself might cheer up a bit if you were with other people."

"Oh, sure! I'll cheer up, that's for sure!" Korniy said, but, nevertheless, he did leave the house.

He walked out of the manor yard into the street and, leaning against a post, just stood there—not looking at anything, not seeing anything, not hearing anything, and not paying attention to anything.

He was thinking his sad thoughts—that he had been recruited and was now enlisted, that his freedom as a young unmarried man was now curtailed. He was thinking that his mother would be left alone with her uncaring stepsons, and there would be no one to protect her now, poor thing, from her harsh stepfather. And he was also thinking about the young woman he had planned to marry, but now, the wedding had drifted off into the mists, for who could tell what might happen in the course of six years . . .

He was overwhelmed by thoughts that were like the autumn fog, and there was no comfort in sight.

People, seeing him as they passed by on the road, said: "Aha, the new recruit has drunk so much in his sorrow that he's leaning against a post already!"

Korniy did not hear the people's gossip, and it would not have bothered him if he had.

Someone tugged at his sleeve, and Korniy came to with a start. Next to him stood Semen Klymchuk, a friend of his who was also a new recruit.

"Korniy, my brother! Let's go, my dear friend; let's at least have a drink in our grief!"

"Let's go—it's all the same now," Korniy replied indifferently.

They set off towards the nearby tavern that a Jewish man had opened right across from the government offices. He most certainly was raking in a sizeable profit today! It did not matter if the men were drinking out of grief, or out of joy, because in either case, money jingled in the tavern keeper's pockets.

The tavern was crammed with people; some were coming in, others were leaving, and a few had settled in for the long haul— probably for the entire night. Those who had been released from military duty were buying drinks for their kinsfolk and for the young men who were less fortunate.

The new recruits were sitting in a group; each one of them tossed in a coin, and then they drank together and sang songs about recruits. There was singing, weeping, and quarrelling in the tavern and, in one corner, a fight was brewing.

"Hey, you there! You slab of fat!" one of the recruits shouted at a young man in a grey, embroidered coat. "Buy us a drink! Let's conclude the deal with a drink, you devil's son—are we supposed to serve for you without getting anything in return?"

"Who the devil is serving for me?" the young man in the grey coat shouted in turn.

"We are! Who else? Do you think that no one knows the size of your father's purse? Or how your mother beat a path to the lord's home? Ho-ho! Even the devil doesn't dare to take a rich man's son. Come on, buy us some whiskey, you son of a bitch!"

An altercation broke out between the young man and the new recruits.

"Hey, you guys! Who'll drink to me? I'm partying!" A young man, who had not been drafted, shouted from the other end of the tavern. "Whoever is in the tavern or outside of it—come over here. I'm paying for everything! Drink until you drop—I won't say a word!"

"Oh, I'm ru-u-u-ined now!" a new recruit wailed.

Semen and Korniy walked in. They had many friends, both among the recruits and among those who had been freed from service. They were invited to join both groups. Semen turned towards the recruits.

"I'll come to you, my dear brothers—we'll drink away our freedom together. Jew! Some whiskey over here!"

Korniy also joined this group and sat down beside Semen.

They all began to sing:

> "They've sown and ploughed,
> but there's no one to harvest,
> For they've herded our young men
> to swear their oaths in the city."

The sad, solemn singing resounded strangely among the drunken cries, the hubbub, and the rattling of glasses and coins.

> "Did we deserve this from God
> or from our community,
> That we young men
> have been bound in chains . . ."

Semen downed glass after glass, and Korniy did not lag far behind. Soon, Semen's head began drooping, but Korniy's kept rising higher. Semen's eyes were gradually becoming clouded, but

Korniy's shone more sharply and seemed to be growing darker.
Semen weakly nodded his head in time to the music, but Korniy
sang in a strong voice, frowning, and occasionally banging his
fist on the table when someone provoked him with an inane joke.

A small group began singing:

> "The unmarried young men
>   are drinking and carousing.
> The men who are married
>   are weeping and wailing . . ."

Semen pressed his head against the table and burst into tears.

"Hey, you! Cabbagehead! Why the devil are you blubbering?
You're not married!" one of his friends shouted at him.

"Oh, it's true I'm not married, my dear brothers, it's true! Who
will show me any kindness in a foreign land? Oh, my dear mother,
my own dear mother—at least you take pity on me! Oh my dear
kinsfolk, didn't I turn out as I should? Oh, my dear betrothed!"

The uproar grew louder; some of the men laughed at Semen,
while others tried to console him and cheer him up.

Korniy was silent; he was no longer singing and, his dark eyes,
burning with grief and compassion, glared angrily at Semen.
Suddenly, he slammed the table so hard with his fist that the glasses
rattled, and Semen fell silent.

"It would be better if you shut up," Korniy said to Semen in a
quivering, choked voice. "Why are you carrying on like an old
woman? Even if I were being slaughtered, I wouldn't cry!"

He rose to his feet, hurled his glass to the floor, and stalked
out of the tavern.

IV

The next day, Korniy and his mother began the trek home,
walking along with a group of other sons and mothers, just as when
they had set out for the recruitment office. But now the group was
smaller. Some of the youths had remained in town "to drink away
their freedom," while others, having drawn a favourable lot, had
returned home earlier.

Ivanykha was walking silently beside her son; their attempts to carry on a conversation had failed. And this was true not only of them—there was very little talking in general. When they reached the village, the group grew even smaller as people dropped out of it, and the conversation became even more subdued. Finally, all the people dispersed to their homes, and Korniy and his mother walked on alone to their cottage that stood near a lake at the far end of the village.

Korniy entered the house first. His stepfather was sitting at the table, eating a breakfast of dry bread and garlic. The old man glanced at Korniy and said: "Well?"

"I was drafted," Korniy replied grimly.

"So, they did draft you, after all," the stepfather said. "Were a lot of our young men drafted?"

"Quite a few. Semen was drafted, Pavlo, and many others."

"What about the old woman, did she beat a path to the lord's door?" Ivan asked, glancing obliquely at his wife.

"Yes, she did," Korniy replied, looking off to one side.

"Well, what came of it?"

"Nothing."

"That's what I thought . . ."

"You thought . . . your mind is like that of a wolf," Ivanykha snapped.

"Watch that you don't lose your mind!" Ivan retorted. Then he turned to Korniy and said more gently: "Sit down and have some breakfast."

Korniy sat down, cut some bread, and began to eat.

"Wait, my son! You aren't going to eat dry bread, are you?" Ivanykha said.

"Have you cooked something then?" Ivan interjected.

Not wanting to get into an argument, Ivanykha did not reply. She lit a fire in the stove and began preparing a thick cornmeal gruel. Ivan got to his feet, took his cap off a hook, and walked out of the house.

"When do you have to go back into town?" Hrytsko asked Korniy.

"On Sunday, two weeks from today."

"Have you heard where you're being sent?" Petro inquired.

"How should I know?" Korniy replied listlessly.

He turned away and sat looking through the window at the lake that glimmered indistinctly in the distance. It was either misty, or an almost imperceptible rain was falling—one that seemed to be passing through a fine sieve. It was hard to tell which it was.

Through the fog, Korniy saw someone moving across the pasture to the lake. From a distance, the figure appeared grey, but there was a red kerchief on its head.

Korniy looked at it intently for some time, and then got up and went towards the door.

"Where are you going, my son?" his mother inquired.

"Oh, I'm just going for a short walk until breakfast is ready. I don't have anything else to do," Korniy said, and he made his way out of the cottage in a leisurely manner.

"Don't stay too long," his mother called out after him.

Korniy left the cottage and set out for the lake. On the shore, the figure of a woman could be discerned. Korniy came up closer, and the figure became more distinct—it was a young woman dressed in a white homespun skirt and a white jacket. She was bending over, filling her pail with water from the lake.

"Varka!" Korniy called as he drew closer to her.

The girl turned around. "Oh, it's you, Korniy! You've come back? Well, tell me, how did things go for you?" she inquired anxiously.

"How did it go for me? I'm going to be a soldier . . ."

"Oh, my bitter fate . . ." The pail dropped from her hands and rolled away. "What are we going to do now?" The girl wrung her hands and looked at Korniy with tear-filled eyes.

"What are we going to do? This is what we'll do, Varka . . ." Korniy hesitated. "Listen, we can't talk here—there are people going by. It would be better if I came to see you in the evening. When I knock on the wall—come out. Good-bye for now." And he turned to go home.

Varka wiped her eyes with her kerchief and picked up the pail. She quickly filled it with water and went home across the pasture, avoiding two women who were heading towards the lake.

When Korniy came home, Petro and Hrytsko were no longer in the house. He once again sat down by the window and gazed unthinkingly at the pasture. His heart was heavy and filled with pain; he remained silent and did not speak to his mother.

"Sonny!" his mother cried. "Why are you so quiet? You might at least talk to me during the short time we have left together."

"What am I to say to you, mother?"

"Are you at least sorry that you have to leave me?"

"And even if I am sorry—will that help matters any?"

"Just like his father," Ivanykha thought. "Will you at least come home for a visit when you're in that army?" Ivanykha asked once again. Her voice was brimming with tears. "Will they let you?"

"If I'm stationed somewhere nearby, then maybe I'll get back for an occasional visit. But if I'm sent far away, then I probably won't come back for at least five years."

"It may be that you won't find me here by then, my child!"

"Oh, don't provoke God, mother! Why do you say things like that?"

Ivanykha wanted to say something else, but she remained silent; tears were choking her. "I've probably wearied him more than enough with my tears," she thought.

After eating the breakfast his mother served him, Korniy did not leave the table; he smoked and continued to sit there—silent and sad—leaning his head on his hand.

"You should go out and be with people, Korniy," his mother spoke up. "You should go and have some fun. What is there for you to do with someone old like me? There's nothing for us to talk about."

"Where am I to find some fun?" Korniy said; but then he thought about it and rose from the table. "Well, perhaps I'll go and see Semen."

On his was to Semen's home, he realised that the young fellows were probably enjoying themselves dancing in the tavern, because it was Sunday, and the last one at that . . .

When he arrived at the tavern, he saw that a large number of young men and women had congregated there, and the musicians were playing the violin and beating a snare drum. Korniy ran his eyes over the girls, but Varka was not among them—her stern, widowed mother did not often permit her to go dancing.

Semen was dancing with Hapka, his betrothed. Today, he was feeling somewhat happier, because Hapka had spoken frankly with him and promised that she would wait for him without fail during the four years that he was to be away—she would not marry anyone else. Well, that was to be expected—Semen came from a well-to-do family, and Hapka was still young and in no hurry to get married.

After finishing the *krutyakha [a whirling dance]* with the girls, the boys began the dance "I was walking by the grove" by themselves. Calmly and in a dignified manner, they paraded in pairs, swaying to the rhythm of the song, and singing:

> "I walk by the grove, but not in it, by choice,
> And I recognize my girl by the sound of her voice."

The girls stood and looked on; some were laughing among themselves, while others were sad. There were also those who provoked the young men with jokes, and sang to them:

> "The swamps have burned, heaps of ashes remain,
> If you aren't recruits, get married, young swains."

This song did not appeal to the young men; they stopped their "parading" and began inviting the girls to dance the *krutyakha*. Once again, they twirled in twos and threes; red kerchiefs flashed and white skirts trimmed with crimson yarn whirled.

Young adolescent girls spun around among the older ones; the young men did not ask them to dance yet, and so they fluttered about with their girlfriends like pairs of bright butterflies— dancing rapidly, with tiny, mincing steps.

Korniy quickly grew tired of watching the dances—he had never liked dancing. He wandered around for a while among the young people and then strolled through the village. None of this cheered him up, and he finally decided to go home.

"Well, my boy, did you enjoy yourself?" his mother asked.

"Oh sure, I took a walk, and that's good enough for me."

Korniy stretched out on the bench and lay there with his eyes shut. It was quiet in the house. The stepfather and his sons were not at home—they had eaten their dinner without Korniy and gone to the tavern.

As he lay there, Korniy thought: "So this is how my life has turned! I grew up in freedom, but now I'll get to taste military drills."

It was true that Korniy had grown up in freedom. After his father died—Korniy had been seven years old then—there was no one in a position of authority over him. His mother had pampered him as an only son, and she was much more likely to give in to him, than he to her.

It was only during the last four years, after a new master had come into their home, that Korniy quite frequently found himself defending his freedom. He never retreated, nor did he argue— but neither did he give in. It seemed to him, however, that his own home was no longer his.

Towards evening, Ivan and his sons came home from the tavern slightly tipsy.

As he walked in the door, Ivan shouted at his wife: "Well, how's it going to be, are we all going to be eating, or just half of us?"

"Not all of us," Korniy replied, "because I won't be here." He rose from the bench, took his cap, and put on his homespun coat.

"Where are you going, Korniy?" his mother inquired.

"Nowhere in particular . . ." Korniy stepped outside without saying anything more.

The fine rain had stopped towards evening; it was turning dark, and a heavy fog was rolling in from the lake. The moon's rays penetrated the ragged clouds that were turning pale and drifting off towards the east, uncovering the western horizon. The air was still. The last few leaves were drifting almost silently from the trees.

Korniy did not walk along the street. He went past the gardens to a yard that abutted the lake, crawled over a fence, and went through the garden to a small cottage with a single window in it. A flickering light from a fire in the stove shone through the window. The small window turned completely dark at times, as human figures blocked it. The widow and her daughter Varka were preparing their supper.

Watching the light, Korniy stood and waited for it to go out. After quivering for quite some time on the uneven ground, the bright streak vanished, and the window turned silver in the moonlight. Korniy waited a little while longer, and then went up to the cottage and thumped on the wall with his fist.

The old widow could not hear such a dull noise from where she was lying on the clay bed atop the oven, but Varka heard it, for she was waiting near the window. She deftly let herself out of the house like a novice nun and silently closed the door behind her.

"Have you come, Korniy?" she asked softly, as she rushed to meet him.

"Yes, I have—to talk things over!" Korniy replied just as softly. Let's go a bit farther away, Varka, so your mother can't hear us."

"Well, she's sleeping, but it would be better to move off a bit."

They walked swiftly down towards the lake and climbed into a boat lying on the shore. Varka glanced at Korniy as if she wanted to tell him something but, instead, hid her face in her hands and began to weep.

"Don't cry, Varka, don't cry. Let's discuss what will happen to us now," Korniy said.

"Oh, how can I know, unfortunate creature that I am, what will happen now," Varka replied tearfully.

"Well, I'll finish my service and come back to you. But will you wait for me?"

"I'd wait even for seven years, if it were up to me."

"Who is it up to?" Korniy inquired painfully.

"Don't you know my mother? She has her heart set on a rich son-in-law."

"Well, I'm not all that poor—I have half a farm."

"What good is that? You'll go off into the army, and your stepfather and his sons will do whatever they want to."

"I'll take care of them when I return."

"If you return . . ." Varka said sadly, and fell silent.

"Oh, my dear girl, you seem to be twisting words around," Korniy said bitterly. "You should just tell me, straight out—I'm not meant for you, and you're not meant for me."

Varka wept even more bitterly, and Korniy rose to his feet and quietly walked away along the shore.

Rushing after him, Varka cried: "Korniy, my dearest Korniy!" Grabbing his hand, she sobbed brokenly: "See what you're like! Do you think I don't care for you? How can I speak more frankly? I'm saying that I would wait, but as for my mother . . ."

"So, stay with your mother . . ."

"How cruel you are, Korniy! Do you think it's easy to stand up to my mother? My mother isn't like yours. She wants to have everything her way. And you're so proud—somehow, you just don't know how to get around my mother. If you tried, perhaps it would be different."

"Eh, Varka, such attempts to get around people are not for me. I couldn't please my stepfather, and I won't be able to please a mother-in-law," Korniy smiled proudly and sadly.

"That's just it! You're always like that—but where has your pride got you?"

"I guess that's my nature. Still, it's all the same—if I try to please her, or if I don't, for when I leave for the army, there won't be a chance to please her. Others will be found who will be able to do this without me."

"May misery try to please them!"

"Misery will take care of us all . . ."

Varka fell silent once again, but she continued wiping away her tears. They walked along the lake in this way for some time. And then they heard a shout from the house: "Varka, where are you?"

"Oh, this is terrible! Mother has woken up—she's calling me! Farewell, Korniy, I have to go . . ." Varka tearfully embraced him and kissed him quickly, passionately.

Korniy did not reproach her anymore; he did not afflict her with his words. He just clasped his beloved tightly in his arms.

"Farewell, Varka! We'll say our farewells and part forever."

"Varka! Varka!" The old voice cried out more stridently now.

Varka tore herself from Korniy's embrace and raced up the incline towards the cottage. Korniy moved silently along the shore of the lake and disappeared into the white fog.

V

The sky was clear the morning the young men left the village. The autumn sun, though not warm, was shining brightly. The trees were outlined in bold relief against the azure sky, but the wind blowing through the village did not bring with it either the sound of the rustling forest or the singing of the birds. It was quiet and sunny, peaceful, but there was no joy. Even though it was Sunday, there was no singing and no music to be heard in the village. The young men were done with dancing for now . . .

The recruits had agreed to go into town together; they were to gather in a fenced-in field and leave from there. It took a long time for them to assemble! The mothers were in no hurry to put together the few things their sons needed for the trip. But they finally got everything ready, and the young men drifted in, one by one, to the field by the mill. Their mothers and wives came with them, but they would not make the trip into town—what would be the point?

As Korniy walked down the street, he was accompanied by his mother, who could not see the road for her tears. When they were passing Varka's cottage, a window opened with a thud, and a girl's face, also awash in tears, appeared. Korniy looked up and stopped; he wanted to say a few words of farewell to Varka, but he did not say anything—he bent his head and continued quietly on his way. The window closed, and if someone had glanced through it into the house, he would have seen a slender blond girl weeping bitterly, her head on the table.

Farther along the way, Korniy met Semen as the latter was leaving Hapka's cottage. His eyes were damp and, as he walked along, he kept looking back at the little yard where his betrothed was standing by the gate. He kept waving to her with his cap, saying good-bye. They were engaged, so there was no shame attached to saying their good-byes in public. Semen's mother, carrying something in a bundle, quickly caught up to him. The little old woman was wailing loudly as she followed her son.

Now they were on the tilled field by the mill, where many young men had already gathered with their kinsfolk. Fragmentary conversations were taking place, and there was the sound of weeping. Some of the young men had no kinsfolk—no one was seeing them off, and no was crying over them—but they did not seem any happier than the others. It was the married men who had the most difficult time! They would have liked the ground to open up and swallow them! Both their mothers and their wives were wailing as if they were seeing them off to their deaths. It would have been better never to have married or become engaged!

Everyone had arrived—it was time to move on. Oh, what a painful parting it was! Six years, four years—it is not a lifetime, but so much could change in that time. Tomorrow, one life would come to an end, and another would begin; at the moment, however, life stood still.

The youths without families stood off to one side, gazing sadly at the grief of others, but their hearts were also moved. The married couples were embracing for the last time. The women were wailing, and some were fainting.

Semen hugged his mother and cried uncontrollably: "Farewell, mother! Farewell my dearest! Tell Hapka not to pine!" He could not say anything more. A friend took him by the arm and led him to the recruits who were ready to set out. Semen obediently followed his friend, weeping and stumbling as he walked.

Korniy, his hands at his sides, was standing and looking at his mother, who was pressing closely to him. He was not crying or saying anything—he was just standing silently. His eyes had darkened, and his lips were pressed tightly together. He had no words, no tears, nothing.

"Farewell, mother," he suddenly said hoarsely and, turning abruptly, as if forcing himself to move away, walked off decisively to join his friends.

Ivanykha clasped her hands and fell to the ground in a faint— her sharp grief had mown her down. Her son did not see this; he did not turn around to take another look . . .

The recruits departed, and they shimmered in the distance for a long time, growing ever smaller to the eye, until they finally disappeared into the forest. They were walking quietly, without singing, and the wind did not carry a farewell song to their kin. Today, they did not feel like singing, but tomorrow, when they walked into the town, there would be singing, inane whistling, and loud music; but those songs would be of a different kind!

VI

Many drably dressed people gathered at the train station in the little Volynian town; short yellow jackets were seen most frequently but, here and there a soldier's grey overcoat was visible. The train was to leave soon, and all the recruits had gathered beside it with bundles in their hands. Some were already moving through the cars, but others were still standing on the platform saying their good-byes to their families.

There was no point in prolonging the farewells—the train was to leave late at night. There was much weeping and wailing to be heard here as well, but those who had heard it on the day of the draft were no longer as greatly affected by it. At that time, they had been weeping as if someone had just been laid out in a coffin, but now they were crying as if they were standing over a covered grave.

The recruits themselves were no longer crying. For them, a new life had begun. They had crossed the boundary, and it did not matter if the new life was going to be better or worse—it had already begun!

"Korniy! Korniy! Where are you? Come on, we'll sit together!" a slight recruit was shouting anxiously as he ran up and down the length of the train searching for his friend in the dim light of the lanterns. "Korniy, where are you?"

"I'm over here, I'm not lost," Korniy spoke up calmly as he stepped out of a group of friends. "What is it, Semen? Are you scared to go without me?"

"No, I'm not, but all the same . . ."

"Get on the train, get on the train, that's enough talking!" a sergeant shouted at them.

They quickly entered a car already crammed with men. A place was found, however, and Korniy and Semen sat down on a bench by themselves.

"Well, they've really packed us into this car," someone spoke up in one of the corners. "We're jammed in so tightly that no one could stick a needle between us. There'll be lots of fun and games tonight!"

The School
(1895)

I had been planning for a long time to visit my friend who was a teacher in a parish school, and now I was finally on my way. But what a day I had chosen! I had scarcely travelled a kilometre from the town of Lutsk—the village where my friend lived was about twenty kilometres from Lutsk—when there was a terrible downpour.

It was still raining when I arrived in the village, and, as I gazed at the cottages and the dam that was overgrown with willows, it seemed as if I were looking at things through a sieve. It was only when I reached the village square that the rain let up a little, and I was able to get a better look at the church, the priest's big house and, a little to one side of it, a small cottage with a porch that had a school bell beside it.

"That must be the school," the driver said, "but how are you going to get to it?"

He had a good point. Immediately in front of the school, there was a huge puddle that resembled a ford in a river. I gazed at it distrustfully and then picked a spot where I could put my foot down without immediately getting stuck in the mire.

In the meantime, my friend had spotted me through the window, and she rushed out to the porch with a loud, cheery greeting: "Well, here you are at last! But what's wrong? Has my Venice scared you? There's only one thing you can do, my friend. Jump into the water."

I had no choice but to listen to her advice, and so I resolutely stepped into the water that reached my ankles. Actually, this was not such a big act of courage, as I was already fairly well soaked, and it would not have taken much to finish the job.

After entering the cottage and exchanging greetings, I took off my wet clothes and was about to hang them on the wall when my friend stopped me.

"What are you doing? Your clothes will get all white from the lime on the walls—especially since they're wet; you won't ever be able to get them clean again."

I had no choice but to spread them out on a chair. I was just about to sit down on another chair when my friend stopped me once again.

"Don't sit there!" she cried.

I stared at her in amazement.

"That chair has only three legs," she explained.

"Well, where is there one that has all four?" I inquired.

"Your clothes are on it, and there are no others. Sit down on the bed. I'll push the table in closer, and we'll have tea."

We managed to get settled, and soon the tea was ready.

While my friend was preparing it, I looked over her little home, but there really was not very much to see—bare walls, a ceiling that was peeling, and a stove that was in an even worse state of disrepair. By the stove there was a little bench with a dipper and a wash basin; next to it there was a small cupboard. By the other wall, there was a table—which was now by the bed—a trunk, and the two chairs that have already been mentioned. And that was all.

"Well," I said to my friend, "I've come to see your academy and to find out how you are enlightening the masses."

"That's too bad, because you won't see anything. You've come too late."

"What do you mean? It's only mid-April. Why did your holidays begin so early? You wrote me that exams would be starting soon."

"There won't be any exams."

"Why?"

"The priest is against it. I prepared a group of the more capable boys, but everything came to a standstill because of the religious instruction. The priest is supposed to look after that. He kept putting it off until Easter, and now he's saying, 'Why do they need exams? Let them go and graze cattle.' That's how things are here! How did you expect them to be?"

"Well, I certainly didn't think they would be like this. Well, it can't be helped; however, I'd still like to see the school."

"We'll do that tomorrow; it's dark now."

"Fine. But listen. Why are you staying here? Why don't you go home if there's nothing for you to do here?"

"Well, you see, I still have to pry some money from the priest."

And she began telling me about the lengthy, involved process of "prying loose" money for a teacher.

First, the priest has to gather money from the parishioners; the parishioners try to avoid giving it, saying that they have no need of the school, that not all of them send their children to it, and that, after all, they have no money. Despite this, the money is collected in one way or another, and the priest hides it away in his home.

This is when the "prying loose" process begins in earnest. The teacher has to go to the priest for the money, and an interminable discussion ensues. After lengthy arguments, the priest finally releases two or three rubles, or, if he really gets stubborn, just one.

"But how is such a thing possible?" I asked my friend. "And why do you get embroiled in such demeaning negotiations with the priest? What right does he have to dole out your money in dribs and drabs as if you were begging money for vodka?"

"Well, what is one to do with him? It's all in his hands."

"Then you should complain about him!"

"To whom?"

"Well, to the parishioners, or the intercessor."

"The parishioners don't care, and the intercessor is useless; I'm happy if he just leaves me alone. Once he came and really blasted me. And do you know what for? Because I wore a Persian lamb fur hat to church in the winter. He said: 'This offends the pious feelings of the peasants.' What was I to say to him? But, all in all, this priest is no worse than the others; he's old, so at least he doesn't cause any problems, and he's quite good-natured. I teach his grandchildren, and he gives me my dinner for this."

"What? Just your dinner?"

"*Just!* In your way of thinking it's *just*, but in mine, it's *even*. If you were sent your dinner in turn by every woman in the village, then you too would say *even*. No, my priest is still so-so, praise God; one can arrive at some agreement with him. He's a trifle stingy . . . and, to make things worse, he doesn't get much income here."

"Nevertheless, he does live in a big stone house."

"Well, what good is a big stone house when it's empty."

"Perhaps, perhaps . . ."

We arranged things somehow, made our beds, and went to sleep. One window had to be stuffed with a pillow because the pane in it was broken.

Early the next morning, after washing with a beaten egg—there was no soap, and one had to "pry loose" some money before it could be bought—I went to have a look at the school.

As soon as I crossed the porch—which was still wet from yesterday's rain—and opened the door to the classroom, I was hit by a cold, damp draft as if it were coming from a cellar.

The classroom was not plastered, and the floor was uneven and peeling even more than in the teacher's cottage. In the middle of the room there were rows of desks; in the corner stood a chalkboard with traces of chalk still on it; at the front of the room there was a table and a chair; and between the grimy windows on the wall behind the table there was a fairly large map that was outdated and covered with a film of smoke.

"So, are your pupils studying geography?" I inquired, looking at the map.

"Geography? Heavens, no! They can scarcely learn to read and write in the short time they're in school."

"Why is that?"

"What can one expect, if they don't start coming to school until a month or so before Christmas? Up to then, they're always busy herding cattle and doing things like that."

"Nevertheless, don't you have some kind of a curriculum?"

"Well, it's like this. The most one can hope for is to teach them to read, to write without *serious* errors, and to do some arithmetic. And then the singing takes up quite a lot of the time."

"What kind of singing? Do you teach them singing?" I was completely bewildered; up to that moment, I had not known that my friend could sing, let alone teach singing.

"Well, yes, I do. It's church singing. It's not very difficult because we pick out what's easiest. But it's difficult to teach boys who don't know anything about notes or choral singing how to sing even the basic 'Lord have mercy.' Sometimes one works up a real sweat trying to teach them, and one's throat ends up aching more than I can tell you . . . Well, anyway, let's go. There's nothing more for you to see here."

But I stood in the middle of the room and listened; there was some noise on the other side of the wall.

"What's that?" I asked.

"Oh, some people have probably gathered for a meeting. There's a meeting room next door, and the caretaker lives there as well. And next to my room, there's a jail. I'm telling you— the kinds of things one can hear at times!"

"But there's no one in the jail now, is there?"

"No, it's spring, and people are rarely put there in the springtime; there's a lot of work to be done in the fields, and people beg off and try to serve their time later, after the most urgent work is done, or until some longer holy period in the church calendar when one isn't allowed to work . . ."

The noise on the other side of the wall grew louder, and the discussion was far from amicable. The sounds echoed dully in the damp air of the school; it became very unpleasant. We returned to the teacher's room.

"Where are your school books?" I wanted to know.

"Over here," my friend replied, pointing at the small cupboard by the stove.

"May I have a look?"

"Of course you may. You must bear in mind, however, that there are banned books there!"

I looked at her and did not know if I should believe her or not. She began laughing.

"Yes, yes, they're banned; you'll see! I trust you won't report me to the 'authorities'?"

I still did not understand. She unlocked the shelf and showed me: "This is the library for reading outside the classroom."

I picked up a book at random and examined it. *The Life of St. Simeon Stolpnyk.* I put it back and took another: *The Life of St. Gregory* . . . I pulled out still another one, from the other end of the shelf, and read: *The Life of the Holy* . . .

"Why are all your books religious in nature?" I asked.

"That's the way it is. We have a *parish* school, and so we have to read the books that are sent to us. Our textbooks are here." She pointed at the middle shelf.

The books that stood there were prayer books, a short catechism, the Old Testament, a book of exercises, an arithmetic text, and a few slim primers. I've forgotten who the authors of the primers were—their names were all unfamiliar to me.

"And here are the proscribed books!" my friend finally said. She smiled and pointed at the bottom shelf where there were a few books and a large empty flask.

I looked at the books: *Our Native Tongue*, by Ushynsky; a series of readers by Paulson; and several publications put out by "Posrednyk" . . .

"You must be joking!" I exclaimed in amazement.

"Why, no! What do you mean—joking? These really are the books that must be 'removed from school libraries.'"

"But these are books that have been approved by the Committee on Literacy."

"So what? The 'Committee on Literacy' means nothing to us." She said this without laughing and with a rather sad look on her face.

At that point, I believed her.

"What is this for?" I asked, pointing at the large flask.

My friend started to laugh again. "This is my inheritance as a teacher! It's also forbidden, you know. My predecessor kept whiskey in this flask, but, of course, since I've been here, it's remained empty. Perhaps some day it will come in handy for someone . . . Anyway, looking at this flask has reminded me of my priest; it's time for me to go and have my dinner. Are you coming with me?"

"Well, no, how am I . . ."

"Well, there's no way out, my dear; you have to come with me because I have nothing to eat here. And there's no need to feel awkward about it; my priest likes to receive guests. He'll be very happy to see you. Let's go."

And so, happy or not, I had to go. Clinging to the fence to avoid falling into the brimming puddles from yesterday's rain, we went to the priest's home. In the yard, large and overgrown with grass, stood a motley array of barns, storehouses, and various outbuildings. Next to the yard, a mature orchard with luxuriant trees surrounded the large stone house that I had seen as I drove into the village.

We entered the stone house through a high porch. In the very first room, we saw the priest with his daughter and two grandsons; they were already seated at the table.

My friend introduced me, and we were invited to join them.

While I was eating my dinner, I looked around the room. It was difficult to decide if this was a poor or rich household. My friend spoke truthfully when she said that the stone house was empty, but it would have taken a good many things to fill it.

It was an old building, a former Catholic convent—the church had also belonged to the convent at one time—with thick walls, deep windows and, instead of a ceiling, a high arched vault that was cold, expansive, and quite dark. Voices and footsteps echoed in these rooms, and it seemed that the masters here were not the priest and his family, but the dark Uniate icons and the wooden angels that looked down at us from the walls with unfriendly smiles or severe frowns.

The icons and angels had been removed from the church when it was changed from a Uniate Church into an Orthodox one—such transformations were nothing new to this church. The priest who, like the church, had belonged formerly to the Uniate Church, had accepted these refugees into his home, and they fitted into it extremely well, better than the master himself. He was a small, withered old man who was dwarfed by his immense dwelling.

But then, everything was dwarfed by it: the people, the furniture, the rugs, the cupboards, and the trunks—all that priestly treasure that in an ordinary house would have created an impression of wealth. Neither our conversation nor our company was suited to that place.

I felt relieved when our little group finished eating and moved out into the orchard where there were neither Catholic walls, nor Uniate icons.

As we strolled down the path among bushes of currants and gooseberries, my friend gradually turned the conversation around to the fact that it was spring already, the school year had ended, and the time had come for her to go home.

"Well, by all means, go," the priest said kindly.

"But you know, Father, that I can't go, and you know why."

"No, how am I supposed to know?" the priest stated in the same innocent tone. "Can't you hire horses in the village?"

"But, Father, it's not horses that are the problem! You know what's wrong. Horses can be hired, but I don't have any money."

"Ah, so that's what you're getting at. Lord, what has this world come to! How greedy our young people have become! Was it like this in our day? Well, well, young lady, well, well!" And he laughed in a low, muffled voice.

It was clear that the young lady with whom he was speaking did not feel like laughing; on the contrary, she was hardly able to restrain her anger.

"Really," the priest continued, after he had finished laughing, "why do you need money, and all at once at that? You're young. So, wait a while, and when you're getting married and preparing your dowry, that's when the money will stand you in good stead. Isn't that right?"

He directed his question unexpectedly to me.

I was forced to enter into the conversation. "Who knows when that will be, but it really is too bad that she can't travel to town with me. I've hired the horses already, but it looks as if I'll have to go home alone. So what shall I tell your mother?"

I turned to my friend. "When will you be coming home?"

"I don't know," she replied curtly.

"Well, that's enough, that's enough, don't worry." The priest began to speak and there was a sudden change in the tone of his voice. "Do you really think I'm such a skinflint? Come over this evening, we'll settle our accounts, and then you can leave tomorrow if that's what you want to do."

After this, the topic of conversation changed, and soon we went home.

In the evening, my friend went to "settle the accounts." I waited for her for a long time. She finally returned, looking neither happy nor sad.

"Well, what happened? Did he give you the money?" I asked.

"Well . . . he gave me half of what was owing to me! He said he didn't have the rest, that he hadn't collected it yet. What's one to do with him?"

"Do you believe him?"

"Of course not!"

"So what are you going to do? Are you coming with me, or are you going to stay here and try 'to pry loose' all your money?"

"Oh no, I'm going. I'm sick of all this. Perhaps I'll manage somehow to get the rest of it later. But that's enough talk about it! I'm sick of it!" And she began to pack her things so that we could leave in the morning.

The following day, we set out after saying farewell to the school and the village, which neither one of us was fated to visit ever again.

The empty school, the empty room, and the empty flask remained behind to await the arrival of the new teacher.

Happiness
A Legend
(1895)

It happened at the beginning of time.

The newly created earth, abounding in harmony and glorious life, glowed with a wondrous beauty. God's blissful and gracious dream flourished. Human life, flowing in gentle waves, merged with this vision into a single, dazzling, tranquil sea. There was peace on earth, and people lived serenely.

It continued like this for a long time.

The Evil Spirit slept in a subterranean land. He slept for many ages, and his dreams were malevolent.

Waking from his sleep, he shouted: "Wicked dreams are tormenting me! My soul is being torn apart, and I can find no peace. But there, on earth, a radiant peace prevails; the vision of my Enemy is flourishing and prospering, and nothing disturbs it. Am I to bear my searing affliction by myself? Am I to bury my dark woe? No, I will cast my grief into the heart of my Foe's dearest children. I will sow sorrow, like a black veil, among them, and the vision of my Enemy will be obscured."

Bursting as black smoke out of the bosom of the earth and soaring over the land in a fiery cloud, the Evil Spirit flew over valleys graced by fields of undulating golden grain and thick stands of trees, their heavily laden branches bowing to the ground.

Wherever he descended, the grain was scorched as if by fire, the fruit on the trees blackened, the grass turned yellow, flowers withered—and a desert came into being.

People, hiding from the blazing-hot wind in burrows and caves, groaned: "Famine . . . famine!"

The Evil Spirit returned to his subterranean land and waited.

A hundred years went by.

The desert was once again transformed into a luxuriant land; once more, golden grain undulated, and thick stands of trees bowed down their heavy-laden branches. A new generation of people still related tales about the hunger of long ago, but the stories were slowly being forgotten. God's vision flourished as before, and peace enveloped the earth.

But the Evil Spirit was not sleeping. He said to himself: "I will go and look at what my hands have wrought."

Rising as a grey fog from the bosom of the earth, he soared over the land in a freezing cloud. He flew over mountain pastures and, wherever large herds grazed and people were encamped, he appeared as an impenetrable darkness, as a pernicious pestilence.

Cattle died, people perished, and a terrible lament rolled through the mountains: "Death . . . death!"

The herds vanished, the camps emptied . . .

The Evil Spirit returned to his subterranean land and waited.

A hundred years went by.

The graves of the people who had succumbed to the pestilence were lushly overgrown with grass, and the descendants of these victims walked serenely over mountain pastures, cheerfully playing the *sopilka [shepherd's flute]* and calling together their countless herds. The camps, gleaming with white tents, teemed with life. No one remembered or spoke about the calamitous pestilence. God's vision flourished as before, and there was peace on earth.

In his subterranean land, the Evil Spirit sat and pondered. And, out of his thoughts, he created a marvellous being. It sparkled like the morning star and, like fire, continually altered its appearance.

The Evil Spirit breathed life into this being and named it Happiness. Lifting it up on his powerful wings, he soared with it high above the earth.

It was the dead of night, and people were slumbering in the camps. Only some young herders—who never slept at night— were sitting around a bonfire, singing. The youngest one was playing a *sopilka* and gazing up at the heavens, and his eyes were as serene as the stars.

A large, brilliant star tumbled down from the sky. Seeing it fall, the young herder dropped his *sopilka* and clutched at his chest.

The star had wounded his heart.

He shouted loudly: "Look! Look!"

And all the herders turned their eyes to where he was pointing— to the spot where the star had fallen. The star, landing on a high mountain, burst into a blaze of light that flamed alluringly and enticed their hearts.

The young herder called out to his brethren: "Come, let us go there!"

And they all walked towards the light. And each one of them saw in that light something that was more precious to him than life itself, and each one saw something different. They felt as if the fire were blazing in their souls.

They went farther and farther, but the light kept moving away from them. They continued walking, piercing their feet on prickly thorns, ripping their garments on sharp thistles, and marking their footsteps with a trail of blood. They kept pressing forward and then, one by one, as their strength failed them, they dropped by the wayside. And the luminous, wonderful being, receding ever farther and farther into the distance, and changing its form ever more frequently, vanished in the fog.

Daylight came, but the marvellous being did not return, and no one found it.

Evening arrived once again, and the herders began singing. They sang: "O Happiness! O wonderful, elusive Happiness!"

And those songs poisoned the hearts of the people. They all longed for happiness, but no one came to know it; they all wanted to see it, to possess it for a moment, and then to die, because for them it had become more precious than life itself.

And they all saw it, if only in their dreams, if only for a moment. For some, it gazed at them with the eyes of a beloved; for others, it glittered with gold; and, for still others, it beamed with glory. It charmed all of them forever, and its charms were poisonous.

It plunged like a falling star into a heart, and that heart was set ablaze. Whoever caught sight of it once never forgot it to his dying day.

Everyone searched for Happiness; everyone wanted to hold it securely in his hands. To attain it, they gave up all that was dearest to them, destroying both themselves and others; in its name, tears and blood flowed in streams.

But Happiness, soaring above the earth like a star, like lightning, like a will-o'-the-wisp, did not stop anywhere for long, and no one ever held it firmly in his hands.

And a great outcry was heard over the entire earth: "Happiness! O Happiness!"

Since then, there has been no blissful serenity on earth, and God's resplendent vision has been obscured.

And the Evil Spirit rejoiced in his work.

A City of Sorrow

(Silhouettes)

(1888)

"Where is the boundary dividing
the normal from the abnormal?"
A scientific question.

I once happened to visit a large institution for the insane.
Everyone who has been in such an institution knows the feelings
of fear, infinite compassion, and—shameful though it is to admit
it—curiosity, that engulf a visitor upon entering this huge
verkehrte Welt [upside-down world].

For me, a special feeling of sympathy for several patients
intensified these feelings. And, because of my heightened interest,
the images of some of these unfortunate individuals stayed with
me at night.

Often, after turning off the electric light and lying down on the
wide couch in the doctor's office that was serving as my bedroom,
I would gaze for a long time at the streaks of moonlight on the
wooden floor and the high, white walls, seeing in them all sorts
of absurd images. It seemed to me that the very air in this place
was filled with hallucinations flying around like sparks of an
invisible fire, like the echoes of invisible instruments.

From time to time, strange sounds—ever so clear in the dead
of night—broke into my room through the window. They
resounded with all the terror and despair that can be contained
in a human breast, and became strangely interwoven with the
moonlight and my apparitions.

Even now, on nights similar to those, my thoughts often fly
across the great distance, penetrate the high, stone walls of "the
city of sorrow," and hover over the bed of a young, dark-eyed girl.
Caught in the throes of despair, she is rolling her head on the

pillow; her loose, black hair covers her shoulders and chest like a dishevelled net. Her dark eyes burn with an inhuman sorrow; and her voice hums monotonously and mournfully, as if someone were plucking a single string: "Mariya, Mariya, a pure girl, a white lily . . . broken, stained, your lily, *elle était pure et belle comme un cygne et fraîche comme la rosée [she was pure and beautiful as a swan, as fresh as the dew]*."

I take her hand and—I don't know why—ask her: *"Êtes-vous souffrante [Are you suffering]?"*

"Oh, comme je souffre [Oh, how I am suffering]," her voice hums. "Our Mariya is gone, she's gone, *les démons l'ont souillée, la vièrge Marie est morte [the demons have defiled her, the Virgin Mary has died]* . . . Mariya, Mariya, a white lily . . ."

I gaze with damp eyes into her feverish, dry ones.

And now I hear an incoherent female voice.

"This . . . this, oh, you don't know! Isn't it true that you must walk towards a virtuous goal on a virtuous path? But what if someone walks on a evil one? Oh, you know! Do you think I'm crazy? Aha, you're asking about my husband? My husband's a dealer . . . He knows how to deal, oh, he knows how. No, you don't understand . . ."

A tall woman, like a wavering shadow, smiles ironically, but her widely staring eyes dart about swiftly, revealing a mortal fear.

In front of me walks a young poetess with blond, wavy hair and wonderful blue eyes in which both her talent and her insanity shine brightly, blending into a single piercing ray of light. From her lips pour forth enchanting musical verses that bring with them the fresh air and the freedom of the mountains. Suddenly, they are cut short by a sadly satirical joke, its black humour, punctuated by laughter that is more like racking sobs.

I recall her words: "It is always thus with poetry, an impulsive flight *ins Blau [into the azure],* betrayed hopes and . . . and an unfortunate love, and then everything ends here, in the best company . . ."

And her laughter resounds again and merges with a distressing accompaniment—the cynical guffaws of an older woman with grotesquely coquettish mannerisms.

They are both drowned out by the din of a dilapidated piano that is being played by an insane woman composer. Her face is evocative of a Byzantine icon, her eyes gaze seriously and sternly at a fixed point, and she is playing the *"Grande Polonaise."*

And now, her majesty the queen graciously gives me some flowers she has made. There are many of them lying on her table, along with a self-made crown.

"It is a small gift, but it has been made by royal hands. When you go there, where my people are, tell them in what a sorry state you saw their queen." And, with a tragic gesture, her majesty pointed to her run-down shoes and her worn skirt. "Tell them how the most gracious of all queens is being treated by her people! Tell them that I do not remember evil—I am simply demanding my rights."

I bow down low before her majesty and accept her regal gift with sincere respect. In what way is my queen any worse than other individuals who wear a crown?

On my cheek, I feel the kiss of an idiot. "Oh, you're my darling!" she shouts and, with a cheerful, loud laugh, she hands me her toy—a slice of bread. "Here, you can play with it like this, like I do. It's fun!"

I hear some wild singing—monotonous and persistent, like wind in a chimney, and I see the dancing figure of a happy maniac. He runs lightly, catches something in the air, and shouts: "Oh, how lucky I am! I don't even wish any harm to anyone, because I'm as lucky as luck itself!"

And now I hear the sad and astonished voice of the genius of Christianity: "In the Gospel it says that the time of liberation has come; however . . . I freely laid down my wreath of thorns in order to save the world from sin. I know that I am dying, but why are these unfortunate ones suffering? When will there be an end to torment?" The face of the genius of Christianity turns dark, and her eyes cast their gaze downwards.

Pale, indistinct shadows are passing in front of me. They moan dully, leaning against a wall or on the shoulder of a nun—a sister of mercy. They weep, throwing themselves down on the floor, or they sit silently, inertly, holding their heads in a grief that is deaf and mute—they are no longer living on this earth. And it seems to me that I, like Dante, have landed *nella città dolente [in the city of grief]*. These are the images that appear before me in the streaks of moonlight.

But there is one silhouette that I recall most often, not at night, but, for some unknown reason, during the day, when the sun is shining brightly, when people are talking loudly, when everything seems so clear and normal.

One day, I was in the park of "the city of sorrow," watching a group of patients doing gymnastics on a wide playing field bordered by pine trees. The instructor was showing them what to do, and they were doing everything obediently, even eagerly, with serious, determined looks on their faces.

One young man, exhausted from jumping over a sawhorse, walked over to one side and began pulling on a frock coat he had taken off because it impeded his movements. The coat had been hung on the pine tree under which I was standing, and so the young gentleman ended up quite close to me.

I did not even consider leaving, because over the past few days I had become accustomed to the residents of "the city of sorrow." Moreover, I had often come across this resident in the park, and I had seen how he sometimes stood for hours apart from the others, and gazed with sad and kindly eyes at the children playing croquet. The children were not afraid of him, because he was "peaceful."

The gentleman put on his coat, but did not go away—he was searching for something under the trees. I stepped aside and, noticing that his cap was partially covered by my skirt, picked it up and handed it to him.

Before putting it on, he bowed to me and said: "Thank you, Miss!"

Then he added in a hesitant voice: "Would you permit me to sit under this tree—because there isn't much shade over there."

"Please do," I replied.

He sat down on the ground and leaned against the tree trunk.

"Did you get tired?" I asked, taking advantage of the exclusive privilege of this exclusive place to start up a conversation with a stranger.

"Yes, a little bit, but that's nothing. Gymnastics is good. I like the fact that we have such a democracy here. We're all equals—both the kings and the common people who are insane . . ." he said laughingly. "You know, of course, that we have very important people living here."

"No, I don't know," I replied. "I've come quite recently, and I won't be here long."

"Ah . . . Well, it's like this—we have kings, artists, great criminals, grand inquisitors, and I, too, am not a person of the lowest degree." His modest appearance contradicted his last words.

"Who are you?" I inquired.

"Oh, I'm the senior madman here."

I glanced at him and did not know what to say. For a moment, it even seemed to me that he was joking with me.

But then he added very seriously: "And, in addition, I'm a professor of the new psychiatry . . . It's a bad time of the year; the students don't want to study, but professors can't be like that; a professor must push back the frontiers of knowledge."

He was gazing into the distance, and it seemed as if he had forgotten all about me. Then he pulled out a pencil and a folded piece of paper from his pocket; placing the paper on his knee, he began to write something quickly, without pausing.

Finally, he raised his head, glanced up, and smiled at me: "It's ready!"

And for some reason, he blushed.

"What have you written?" I asked.

"An outline of my lecture for tomorrow. Here, take it, if you want to. You're probably a student as well, right?"

"Why do you think so?" I said, avoiding a direct reply.

"You're wearing glasses," he said quite simply, looking at my pince-nez.

"That kind of 'studentship' can be hidden in one's pocket," I said, putting away my pince-nez.

"Well, then hide my professorship as well," he said laughingly, as he handed me the paper on which he had been writing. I took it and thanked him.

He rose to his feet. "I'm going now. Good-bye."

He started moving away; however, after taking a few steps, he came back and whispered: "I beg of you, don't show this to any of the doctors here—they're such obscurants!"

"You may be assured that I won't," I replied.

"Word of honour?" he inquired anxiously.

"Word of honour," I said, and I gave him my hand. He pressed it, bowed, and departed.

"Tell me, if you would be so kind," I later asked one of the doctors during the course of a conversation, "is it a good sign if a patient understands that all is not right with his mind? It is said that understanding one's illness is already half the cure."

"Well, not always," my conversational partner replied. "At least our experience has been that this kind of 'self-recognition' is often connected with the most hopeless conditions . . ." And he began to tell me all about the various degrees and stages of *Folie raisonnante [reasonable madness]*.

In the evening, after returning to my room, I read what was in the "professor's" paper. In his large, firm, but rather uneven handwriting, he had written the following:

MANIA EROTICA
Systematic gibberish

Symptoms: Idealization of the object of one's affections, Platonism, intensity, pessimism, hopelessness (for examp[le] *I*), in its act[ive] form—wild attacks, murder and suicide. Forms: lateral and expansive.

Etiology: Uneven connections of the heart to the mind. Not well researched (here there were some unclear initials and marks, probably citations).

Degree of distribution: Not as rare as *they* think (more marks).

Medicinal remedies: Palliatives: *Aqua Lethae [water from the river Lethe],* change of locale, work, *autosuggestio [self-suggestion]*. Radical methods: the famous Dr. Heine advises Pulv. B. Schwarzi in the form of *instant* chest and head compresses. Can also use Tinct., Or., Stroph., C. Cian (ars., phosph. is *not recommended*). In ancient times surgery was used, e.g., *perforatio pectoris [perforation of the chest cavity]*—it is now outdated. Results: *Beatitudo neutralis [neutral blessedness]*. It is better to leave natural currents. (Initials, among them, once again, *I*).

Prophylaxis, prognosis: It is all the same; it is not worth thinking about it.

The writing concluded here.

I stared for a long time at this writing, and I pondered it for a long time afterwards—what was it? Gibberish, or a joke? But in this city, all jokes are serious . . .

And I recalled Lear, the mad king, and his request to those who were accompanying him: "I'll talk a word with this same learned Theban . . ."

The Farewell
(1896)

*In the living quarters of a young man. A young lady is visiting him.
She is his sweetheart—not his mistress, nor his fiancée—just his
sweetheart. On the table stands a large photograph decorated with
flowers; the photograph is of a beautiful young lady—but not the
one who is visiting him. The scene is a tender one.*

Young man: "Nevertheless, you're sad. Oh, how sad you are!"

Young lady: "I? No! Look—truly I'm not!"

Young man: "You're smiling, but I can see that you're sad."

Young lady: "It just seems that way to you. Why should I be sad?"

Young man: "I don't know. But it seems to me that, at any
moment now, you'll start saying those things that I so dislike
hearing."

Young lady (puzzled): "What kind of things?"

Young man: "Well, you know . . . as if it were inevitable that
with time I'll become indifferent to you . . .

Young lady (calmly): "No, I'm not going to talk about that. You
have, after all, forbidden me to ever talk about anything like that."

Young man: "Only because I've forbidden you?"

Young lady (hiding her face on his chest): "I won't talk about it;
I'll never talk about it."

Young man: "Do you have faith in me?"

Young lady: "I trust you."

*There is a knock on the door, and the young couple separates. A
servant brings in a letter, and the young man reads it. The young
lady paces the room; coming to a stop in front of the photograph,
she looks at it for a long time. The young man smiles, puts the letter
away, and gazes thoughtfully into the distance.*

Young lady: "Tell me, where do you keep my photograph?"

Young man (pointing at a drawer in the table): "Here."

Young lady: "You never display it on the table?"

Young man: "No . . ."

Young lady: "Why? It's framed."

Young man: "I don't display it, because I fear it might be profaned. It has your inscription on it. Do you remember what you wrote?"

Young lady: "Yes."

Young man (kissing her hand): "Not all eyes are worthy of reading that inscription. If anyone—even my very best friend—took the liberty of making a joke about you, I would throw him down the stairs."

Young lady: "But can't you vouch for your friends?"

Young man: "N-n-not for all of them . . . Do you find it strange that I am not able to vouch for all those I call my friends? But, you see . . ."

Young lady: "I don't find it strange. May I ask who sent you the letter?"

Young man (pointing at the photograph): "She did."

Young lady: "Who is she?"

Young man: "My childhood friend."

Young lady: "I can see that; it's written right here: 'To my childhood friend—in fond remembrance.' But who is she—not just for you—but in general?"

Young man: "In general? Well, she's a recent high school graduate, the daughter of the principal of the high school that I attended in N. . . . and, as for anything more . . . Well, that's all that can be said about her 'community standing.'"

Young lady: "Is she an interesting girl?"

Young man: "How can I put it? I really don't know her all that well. We didn't see each other for about five years and, at the time that we parted, she was just an adolescent in that 'awkward stage.' And so, when I encountered her this summer, I scarcely recognised her. She was a grown-up young lady."

Young lady: "And beautiful as well?"

Young man: "Do you find her attractive?"

Young lady (peering intently at the photograph): "She is very beautiful . . . Is she much younger than you?"

Young man: "Five years younger."

Young lady: "Exactly the same number of years that I'm older than you."

Young man: "Why did you say that?"

Young lady: "But, after all, isn't it true?"

Young man: "Well, what if it is?"

Young lady: "Nothing. It's true, and that's that. So why can't we talk about it?"

Young man: "But why is it absolutely necessary to talk about it?"

Young lady: "The same can be said about all conversations."

Young man: "No, not about all of them. The same cannot be said, for example, about the conversation we had yesterday."

Young lady: "I don't recall what we talked about yesterday."

Young man: "About our engagement. And I'm saying once again that . . ."

Young lady: "No, that's enough, that's enough; there's no need to say anything more . . . Why do you talk about this so often now? After all, you yourself once said that you're opposed to all kinds of bonds and shackles."

Young man: "But we're not talking about shackles."

Young lady: "All the same—why should I bind you?"

Young man: "Only me? What about you?"

Young lady: "I'm already yours."

Young man: "And am I not yours?"

Young lady: "That's not what I'm saying . . . Listen . . . What did I want to say? Did your mother really pamper you when you were little?"

Young man: "Yes, very much so."

Young lady: "Did you have a happy childhood?"

Young man: "Oh yes, very happy."

Young lady: "Nevertheless, you grew up as an only child; it must have been sad and somewhat lonely."

Young man: "I always had a lot of childhood friends."

Young lady (pointing at the photograph): "Did she belong to your circle of friends?"

Young man: "Yes, but a little later on; I was in high school when we first met. She was such a funny little girl then, with hair that was always tousled. We used to tease her, calling her 'a little flaxen doll.'"

Young lady: "Did your teasing make her cry?"

Young man: "Not always; she got used to it after a while. And now, as is usually the case, she finds it pleasant to recall those *Kinderspiele [childhood games]*; she even signed this letter to me as 'your former flaxen doll.'"

Young lady: "But now she no longer resembles a doll made out of flax."

Young man: "Well . . . Now she's a grown-up young lady!"

Young lady: "Nevertheless, you're still laughing at her. Do you show the same respect to all your former childhood friends?"

Young man (suddenly turning serious): "No, actually, I respect her greatly. I was just laughing about the *Kinderspiele* that I called to mind. She's a fine young lady—that is, as far as I could tell, because she's very shy, a veritable mimosa blossom; one doesn't dare to touch her for fear of offending her."

Young lady: "You're always afraid of offending someone."

Young man: "Afraid? No, I just don't like to offend someone who doesn't deserve it."

Young lady: "And who does deserve it?"

Young man: " . . . Let the one who deserves it, blame himself."

Young lady: "I always blame myself."

Young man: "Why do you always take everything personally? You know, that's not an attractive habit."

Young lady: "It's a habit of egotists?"

Young man: "You're the one who said it, not I."

Young lady: "Yes, of course, I said it . . . But then, I have many unattractive habits. You . . . you yourself have asserted this."

Young man: "I asserted this? When?"

Young lady: "At various moments; not all at the same time."

Young man: "You're in a strange mood today. You're pouncing on words . . ."

Young lady: "What word have I pounced on? Maybe on a fact, but not on a word."

Young man: "I've noticed for quite some time now that you can't tolerate even the slightest allusion to any of your faults."

Young lady: "Perhaps it's because I feel these faults of mine all too deeply and painfully."

Young man: "It would be easy to remedy that."

Young lady: "How, precisely?"

Young man: "Mend your ways."

Young lady: "That truly is very easy."

Young man: "Well, isn't it?"

Young lady: "Did I say it wasn't?"

Young man: "No, you didn't, but . . ."

Young lady: "But what?" *(She looks directly at him.)*

Young man: "Well, there's that look again, that look. *(The young lady closes her eyes.)* "Why have you closed your eyes? Are you ill?"

Young lady: "No, but you don't like my look."

Young man: "How can you say that? *(He kisses her closed eyes; she smiles with trembling lips.)* "It's not that I don't like it, but you seem to pierce one's soul to its very depths with it."

Young lady: "And that's not pleasant."

Young man: "It's wearying . . . It isn't possible to live in a perpetual state of self-examination and confession, is it? Why can't you relate in a straightforward manner to what life has to offer? Why must you torture yourself with such close scrutiny and questioning?"

Young lady: "But was I inquiring about anything?"

Young man: "Not in so many words, but by the way you look and . . . just everything. No, truly, you are torturing yourself to no avail."

Young lady: "If I'm torturing only myself, then it really isn't a problem. But perhaps it's not only myself that I'm torturing?" *(The young man remains silent. The young lady wants to say something but restrains herself).*

Young lady: "Give me your hand." *(The young man gives her his hand; she presses her face to it and speaks in a quiet, even, and controlled voice):* "You're so very good; you put up with so much from me."

Young man: "Come now, that's enough, enough . . ."

Young lady: "No, no, it's nothing. I want to say that I will no longer torture you and, as a reward for your past suffering, I promise you that I will not ask about anything. As soon as I see that you've stopped loving me."

Young man: "There you go again!"

Young lady (keeping his hand): "No, no. That's not what I'm saying . . . I promise you that when this happens, I will no longer ask you about anything; I will see it by myself, and I will quietly go away."

Young man: "What do you have in mind?"

Young lady: "Nothing; just what I'm saying."

Young man: "Well, why are you saying that?"

Young lady: "Just in case . . . *(Changes her tone of voice.)* That's what my mother always said as she gave me a parasol whenever I was going for a walk. Do you remember that big black parasol under which both of us used to hide to shield ourselves from the rain? It took me a long time to learn to hide under a parasol. When I was little, I always got soaked to the bone, no matter what kind of a parasol I had in my hands. And even now, it's only thanks to you that I could escape from the rain."

Young man: "That's strange. Just from looking at you, no one would think that you're so helpless."

Young lady: "Oh, there are times when I'm very helpless, completely helpless. At times like that, it seems to me that there's no one in the whole world who could save me."

Young man: "That must be how it seemed to you a long time ago, before you met me, right?"

Young lady: "Yes, that's how it seemed at times . . ."

Young man: "Tell me . . . Were you . . . Were you ever in love before?"

Young lady: "You yourself said just a moment ago that one can't be in a perpetual state of self-examination and confession."

Young man: "Well, I won't press the matter, if it distresses you. But you know, there sometimes are souls that are—one could say— so transparent that there is no need for them to make a confession, because one can see right through them. And, from my observations, I've noticed that the eyes of these people who have such transparent souls are neither light grey or blue, but dark brown or black. That's interesting, isn't it?"

Young lady: "Is that really true?"

Young man: "According to my observations—yes, it is."

Young lady: "What colour eyes does this girl have? *(She points at the portrait.)*

Young man: "Her eyes are brown, and she gives credence to my theory—she can hide nothing."

Young lady: "But you just said that she was like a mimosa blossom."

Young man: "That's just the point! It's instantly clear what touches her to the quick, and why. For her, everything is very simple and straightforward; no words whatsoever are needed to explain her actions."

Young lady: "And was she always like that?"

Young man: "Always, as far as I know. I remember that in our circle of childhood friends she settled every argument so quickly and easily that we often found it funny that we had set upon one another in the first place. Once, when she was still quite young, and I was already a teenager, I became angry with her because she laughed at me when I fell out of a tree. I have to admit now that it truly was funny, but it was quite painful at the time, and I didn't speak to her for three days. She would walk by me, smiling hesitantly, until finally, she came right up to me, hugged me, and said straightforwardly: 'Peace; for everyone—peace; dumplings in butter, turnovers with cheese; we're the best of friends, let's kiss and make up.'"

Young lady: "And you kissed?"

Young man: "Of course."

Young lady: "And that was the end of the quarrel?"

Young man: "We immediately ran off to the swings on the best of terms."

Young lady: "I think that things can be settled so simply only between children."

Young man: "Well . . . 'If ye be not like children . . .'"

Young lady: "I know, I know . . . But what do you think—is there a person who has never been a child?"

Young man: "Perhaps, but it's a great misfortune . . ."

Young lady: "It's far better to be a child forever."

Young man: "Yes, in some cases."

Young lady: "Yes, it's true, there's no need for examples, for analysis, for anything!"

Young man: "You're sounding a bit strange again . . ."

Young lady: "No, no. I'm not at all 'a bit strange.' You love me now, what else could I want?"

Young man (embracing her): "Well then, 'Peace; for everyone—peace?'"

Young lady (with a tortured expression, but in a cheerful voice): "But we haven't been arguing. *(She draws herself up straight in his embrace and moves away slightly.)* "I think someone is knocking."

Young man (suddenly on guard): "No, they're knocking on the neighbour's door."

Young lady: "Nevertheless, it's time for me to go home."

Young man: "Why so suddenly?"

Young lady: "Suddenly, or not so suddenly, but one has to leave sometime . . ."

Young man: "Why put it so dramatically? 'One has to leave sometime . . .'"

Young lady: "Because one has to . . . Well, farewell."

Young man: "Why not say 'until we meet again?'"

Young lady: "That expression is foreign to us; what I said is more native to us. Even the song says: 'Farewell, my friend, who is not destined to be mine . . .'"

Young man: "What was that for?"

Young lady: "Ah, today you're always asking, what for, what for? For no reason; simply—farewell."

Young man: "No. Until we meet again. *(He embraces her.)* I'll come to see you tomorrow."

Young lady: "Come."

Young man: "And, I expect that I'll finally be able to convince you that it would be best if we were engaged."

Young lady: "No, no, no. Don't talk about that, don't talk about it. I don't want you to. There's no need to, no need, no need at all. *(She gestures suddenly . . . in the doorway):* "Farewell! Farewell! *(She disappears.)*

Young man: "But listen . . ." *(He frowns, shrugs indifferently, and, stepping up to the photograph, adjusts the flowers around it.)*

Sonorous Strings
(A Sketch)
(1898)

Whenever she walked down the street, everyone turned to look at her. They all looked at her in their own way—some with derision, some with astonishment, some with pity; most often, it seems, with pity; but then, this is hard to judge.

She was a hunchback—and this word says it all. This word is distressing. It is a distressing word to say, but even more distressing to bear. But it was borne—borne as a label—by this girl with big blue eyes and long blond hair.

It is difficult to judge what it was that passers-by stared at the most—those wonderful blue eyes, or the partially unbraided wavy blond hair, or . . . No, let us forgo this distressing word! It seems that the girl, upon hearing it, always wanted to hide from the merciless stares of people; her blue eyes would instantly dim and grow misty with tears.

This is how she was walking now, with lowered eyes; these lowered eyes gave her face, which was involuntarily drawn upwards, a strange expression. A faint rosy hue would colour her face and then recede, leaving it pale.

This is how she was walking amidst the bustling city crowds that were winding their way around her, jostling her, passing her, and—turning around to stare at her!

Over there, two young ladies were moving along swiftly, chattering loudly, engrossed in their conversation and apparently not seeing anything.

"Oh, excuse me!" one young lady said offhandedly, as she accidentally bumped into her.

The latter did not respond; she just blushed lightly. The two young ladies took a few more steps, and then, of course, they turned around to take another look.

"My dear, just look what beautiful hair she has!" the young lady who had excused herself could not help exclaiming loudly, and she involuntarily slowed her pace.

The girl's blue eyes once again lit up her face. She appeared to grow taller, and her walk became more confident.

"What extraordinary hair!" the young lady continued. "That is, if it isn't a hairpiece."

"Oh, no!" the other young lady spoke up, as she hurried along beside her friend. "I know that girl. It's Nastya Hrytsenko. She attended our high school once; I was in the third form at the time. She enrolled in our class, but she didn't stay long. Shortly afterwards, about half a year later, she left our school. I really can't say why, but she may have been afraid of the exam. I hear she's enrolled in a music school now.

"She's really very touchy! It was difficult to approach her, because she was offended by even the smallest little thing. They're always like that, these . . ."

It is just as well that by now Nastya was a fair distance away and did not hear the rest of what her former acquaintance said.

Nastya turned off from the main street, walked another three blocks, then opened a gate that led to a small, enclosed garden in front of a single-storey house. She strode quickly through the garden, stepped up on the low porch, and rang the bell.

A young gentleman in student attire opened the door.

"Ah, my dear Nastya!" he said, smiling joyfully.

His blue eyes, which were similar to Nastya's, gazed warmly and sincerely into the girl's eyes.

"Are you tired?" he asked.

"Yes. . . ." Nastya replied breathlessly.

"Oh, what a stubborn person you are, my dear Nastya!" the student said half reproachfully and half jokingly. "How many times have I told you not to walk here on foot from your school, but you just won't listen to me!"

"But it's nothing . . ." Nastya said softly.

"It's nothing, it's nothing!" the student mimicked her; however, he did not say anything more.

He took Nastya's heavy, music-filled briefcase and followed her into the house.

In the front room there was a piano and, above it, there was a shelf on which busts of Chopin and Beethoven stood between potted laurel trees. There was also a bookshelf with notes, and another one with attractively bound books—for the most part, the works of well-known poets.

The room was furnished quite inexpensively, but it had an air about it that was fresh and appealing. The profusion of flowers in it enhanced its charm.

Under the window stood a fairly small table, and on it were scattered some texts and tattered notebooks in which Nastya's brother took down notes from his university lectures. Not far from the table, a dusty violin and bow were hung on a wall above a desk with sheets of music on it. An even smaller table stood by the other wall, and on it lay rolls of music paper, some sheets with notes written on them, and a few small scraps of paper covered with fine writing.

The young gentleman placed the briefcase on the piano and helped Nastya off with her coat.

"Well, my dear Pavlo, did Olesya drop by while I was away?" Nastya asked her brother as she took off her little hat.

"No, she didn't. I thought she might, but since she hasn't come here as yet, I must dash over to her place for a moment to tell her that tomorrow we're all going out together for a boat ride. Wait for me, and we'll have our tea when I return. I'll hurry right back."

Pavlo lit the lamp on Nastya's table, took his cap, and was ready to leave. "Oh, yes, I forgot. Here's a letter for you! I think it's from Bohdan—it's his handwriting," he said, taking a letter out of his side pocket.

"See what you're like! You were just about to go away with my letter. You know, you're very absent-minded, my dear Pavlo."

"Well, don't scold me! After all, I didn't take off with it!"

Pavlo gave her the letter. A moment later he was already walking rapidly up the street, singing a lively tune sotto voce.

Nastya hurriedly opened the envelope and, still standing, eagerly scanned the letter.

It began without any salutation: "Forgive me for still not returning your 'Duet.' The problem is that the sister of one of my pupils is determined to learn it at all costs, and she has been playing it nonstop for two weeks now. If you aren't in any great need of this piece, permit me to keep it a little while longer . . ."

This was followed by a brief description of life in the village, and then the letter moved on to a written debate they had begun some time ago about a certain writer who knew how to use his words to touch more than one chord in a human heart.

But the letter was not long: "Don't be surprised if my arguments are not very cogent this time, because the barbarous sounds of the piano and the shrill soprano voice emanating from the living room—they are learning your 'Duet'!—are confounding my thoughts and spoiling my mood. So, I'll save my arguments for another time!"

At the end of the letter, the first part of his surname was scribbled illegibly.

Nastya rapidly reread the letter and laid it down on the table. Then, picking it up again, she read it once more, slowly this time, as if she were examining every word separately. She continued staring at the letter for a long time without reading it. After that, she put it down and began walking agitatedly around the room. At times, she stopped and pressed her hand to her breast, as if she were calming her heart.

She drew closer to the window and gazed through it into the translucent twilight. Tears were clouding her eyes but, frowning proudly and painfully, she turned away from the window in deep thought.

Deciding to write a letter, she got a pen and some paper and sat down at the table. She sat for a long time, occasionally picking up the pen as if she were about to write with it. But the paper remained blank. Not a single word appeared on it.

She sighed and, her hand trembling, laid the pen down on the table. Then, rising to her feet, she walked out of the house into the dark orchard. As she strolled quietly along the path, she kept thinking unspoken, unwritten thoughts. Her unshed tears oppressed her heart. She continued thinking, pondering.

"No, I can't write to him. What could I write to him? A soulless letter—about various issues, about the latest happenings in town—a letter adorned with witty phrases, carefree humour; the letter of an acquaintance, not even that of a friend.

"But why would I do that? Why indulge in these mental exercises, when my soul is groaning and breaking with sorrow? Whenever I sit down to write to him, I can only think that I love him immeasurably, boundlessly. This love is like a knife in my heart; remove that knife—and my heart will bleed to death.

"I think about the fact that I'm doomed to be unhappy all my life. While love is still alive, it flames with fire; when love dies, only the dead, charred ruins remain.

"He doesn't love me, and therefore I'm unhappy; but if he did love me, we would both be unhappy. I know this, but nevertheless, I love him. I am consuming myself in my own fire. I can't write anything else, nor do I want to write anything else.

"And so I have to remain silent, even though my heart is full of things I would like to say. I must remain silent, and I must renounce my one joy, the letters from him, even if they are short, casual notes.

"In his letters there is not a single, sensitive, friendly word, not even one that is said in jest . . . But no, I don't want such a word, one that is tossed out in jest.

"Oh, if I wanted to, it would be easy for me to hear more than one such jocular word from him! More than once I have heard him flirt jestingly with my girlfriends, and it is very distressing for me to listen to how they carry on. I would not be able to tolerate such a bitter comedy, and I am grateful to him that he has never indulged in that vaudeville brand of love with me.

"His respect for me is decorous, but still, it is a form of respect. He never addresses me in an offensively gallant tone. Does he perhaps realize that this would sting me to the quick? No, I'm sure he doesn't. It's simply, simply . . . he does not see me as an interesting toy. And it's true that I have neither the desire nor the talent to take part in such conversations. Of all the young ladies, I'm the only one with whom he conducts himself in this way— no, he is also like this with *her*, with that other one . . .

"Yes, he talks the same way with both of us, but his eyes do not say the same things, and his voice rings differently as it says the same things . . .

"Who knows? If I were to tell him about my suffering, if I were to pour out all my grief before him, perhaps he would find a kind word for me as well, a word of comfort. Or at least he might pity me with his eyes, because he does have a kind heart in his proud chest. He would not laugh at my love, for he knows what unrequited love is. Yes, he knows it only too well . . . but he bears his love with dignity, concealing it from everyone . . .

"Perhaps he would give me a word of comfort from a sincere heart, like a piece of bread is given to a hungry beggar; but I would sooner stretch out my hand to beg for bread than to beg for a word of love. They say begged bread burns the hand—but a begged word of love freezes the soul. And I do possess the courage to die of hunger, without extending my hand for such bread . . ."

The darkness in the orchard deepened. Nastya did not like being alone among the dark trees. Like all infirm people she found the expansive darkness disturbing. She walked swiftly into the house.

When she approached her table, her eyes fell once again on the letter she had read earlier. She picked it up and put it away in the little chest that stood on her table. There were many letters there, including some written in the same handwriting as the one she had just received. There were not too many of those, and almost all of them were short. Only a few of them had a date on them, but Nastya knew exactly when every one of the letters had been written.

Take this brief note, the very first, written just after they became acquainted. In it, Bohdan had asked Nastya when she would be at home—the note had been written in the city—so he could come over and they could learn a romance he had been invited to sing at some small social gathering.

Nastya still remembered, as if it had been only yesterday, both that song and that first rehearsal, even though it had taken place four years ago. It was Schumann's romance, *Ich grolle nicht [I do not grieve]* and they learned it together—he sang, while she accompanied him on the piano.

At first, she found it difficult to follow his whimsical singing. He became annoyed, impatiently raised his voice, and then immediately smiled in confusion, as if asking forgiveness for his impatience. At that time, Bohdan was a young first-year student; she was seventeen years old and was not yet enrolled in the music school. Her mind was still full of immature, youthful dreams. All these dreams had withered in those four years . . .

She played in a decadent fashion, with great feeling, and without always keeping strict time. He sang with a vibrato in his voice, knitting his brows and raising his forehead as befits a young singer. At times, when he became weary, he seated himself beside Nastya and, softly singing some of the phrases, leaned over her shoulder to see the notes better and point out where she had made a mistake.

A few rehearsals went by like that and, towards the end, Nastya sometimes made more mistakes than she had at first. Bohdan's singing kept improving.

"This romance," Nastya thought now, "was to me what the novel about Lancelot and Guinevere was to Paolo and Francesca; but, alas!—my Paolo was seeing his other Francesca in his mind!"

The evening of the social finally came—Nastya probably would never forget it. When *Ich grolle nicht* was sung, it was not Nastya who played the accompaniment, but another girl, while Nastya sat in the farthest corner of the room, the spot she always occupied when she found herself in a large gathering.

The girl who sat at the piano was young, slender, and dark-haired, with a serious but vibrant pale face. Her dark, bold head was bent forward, and her intelligent, dark eyes seemed to light up her countenance. She played energetically, but not stridently, and her slim, white hands flew over the keys lightly and nimbly.

Bohdan sang well. He was emotional, and that emotion greatly enhanced the meaning of the phrase "I do not grieve!"

Nastya gazed at his face, and at first it seemed to her that she had never seen him like this, but then she suddenly remembered every moment she had spent with him, and something heavy pressed down on her soul.

The singing ended. The gathering of young people rewarded the singer with applause.

As Bohdan walked by, someone said: "Wonderful!"

But he was dissatisfied, and replied: "No, it wasn't quite right."

Looking troubled and gloomy, he moved away—as if he wished to hide in the midst of the crowd.

The evening's program continued, and Nastya forced herself to listen to the other items. When the intermission came, she felt cold and unwelcome in the bright room among the noisy guests; however, she stayed to the end of the evening.

She did not recall too clearly what happened after this; there was much singing, then a lot of dancing. Pavlo danced with various young ladies, and so did Bohdan. He danced most often with the girl who had accompanied him on the piano.

Nastya watched the dancing, but all of it drifted before her eyes as if in a cloud of smoke. Now she only remembered that a piercing anguish tore at her heart the whole time, as it always did when she was in a large crowd at a festive social; but that evening, it was much worse than usual . . .

Now Bohdan was once again approaching the dark-haired girl to ask her to dance, but she refused him. Bohdan walked away in confusion. The dark-haired girl danced with a few other young men, but she did not remain at the social much longer. She went home early with her mother, before supper was served.

For a while, Bohdan stood in the group of those who were not dancing. He leaned against the wall and stared straight ahead pensively, without noticing anything—but not for long. He went up to a pretty, animated young lady and merrily danced away with her. Then he danced with many others, almost without resting, right until supper.

Nastya did not wish to interfere with Pavlo's dancing, and so she sat and watched as other people enjoyed themselves, or pretended to enjoy themselves.

Later, during supper, there was much noise, many speeches, and many conversations. Bohdan was witty and humorous, and talked without stopping. But it was painful for Nastya to listen to what he was saying. He was sitting quite close by, and she could see him; but he did not address her even once as he drank to the health and success of the assembled guests.

It was only when they raised a toast to young artists that he turned to Nastya with his glass and a joke. As he did this, their eyes met. Nastya silently raised her glass and touched his, and he, without completing his anecdote, bowed his head and placed his glass on the table; but then, after a moment, he raised his eyes, and there was a smile and a new witticism on his lips.

After that incident, however, the conversation at that end of the table seemed to die out. Bohdan did not speak to Nastya again; she hardly conversed with anyone . . .

"Enough memories!"

Nastya picked up a book of poetry by Nadson, her favourite poet, opened it, and walked around the room as she read. Noticing that something had fallen out of the book, she bent over to pick it up; it was a withered, dried flower of an indistinguishable colour. Looking at it, she quietly nodded her head, as the memories she had tried to smother with the lyrical poems of her beloved poet once again blossomed in her heart.

"How dry and unfortunate this flower is!" Nastya thought. "Who would have thought that this was a flower from the periwinkle plant, that once it was as happy and as blue as the sky!

> Is this you, my poor little faded flower?
> All pale, and faded like a distant dream . . ."

Nastya smiled bitterly:

"What am I doing? Have I begun to compose verses? It's no use, for they will never see the world, except perhaps, for the fire that will read them. Oh, it has read quite a few of them already!"

She gazed at the flower with a rueful smile. At one time, she had never thought she would be able to recall her past feelings so clearly—not just the images, the conversations, and the deeds, but the very feelings themselves.

Perhaps it would be better not to have such a memory. But if so, why hide the withered flowers? Why bring back to life one's dead dreams? Memories swarmed over Nastya; she contemplated them, leafing through them in her mind.

It had happened . . . quite recently, last year. In the spring, when the periwinkle was blooming.

It was an enchanting, blissful spring. Her dreams revived—her hopeless, precious dreams. Those nights that she would never forget, those spring nights—dark, or bathed in moonlight—were warm and secretly troubling. On such nights, mysterious flowers blossomed in her heart; they unfolded, flourished, murmured, and enthralled her. And she slept and listened to the beating of her heart. Her heart was pulsing, throbbing, rushing to embrace life, yearning to live it fully . . .

At that time, Nastya was living virtually alone. Pavlo sat for days on end in the town park, studying for his approaching exams. He came home late in the evening, and dropped in once or twice during the day. Nastya did not go anywhere, and no one came to see her—and that was good! It was quiet all day long, and she was alone with her dreams and her work. Now, she could no longer remember what that work was.

In the evenings, she sat beside the window and listened as people walked along the street. She listened closely to the sounds of footsteps, and she could tell when Pavlo was coming, and if he were coming alone. Usually, he came alone. One evening, however, after an exam, Nastya overheard Bohdan tell Pavlo that he would come to the house the next day.

Early the next morning, the sky was incredibly blue, the little garden was happy, and the periwinkle smiled. Nastya loved flowers—she forgot that flowers did not bloom for her. That morning, there were violets on her table and lilies of the valley on the piano. She carefully tidied up the house, and then laughed at herself when she realised what she was doing. She spent a long time combing her blond hair, "her one claim to beauty."

It was a wonderful day, but it was very long. Nastya played some spring songs, many songs, as brief as happiness; and the day, it seemed, wanted to listen to all of them.

Towards evening, Nastya left the piano and walked restlessly around the house and orchard. She could not settle down to anything; she was thinking, pondering, and waiting for someone. It seemed to her that this was the evening when something was going to change, something was going to happen—and it would be something joyful.

She went out into the orchard, picked some periwinkle with blue flowers on it, braided a wreath, and placed it on her head. When Pavlo saw her in the wreath, he kissed her and said she looked very pretty today, that her eyes were like the periwinkle, and her hair was like the rays of the sun. He truly was quite an eloquent young man! Nastya smiled as she walked into the house and caught a glimpse of herself in a mirror wearing the wreath.

Suddenly, the doorbell rang and Pavlo opened the door.

Bohdan came in and extended his hand to Nastya. He glanced at her, then at her head, then at her face again and, without saying anything, sat down at the table. But the expression in his eyes was all too familiar to Nastya! It was the same look people on the street gave her when they passed by . . . and then turned around to have another look . . .

It seemed to Nastya that the house became darker, colder, and that she was the only one who was so alone, forgotten, superfluous. Here in the house, two people, both of whom she loved, were talking, but she heard their voices as if in a dream, as if they were far away, even though she was sitting at the same table with them.

Almost immediately the young men got into an argument about one thing or another, and, more than once, asked for Nastya's opinion. She replied, but thinking back, she could not remember a single word of the discussion; all she could remember was that her contributions to the discussion were, in her view, inappropriate and intemperate.

Quietly removing the wreath from her head, she put it down on the table, walked up to the piano and, still standing, began playing fragments of melodies; then she sat down and began to play her favourite piece. At first she played to smother the weeping welling up in her heart; then, little by little, the pleasant sounds conquered her heart and her mind, and her thoughts, following the music, flew far, far away.

The arguing at the table quieted down—the two young men had fallen under the spell of Nastya's music.

Bohdan listened as she played, and then said: "If you would be so kind, please play *Ich grolle nicht*. I haven't heard it for a long time."

"Perhaps you'll sing it?" Nastya inquired.

"No, I'm not in the mood for singing today," he said apathetically.

He was pale and listless that evening—as he had been all spring. Nastya played, and she put her whole soul into the music, for it was *he* who had asked her to play.

After she finished, she turned around and, smiling tentatively, looked at Bohdan.

He was sitting deep in thought, unconsciously plucking the tiny periwinkle flowers from her wreath; most of them were already lying on the table, and only a very few still graced the green circlet.

Shortly thereafter, Bohdan rose to say his farewells.

"Where are you off to? It's still early!" Pavlo tried to convince him.

"No, my friend, it's late," Bohdan declined, extending his hand first to Pavlo and then to Nastya. "You must certainly be tired after your exams, so you should have a good night's sleep; I don't want to be in your way."

Nastya silently gave him her hand and turned away to close the piano. Pavlo locked the door and asked her to continue playing, but she excused herself, saying that she was tired. As she cleared the table, she picked up the plucked blossoms and tucked them away in a book. Then, bidding Pavlo good night, she went to her own room.

That night, Nastya could not sleep for a long time. She cried bitterly, restraining her sobbing, so as not to awaken her brother. Why was she crying? What, exactly, had happened that evening? What new worry had been added to the others? Nothing at all had happened. Everything was as it had been, and the worries were the same. Nothing had happened . . .

Vanish, O memories!

Pavlo returned from Olesya's.

"Nastya, my dear!"

Nastya did not hear Pavlo until he was quite close to her. Lost in thought, she had not heard him come in—he had not rung the doorbell because the door was unlocked. She jumped up, quickly closed her book, and changed her demeanour.

"What is it you're reading so intently?" Pavlo asked. "Did you have your tea? No? You were waiting for me? Oh, I'm terrible! But you see, when I'm at Olesya's, the time just flies. I arrived when she was singing, and I didn't want to interrupt; then I somehow became involved in a conversation. But it's a long story. Then Olesya sang again—you know, that Polish song: *Gdyby ja była [If I were]. Gdyby ja była gwiazdeczka na niebie [If I were a star in the sky]...*"

Pavlo began to sing, but then he immediately interrupted himself: "She sings that song wonderfully! It's too bad you didn't go with me."

"But why would I have gone? You said you were going for just a minute," Nastya said, smiling and gazing tenderly at her brother; she knew only too well how that "for a minute to Olesya's" always ended.

After clearing away the books and notebooks on Pavlo's table, Nastya prepared tea. She sat down, and Pavlo, having foregone tea at Olesya's, joined her.

Nastya peppered him with questions, inquiring if the party would take place tomorrow, what had been said at Olesya's, if anyone had been visiting her, and so on. Pavlo animatedly told her everything, recalling various witticisms, singing bits of songs, and talking incessantly about Olesya—what a marvellous voice she had, how beautifully she sang, and how everything she said was so interesting.

Nastya looked at him with kind eyes and thought: "Now, this is happiness! It's sparkling like a wave that is free!"

A thought crossed her mind—soon that wave might part her and her brother. It would carry him to a beloved wife in a safe harbour, and it would leave her, Nastya, here on this deserted beach where she would be all alone and even sadder . . .

But then she became ashamed of her thoughts.

"Surely I'm not grieving over his happiness?" she asked herself.

She began to inquire if Olesya had finished reading the books she had loaned her, if she could go with them to the theatre, and if the Italian troupe would be coming soon during its touring season. But the conversation had become somewhat forced, and eventually, even Pavlo noticed this.

"What's wrong, Nastya? You seem to be sad, and your eyes look so tired. Are you ill, or are you worried about something? Today isn't the first day I've noticed this. What's wrong?"

Nastya glanced up at him; his eyes were sincere, and they seemed to be gazing deep into her soul. She lowered her eyes and said quietly: "Nothing; there's nothing wrong. But it's true I'm tired. I walked a lot today, and they kept us late at school."

She felt slightly ashamed of her insincere response, but what else could she have said? Pavlo was so happy, so fortunate . . .

After they finished their tea, Nastya tidied up. Pavlo sat down to write something on paper cut up into small pieces.

"Would I bother you, my dear Pavlo, if I played the piano?" Nastya asked.

"No! You know it never bothers me; I even work better to the accompaniment of music."

Nastya sat down at the piano. For some time, only the scratching of Pavlo's pen could be heard. Then Nastya began playing with a loud chord; the first phrase of *Ich grolle nicht* resounded clearly, and then broke off abruptly.

A tender, soft, crystal clear theme emerged faintly like a luminous memory from the depths of a soul. At times, this gentle melody resembled a stifled moan; then it flowed on like a transparent stream, rising in melodious waves, then dissolving like a dream.

Precious, long-forgotten fantasies reawakened, only to be transformed instantly into grievous weeping; the sounds mourned quietly, weeping despairingly, but the dull chords smothered the sorrowful moaning, gradually decreased in volume, and became silent of their own accord . . .

Then a sonorous melody, proud and wild, and filled with pain and despair, erupted in a blaze and awakened all the strings.

The storm raged, and through it echoed the first haunting melody, but it was sad and fragmented, and then it disappeared completely in waves of proud despair. Everything drowned in it— the bright dreams, the sad weeping, the bold impetuous flights, and the quivering tears.

The waves roared still more loudly; they became more and more disquieted and alarmed, deafening even themselves. Rolling at an ever increasing tempo, they flooded everything and spread more widely, and then they began to calm down. They murmured much more quietly, and from their murmuring arose a song, hopeless and gloomy, like a foggy night at sea. It was barely audible, like a breath, and then it fell silent . . .

Suddenly a loud moan issued forth, like a cry from the heart, and then broke off on a low note.

Silence reigned.

Nastya's hands dropped from the keys, and her head fell to her chest. She was pale and silent.

Pavlo turned around. Then he rose to his feet, went up to his sister, and leaned over to see her face.

"What's wrong, Nastya? Are you ill?"

She did not reply.

Flinging her arms around her brother, she collapsed on his chest, and began to weep loudly, unrestrainedly.

Her brother did not ask her anything else. He kissed her silently, and caressed her as one caresses a little child.

From her heart-rending sobs, he sensed the futility of trying to console her.

A Letter to a Distant Shore
(1898)

You most certainly will never have the opportunity to read this letter, but even if it should so happen that you do—and I am not at all convinced that it could ever be possible—you would not, in any event, be able to find out who wrote it and to whom it was addressed.

Of what use, then, is such a letter? Truly, I do not know the answer to this question and, for the moment, I do not wish to think about it. There is a French saying for such conduct: *c'est plus fort que moi [it is something more powerful than I am]*. And so, this *c'est plus fort que moi* is what is behind my desire to send you a letter somewhere on a distant shore.

I do not know your name, and it is quite likely that I will never find out what it is. We met during an ocean voyage. For me, it was a journey to a foreign land; for you, it was a homecoming; but the road was the same for both of us. We were like two waves that float along together for some time until an obstacle appears— a ship or a rock—that parts them forever; they never try to find one another again, for nothing impels them to do so. This is what is happening to us.

I would really like to know: do you still remember our encounter—the encounter that was our first and our last? I have no way of knowing if you do or not, but I will never forget it, even though I have forgotten countless other such accidental encounters that I have had since then.

I often see you in my mind's eye—your head slightly tilted forward, a serious look in your eyes, and your voice, clear but not strident, perhaps a trifle husky. When I close my eyes, I see you in a distant perspective—as one sees objects through opera glasses when they are turned the opposite way—but to me your image always looks pleasing, refined, and clear, like a photogravure executed with an engraving needle. I am not able to explain to myself why I always see you like this, but I cannot imagine you in any other way.

I recall very precisely how you approached me. You noticed that I was maintaining my balance with great difficulty, and that I was almost falling because the ship was rocking so violently. You offered me your assistance then, and we strolled together, arm in arm, the entire afternoon until nightfall.

There is nothing exceptional in this—that an arm is offered to someone who is feeling dizzy . . . As soon as you offered me your arm, however, I had the feeling that we had strolled together this way more than once. I was not the least bit surprised that you were able to maintain your balance so wonderfully on the swaying deck, and that your arm was a better support to me than the iron railing of the stairs; it seemed to me that I had known this for a long time.

You did not permit me to walk alone even once, and when I swayed your hand came up quickly, and you looked into my eyes in alarm, saying in a quietly reproachful voice: "I beg you, hold on more tightly to my arm!"

And whenever we came up to a bench, and I sat down, you seated yourself at some distance from me, or stood beside me— whichever you thought was more convenient—and we engaged in conversation.

We interacted very naturally, without that banal, artificial politeness that tends to characterise relationships between men and women—and which I find so odious. It did not even occur to you that it might be impolite when, instead of conversing with me, you paced the length of the deck with your hands behind your back. I understood that you were sunk deep in thought or, perhaps, preoccupied with some worry, and I did not intrude upon you then.

From time to time, and always unexpectedly, you stopped beside me with a question or an observation, and we would immediately begin talking again. I remember those conversations very well, but I do not want to recreate them here; it is boring to repeat what has already been stated—to me it would seem like dictation.

Yes, I remember our last long conversation when I stood leaning against the ship's railing, looking down at the dark, chaotic sea and talking about something that seemed as dark and chaotic to me as that sea. We were discussing a challenging concept: "predetermination—the fatality of life . . ."

You spoke seriously the whole time, and not even once did I detect so much as the slightest hint that you might be making fun of me. You also did not resort to any jocular comments, as so often happens when one is enjoying a cup of tea in the company of friends. It was more like academic discourse.

You discussed the matter calmly, but I was conscious that my eyes were blazing and my face was flaming. I bent down so low over the side of the ship that salty droplets of water struck my face; the fresh nocturnal breeze blew at my summer dress, and I started to tremble.

You noticed this immediately, and I once again saw in your eyes your kind concern; you instantly halted the conversation, but so swiftly, so straightforwardly. You simply said: "You're tired, cold, and it would be better if I took you to your cabin. Give me your arm and, for God's sake, hold on tightly."

There, down below, on the threshold of my cabin, you extended your hand in farewell. I wanted to say to you then: "Thank you, my friend!" But I managed to utter only the "thank you," and that was all.

You raced up the stairs swiftly and nimbly—and vanished into the darkness.

We never again spoke to each other.

The next morning, I saw you one more time, as you were standing in the most distant corner of the ship. You, however, did not see me, and no new encounter took place.

When we arrived in the harbour where you were to disembark, I wanted to find you to say a word of farewell, but you were lost in the crowds, and I could not spot you.

Since then, we have not seen each other and, I think, we never will see each other again. Perhaps it is better this way.

On another occasion we could be in a very different mood, and our second encounter could simply serve to spoil the good impression created by the first one. Perhaps, on the evening that you conversed with me, you were in a special mood—a mood that rarely overcomes you. And I, in a second encounter, could also seem completely different, boring, and hardly worthy of your attention. Then we would have regretted that chance had brought us together again.

So, let it be the way it is; at least, this is what I am assuming theoretically.

But still, whenever I recall you and see your figure in the distant perspective, I have an overwhelming desire to say to you: "Thank you, my friend!"

And I truly regret that you are not able to hear me say it.

By the Sea
(1898)

As I reclined under an outcrop of rock at the very edge of the sea and looked out at the phalanxes of waves and the clear horizon, it often seemed to me that I had arrived in a country where there never had been, or no longer were, any people. I must admit that such an illusion was pleasant.

I am not a misanthrope by nature, but at times one does want to escape from people for a short while, just so that one does not begin to hate them. I have heard the expression somewhere that a landscape without people is like a painting without a frame; but I sometimes think it is a painting without a blemish.

Gazing at it from afar, the city that was scattered on the slopes by the sea did not appear to me to be the work of human hands, but simply part of the panorama. In the evening, when the buildings were hidden in the darkness, and only the lights of the city could be seen, I was reminded of fairy tales about an enchanted mountain, replete with gold and precious jewels, that opened at the magic word of a courageous adventurer.

Indeed, the mountains that loomed darkly all around the bay appeared to become translucent, as if hundreds of bright windows had opened, revealing gleaming caches of sparkling gold. On the mountain tops, the bonfires of the shepherds flamed in the distance, and often I could not decide if it was a star rising from behind the mountain, or the flame of a beacon.

The sea murmured, and tiny pebbles, caught up by a wave, clattered incessantly, as if complaining that the capricious water was not giving them any peace. The sea gulls flew in flocks above the water, crying mournfully day and night, in both good weather and bad.

The stately Crimean orchards stood quietly—only a violent storm could have made them rustle like our groves at home. The stones and cliffs on the shore appeared even more inert against the eternally animated, eternally restless sea that altered its appearance with every passing cloud and with every change in the heavenly light, without ever disturbing the harmony of the painting.

It was only when the piercing brassy sound of a military band, a fragment of a soldier's song from the tsar's palace, or the whistle of a steamer broke the silence, or when the angry waves cast out corks, peelings, old shoes, and all sorts of human refuse on the shore—that the harmony was suddenly broken, and the illusion of being in an uninhabited country vanished.

There are people everywhere!—screamed my offended thought, dismayed by its encounter with the filth, the poverty, and all the misfortunes of humanity; but I restrained it with ancient and modern aphorisms, with recollections, and with paintings that had people in them, but no blemishes.

My thoughts were gradually subdued, and they even had to submit completely, when, compelled by my own incapacities, I came to dwell in that very city which, from afar, seemed to me to be part of a landscape without any inhabitants. There, people were present everywhere, and at all times.

Even when I sat by myself in my solitary room, I could hear their movements behind the walls, or above the ceiling, or in the room below me. There were people, but along with them, there was also work, and there were ideas, and these new ideas dulled the older thought—the one that was hostile towards people. What from a distance had appeared as a blemish, as a disharmony, did not strike me as such from closer up. This often happens.

When I viewed art exhibits as a child, the huge oil paintings that were full of cruel realism, such as those of Repin, distressed me terribly; to shatter the disturbing illusion, I would come up very close to the painting and then—I would cease to see it. In front of me there were simply daubs of paint, with the thick threads of the canvas peeking out from under them, and it even seemed strange that they had appeared terrifying from a distance.

Now, when the daubs of colour have once again blended into a distant landscape, I want to capture this painting on paper. I want to examine it more closely, once again, for it has dominated and consumed my thoughts far too long, and is beginning to weigh heavily upon me.

One day I went to a certain villa to visit a young lady with whom I was casually acquainted. Since she had invited me for the whole day, I brought some sewing with me, and the two of us, my hostess and I, sat in the gazebo in the orchard and busied ourselves with our work.

I did not know the family or background of my chance acquaintance; indeed, I hardly knew her name—it was a fleeting summer friendship, the kind that is established casually, and then vanishes quickly, without any regret.

Someone watching the two of us from a distance might have thought we were close companions, or even friends. We were sitting at the same table, sewing the same item, and conducting an animated, incessant conversation; moreover, my speaking partner often touched my shoulder, or leaned over to gaze into my eyes.

But if that same person had been able to listen in on our conversation and come up closer to us, he would have heard that our conversation was more of a monologue—interrupted with brief responses—than a dialogue. My conversational partner spoke rapidly, affectedly, and in a shrill soprano voice, interrupting herself time and again with either some singing, or a strange interjection she called a "Gypsy vocalism."

These vocalisms were used mainly to gain my attention or, more likely, to draw me into the conversation. My attention, however, was not wandering; it was simply being involuntarily dissipated over the orchard and the mountains, and if it had not been for the piercing soprano voice of my loquacious interlocutress, my work that day most certainly would not have been finished.

Whenever I lifted my head to find some item I needed for my sewing, I found myself looking straight ahead down a long, dark path that lay between two thick walls of cypress trees. This walkway continued on and on, and then it either came to an abrupt end or dropped down; in the narrow space between the cypresses, the sea was laughing with a fresh, sparkling smile that evoked a bright smile in me as well . . .

"Why are you laughing?" my companion exclaimed. "Does my song seem 'trivial' to you? Well, here's a romance, a Spanish one: 'O sea, O sea, O night of love!'" And she began to sing in an unnatural, husky voice, like the cooing of Egyptian doves.

I once again lowered my eyes to my work and, while straightening out a sleeve and adjusting the collar, reflected on the kind of person my acquaintance was.

She was young, less than twenty years of age, and "a young lady from a good family," as she herself told me more than once. She had not come alone to Crimea, but with an older woman who was not truly a nanny, or a companion—she was there strictly for the sake of appearances!—but she went everywhere by herself, and sent the so-called nanny to do the shopping.

She spoke with disgust about "the young women who go off by themselves with Tartar guides," but her fondest memories were of Gypsies and of Moscow restaurants of dubious reputation called "Yar" and "Strelna," all of which, it seems, she knew very well. She did not have a profession.

"In the winter I leave the country, and in the summer I return," she said.

All her conversations began with the phrase: "Back home in Moscow . . ." and ended with: "Oh, your horrible Yalta!"

"Well, tell me, what do you do when you're here?" she asked me. "What can you possibly do in this boring hole?"

Without waiting for my reply, she continued: "In my opinion, there's only one way to cope—to fall in love! But with whom? I know one man here . . . Oh, you probably know him as well. He's the notorious heartbreaker, Anatole B.! You don't know him? O my God! Where are you living—on earth or in heaven? But he's only good for flirting with . . . 'I wander, I never cry, I sing without end' . . . Oh!"

She interrupted herself with a Gypsy vocalism.

"This Anatole is such a lout; just imagine, he tells me straight to my face that I don't have any voice at all, but that I'd be a wonderful music hall star, because *j'ai du diable [I have something devilish about me]*! He takes too many liberties; I told him yesterday he is not to come and see me anymore . . . Nastasiya Illinichna! Nastasiya Illinichna!" she suddenly shouted.

An elderly woman in a white headdress, with a serious but kindly old face, glanced through the window into the verandah where we were sitting.

"What is it?" she asked in a dejected voice, as if she did not expect anything good to come of this.

"May the devil take me!" the young lady shouted, bursting into gales of laughter.

The head of the old woman vanished instantly, and the window was abruptly banged shut.

"Ha-ha-ha! My devils really scandalize her!" the young lady convulsed with laughter.

"Why do you cause her this unpleasantness?" I inquired.

"Oh, my God! What won't one do out of boredom here?" she replied, still laughing, and then she turned serious. "But perhaps this really is wicked? Everyone always tells me that I invoke the devil too often. Are you religious?"

I glanced up at her, and for some reason I was not able to refrain from shrugging my shoulders.

"Why aren't you saying anything? This isn't a forbidden question, is it? I can already see you're not religious; that's bad—you're depriving yourself of a great joy. I couldn't be that way. I'm very religious; all of our family is. We're Muscovites, and every year we hold the service of the 'Miraculous Icon of the Virgin Mary' in our home.

"Have you ever been in Moscow? No? You've missed out on a lot! So, you also haven't heard any Gypsies? But I've heard them—real ones! My mother doesn't know about it. O God forbid! I slipped out with my brother and his friends, supposedly to the theatre, but instead we went by troika to Strelna—it was ever so much fun!

"You don't like Gypsy romances, but if you had heard them sung the way the Gypsies themselves sing them:

> We are in the silence
> All alone . . ."

Her attractive face, with its delicate features, took on such a "Gypsy-like" appearance that I felt unspeakably sorry for her, just as one feels sorry for little children in the circus who display their broken little bodies to strangers.

The young lady had wonderful dark eyes; they were black, like velvet, and their gaze could have been deep and calm. Her figure was supple, and her face was pale, with a faint rosy hue. She was so young, but she was already infected . . .

"Tell me, is it true *que j'ai du diable*? I'm really very much like the Gypsies. Come, and I'll show you my photograph—everyone says that it's been touched up too much, but I don't think so. Come on. You can try your blouse on in there, and I'll change my clothes as well; I'm tired of wearing these rags." And she pointed to her batiste sailor outfit.

We went into her room. Actually, the young lady occupied three rooms. In the first room, the photograph she wanted to show me stood in a prominent spot on a table. It was between two other photographs: an older military man with ornamental epaulettes, and a haughty, not so young lady, who was sitting bolt upright in a black visiting gown.

"My daddy and my mummy," my hostess introduced the photographs to me.

Her own photograph was grander in size—bigger than those usually kept on desks—and portrayed her photographed to the waist. She was wearing a white, diaphanous ball gown, and her thin arms and supple, childish neck were etched like alabaster against the dark background of the photograph; her narrow bust was covered copiously with elegant lace, and her head was tilted upwards in a stiff pose.

When looking at her face in the photograph, the first thing one saw were her white, perfectly even teeth and her artificial smile; because of her pose, her chin appeared wide and thick, and the features of her face were foreshortened and rounded. Her eyes, gazing upwards, were heavily made up to look larger, her eyebrows were glaringly black, and her hair loomed like a huge cloud over her low forehead.

I told her that the photograph was not at all touched up. The young lady was very happy to hear this.

"It's a good idea, isn't it—to take photographs in white?" she began her chattering once again. "I always go to balls in white, *rien que du blanc [nothing but white]*! My friends are annoyed their mothers dress them like that, but I like it. I feel so white and pure then, so wistful. Tell me, isn't it true that I'm pretty? My sister says that's a stupid question—she's our 'prude'—but I don't see anything wrong with it. I can ask, can't I, if a dress is becoming to my face? So, why can't I ask if my face is becoming to my face?" she laughed, delighted with her witticism.

I felt as if I were becoming entangled in a finely spun cobweb that was spreading over my eyes and interfering with my breathing. My head was growing dizzy. In order to avoid pursuing the conversation, I began trying on my blouse.

In the meantime, the young lady, having put some straight pins between her lips, was preparing to help me with the fitting, all the while talking through the pins and paying me the most childish compliments, without any real idea about fashion or fabrics.

"I should be a milliner, a tradeswoman," she spoke up as she pinned the blouse on my shoulders. "Just look how nicely I've fixed it for you. It might be a good idea . . ."

She said this smilingly, but when she said it, her eyes were no longer like those of a Gypsy. They were quiet and deep.

"What might be good?" I asked. "The way in which you've fitted it?"

"No, I wasn't talking about that, but about becoming a tradeswoman, because what am I now? 'She's like a billy goat—there's neither wool nor milk from her.' But how come you're not frowning? It is a trivial saying, isn't it? Oh, to hell with it all!" she shouted once again, and the quiet expression vanished from her eyes. "Nastasiya Illinichna! Nastasiya Illinichna!"

The old woman appeared in the doorway; she did not say anything, but her eyes spoke eloquently: "Well, what is it this time?"

"Where is my grey silk skirt? Where the devil has it gone to?" the young lady turned to the old woman.

"But why, my young lady, do you always mention the name of that black creature?" the old woman asked in a quiet, reproachful voice.

"Where is my grey skirt?" the young lady repeated, paying no attention to the old woman's reproach.

"It's in your closet, of course. Where else would it be? I shook it out last night after you came home, and early this morning I fixed the hem and hung it up. I keep everything neat and tidy, you know."

"A delicate hint," the young lady whispered to me.

In the meantime, the old woman took the skirt out of the closet and, after examining the hem once again, laid it carefully on a chair.

"Which blouse are you going to put on?" she asked the young lady.

The young lady placed a finger on her lips and became thoughtful for a moment.

"I don't know yet; I'll pick one out myself," she finally decided.

"Well, what am I to do then? Take them all out?"

"Yes, all of them. Why are you so surprised? Why the deuce would one sew them, if not to wear them?"

The old woman, with a martyred expression on her face, began pulling the blouses out of the closet.

"Here, have a look," the young lady called out to me. "Are you finished already? Well then, come here and give me some advice. Take this white one here—the fabric is nice, but it's sewn like a sack. The confounded seamstress, may she be damned! Just look, I'll put it on. Isn't it true, that it's a sack?"

I agreed that it really was sewn a trifle inelegantly.

"Well, the devil take it, if that's the case!" the young lady decided, tearing off the blouse and flinging it to the floor.

The old woman immediately picked it up, shook it out, and hung it back in the closet. The young lady began trying on one blouse after another, sharply criticizing each one, while keeping a close eye on me to see how I was reacting to the size of her extensive wardrobe. Of course, she did not remain silent as she kept slipping them on and off.

"This red one isn't too bad, but it's not for daytime; it's for evening. This sky-blue one suits me at times, but not today. You're probably thinking that sky-blue never suits me, right? You're mistaken; I'm one of those dark ones who is able to wear sky-blue as well . . .

"Well, tell me, what am I to put on? Perhaps this Scottish one? It should appeal to you: it's simple and austere."

"Well, it's not all that austere," I smiled, glancing at the silk blouse in a red and blue Scottish plaid fabric, with expensive stitching and ribbons.

"Even this isn't austere enough for you?" the young lady asked in astonishment. "Well, if that's the case, you're a Quaker. But all the same, I'll wear this one, because it's simple *'et distingé'* *[and genteel]*. And, just to please you, I'll put on a black wool skirt instead of the grey silk one. Nanny, give me my black skirt!"

"Now you want the black one? It's not cleaned yet; you did a good job on it this morning . . ."

"Then clean it immediately, but do hurry! Wait, wait, first pass me my red taffeta underskirt, because I won't be able to find it. Even the devil himself would break a leg trying to find something here . . ."

The nanny quickly found the requested article of clothing and went out into the orchard to clean the black skirt. As the young lady dressed, she made the taffeta rustle and squeak loudly, a noise that I have always found unbearable; my nerves could not tolerate it, and so I followed the old woman outdoors.

The skirt was spread out on the chaise lounge in the orchard, and the nanny, muttering to herself all the while, was alternately beating it and cleaning it with a brush.

Upon seeing me, she immediately addressed me in a familiar manner, something that older servants often do, especially Muscovite ones: "I've nothing but grief with the young lady— that is, with Alla Mykhaylivna. Day after day, it's as you saw just now: 'Clean this one! Shake that one out!' And, what's more— you work, you try your best, and you think you'll please her! But then, you see, it's no longer needed; fetch her something else. This wouldn't be too bad yet—that's the way it is with lords and ladies—but the way this family goes about things, God forgive me, just doesn't make any sense at all.

"Whom does she take after? Her parents seem to be decent people, your regular upper-crust types; her father's a general, her mother's the daughter of a professor, and the older sisters studied at an Institute and married well. Oh dear, oh dear, she's really been spoiled! She's the youngest, the baby in the family, and, to make matters worse, the Lord has sent her a trial—her health is failing. If only the Queen of Heaven would help her get well here. So much money has been spent on doctors, and so much has been frittered away here and there and everywhere. Oh . . . it's more than can be counted!"

Alla Mykhaylivna's voice could be heard through the open window as she sang, with emphatic pauses:

> "Until daybreak, until the dawn
> He passionately kissed me . . ."

The young lady was sitting in front of a mirror at a table near the window; a gas lamp was burning on the table, and tongs were being heated in it to curl her hair. From time to time, she parted a strand of her wonderful black hair and wound it on the tongs, making it crackle.

The nanny carried the cleaned skirt into the house and, after a while—a fairly long while—Alla Mykhaylivna walked out of the house all dressed up, wearing a little crimson hat and carrying a matching red parasol.

"Let's go for a walk," she said, taking me by the arm.

"Fine," I replied. "It's time for me to be going home anyway. As you can see, I've overstayed already."

"Well, you'll still have time to get home! We'll just stroll through the park of the hotel 'Rossiya,' and then we'll go to the city park to listen to the music—it will soon be six o'clock." She glanced at her small watch that was attached by a ribbon to a brooch on her bodice. "Yes, we'll listen to the music, we'll look at the people, and we'll probably meet Anatole there. I'll introduce him to you."

"No, spare me from making that acquaintance, at least for today," I said laughingly.

"Aha, you're begging to be spared. You're concerned about your peace of mind!" Alla Mykhaylivna teased me.

"I truly am concerned," I replied. "The sea is so beautiful today—just look at it—and I'm concerned that this gentleman, this Anatole, may spoil my mood, both with his person and his conversation."

"Why are you judging him so severely? Do you perhaps know him?"

"I don't know him, but I've seen more than enough of his kind; 'heartbreakers' are neither new nor original."

Conversing in this manner, we strolled down the cypress path to the street, along the path that had seemed to end abruptly in the sea, but which, in reality, ended in fairly steep stairs that led to a green gate—a gate that demarcated the boundary of the verdant countryside we were leaving behind us.

The street that we entered was terribly hot. With every step, a fine, powdery white dust rose like smoke and lingered above the road. To make matters even worse, two big stone buildings were under construction, and wagons loaded with building materials kept driving by with a maddening clatter. Because of this, tall columns of dust spread over everything and settled in grey layers on the cypresses, the thuyas, and all the other trees that lined the road and encircled, like a high wall, the numerous lordly villas situated on this street, so far removed from the centre of town and the markets.

Alla Mykhaylivna picked up her pace and tried to protect herself with her parasol. She lifted up one side of her black skirt quite high, and her crimson underskirt shimmered like red-hot coals; the other side of the skirt dragged along the ground and was already grey from the dust, but the young lady did not notice this.

"Phew!" she said, wrinkling her nose. "How ugly this street has become since they started building those homes. What a stupid notion—to muck around with building at the beginning of the season. They should do their building in the winter, when there's no one here."

"What do you mean, when there's no one here?" I said. "People live in Yalta all year round."

"Oh, I'm not thinking about those people! In the winter, there's no one here *de la société [from society]*. Just imagine what I'll look like by the time I arrive at the bandstand!"

"It really is a shame about your clothes," I observed, thinking about Nataliya Illinichna, who had put so much effort into cleaning the skirt.

"It's not the clothes I'm worried about; here, in this disgusting Yalta, I dress like a cook. I would never appear in public like this in Moscow! I'm worried about myself; when you have to wear such shabby outfits, your natural beauty must make up for it!"

It almost sounded as if she might be fishing for a compliment, but her tone was sincere.

"Truly, it's impossible to dress fashionably here. Take my little hat, for example: yesterday I went through all the shops in Yalta, and all I could find was this rag for ten rubles. And what can one say about the seamstresses here, and the stores? It's all so expensive and disgusting! It's terrible, how expensive everything is here!"

I was taken aback by her unusual concern with economy.

"It seemed to me," I remarked, "that the high cost of things did not perturb you."

"Yes, that's true, but all the same . . . Daddy gave me a thousand rubles for the entire season. And after two and a half weeks, do you know how much I have left? Two hundred rubles! Ha-ha-ha!" she laughed gaily and resoundingly.

At this moment, a young worker with a pail of green paint in one hand and a big brush in the other was coming towards us; paint dripped from the brush and left a green trail that looked very much like tiny leaves scattered on the dusty white sidewalk. The worker was quite a young, frail boy; the pail was too heavy for him, and sweat was streaming down his dark, bronze forehead from under his low, lambskin Tartar cap.

Just as he came abreast of us, the boy began wiping his brow with his bedaubed arm, and the brush he was carrying came up level with Alla Mykhaylivna's little crimson hat, almost leaving a little green leaf on it.

Alla Mykhaylivna, jerking to one side so suddenly that she almost shoved me off the sidewalk, yelled at the boy: "Move over, my man, move over!" Then she added, a trifle more quietly: "What a dolt!"

The boy moved sideways a little and put his hand behind his back, so that he would not touch the young lady; but, at the same time, the hatred in the look that he shot in our direction made me uneasy.

I do not know if Alla Mykhaylivna noticed this look, or if she could perceive and comprehend the antagonism, terrible and fatal— blacker than the dark eyes of the young worker—that was in it. And I do not know if the boy saw the look that the young lady cast at him along with her words. But I saw both looks, and I felt terrified—they encompassed all of history.

Long after the boy had passed us, I continued thinking about his dark look, and perhaps, because of that, the mindless talk and the carefree chattering of my companion made a distressing, almost a tragic, impression on me . . .

"Poor 'Little Red Riding Hood,'" I thought, "she is running around in a dense forest, chasing after brightly coloured butterflies, without ever stopping to think what could happen when the sun sets, and the redness of the setting sun spreads over the forest, and the birds stop singing, and the butterflies hide under leaves, and the eyes of wolves light up with a wild flame among the dark bushes.

"Mon petit Chaperon Rouge, ne vas pas dans la forêt [My little Red Riding Hood, do not go into the forest]!" I did not realize I was saying these words out loud.

"Il y a le loup qui va te manger [There is a wolf there that will eat you]," the young lady finished what I was saying and burst out laughing. "Oh, don't be afraid, I'm not afraid of that wolf; I have my own plans for him."

I glanced at her in surprise and thought: "What plans? What kind of plans could she possibly have?"

She smiled happily. "I know you're hinting about Anatole."

Oh, so that was it! I had no choice but to accept, without comment, this abrupt change in the conversation.

"Perhaps you think I'm 'suffering'? Oh, no! But it's true he intrigues me. Do you know what I'm thinking about now? I would like to make him fall in love with me, make him love me so much that his head would begin spinning, and he would simply go mad, and then I would say: 'Adieu!'—and I would depart for Moscow and leave him 'to suffer' here. That would be some joke! The devil take it!"

She was all set to vocalize in the gypsy manner, but stopped just in time and covered her mouth with her hand. "Have I gone mad or what? After all, we're out on the street!"

Actually, we were already standing in front of the entrance to the park of the Hotel "Rossiya." Alla Mykhaylivna came to a stop, folded up her parasol, used it to beat the dust out of her skirt, wiped the parasol and her blouse with a handkerchief, and asked me to check and see if her hat and hair were in order. Then she put away her handkerchief, unfolded her parasol once again, and picked up her skirt a little, this time paying more attention to its symmetry. There really was no great need now to pick up one's skirt, for the paths in the park were strewn with coarse sand from the sea, and the dusty street was left beyond the gate.

We walked down the path through the park, continually meeting proud-faced ladies dressed in all their finery, and gentlemen who were walking with a modern gait—raising their shoulders, stepping on their heels, and swaying from side to side.

"Alla Mykhaylivna," I said, "why would you want to bother with this Anatole? It would be better if you dropped this 'joke' as you call it."

"Why would I bother with him? But I'm trying to tell you—he intrigues me. Do you know what else I'm going to tell you? You should like this; I'm doing it partly as a matter of principle."

I just stared at her in astonishment.

"That's right—the principle of revenge. He most certainly has made more than a few women suffer, so let him pay a bit for his sins now."

"No, Alla Mykhaylivna, your 'principle' does not enchant me."

"Why not?"

"Because your 'revenge' . . . How can I say it? Here's how it's said in your Muscovy: 'The sheepskin is not worth the tanning.'"

Alla Mykhaylivna blushed instantly.

"It can't be helped! I'm not capable of any other idea; ideas aren't my forte . . . But how do you know he's not worth the 'tanning'? After all, you don't know Anatole."

It seemed to me my tone had offended her slightly, and I tried to change the subject. On the whole, my conversation with Alla Mykhaylivna was beginning to weary me; topics changed frequently, rapidly, and without any purpose, like the tiny bits of multicoloured glass in a kaleidoscope. I was happy when we finally stopped in front of the gate to the city park, where people were milling about, entering and exiting.

I extended my hand to Alla Mykhaylivna. "Good bye! We'll part company here. I'm going home now."

"What do you mean?" she protested, holding on to my hand. "But I thought you would keep me company in the park! It's not even proper for me to stroll alone."

"Well, you don't have to worry about that. You have many acquaintances, and you'll soon find somebody," I began to reassure her. But then I noticed she was not listening to me.

She was staring excitedly into the depths of the alley that led into the park. "Anatole is coming!" she whispered, tugging at my arm.

In the distance appeared a young gentleman in a riding habit and a jockey cap, toying with a whip in his hand. He was walking with the same modern gait as the young gentlemen at the hotel

'Rossiya.' I could not see his face very well, as he was still quite far off.

"Well, this is all the more reason for me to bid you farewell!" I said, and I freed my arm.

Alla Mykhaylivna no longer detained me; she did not even glance at me as she said good bye. She stood in a haughty pose, with her head tilted upwards in the same way as in the photograph I had seen in her room. The expression on her face was also the same, but against the background of her red parasol and her little crimson hat, it took on an even more "Gypsy-like" appearance.

The young gentleman approached the gate, casually swinging his whip. I walked away, but I did not go home as I had told Alla Mykhaylivna I would, and as I actually had intended to do. The sea lured me to itself. It stretched out ever so far and wide, and it was so calm and tenderly rosy. I longed for that rosy peacefulness; I truly needed it after my mentally fatiguing day.

I descended the steps that led from the bank to a small space between the so called square and the city bathhouse, and walked to the very edge of the sea. This was the only spot where one could sit, not on a bench, but on the sand, and watch the waves as they unrolled on the bank without breaking up either on the retaining wall of the shoreline or on the huge boulders that had been placed intentionally along the whole length of that wall to protect it from the sea. This was the only place where, during "the season," one could spend five minutes in solitude.

It was not late, but the sun was already disappearing behind the mountain ridge. The city was now lying under the long shadow of the mountains, and only the narrow edge of the shore in front of me was still gleaming in the dying rays of the setting sun. The distant slopes beyond the quay were sinking gently into the sea like a dark blue cloud, and everything was becoming darker and darker.

Gold and blue sparks flitted over the flushed surface of the sea; they fluctuated and faded, and the roseate glow of the sea also grew dim. Then the warm rosy hues vanished entirely and, almost instantly, a breeze arose, the waves splashed more noisily, the illuminated edge of the shore turned dark, and a shadow sped swiftly to the very middle of the sea that was now covered with tiny, white crests. Then both the breeze and the crests disappeared simultaneously, and the sea once again became calm and smooth, but it had turned a dark steel-grey, like the wing of a dove.

It was the summer twilight that had fallen so abruptly; it had fallen, trembled, and then calmed down again. Far, far away, on the very horizon, an opal light—the reflection of the sun—was glimmering.

The sun had already set over Yalta, but on the steppes beyond the mountain ridge it was still sunny. Another moment, and the horizon would turn violet; still another moment, and the moon would swim grandly out of the sea and pave a broad, gold, translucent path all the way to the shore; the stars would rise above the mountains and, in a golden horde, would follow the moon, always keeping their distance, as if respecting its magic power. I waited for these moments, that silent, grand, triumphant march of the heavenly lights.

"Ta-ra-ra-boom-tee-yeah!" the brass band suddenly burst forth from the city park, cutting through the din of footsteps and voices. I jumped as if I had been startled out of a sleep. Right here, above the stone barrier of the square, ever so close to me, a restless crowd was milling about, eagerly seeking joy, noise, smoke—and I was still dreaming about peace, about natural joys! A vain dream!

I rose to my feet and was about to go home, when I heard the voice of Alla Mykhaylivna directly above me by the stairs. I stood still in the shadows of the bathhouse, because I did not want to encounter her. I could see the outline of her figure quite clearly in the diffused evening light. She was standing with Anatole, holding his arm and tapping the stone barrier with her parasol.

I could also see Anatole's face distinctly. For some reason, I had come to the conclusion that he must be handsome, more handsome than he now appeared to me. In reality, he had an ordinary, vacuous face . . . When we see such faces in paintings, we say they were painted by an unskilled artisan, or cut out of paper and affixed to the painting with lacquer. But such faces do occur quite frequently in nature.

The two of them, Anatole and Alla Mykhaylivna, were standing very close to one another. He was pressing her hand to himself with his elbow, and she was grazing his jockey cap with her little crimson hat.

"So, tell me, what were you saying about me when you talked with Trapinsky? Tell me at once!" she wanted to find out from Anatole. "Tell me, or I'll throw your cap into the sea!"

She reached out to grab his cap, but he intercepted her hand. "Aha, now you're caught in a trap! But victory makes me magnanimous: I don't have to tell you, but I will. Trapinsky and I made a bet that you wouldn't dare to sing this song with me when we're alone: 'We're in the silence, all alone.'"

"Oh? I wouldn't dare? I would sing it right now, if we weren't out on the street."

"I'm taking you at your word; let's go into the park, into a side lane!"

"Fine, let's go then!"

Setting out at a fast clip, the couple crossed the street and disappeared into the park.

About two days after that evening, I was sitting and reading on a balcony in the public hall in the city park. Suddenly, someone called out to me by name. I glanced down and saw Alla Mykhaylivna waving her hand at me.

"Come down here to me! The devil take your magazines! Come and save a human soul!"

"Save whom? Who's dying?" I asked.

"Save me! I'm dying of boredom!" A note of nervous strain vibrated in the voice of the young lady.

I went down to her. From closer up, I noticed at once that she was agitated, and her eyes were troubled. She was holding a large, thick leaf of a magnolia plant and was absently shredding it into tiny pieces; her open parasol was lying on the ground.

"Why are you so bored?" I asked her after I had greeted her.

"Well, what am I supposed to be doing? There are no evening balls in this hellhole where dogs go mad from the heat, and people from boredom!"

"But I thought you'd found yourself a form of entertainment. Didn't you?"

"Are you referring to Anatole? May the devil take him! I'm going to break off with him."

"You should have done that long ago!" I remarked, but the young lady carried on without listening.

"Who does he think he is? Do you know what he snapped at me when I didn't agree to go with him to the waterfall at Uchan-Su? Just think about it! Is it possible for a decent girl to go alone with him way up into the mountains?"

"If you're asking my opinion . . ." I started to say, but the young lady interrupted me once again.

"It goes without saying that I did not want to go, and I didn't go; then he became angry and shot his mouth off: 'There's nothing more annoying than the eternal subterfuge used by you fashionable young ladies of the world! You don't know how to be either completely virtuous or completely dissolute; you do everything by halves.' That's what he said: 'dissolute'! The brute! What does he take me for?"

"Listen, Alla Mykhaylivna, I don't want to preach a lesson on morals to you, because you won't listen to me anyway; so, I'll only say that revenge is better left to French women—we Slavs don't have the temperament for it."

Alla Mykhaylivna shuddered. "French women? Do you know something? Did you hear something about her?"

"About whom?" I asked in amazement.

"About Mademoiselle Girod, that red-haired Frenchwoman! She has flaming red hair and almost always dresses in green."

"I did see someone like that, but why should she concern us?"

"Yesterday, Anatole said: 'I'm sure that Mademoiselle Girod would be braver than you, *il n'y a que les françaises pour ces escapades là' [there's no one like French women for escapades like that].* It's as if you had heard him say this. Tell me, what does this Girod seem like to you? She's quite ugly, as ugly as sin, isn't she?"

"I don't know, I didn't look at her that closely. Anyway, Alla Mykhaylivna, it's too hot to stand here. Perhaps we could go into the reading room?"

"Oh, what can one see in there? Besides, it's even worse there, because it's stuffy."

"Then let's go for a walk in the park or something."

"Heaven forbid! It's so hot! I've just come down from there, and you want me to go back up?"

"Well, if you don't want to walk—let's go out on a boat; there's a breeze today, and it will be wonderful under the sails!"

"Do you expect me to go out on a boat, and one with sails, no less?" Alla Mykhaylivna fluttered her hands. "Not for anything in the world! I'll most certainly become dizzy. I really don't like your 'most beautiful' sea; when I look at all that rocking motion I get sick to my stomach. It seems to me it's more as a matter of form that people say: 'Oh, the sea! Oh, the sea!' But, to put it bluntly, it's water and nothing more. We're not amphibians . . ."

This conversation and the heat were beginning to irritate me, and I was trying to think of a way of escaping from Alla Mykhaylivna.

But, at that very moment, her tone changed.

"My dear, my little dove, let's go have some ice cream."

She said this so ingenuously, so sincerely, that my impatience with her melted away.

"Fine," I agreed smilingly. "Only I don't want to eat it here in the park; it's not very pleasant to eat in the middle of the road."

"No, no, we'll go into the pavilion. It's by the sea, so you should like it there. You can gaze at your beautiful sea, and I can look at the people."

"I wonder who will see more!"

We went to have some ice cream in the seaside pavilion. Alla Mykhaylivna found a place at a table situated close to the street; I sat down on the opposite side of it. The sea was beating against the post next to us. I looked down at it, and I felt sorry for my "beautiful sea."

Its velvety, dark green waves could barely be seen from under all the garbage—watermelon rinds, sunflower seeds, yellow streaks, and some kind of red strings that were floating in from the ferry boats and the petroleum steamer that was being loaded at the dock. Another steamer, transporting coal, was also standing there, spewing steam; black, and flat like a turtle, it was coughing up bursts of smoke from its smokestack and spreading soot over the entire harbour. A small ferryboat, whistling shrilly, was chugging its way beyond the quay; boats with oars, and some with sails, were milling about the bay.

Noise, whistles, shouts, bells . . .

Nevertheless, all this racket could not muffle the roar of the conquering sea; and the filthy refuse littered only the waves on the shore. But out there, beyond the harbour, stretched a clean, blue expanse, and there were no blemishes on it; only the reflections of the gilded clouds danced over it and, in the distance, the sailboats looked like huge, white butterflies. The horizon was beginning to draw me to it irresistibly . . .

Just then Alla Mykhaylivna poked me and cried out. I turned around.

"Look, it's them!" Alla Mykhaylivna pointed, her eyes riveted on the shore.

In the middle of the street, two equestrians—a gentleman and a lady—were galloping along quite quickly, smartly brandishing their whips. It was only when they were in line with the pavilion that they slowed down, and I recognized Anatole. I did not know the lady. She was a chic girl; on her carroty red hair she wore a green jockey cap—like Anatole.

Evidently, Anatole had caught sight of Alla Mykhaylivna; he took off his cap, waved it broadly, and then bowed down low, almost to his reins. The lady turned her head in our direction, laughed, and bent over to Anatole, obviously sharing a confidence with him. Then they both flicked their whips once again, and galloped off.

Alla Mykhaylivna was sitting red-faced, and the glass spoon in her hand kept clinking against the dish with the ice cream. She silently took out her money, paid the waiter and, just as silently, started to leave the pavilion. I stopped her to say good bye; she gave me her hand, still without a word, and left without raising her eyes.

I watched from the pavilion as she walked down the street. Her head was lowered, her parasol lay forgotten in her right hand, her free hand was hanging limply, and her light-coloured dress was dragging on the ground. Her pace was hurried and uneven; then, after coming to a complete stop, she turned sharply away from the shore and, as if fleeing, walked rapidly up the incline of a narrow side street.

A few days passed by before I encountered Alla Mykhaylivna again. Then, one afternoon, I saw her as I strolled through the square; she was sitting on the stairs that led to a small dock where boats were tied. Her head was leaning on her hands, and it seemed she was staring out at the sea which was restless that day, changing from blue steel to green emerald, rising up in angry billows, and crashing ever closer to the retaining wall of the square.

Dressed in a black riding outfit, she had a small cylindrical hat on her head, and a whip in her hand. Although she was sitting on the highest step, the train of the riding outfit trailed down much lower, so that the waves splashed occasional droplets of water on it. Looking at her from the side, one could have thought she was engrossed by the sea. This seemed quite strange to me, because she had said more than once that she did not like "to get sentimental over nature."

I walked up to her. "Well, Alla Mykhaylivna, has the 'beautiful sea' conquered you as well?"

She turned around and glanced at me with a clouded look. Her eyes were either tired or tearful, and small red spots were clearly visibly on her pale, exhausted face.

"The sea?" she said gravely. "No, it's little Liza who has dragged me here."

I now turned my attention to a thin, blond child of about seven, the daughter of Alla Mykhaylivna's neighbour. I knew this girl. Her mother was a teacher and spent almost the entire day giving lessons; the little girl, bored with staying home alone, kept running in to see "Auntie Alla," who spoiled her, fed her candies, and often took her to listen to the music in the park.

The two girls, the young one and the older one, had developed a genuine friendship, and I often found them conversing or playing some childish game; at those times, Alla Mykhaylivna forgot her "Gypsiness" and looked like Liza's older friend—perhaps no more than two or three years older.

The little girl felt completely unconstrained in the company of "Auntie Alla," and now she was happily hopping down from the steps to the stones, trying to jump over as many stones as she could and still make it back up the steps before the waves rolled up on the shore. Her yellow shoes and the bottom of her blue sailor outfit were completely splashed with water; I drew Alla's attention to this.

"Oh, that's right. Liza dear, that's enough jumping for now; and it's actually quite damp here, as well. Let's go." Alla Mykhaylivna rose to her feet. "It's a good thing you came by, because if I should be delayed in town, I'll ask you to take Liza home. But now let's go into the park. It's unpleasant here—it's wet, and there's that roaring . . ."

We crossed the street and went into the park. There were very few people there at that time, mainly nannies with children, and most of them were by the jungle gym and the swings; Liza also ran off to the playground.

"Are you planning to go horseback riding, Alla Mykhaylivna?" I inquired.

"No."

"Then why are you wearing a riding habit?"

"Just because. It's fashionable to walk around in a riding habit these days."

We were walking on the main path and had already passed the building with the musicians, when she suddenly turned back to the jungle gym.

"Liza, my dear!" she called out.

The little girl ran towards her.

"Listen, Liza dearest . . . go," Alla Mykhaylivna was speaking incoherently, hesitantly. "Go down that wide path, over there . . . on the long bench . . . a gentleman is reading a newspaper . . . a gentleman, you know . . . tell him that you . . . that you were just on the jungle gym and that . . . Auntie Alla is with you. Go!"

"Alla Mykhaylivna!' I shouted. "Liza dear, don't go!"

But the little girl was already running swiftly among the benches on the main pathway and did not hear my call.

"Alla Mykhaylivna!" I involuntarily repeated reproachfully.

The young lady was striking the pebbles at her feet with her whip. Blushing furiously, she attempted to justify her behaviour. "So, what did I say? I didn't say anything . . . Liza knows him herself, and she's gone up to him of her own accord . . ."

I kept silent and tried not to look at her face.

In a moment the little girl ran back to us.

"Well, what?" Alla Mykhaylivna asked her, forgetting about her confusion.

"Nothing," the little one replied.

"What do you mean, nothing? Did you see the gentleman? What did you tell him?"

"I told him I had come to the swings, and that you had come with me, and that you were sitting over here."

"Well, and what did he say?"

"He said: 'Oh, she's sitting over there? That's fine, let her sit.' Then he got up and left."

"Where did he go?"

"To the public hall."

Alla Mykhaylivna turned pale and stared straight ahead with wide-open eyes. Anger and despair were reflected in them.

I sent little Liza off to the swings and tried to convince Alla Mykhaylivna to go home. But she did not want to.

After some time, on a path that was secluded from us by bushes, we heard someone's footsteps and a voice that was humming a chanson:

"C'est pas de la soupe ça, [This is not soup,]
C'est pas de la soupe ça." [This is not soup.]

"He's coming . . ." the young lady whispered, and she suddenly straightened up proudly.

And sure enough, Anatole emerged from the bushes and approached us with a careless gait; as he came abreast of us, he touched his cap with his hand, cast a vague look at Alla Mykhaylivna through his pince-nez, and kept on walking towards the gate. After he had gone a few steps, he once again sang:

"C'est pas de la soupe ça, [This is not soup,]
C'est — du— chocolat!" [It is chocolate!]

He then stepped through the gate, walked out into the street, and vanished in the crowds.

Alla Mykhaylivna grabbed my hand and squeezed it so tightly that I almost shrieked. I glanced at her; she looked as if she might burst into tears.

"Alla Mykhaylivna! Control yourself! Let's get away from here!" And I led her into the washroom in the public hall.

Once she was there, she collapsed on a couch and began to weep spasmodically. Then she jumped to her feet, grabbed my hands and, falling headlong into my arms, wailed indistinctly, as if she were delirious.

"Yes . . . that's just how it should be . . . I hate . . . him . . . and myself . . . Oh, it hurts, it hurts, it hurts here . . ." And she clutched her chest.

I gave her some water and waited until the attack passed. Then I advised her to hire a carriage, for it was doubtful if she could have made it home on foot. She got up and started walking to the door, then stopped, as if she had forgotten something. Stepping up to the mirror, she fixed her hair and hat, asked if she could borrow my veil, pinned it on, and then left.

I called little Liza, settled her in a carriage with Alla Mykhaylivna, and hurried home myself. The wind was whistling along the shoreline, and the furious sea seemed to be tossing raindrops right up to the shops on the shore. But the sky was blue, as it had been formerly, and the sun sparkled like molten gold on the breakers of the giant waves. It was a refreshing summer storm.

The next evening, I was sitting at home writing letters when someone knocked on my door. I was not expecting any guests; thinking, therefore, that it might be the maid who wanted to enter, I did not interrupt my writing as I said: "Come in!"

The door squeaked, but no one walked in. I turned around and saw Nastasiya Illinichna standing on the threshold! "Nastasiya Illinichna! It's you? What's wrong? Is something wrong with the young lady?"

"Oh, there is something wrong, there is something terribly wrong, my dear young lady! I simply don't know what it can be. Yesterday she was still completely well, but this morning her head started to ache. I said: 'Don't go out into the wind, my young lady; don't go dancing, because you're not well.' But what was the use of that? She didn't listen. And now that little Liza is hanging around . . . Oh, what a lot of trouble! Oh, our sins, our sins!"

"Is Alla Mykhaylivna very ill then?"

"She's in bed. The doctor came by and told her to stay there. And I came to you." Here the old woman bowed down to me. "Alla Mykhaylivna is asking you to visit her. She's all alone here, and there's no one to advise her, to comfort her. What kind of advice can I, such an ignorant creature, give her? I just don't know what to do."

The old woman began wiping her eyes with her apron.

"Don't worry; perhaps it's not as bad as it seems," I tried to cheer up the old woman as I dressed to go with her.

All the way there, while we were in the carriage, the old woman groaned and moaned. She felt sorry for the young lady but also for herself, as she imagined what "daddy and mummy" would say to her for not looking after their child.

When I arrived, Alla Mykhaylivna was in bed in the same room in which we had once tried on blouses. As I entered, the first thing I saw was the picture in its golden frame, with a candlestick in front of it. The last time I was there I had not noticed it. Alla Mykhaylivna was lying listlessly on the bed, and her black hair covered the pillow like a dense net; her eyes were burning, her face was flaming, and her breathing was rapid, shallow, and hoarse.

"Oh, you've come!" she greeted me, extending her hot damp hand. "Tell me, advise me, what am I to do? I'm going to send my mother a telegram asking her come, because what good is this? I'm here alone. I'm sick. I might die . . ."

Her voice grew faint, and became soft and high like a child's. One could see she was very alarmed, but the arrival of a new person seemed to give her a bit of courage.

I assured her she did not look at all ill, and advised her against sending the telegram. Asking what medicine the doctor had prescribed, and what was usually done for her in such instances, I placed a compress on her forehead. She calmed down a little and ordered Nastasiya Illinichna to give me some tea. Then she took my hand and pressed her hot face to it.

"You know, I didn't think you were so kind. At times, you have such a forbidding appearance. Don't argue. I know I often seem like a complete idiot to you; well, that's not surprising . . ."

I asked her to stop saying things like that, and not to upset herself.

"No, no, I'm not upset," she protested. "I want to tell you that I feel completely at ease with you. I knew people like you in Moscow as well . . ."

"What kind of 'people like me'?"

"This kind . . . Different, than I am . . . Only they are all so unfriendly and cool; they talk as if they begrudged their words, as if they didn't want to 'cast pearls.' And they're always hurrying somewhere, they never have time . . ."

I smiled: "Well, you see, I'm not like that, for I am not hurrying anywhere, and I have all the time that is necessary, and even more."

"Oh, I'm not saying that . . ." she fell back on her pillow, closed her eyes, and fell silent.

Then, after a moment, she started up once again: "You know, one of my cousins is presently taking a course to become a medical assistant . . ."

I thought she might be becoming delirious, but she was fully conscious.

"This cousin tried to talk me into taking the same course. She says it's interesting—the knowledge, the friendships, the study groups . . . Father and mother would permit it, because such courses are even fashionable now—of course, medical assistants are a little different.

"Well, I tried it. I got the course of study, but it was all so boring. I didn't understand anything; I'm not used to studying. I felt even more stupid when I looked at those courses . . . No, nothing will ever come of me . . . So my mother said: 'Study music.' Well, what's the good of that? My sister graduated from the Conservatory; she struggled and struggled, ruined her fingers, and poisoned the life of everyone around her with her exercises, but now she doesn't even play anymore—she got married.

"But why aren't you drinking your tea? Nanny, bring some jam to sweeten the tea!"

After I was done with my tea, she returned to her theme.

"They say I'm an egotist . . . It's true that I can do only what pleases me. It's just that sometimes I don't know what it is exactly that I like doing. I wonder if everyone is as bored and disgusted as I am? You probably think I'm saying all of this capriciously because of that . . . Oh, you know what I'm hinting at . . . but at times I think like this even without that . . . And as for *that*, I'm just angry with myself. I acted like a foolish peasant girl, and he may think I'm truly dying for him; but I would just like to spit on all that!"

This was the first sharp expression from her during the entire evening.

"Alla Mykhaylivna," I interrupted her. "I think all this talk is upsetting you. Might it not be better if you read something?"

"I suppose so," she agreed. "Over there on the table there's a new novel by Gyp that I bought recently, but haven't read as yet."

I picked up the book: *'L'amour moderne' [Modern Love]*, I think it was called.

The book was of a small format, nicely published, with delicate illustrations, and on the cover there were some figures in reddish hues and contorted poses, barely covered by veils, with wild expressions on their faces, as if they were rushing off someplace in a hurry or having an attack of St. Vitus' dance.

I began to read the book out loud. The French puns, the brief conversational exchanges, the eccentric aphorisms, the descriptions full of a refined intellectual debauchery, and the fantasies all stuck together like links in a colourful paper chain.

In the middle of one particularly risqué scene, I glanced up at Alla Mykhaylivna. She was no longer lying still, with closed eyes, the way she had been earlier; she was leaning on her elbow, her head was raised, and she was wide-eyed, gazing at me animatedly, holding her breath, and hanging on to every word in the novel with avid interest.

"Well, why have you stopped?" she protested querulously when I paused.

"I think that's enough for today," I said, closing the book.

"Oh, no, read some more, read some more, it's so interesting! You should be ashamed of yourself; you've stopped reading just at the most interesting place in the book!"

"It seems to me that this novel is unsettling your nerves, and you're ill. Don't you have any other books?"

"There are some on the shelf, but they're all old, and I've read them all."

I walked over and looked at the books. For the most part they were in French: *Demi vièrges [Semi-Virgins]. Contes jaunes [Off-Colour Anecdotes], Pour lire au bain [For Reading in the Bath]* . . . There were also the *Russian Tales* by Leykin, the novels of Yasinsky . . .

"Are these your books from home?" I asked.

"No, I got them here, in Yalta."

On some of the books I saw the words "Anatole B."

"So you're not going to read any more of Gyp?" Alla Mykhaylivna asked again.

"No, I'm not. Perhaps you will allow me to bring you another kind of book tomorrow?"

"Another kind? What kind?"

"I don't know yet; something more peaceful."

"I don't like 'virtuous' books which are intended *pour les enfants sages [for wise children]*!"

"We'll select something without 'virtue and vice'."

"Well, of course: literature for the ill, for tubercular patients. Why, that's exactly appropriate for me now . . ."

She was beginning to be capricious.

"If you like," I said, "we'll read Gyp, but not today. It's late already. It's time for you to sleep, and I'll be afraid to walk home. Good night!"

I put on my coat, said my farewells, and started walking towards the door.

Alla Mykhaylivna made me come back: "Come here. Are you angry?"

"I assure you, I'm not."

"*Quelle cachottière [What a dissembler]*! Well, good night. Bring me a book tomorrow, and we'll read it." she smiled, and pressed my hand weakly.

When I returned the next day, Alla Mykhaylivna, dressed in a greyish blue peignoir, was still lying down, but she was on the couch, and not in bed. Her face was fresh, and her demeanour was calmer.

"Well, did you bring me a book?" she greeted me.

"Yes, I did."

"What is it?"

"Turgenev."

"Oh, Turgenev . . ." she drawled apathetically.

"Forgive me. Really, I should have known you probably had read him not too long ago."

"Him? No, I haven't read him. We only read the classics up to Pushkin. It's true there was something in the anthology, 'Bezhin Meadow,' I think, and something else that I don't remember . . . Yes, something childish . . . Is what you brought me interesting?"

"I don't know; we'll see what you think."

"Well, start reading, and we'll see."

I opened the book and read the epigraph.

"The good years, the happy days,
Have sped away like the waters of spring . . ."

Alla Mykhaylivna adjusted her pillow and made herself more comfortable.

After reading two or three pages, I stopped to give my voice a rest, and I heard the even breathing of Alla Mykhaylivna. She was sleeping with her hand under her cheek.

From under the pillow peeked the reddish cover of "*L'amour moderne.*"

Alla Mykhaylivna improved rapidly, but she did not go into town. She often sent me notes asking me to visit her. In the notes there were always complaints about her oppressive boredom.

When I visited her, one could see that the young lady truly was bored; her movements were apathetic, and her voice had a nervous quality to it. Her conversation was often interrupted by yawns, and sometimes we spent hours working at some sewing without uttering a single word.

She even began to display carelessness in her attire, walking around in a peignoir, and with her hair uncurled.

This is why I was somewhat taken aback one day to find her all nicely turned out, her hair curled, sitting in front of a mirror. She was powdering her face, cocking her head first this way, and then that way, like a sparrow.

Seeing me, she leapt to her feet and quickly called out: "Oh, my dear! How splendid that you've come! I'll show you the new things that I received! Mother sent them to me today. Look! But where are they? Nastasiya Illinichna! The devil must have taken off with them!"

"Well, well, you're mentioning the evil one again, may God forgive you!" the old woman muttered, but it was evident she was happy that her young lady had her health back.

Nastasiya Illinichna took out some carefully folded items from the closet—blouses, ribbons, lace, a new bathing suit, and so on. Alla Mykhaylivna was as delighted as a child with everything.

"Oh, they have brought the scent of Moscow with them! This is all from 'Kuznetsky's Bridge'! And if only you had seen who brought me the package!"

"Who was it?"

"A little red devil!" the young lady said laughingly. "I never expected to see him here, and to tell you the truth, I'd forgotten all about him. I knew him as a military student, and he was ever so awkward and funny then—like an oyster! But you should see him now! He's a soldier of the guard and dressed to the nines, *fichu turlututu [ever so dapper]*! There's no comparison!

"I was so embarrassed that he caught me looking like such a mess, uncombed, and in my housecoat. Well, that's nothing; he's coming by later today to take me to the lottery, and this time we'll make sure he sees something totally different!" She winked and laughed once again.

I remarked that I had not seen her so happy in a long time.

"Well, why shouldn't I be? I'm not about to wear mourning clothes. *Plaisir passé, joujou cassé [The pleasure is gone, the toy is broken]*! We'll push the wedge out with another wedge.

"Oh, burn! Talk! Talk!

"Phew! Tell me have you ever been in love? Ha-ha-ha! How bristly you've suddenly become, like a porcupine! Ha-ha-ha, how amusing this is . . . Well, tell me at least, which ones appeal to you more, brunets, or blonds? As for myself, I prefer blonds— for now! Listen, why are you looking at me like that?"

I did not know what to say, so I kept my counsel.

Alla Mykhaylivna began to pout. "I can see my manners shock you. Well, I'm not an English woman, and I'm not a fish. But I'm not at all sure that it's polite to make it known to a person that you consider her to be a complete idiot."

"Alla Mykhaylivna," I protested, but she interrupted me.

"Oh, there's no need for that; it's better to be 'honest.' I'm not all that stupid; I also understand a thing or two. And, to tell you the truth, you're beginning to irritate me with '*votre petit air de soeur grise [your slight grimace of a sister of charity]*'."

"Alla Mykhaylivna," I began, and the sharpness in my voice startled even me. "I simply do not understand: what it is that you want from me?"

"Simply that I hate secrecy and contredanse. I was very frank with you."

"It was your desire to be so . . ."

"By that you mean that no one forced me to talk . . . But I was so alone . . ."

"By that you mean that if there's no one else, any one at all will do? Well, in that case, we've settled our accounts when it comes to compliments."

I felt I was losing control of my voice and of the tone in it.

"It's not a matter of compliments. I simply want you to know that I've noticed you're contorting yourself into another 'Miss Forster'."

"What does that mean?"

"That was the name, wasn't it, of the English lady who travelled to be with the Yakuts? 'The Teacher of the Lepers'! She even collected money in Moscow to build a church for them. She probably read them spiritually uplifting books as well . . . After all, let them hear them as well . . ."

"If they don't fall asleep!" I interrupted her.

"Exactly, if they don't fall asleep!" Alla Mykhaylivna leapt in. "Well, what's to be done? 'It's not for fools like us to drink tea'! The sea, poetry, nature, ideas . . ."

"As far as I recall, we never discussed any ideas with you."

"Oh, of course! 'Don't cast pearls before swine!'"

"Or, as we say: 'It's a pity to waste one's words!'" This flew out of me involuntarily.

"How dare you?"

I did not repeat what I had said and lowered my eyes, because they had "a dark look," full of irreconcilable, fatal antagonism.

At this moment a voice could be heard, and the jangling of spurs.

"You have guests," I said. "Farewell."

"Farewell!" Alla Mykhaylivna replied, returning to her mirror. I made my exit.

As I walked through the next room, I saw a young officer in a guard's uniform. He was standing by the window with his hands behind his back, and I could see only the back of his head and the part in his hair. He turned around to glance at me, then once again turned quickly to the window.

I strode through the orchard at a quick pace, and began to wander aimlessly through the streets, not knowing where I was going. I was angry both at myself and at Alla Mykhaylivna; this conversation had left me with a bitter taste in my mouth; but I had no desire to make peace, to take back what I had said. What had come between us was not just a misunderstanding; I realized this, and I only wanted to get over it as quickly as I could, and then to forget it.

Wandering through the streets, I found myself at the city park. By the gate, there were posters announcing the lottery that was to take place in the park that very day. The people were already gathering, and the musicians were seated in their places in the pavilion. I mixed in with the crush of people; I was prepared to go to any lengths to change my mood.

It was crowded in the park. The booths, built especially for the lottery and the charity bazaar, made the already narrow paths still narrower, and the people, walking in pairs and in groups, involuntarily shoved one another. The crowd had whipped up the coarse sea sand with its feet, and now a yellowish dust was rising in the air and swirling over heads attired in gaudy little hats, bright caps, straw hats, and black top hats.

It was hot in the lanes, even though the heat was no longer very intense; the sun was already edging its way behind the mountains. The fragrance of the flowers, the perfumes wafting from the ladies and their handkerchiefs, the gas from the lamps that were lit early today for the parade, the aroma of the resin of the cypress trees, and the dust—all of this blended together and made the air heavy, as if saturated with chloroform.

The people also looked as if they were drugged; they walked from booth to booth, bought tickets, selected prizes, threw bits of paper at one another—that "confetti" of Yalta—but it was all done languidly, lifelessly. Others were sitting on benches, gazing at the passers-by; some ladies—in diamonds, with décolleté dresses, incredible hairdos, and hats—were decked out as if they were attending a ball. They gesticulated and smiled, but for some reason, it looked as if they were not real people, but artificial, like wax figures.

Some kind of compulsion held sway over everything, like in a dream, and it seemed that in a moment or two all of these people would yawn, rub their eyes, glance in amazement at one another, and disperse.

But no, the music began, and the crowd shuddered, but it did not disperse; it only began walking more quickly. The bits of paper flashed like a multicoloured snowstorm, and the wheels with the lottery numbers began spinning like windmills. The noise of human voices vied with the music. It became even more crowded, and somewhat dizzying . . .

I sat down in the first free spot I came across. Some ladies were seated beside me; one was in a gaudy orange outfit, with hair to match. Next to her was a gentleman; it was Anatole.

The lady was conversing loudly with him in French in a low contralto; she had a native, but vulgar, French accent. She referred to her young man as Monsieur Toto and kept ordering him to buy lottery tickets, and flowers, and oysters, and so on, from every young lady who walked by with a basket or a wheel. Monsieur Toto bought tickets, and flowers, and oysters, but he had quite a displeased look about him as he catered to her whims.

New groups of people were continually coming from the gate towards the pavilion and the music. In one of these groups, bright buttons and epaulettes flashed, and ringing laughter resounded. I immediately recognized the laughter of Alla Mykhaylivna. Attired in a sky-blue dress of eyelet embroidery, she was walking arm in arm with the guardsman; on her head, she was wearing a little white hat that resembled a tuft of soft feathers.

Their eyes were sparkling, their smiles radiant. The officer, carrying her white cape in his free hand and waving it gently, beamed and gazed into her eyes. From time to time, she stopped, moved away slightly from her young man, and raised her head in happy laughter; her slim figure swayed, and then she once again drew nearer to him with the gracefulness of a little cat. It was clear that they already knew each other well, and that there was an understanding between them.

As she walked past Anatole, she lifted her head and glanced at him haughtily, narrowing her eyes. Anatole hurriedly lifted his cap.

The guardsman bent over to Alla Mykhaylivna as if he were asking her something.

"No, I don't know this gentleman; he must have made a mistake," she responded loudly, shaking her head so violently that the tall, pale blue flowers on her hat waved back and forth.

The couple passed by, and other couples followed with similar gestures, similar laughter . . . Often that laughter was interrupted by coughing, but eyes shone and faces flamed, perhaps from happiness, perhaps from asthma, and perhaps—from tuberculosis? These were people who had come to a health spa. They had come here to leave their pain with the sea and with the mountains, and to free themselves from their illnesses. Would they free themselves? What would free them?

I forced my way through the tightly packed crowd, came out on the shore, and then walked out into the square. There were many people there as well, but not quite as many as in the park. A fresh breeze was softly blowing, rocking the sailboats near the dock. Sculls were gliding over the bay and, farther away, white Turkish boats gleamed. Like a flock of swans, they silently floated towards the horizon and dissolved in the distance. Suddenly, I longed to float away in their wake.

I hired a sailboat.

"Where do you want to go?" the oarsman asked.

"Just out there." And I pointed my hand at the horizon.

The sail caught the wind, the waves began to hum, and the boat flew forward swiftly, like a seagull. It sped across the bay, passed the quay, and began to rock in wide oscillations. We had come out on the "open sea," as sailors say. It was not necessary to steer—the wind and the waves did all the work. The boat lifted itself up high, and then descended, softly and gently, making its way from wave to wave.

I looked at the shore and the city; with every motion of the boat, the city appeared to sway, as if it were saying its farewells to me. And the sun was also bidding its farewells. From the shore, trembling red ribbons ran out to us; they twinkled like tongues of fire on the dark green waves. The shadow of the mountain slopes trembled along with them; it seemed to be trying to catch up with us . . .

I gazed at the sea for a long time. The twilight faded, and the dark night unfolded its tent over the sea.

"It's a dark night—the sea will shine with phosphorescence," the oarsman said.

And truly, sky-blue phosphorescent streaks began to tremble beyond the stern, and the oars ignited fires. I gathered some water in my hand and flung it upwards, and a fantastic fountain of cold fire flashed through the air. Dolphins dove and splashed, churning up geysers of light on the black water. Falling stars dipped and sank into the sea.

The shore was not visible in the darkness, but far away in the distance, a group of fires burned like the Pleiades. The deep sky appeared to be speaking with fiery words to the sea, and the sea was singing its powerful, sublime, eternal poem to the magnificent night.

The Blind Man

A Complementary Sketch: A Response to
Olha Kobylianska's "The Blind Man"
(1902)

Motto: No one can see a soul, and—
not everyone can hear one.

It is strange, but I have never been quite sure if I am blind, or if I can see. People have often thought of me as blind, but to me it always seemed that I could see; my belief, however, did not bring me any happiness, because I could not gaze upon the sun. I tried looking at it through multicoloured lenses and, at times, I discerned its outline, but I could not tell where its surface was clear, and where it was spotted; the lenses confused me, because they altered the colour of everything. And, whenever I attempted to look at the sun without any glasses at all, the light dazzled my eyes and made them ache. This pain pierced my brain; from my mind, a feeling of despondency flooded my entire body, and I became ill and unfit for life.

I had to give up trying to look at the sun with my naked eye for I knew it could kill me, and I did not have any desire to view it through glasses, for they, after all, also dazzled me—and very greatly, at that—without letting me see the *sun*. So then I tried to see at least the light—not the actual sun, but the light of the sun. Alas! How it dazed me!—to the point of squeezing tears of blood from my eyes.

I tried gazing at a white marble statue that stood in the sunlight, high up on an inaccessible pedestal. Oh, it was so incredibly beautiful that it looked as if it might come to life at any moment and utter a word. But then, my eyes began to ache, and I no longer knew if it was my eyes that were turning dark, or if the statue was being covered with mould and cobwebs. And, once again, I wept in pain and in grief.

I tried to look down at the white snow with its delicate shading . . . It was changing, transmogrifying, turning first grey and then black. I do not know if it truly did melt and turn into mud, or if it just appeared that way to me, but, once again, I wept.

I tried to look up at a silvery pink cloud in the western sky—it was so lovely and bright. And I did look at it, and it seemed to grow still rosier, but then my eyes began to ache terribly, and I regained my senses only when the cloud was no longer there, and when a gloomy, pitch-black night hovered over me, in front of me, and all around me. And it was then that even I believed that I had gone blind, because the night lasted for a long, long time, and I could see nothing—nothing luminous, nor white, nor colourful— only the night . . .

I wept, and asked people: "Have I gone blind?"

Some shrugged their shoulders and replied: "I do not know."

Others said: "Do not think about it."

A third group comforted me: "The blind also live upon the earth; there are those who have not seen the sun from the day they were born."

I saw that no one would tell me the truth *in a straightforward manner*, and so I fell silent.

I had long been in the habit, after the sun had tortured my eyes, of hiding in all sorts of dark crannies and caves. I would sit there all alone and wait until my tears stopped flowing, and then I would set out once again in search of the light.

Now I no longer wanted to hide like that—I longed for the company of others who were like me. I was terrified in my isolated corner, but I felt unhappy among people unafflicted by blindness, and it may well be that they also were unhappy when they were with me.

And so I went to a hospital. It felt so good to be there. In that hospital there was a child, afflicted by blindness, who had not seen the sun from birth. Hope was still held out for her that she would see it one day, but she did not believe it. Instead, she tried to become accustomed to the night, to accept it; but she often stumbled in the darkness, and then she cried. There were times when she played plaintive melodies for a long, long time—she had a silver harp, one that was a trifle too heavy for her and had tough strings—and then she would weep again.

Whenever I tried to comfort her, she would ask me in a soft voice: "Have you ever seen the sun? What is it like? I think it is terrible, because it burns . . ."

"I think so too," I replied, even more softly.

"But have you seen the light?" the child persisted.

"I do not know . . ."

"How can you not know—was there not a time when you could see?"

"I do not know if I could see."

"But you saw *something*?" the child insisted, upset now. "Tell me, how did you see?"

I began to describe how I saw and then began to weep with grief; and the child also cried, both because of my tears, and because she could not *understand*—she simply could not understand how it was that I "saw" *something*.

She often told me: "Why did you 'look' at that something that you call 'white?' Is it really necessary to 'look?' Perhaps you could have 'listened' to it?"

I remained silent, for I could not bring myself to tell her: "To listen—this is not enough for people."

The child continued her questions: "Why 'look,' if your eyes ache from it?"

Once again I simply could not say: "But what are eyes for, if not to look?"

And so, I remained silent once more.

The child said: "You at least should not have looked at the so-called 'cloud' that you saw last of all; it is because of it that your eyes ache so badly."

And, after searching out my eyes with her hands, the child kissed them tenderly, even though she continued to speak in an angry tone of voice. "If you had not been so interested in various 'clouds' and in that something that was 'white,' and if you had not 'looked' at them, then you would be healthy, and nothing would ache, and you would not have to stay in a hospital. You would be at home, and you would be working."

I could not say: "But you are in a hospital, even though you have never 'looked.'"

I only said: "At least we shall do whatever we can here, my child."

And we wove baskets together and did the kind of work that the blind do. But I was still afflicted by blindness and ached all over because of those unseeing eyes of mine, and the child was still small, so the work that we did was not very good.

The child's hearing was very acute, and she could tell by the slower rustling of my work that I was becoming weary.

Then she would place her hand on my work and say: "Leave it; I'll finish your basket. There is not much left to be done here, and it is the kind of work that I can do. You never know when to stop working."

Her words often sounded angry, but at the same time her hands pressed my hand most tenderly and sincerely, and I truly pitied those poor, kind little hands that were prepared to do my thorny work.

"The basket can wait until tomorrow, but if you have finished your work, I would like you to play something for me, and I'll lie down for a while. Whenever you play for me, I feel less pain."

And she would immediately bring out her heavy harp—too heavy for the thin hands of a child—and she would play for me, and my pain would subside, and my dreams would be about something nebulous; and I no longer thought about the cloud that had vanished, or if I was blind, or if I could see. And I was happy and contented . . .

But I felt sorry that she was wearying her little hands, holding the heavy harp and strumming the tough strings that raised blisters on her fingers; moreover, she often cried after she finished playing, and then she would once again ask me what the sun was like, what light was, and how you "look," and why you "look."

Such conversations fatigued both of us and, afterwards, my eyes always ached. In time, she learned not to ask about these things, but I knew that she was still thinking about them, and so I did not feel much better . . . And neither did she . . .

At times like that, I would send her to play with other children afflicted by blindness—for the most part they played "hide-and-seek"—while I went to see the nurse, the sister of mercy who looked after me in the hospital.

Oh, she was a true sister to me—kind, tender, and gentle. Her musical voice made me think—in keeping with what my little friend thought—that it was enough for people to "listen." Her slender, silky hands created the illusion for me that, through them, I could "see" to the very depths of her soul.

As we walked together in the orchard, with the spring blossoms and the dew from the grass drifting down on us like a gentle rain that barely touched our faces, and the fragrance of the flowers washing over us in waves, there were times when I completely forgot that I could not see, and I did not torture myself—I did not wonder if I were blind, or not.

At those times, I felt as I had felt when I was young and could still see. Back then, I used to stroll through our orchard on opaquely dark summer nights to listen to the songs of the nightingales and, as I listened to their songs, I never stopped to think which was better—day or night.

This is how I usually felt in the company of my sister of mercy; even my eyes stopped aching. And if they ever did start to ache, she said that she knew how and why they hurt, and did not ask me about anything; she would just place her delicate silky hand on my eyes, and the pain never reached the point of issuing in tears of blood. She did not ask me anything, but I voluntarily told her much, very much, of what I wanted to say; and I found that this sharing of confidences was less painful than the solitary monologues I used to indulge in, when I had sat in a corner, hiding from people and from the light.

Oh my dear sister! How good it felt to be with you! You healed everything that lies within human power to heal. Even if you and that angry, but good, child did not restore my sight fully—I really do not know if I ever will be free of my affliction—then you at least returned me to life; you freed me from the fierce pain, from those tears of blood.

And so I walked out of the hospital into the world. I was still afflicted by blindness, but now I at least had some hope. It would have taken too long to wait in the hospital until my affliction was completely cured. I still have qualms about looking at the sun and, to avoid seeing the light, I do not open my eyes during the day; but I know when it is daytime, and when it is night, for sometimes my eyes discern red, while at other times they see black—and then there are those times when there is something indistinct, something that is not quite white, but neither is it grey . . . something like dawn, or dusk . . . As yet I do not know what it is; I am still afraid to look . . .

I am uneasy that I may still be blind, for even the blind sometimes know when it is day and when it is night. I do not have the courage to open my eyes . . . But perhaps some day I will overcome my affliction! People say that I must be able to see already, but I do not know if I can—I am afraid to know.

I have not seen my little friend for a long time, but I have heard that she has grown up, and that now, not only her parents, but she too has begun to have some hope that one day she will be able to see. I would give her all *my* hope so that *her* hope might become bright and true.

And as for my sister of mercy . . . Alas, I have heard that she . . . No, I am not able to utter that terrible word about *her*, that I have used to describe myself. I would like to know if she really did contract some eye disease—in the hospital there are often contagious patients . . . Perhaps I was one of them?—or if the weariness of a difficult life affected her in this way—this often happens. If it is only weariness, then it *must* pass, and I will help to make it pass.

I often think about her, and my dream goes like this—I'll take from her hand the heavy cane that her "friends" have given her, and I'll toss it on the woodpile; and then I'll take her by the hand, and we'll walk, just as we used to walk in the orchard. We do not need "alms;" we are capable of doing *something*—and it will seem to us that neither of us is *leading* the other one, that we are simply *walking*—alone, but alongside each other.

We will walk either down the path that she knows, or along the one that I know. She knows the forest path, and I know the one beside the sea—and, on both paths, there is the freedom of the open air and a roaring sound; we will *listen* together and say, loudly and clearly, what we *think* about the forest and the sea. She will pick a flower—she can find flowers even at night—and I will inhale the aroma of the "forest's soul." And I will find a seashell and give it to her, so that she can hear how the "soul of the sea" roars in the shell and, in this way, we will *listen to a soul*.

And when we both start longing for the sun, my little friend will play for us on her heavy harp—on those tough, silver strings— the melodies that change tears of blood into silvery dew. My little friend has grown, and her hands have become stronger; she is more mature now, and will not ask any more childish questions. She will play and remain silent—of this I am sure.

But perhaps, we . . . the two of us, I and my dear sister, will see . . . We will see *it* . . . "Our dear sun, our divine and holy sun!" And, if not the sun itself, then at least *its* light, or at least a pale hue . . .

The one who sees it first will remain silent in order not to offend the other, who as yet is not able to see. And the seeing one will remain silent, but will walk more carefully and will lead the other more assuredly, and will make it possible for that one *to hear* all the beauty of the sea, all the delights of the forest; yes, the seeing one will make it possible *to hear* them. But, both the beauty and the delights will not be more beautiful than the soul to which we both listened when we could not see. I know this.

I do not *see* you, my most beautiful sister, but *I* can hear you, and because of this, I am certain that I love you more than all your friends.

I do not have a cane to give you, but I am giving you *myself*, as weak as I am. Will you accept me?

The Apparition
(1905)

I see them as they pass by; coming from afar, from distant ages, they advance continuously, unendingly, in an interminable throng. The beginning of this horde is lost in the distance, the end is not visible in the darkness, and an uncertainty comes over me as to whether there is an end and a beginning, or if this is a gigantic, impenetrable circle that is revolving before my eyes—revolving and revolving, without ever ceasing.

A host of them—dressed in the attire of unknown ages and peoples—passes by me; thick, long hair undulates under helmets, strange wings flutter over them; tips of shaggy caps flame like poppy flowers; sparks flash on pointed copper casques; white tassels on chakos, like heather on the moorland, fly by; and now flat round caps like specks of oil on still water are approaching, and they flow on and on for a long time . . . There are the most of these.

Behind them, in the distant darkness, once again appears the apparel of unknown ages and peoples, different ones—not those who had passed by me already—but, in the darkness, it seems as if it is the same ones who are going from the distance into the distance, from the darkness into the darkness, and that this enchanted circle revolves and revolves unceasingly, until one loses one's sanity watching it.

They all walk with the same gait, and at first glance it seems that this apparition is an eternal boa constrictor, vanquished but not subdued, that has crawled out and is silently winding itself around the earth, slowly squeezing it, trying to strangle it. But, from close up, it can be seen that it is people who are passing by, and even though they are walking in an endless multitude, covered with the same dust, wrapped in the same dry mist and immersed in the same national colour, like countless figures on a single painting, every one of them is unique—there is not another like him in the entire word, there is not, there was not, and there never will be, from ages unto ages.

And every one of them holds a whole world in his eyes, and no one else has a world like it. And that world perishes forever as soon as he closes his eyes in death, and no one else will ever be able to reconstruct his world in the way that it was, even if a million new worlds were to come into being.

Where are they going—these people with worlds in their eyes?

They are going where the darkness blends with the distance, from where no living voice can be heard, where eternal terror stands guard to ensure that people are not allowed to pass through the gate of their own free will without blind guides—old age, sickness— for these guides want to receive their payment from everything that lives, but not everyone gives them their due.

The people who are encircling the earth like a boa constrictor press forward without leaders, but they have drivers who chase them from behind. There are so many people and so many herders, and far away behind them, completely hidden from view, terror is racing—the same terror that guards the accursed gate—and, as it guards this gate, it pushes the people towards it. Like a demented beast, it shouts absurd words at them—go back forward!

And they, like madmen, stupidly listen to it and press forward. Everyone of those persons in various caps and garments is carrying something sharp, something shiny, either cold or hot, and terrible and heartless in either its coldness or its heat. And everyone of them can bring death to the one who is walking ahead of him.

Perhaps there are those who might want to stop in front of the gate where eternal terror stands on guard clacking its sharp cold teeth, threatening with its twisted lips, and flaming with the fire of impure breathing—but no one can stop.

No one is able to stop; they must go on, and on, and on. For there are as many herders as there are people. Everyone feels the weapon of his friend at his back, and his muscles quiver, for he knows that if he were to stop, the point of the weapon would almost instantly pierce him in the neck, and his eyes would immediately grow dark, and his world would perish along with them. And he is afraid to look back at his friend, for he knows that the latter will utter, with his eyes, the absurd words—go back forward!

And whoever does not go back forward and takes a look back, will be stabbed in the eyes by the weapon of his friend, and his world will be ruined forever. Whoever dashes off to one side, way out into the wide open field, will be stabbed in the heart by the tip of a weapon, and even if he does not fall on the wide open field like a mown, blood-drenched flower, his eyes will nevertheless grow dark, and the world in them will change and will never again be as it was, and the wide open field will always remain a foreign land for him who has fled, and his native tongue will be to him the curse of his friend who had to pass through the gate before it was his turn.

Whoever joins the throng willingly is no longer his own master.

The friends who are now behind him greet him with praise, for he has stayed their turn for a moment, and so he dreams that he is their leader, but he would be unable to lead them back even if he suddenly wanted to, because the weapon of his friend is already threatening the nape of his neck, and he is terrifying only to those who walk before him. He has become a herder!

The armed people press forward, and everyone curses the one who fell before him, for he then takes that one's turn while walking over his corpse.

And it does not matter how many of the ones who are behind have fallen, the one who is ahead knows that the unavoidable weapon of the fallen one's friend is always close at hand, always ready to stab him in the neck.

Who knows who will come last of all and what the words in his eyes will be?

I can see that the boa constrictor is crawling, but I am not able to discern its head.

Who was that *one*, who was the head of the monster? Did he ever find himself alone in the middle of a field? Did he ever call his friends to him and then lead that mob? Did they go willingly to that gate of terror, and was every one of them the leader of his friend—the who followed him?

When, at precisely what moment, did the leaders turn into herders?

Why did they not turn back from the gate, while they were still leaders?

Or, did that very first one already feel, perhaps, the weapon of his friend behind him, and so did not dare to look back into his eyes?

Or could it be that this boa constrictor has always been—from time immemorial—headless, and blind, and as terrible in its hopeless blindness as chaos itself?

Who can stop it?

Who will release those who can see from the constricting coils of this blind monster?

The Mistake
The Thoughts of a Prisoner
A Fragment
(1905)

And now I am here, in this stone box, in this cage barred with iron, and I have time to think, not only at night, but also during the day. I had grown unaccustomed to thinking during the day, and this is probably why my daytime thoughts are so distressing, drab, uncouth, coarse, like unrefined stones . . .

If only it would turn dark more quickly . . .

But no, the evenings are also bad, because once again those pale bloody images will begin to peer into my soul, once again they will torment me with their silent reproaches, and once again I shall try to justify myself before them, hiding behind that prosaic, weak word, "a mistake," but they will remain standing before me, like creditors before a person who is bankrupt.

Well, let it be that I am bankrupt, a bankrupt person; let it even be that I am wicked—you have this admission from me, but just give me some peace! Oh, yes indeed, peace! What a thing for me to wish for! It is not at all insignificant. Can a bankrupt person have any peace?

But no, I am not a bankrupt person—at least not an evil one. I simply strove to succeed, and any attempt can meet with failure. I certainly am not resting on my laurels—I cannot be reproached with this. And I am certainly sitting in prison just like some of the others, and the fact that my head was not crushed with the butt of a rifle, my stomach was not ripped open with a bayonet, and my chest was not pierced by a bullet like some of the others— this is simply a matter of chance— a fortuitous occurrence . . .

I cannot even bring myself to say "a fortunate occurrence," because I truly see no good fortune in it for myself.

I did not seek safety at the time that bullets were whizzing around me, and I did not flee when the crowd—that until that moment was so fired up—began running away in all directions. And afterwards, I did not betray anyone. Hmm . . . that is all I would have needed! I did not blurt out a single foolish word at the interrogation, as happened with some others . . .

Well, then, why should *they* be reproaching me, instead of *me* them?

But all the same, I am sure that those who managed to save themselves and are now sitting safely in their homes—even though they know I am in jail—are thinking about this calmly, or with a pleasant sadness that softens the soul and increases one's respect for oneself. "Oh, our poor companion! I wonder how he is getting along, what he is doing at this moment. He is a fine fellow, a good soul . . ." —and other such banal thoughts without a single reproach against themselves, without assuming any blame for what has happened to me, even though they are guilty for that mistake along with me . . .

There is just one thing I would like to know. Let us say that they do not care about what happened to me; that is fine, let it be, perhaps that is even fair—but do they not blame themselves in the least for what happened to those . . . to those about whom I am thinking, and whom I fear to recall, but whom I do nevertheless recall, both during the day and at night?

Oh, how all this has exhausted me!

But would it make things easier for me if I knew that they, my companions, the participants in this "mistake," were also suffering and reproaching themselves for it?

It might be easier, it seems . . . Oh, no, no! This would mean that I am guilty, not only for their physical wounds, but also for the ones inflicted on their souls. Because it would be I who was to blame, I, only I, and no one else . . .

Well, really what am I going on about? What kind of "self-flagellation" is this? What good are these "self-torments," this "gnawing away at oneself"? That is what we used to call it at one time.

It is just a prison mood, that's all; that is the only reason for it. No one is blaming me.

Even today, during our "walk," Sanko and Nedostatny greeted me ever so sincerely, and that worker—what is his name?—said the word "comrade" with real feeling. Certainly all the people that

I see, and from whom I hear anything, are kind to me; they are all friendly. Well, perhaps some are indifferent, perhaps some have forgotten about me, but no one is blaming me. And in the "pamphlet" that I was handed today, my name is mentioned among the "fighters, martyrs, heroes."

Oho! I am gaining in self-respect! Well, not really, but one has to be fair to oneself, and not give in to neurasthenia. Yes indeed, neurasthenia. I even feel the pain that is typical of it in the nape of my neck, my neck itself, and between my shoulders; and there is a burning sensation in the top of my head. This is exhaustion, an ordinary exhaustion from thinking, from the monotony of my present life and the tension of my previous one. This is what is giving rise to various pseudohallucinations.

I must gain control over myself. I shall knock on my neighbour's wall . . .

He is not answering. Perhaps he is sleeping, or having an attack of misanthropy . . . It happens . . .

Was I thinking, or was I not thinking during these past few minutes? I do not think that I was thinking about anything, praise God.

Twilight is approaching . . .

Oh, Sanko has begun singing his usual song:

> "Do not rustle your thick leaves
> O lovage so green,
> My heart aches with heaviness,
> When evening draws near."

He sings well. Exactly what kind of voice does he have? It seems to me that it is a baritone, or a low tenor. But can a tenor be low? Who can say?

I know what words will come next:

> "If you, my dearest, do not wish
> To be my wife so true,
> Then give me an herb, a healing herb,
> So I can forget you."

Why does he always sing this song? It must be because of the first couplet, because the second one does not suit him at all. Sanko got married quite recently. His wife often comes to visit him . . . They are in love . . . So why does he choose this song? But then, does every song have to "suit" one? A man just sings whatever comes to mind . . . But why the same song every evening? As if it were intended specifically for me . . . Well, really, intended for me! How would he know? "An awl cannot be hidden in a sack." Phooey, what trivialities are filling my head—"an awl in a sack"—the devil only knows what this is all about!

Ah, yes, there it is:

> "If you, my dearest, do not wish
> To be my wife so true . . ."

Ah! There is no point to it; there is no point in fooling oneself; there is no point in deceiving oneself with trivial phrases, unnecessary thoughts. This is not what I am thinking about, and it is not how I am thinking, and it is not me that I am thinking about!

I am thinking about you, my dearest, my beloved, my Halya who is not mine! I am thinking frankly, more frankly than I have spoken for a long time . . . a long time—perhaps, never? And I often think this way—every evening—as soon as I hear this song. I know, from the first note, that I will once again be *thinking about you*. It is becoming a habit. This is the way a true believer begins to pray at the call of a muezzin . . .

God, what sentimental romanticism! Well, let it be romanticism, let it be even supersentimentalism. If that is how I'm thinking—when one does not think differently—then it is sincere and natural, and the devil take all models of realism, naturalism, and whatever else they are called. I am not writing an "ideological" story; I am simply thinking, and why should my "style" be anyone's business?

Halya, my dearest friend, my beloved, who was not meant to be mine, my most deeply desired but unattainable wife, tell me—why all this suffering? What for?

Did you wish this for me? Did your heroic soul, your farseeing eyes, foresee this?

You sacrificed me knowingly, but was it *this kind* of a sacrifice that you desired?

No, you could not have wanted a sacrifice like this; no—I know you, I believe in you, probably even at times when no one else would believe in you. But all the same, my sincere one, my pure one, my holy one, I cannot help thinking that you are guilty along with me—perhaps even more guilty than I am . . .

It may be that you realize this yourself. Perhaps you are reproaching yourself for my misfortune, and copious tears are flowing from your proud, bright eyes, but nevertheless, those eyes are proud because they do not know what it is you are most guilty of; they know my *misfortune*, but they do not know my *guilt*; they think that I am just "an innocent victim" and that, except for me, there are no sacrificial victims.

But if they knew! No, I will not tell them. I will never tell you to your face what I now want to write to you, and I will not show this to you, because my hand will not lift itself to pierce your heart with the sword that pierced mine long ago. My wound cannot be healed by anything or by anyone, including you.

If only you could place your hand on my heart . . . I would remain silent, I would not say anything to you, but it would not be as hard for me to bear this pain, for it would not be provoked by such fierce paroxysms of rage—forgive me, my one and only love—rage against you. Even so, it is difficult at times to quell them, and the pain is so terrible; it hurts me twice, three times as much, and I cry then; I weep painfully without tears . . . Oh, if only I could shed tears! How I envy women who always have tears at the ready!

And then there is this constant fooling of oneself, this fear of being "sentimental," "like a woman,"—how senseless it all is! The epic heroes of old wept without being embarrassed, but nonetheless, they were true, genuine heroes—but what about us? We can only control our tears, and nothing else . . .

If only they would light the lamps sooner.

I shall write, because it seems to me that otherwise I will not be able to bear it; I will go insane, and I do not want this "style,"—it has been becoming "banal" among prisoners for some time now.

I want to be, when all is said and done, conscious, completely conscious, and to explain everything to myself properly, and then—what will happen, will happen. If it turns out, for example, that I must hang myself, then we will find a way to do just that. And if it turns out that even this will not suffice, then we will consider what should be done next. It will be clear later.

Well, they are finally coming to light the lamps!

I will write this to you. I do not know what else to do; I cannot think of anything else. At the same time, I bear in mind that you will not read this, and that is good, because otherwise I would feel strange writing to you about things that you know well yourself; but all the same I must write about them, or else it will not be "methodical," or whatever one might label it.

I have to understand everything, examine everything, and to do that—I have to recall everything.

This "form" of writing "to another person" will detract from "realism," but I cannot do otherwise, and is it not all the same? I am not writing for anyone else, and I have the right to write as I please. It is true that I would like to write well, better than I have been thinking all along, and I would like it to be worthy of you at least in form, if not in content. To write well—does not mean to write insincerely; quite the contrary . . .

In any event, this "preface to an invisible reader" is beginning to be ludicrous, especially when one considers the fact that, except for me, there never will be another reader. And, finally, how am I to know if it will turn out well, or badly, unrealistically, or otherwise, and where the boundary between the sincere and the insincere lies—I am not a literary person in vain, and we are so thoroughly spoiled by various "styles," "moods," and "tendencies," that we have truly lost all "sense of reality."

I will write as I want to, and primarily, so that I do not go out of my mind—this is a goal that can justify all means.

There is no need for a heading of any kind; I do not know how to dream them up, and the ones I come up with are always inappropriate.

***

You perhaps do not even know on what day it all began, even though that day is probably engraved in your memory as it is in mine. It was when I sent you *that letter* early in the morning—I spent the entire night writing it—and in the evening you came to see me.

As soon as I saw you, my heart fainted. You were serious, ominously serious, and your clear blue eyes were gazing directly at me, far too resolutely. At that moment, I would have preferred it if they had been lowered bashfully to the ground. I would have preferred it if your hand had trembled as mine did when I helped you off with your fur jacket, but your firm little hand that seemed to have springs inside it stretched out unwaveringly, and without trembling at all, pressed my ill-fated, limp hand.

Then you removed your little hat and shook off the snow, and it seemed that your hair turned grey—and this gave you a tragic appearance. A little bit of snow remained; it quickly melted, and when you sat down at the table it glittered in droplets in the light of my lamp.

How beautiful you were then! My elf, bedecked with dew . . . It is thus that I see you most often in my thoughts . . . Oh, Halya!

You were sitting, and I felt your gaze on me, but I remained standing, leaning weakly against the table. I did not dare to raise my eyes to you, and I did not utter a word. But you spoke up swiftly.

"So you see how different we are—you would sooner muster up the courage to write than talk, and I'm just the opposite—I thought and thought how to reply to your letter—you specifically requested me to write a reply—but I finally decided to come and say it just as it is. I don't know how to write. And it would have taken a long time."

My heart fainted once again upon hearing the words "a long time."

"Why should it take long," I said in a quiet voice, as if I were gravely ill, "when it would suffice to say either 'yes,' or 'no.'"

"That's not enough, because I have to say both one and the other."

It was then that I first raised my eyes to you, and under my gaze a blush crept over your cheeks. It was in vain that you frowned angrily, and brushed your hand over your forehead a couple of times—the disobedient flush flooded your face right up to the clouds of your black curls; it was as if a reflection of a rosy star fell on your face, and hope awoke within me. I even smiled timidly.

But you suddenly raised your head even higher, and you gestured with your hand and your entire body in a way that is so well known to all your friends—"an imperious gesture," they used to say jokingly. This gesture always seemed to make your small figure grow taller and more dignified. And along with it, your voice became bold and proud. It was in such a voice that you spoke to me then.

"Well, what's to be done? I'll tell you the whole truth, come what may. This is what you are requesting, and you are worthy of it. Perhaps your suffering will increase because of this, but it seems that it has to be so; it can't be any other way, and I don't know how to do it differently."

Despite your "imperious gesture," I could tell by your voice that it was very difficult for you to say the words that constituted "the whole truth." I attempted "to assist" you, but I could hardly hear my own voice, and now I no longer remember a single word of what I said.

I only remember very well that you shouted: "No, no, it's not like that; you don't understand. I love you, believe me!" And your strong, firm fingers painfully squeezed my hand.

And here again, I do not remember what I said, and how it happened that you were standing already, and I was still sitting and pressing your hand to my lips—silently, it seems, and, I think, with tears in my eyes.

You were stroking my hair with your left hand, awkwardly, and with a slight trembling; perhaps it was because of the quite ordinary ineptness of your left hand, but I found it very pleasant, more charming than your "imperious gesture."

I was afraid to speak. I really do not know why, but I understood that your confession had not ended with this, and that it would be easier for me if I never had to live to hear it. But I did live to hear it . . .

Your hand stopped moving; you sat down on another chair by the table, leaned on your hand in such a way that I could no longer see your eyes, and began to speak.

"I replied to one question in your letter, and I'm not taking back what I said, even though I didn't intend to say what I did in this way . . . It came out rather strangely, didn't it?"

"No, no," I whispered.

It seemed you did not hear me, and you continued with what you were saying.

"All the same, it's true that I love you. I wanted to conceal this from you and to write to you that I would not be your wife, because I loved someone else, not you—*in this way* you would leave me sooner, and forget everything sooner . . ."

"No, no!" I said, more loudly.

"You would probably forget . . . and be happy . . ."

"No!" my voice rang out so loudly that you stopped and changed your tone.

"Forgive me, I believe your sincerity, but I think that . . . no, I won't try to convince you that you're mistaken, because I don't know. Perhaps you're right . . . perhaps you're right . . . It does happen—some people don't forget as long as they live . . . I also think that I'll never forget you . . . And it also would not be easier for me if I thought that you did not love me."

"Then what's the point, Halya?" I groaned.

"The point is that I cannot be your wife."

"But you . . . but we love each other!" I cried.

You dropped your hand, and I saw your eyes. They were ever so sorrowful, and they gazed at me so intently that their widened pupils had turned black, but it seemed to me that you did not see me, and I became terrified, especially when I saw the smile on your lips—the frozen, lifeless smile.

"Not all the orchards blossom that bud in the spring." You uttered the words of the song in a quiet, low, flat voice.

I shivered. Do you know, Halya, that since that moment, I cannot listen to this song—an insane terror comes over me when I hear it.

"Halya!" I cried out.

You were startled. "Really, why am I speaking in riddles like some romantic heroine? Forgive me. I shall tell you everything straightforwardly and sincerely."

And you told me; I will never forget how sincerely and matter-of-factly you sentenced me to the most inhuman suffering, how straightforwardly you proved to me that we did not have the right to human happiness, how sincerely you assured me that we were obligated to be martyrs, heroes. There was not a single pretentious phrase.

You made your point logically, almost prosaically, that in our times there had to be "a division of labour" in everything, that harmony in life was truly an ideal to which the people had to be led, that one day it would exist, there, in the golden age in which we both believed; but now, such harmony was impossible, just as work was not possible without a specialization, given our present state of technology and our social order.

The time had not yet come, you said, especially for women, that with an average capability one could carry on with the struggle of the common people and at the same time live for one's marriage, for one's family—it was impossible to combine and balance such broad responsibilities.

"Well, let them be unbalanced," I defended myself. "I wouldn't demand that my wife 'stay home and take care of the house.'"

"Nevertheless, someone has to stay home and take care of the house, so that it doesn't become a wasteland, doesn't become hateful to both of its masters."

I remember that you smiled as you this, and that the terror that held me in its cold grip suddenly left me. And this time it was I who recalled the words of a folk song:

> "I'd go to fetch the water myself,
> I'd lead my dear one by the hand."

"I'd feel sorry to see you in a role like that," you replied seriously, "and . . . perhaps it's our conservative nature as women, but I, for one, do not like 'household' husbands; it all becomes even more prosaic with them, than with us."

And you brought up a few examples among our mutual friends where the husband was a househusband," and the wife "had a role in the community." I silently agreed that such marriages were not to my liking. But I did not concede defeat immediately.

"Well, this is nonsense; we could have a division of work in the home, and this would mean full equality. Or doesn't 'women's conservatism' permit even this?"

You found it easy to refute this comment by observing that in my five years as a student I had not learned how to serve tea properly, so this meant that at least a quarter of a century would have to pass before I could fully aspire to "a division of work" in even the most rudimentary household matters. I had been raised in this manner, and I had to accept this fact! So it meant that there was a dilemma—either let the wife do the housework, or let the house become a wasteland.

"So, let the house become a wasteland!" I did not surrender. "After all, does a comfortable home mean more than everything else? Of course not—it's rather funny! I wouldn't notice what the house looked like if you were in it!"

Even though I was greatly caught up in this argument, I did not dare to speak to you using the more familiar form of "you" that had burst out of me at the height of my confession of love.

"It seems that way to you . . ." you began.

But I was overcome with such bitterness, I was so offended by your "reasonableness," that I leapt up from where I was sitting and, leaning over to almost touch your face, shouted in a choked voice: "What kind of love is this? How can I believe in it?"

You turned white as a sheet and also rose to your feet.

"If you can't believe, then don't," you said firmly, but your lips were trembling, and your hand reached for your hat with a nervous gesture.

I detained your hand. "Forgive me . . . Forgive me . . . This is all so painful for me."

Hiding your face in your hands, you stood still for a moment; and when you uncovered your face it was completely calm.

"I really don't have the right to be impatient, because, inadvertently, I am performing a painful operation on you . . . *You* must forgive me."

I simply bowed my head.

And you once again began to prove to me, calmly and seriously, that the trivialities in life have a great, ruinous power.

"I would prefer to have love itself ruin me than to have love ruined by life's trivialities." My throat was choked with weeping, but I could no longer be angry with you . . .

"I know," you continued, "that there is a common solution to this problem—to cast all this work on 'a white slave,' but even if I had the wherewithal to do this, I could not condone it morally. I'm no longer accustomed to having people work for me, and actually I never was accustomed to it. You knew my father. You know how I was raised."

The stern figure of an old, "plain living" man rose before me. I remembered how the members of our organization had buried him, the kinds of things his companions had said in parting with that "true revolutionary of the 1860s," in whom "the soul of Rakhmetov" lived on. I recalled the simple, nunlike outfit you wore then, that one black outfit that you used "for good wear" while your father was alive, and as mourning attire after his death.

Truly, it would be pointless to try to convince the only daughter of such a father, bereft of a mother's influence early in life, that her "principles" were utopian and not suited to our circumstances. These were no longer "principles," but habits, strongly ingrained habits of living. This had to be "accepted as a fact."

"Miss Halya," I began, mustering up my strength, and even attempting a smile, "all of this isn't as tragic as it seems to you. There's another way out—I'll ask my mother to move here with my sisters. My sisters will be delighted, and mother will agree because of them. My mother is very housewifely by nature, and it probably wouldn't even occur to her that her daughter-in-law should meddle in the affairs of the household.

"You wouldn't have to concern yourself about anything, and your conscience would be free of any guilt. In any event, my mother and sisters won't change their way of keeping house if we live together or not, so it seems to me that we can quietly take advantage of the benefits that accrue from such an arrangement.

"We'd pay them what we now pay strangers, but strangers take care of us a thousand times worse, and their order is just as bourgeois; and we contribute to maintaining that order by paying for our board and room; there's no point in denying that," I tried to talk just as logically and simply as you, and it seemed to me that I was beginning to master this tone.

Then suddenly it seemed to me that you had stopped listening to me. I noticed that you were not looking at me, but at the wall, where a picture of my mother was hanging.

"What a severe profile your mother has," you said, as if you were thinking out loud. "You don't resemble her at all."

"I resemble my late father," I answered, and then I fell silent, abandoning all my arguments.

I do not know how things would have gone if I had been successful as a publicist; perhaps passionate polemics, conducting a political struggle with a pen, would have given me the self-forgetfulness that I longed for. But I was not successful as a publicist. I do not know how "to think collectively," especially when I pick up a pen to write.

I do not have the strength to be the literary leader of a movement, and the independence of my pen does not permit me to be a common writer in the ranks of literature, to write within the framework of someone else's program, to function in accordance with plans that were formulated by others, not by me.

In my life, I was never so independent that another person's nature would not depress me, or at least "annoy" me—and I cannot say that the other person's nature had to be stronger than mine; no, often it was noticeably weaker, but in that case its oppression was even worse. Your oppression, my unwavering Halya, never "annoyed" me precisely because it was strong, well-defined, and, I even think, often *conscious*. That is right, is it not?

And I consciously bowed to your will. I placed the yoke on myself, and it seemed to become light. At least it seemed like this until . . . But, more about that later.

What I really wanted to say was that I was more oppressed by natures weaker than mine than by the wills of those that were stronger. For example, no one made me suffer more than one of my school friends who was completely without a will—this lack of will resulted in true insanity later—a neurasthenic with hysterical outbursts.

Even now I find it hard to determine what it was exactly that made me submit to this unfortunate nature—it was not that I liked him above all my other friends; indeed, there were moments when I did not like him at all, but only suffered him, like an illness. And it was not that I consciously decided to sacrifice my independence for him; on the contrary, because the sickliness of his nature often assumed the unattractive forms of petty egotism and even cruelty—I did not deem him worthy of it, and regretted that I was wasting my strength on him, strength that I could be putting to more advantageous use. I knew all this very well, but nevertheless, I lived in a state of real subjugation to him, for which my family and close friends hated the unfortunate fellow.

My main feeling for him was pity, a fine, burning pity that permeated every moment of my relationship with him, even though I did not like to admit this even to myself, and determinedly disavowed this feeling in front of others, trying to convince everyone that there was no "servitude" on my part—as they claimed—that I simply liked and respected my friend and that, as a person in completely good health, "it did not cost me anything" to give in at times "to the innocent demands" of a sick person.

At the same time, "it did cost me" so dearly that another year or two of it, and I would have kept my friend company in the home for the insane . . .

It is painful for me to think and write about this, but what is true, is true. It was only the home for the insane that, in taking away my friend, returned my will, my freedom. I immediately sensed this. I am still annoyed with myself when I recall what an effort I made to crush the feelings of relief as I departed from the doctor to whom I committed my ill friend . . . But perhaps this "annoyance" is the remnants of "my servility?"

This is what I am like "in real life." It is actors who use this expression as an antithesis to the phrase "on the stage," as if the stage is not part of life—what stupidity! But in that other life that takes possession of me when I pick up a pen, I am not like that at all. At those times, I do not submit to anyone, I do not pity anyone, I do not aim my deeds—that is, my words—at anyone. I think as *I* think, I alone, and I have nothing else to do with anyone. At that time I hate everyone who prevents me from being by myself.

You should know, Halya, that even your influence vanishes at those moments when I am armed with a pen. Well, and that is why my work did not appease me. I needed something that would make me forget myself, but instead I had to be myself as clearly as was possible. In my stated words, in my deeds, even in my unwritten thoughts, I agreed with you; I lived as you lived—it seemed to me then that I was living in my own way—but I wondered why I could no longer write as I once did.

No, I positively could not write—I either could not write anything at all about those "burning" issues that we so often discussed and which I, it seemed, understood so well and even felt—they often prevented me from sleeping at night— or else I wrote something lifeless about them, "alien," or "too subjective," which "could not convince anyone except the one who was already convinced," as you said. I feared those moments when you read my journalistic articles—at those times you had a most displeased look on your face. You frowned, in such severe pain, that the corners of your eyes quivered, and your lips pressed tightly together as if you were offended.

I sat as if I were on the bench for the accused, and it took everything you had to force yourself to utter, occasionally, a few words of something that resembled "praise," such as: "Well, it's not too bad . . ." or "Hmm, perhaps it will be all right when it's fixed up a bit . . ."

But it never was "fixed up," because after such a "review," I would silently take what I had written, methodically tear it into four pieces and start a fire with it in the fireplace, sometimes before your very eyes.

Then you would protest feebly, trying to defend my work. But I would smile malevolently, blow on the coals, and say: "That's where it belongs!"

In my heart, however, anger mixed with offended feelings started boiling quietly, anger directed neither at myself, nor at you . . . Probably more at me . . . No, in actual fact, at you!

I felt a dull, offended feeling rise up against you for trying your best not to like "my children," "the children of my soul." This is how I refer to my belletristic writings in my mind. For I knew only too well that you were trying not to like them, even though I never spoke to you about this—out of pride, because I never impose my children on anyone, least of all on you. For I once saw you crying over my verses, and I once heard you reading someone a story of mine out loud—you do not know about this. One can read in that way only what one likes with one's entire soul; there are certain notes in one's voice that betray this conclusively.

So, as I burned my unsuccessful works, I experienced a certain feeling of revenge for "my children"—the miscarriage and premature death of the children that you would have wanted to acknowledge as yours if they had been a success. But at the moment, I was overcome with grief—why do we not have anything we can call *our* children? Why was our spiritual marriage so unproductive? I was envious, and I am envious even now of the writers and poets who have their "Muse." What I would not give if I could say about you what, for example, Mills said about his wife! I would be even more pleased if we could have melded into one literary soul like the Honkur brothers.

But in my literary work, in the most intimate life of my soul, I was always alone, without any family, without a wife. You did not want to enter as a wife into the secret home of my poetic feelings, while I could not become part of what you called your "feelings of collectivity."

I could not comprehend this collective soul; that is, I understood theoretically what it was, and what elements it was comprised of, but I could not feel it artistically. It seems to me that if you had some literary talent you would create something on this basis that was more passionate than Ada Negri, something stronger than Herzen, something that was "world-shattering and world-building" —something that you wanted to find in my writing.

But in reality, you are not a literary person! I liked your letters, but it was because of the fact that they were written in your energetic, firm, exuberant handwriting—it reflects your nature so accurately—and also because I love everything that is *yours*.

At the same time, I am too much of a literary person not to notice that you have no inkling about writing, not even letters. It is not that you do not know how to do it as poorly educated people do not—those who do not understand how to turn a literary phrase. No, you are hopeless when it come to writing in a literary manner, in an intelligent manner.

Your phrases are bookish, heavy, pedantic; all feelings freeze in them.

I will never forget what you once wrote me: "Insofar as my feelings towards you are candid, they are just as much unconscious, but neither the first nor the latter ought to have a dominating influence on our relationship" and so on. Truly, this is almost a caricature, but I saw it written black on white!

Why is it, Halya, that your written words were not given the passion that is in your eyes, the delicate and tender shades that are in your voice, the charm that is in your laughter, the gracefulness that is in your gestures—the gracefulness that has a touch of steel in it, like a slender Spanish sword! Why did your genius not find expression in at least one human capability that would pass your soul on to your descendants?

Your soul is immeasurably better, stronger, richer than mine. Why will mine live on, as I know it will—what's the good of false modesty here!—while yours will perish or be dissipated into fragments, to live for a time with a partial, fragmentary life in the memory of those who knew you, and then become nameless and enter imperceptibly into the souls of those who come after you and can hardly recall those who did know and remember you.

I know that your brave "collective soul" does not fear such a fate.

You say: "That's how it has to be, because my nature is also comprised of aspects of people who lived before me."

This is true! But my soul does not accept this, will never agree to this! Palya, my most esteemed, my unattainable love!

How fortunate I would be if I could transmit to you my fire, my "spark of the divine." It would be better if I were to disintegrate into nameless atoms among the "human dust" of the unknown generations of descendants of those who were indifferent to me—such a fate would be much more just! And you would shine for them like a bright star, with a full and perfect light, so that all who lose their way could see you and find the right road.

But it will not be so . . . It will not!

Oh, if it is impossible to pour my fire into you, then let it light up all of you for me—all your soul to its very depths—and sear your image into my heart with flawless lines, so that I could depict you as you are, and so that your soul would speak through my words for a long, long time—I'm sure that *then* my works would be immortal. But it is not for myself that I would want this.

But my fire does not have such power! And this why it did not comfort me in my great anguish, in my loneliness, in the hunger of my heart. If I could have submitted to you in literature as I did in life, if I could have lived with your soul, perhaps I would have been happy, but I still lived only for myself, and I wrote—oh, woe is me—only for myself. I often did not realize this at first; it seemed to me that I was depicting you, your beauty, your soul. But my heart quickly surmised that I was writing about it—my heart—about its love, that you were not emerging from under my pen as nature had created you, and as you live in my heart. I wanted to relate how dear you are, but I wrote only that I love you; I wanted to show how strong you are, but I only wrote that I am dying of love for you . . . And this irritated my wound even more and gave me neither oblivion, nor peace.

For some time I stopped writing altogether. I even found another way of earning a living, so that I would not be compelled to write. But this did not last long. I was much too accustomed to this poison; the *"mania litteraria [literary madness]"* was too advanced in me.

I was weary of life; it seemed that I had become "extinguished," insignificant, exhausted, and, instead of a literary mania, another mania was about to develop in my head—a mania for self-destruction. But I did not want this; I did not want you to think that I had killed myself "because of hopeless love." I knew that you did not respect such a death, and I knew that I could not convince you of another reason for my suicide. I did not want your memory of me to be muddied by a feeling of guilt and an importunate disrespect for my character.

And I began to write once again. I changed my "manner," and this surprised my acquaintances and critics, who searched for all sorts of "civic duty" reasons for this "new phase in my creativity." But, in actual fact, there was no new phase.

I purposely chose "objective" themes, either from history or from a milieu that was foreign to me, but this was only a "masquerade of the soul." People did not recognize it, this "subjective, individual" soul; at times they even accepted it as a "collective conscience," but if anyone knew it to its depths, they would say: "I've recognized you, O mask!"

I parcelled out fragments of my heart to my heroes. And in the various confessions of their love to the heroines—in such seemingly diametrically opposed confessions—it was possible to put together my great and complete love for you.

This "collective conscience" was my own conscience, trampled, shattered into splinters, refracted a hundred times through the prism of tears in my heart and scattered over a thousand fantastic, imaginary souls, the closest sisters of my intemperate and inconsistent soul.

I saw myself in them as in a broken mirror, and I guessed at and recalled what I could not see. When I depicted them as not being in love with anyone—this meant that I was like this until I met you. When I made them happy in love—this meant that this is how it would be if you would be mine! When I made them heroes of renunciation—this meant that they were as you wished to see me. When they died in battle for an idea—this meant that this is how I would want to meet my death, and how you will most certainly meet yours.

And everywhere and in all things, it was you and I, you and I, but mainly I, I, I . . . Finally, I no longer could stand living in this way.

My "other manner" was more appealing to you, that is, you permitted yourself to tolerate it, even though you regretted that I was incapable of expressing my ideas in a popular journalistic form; "so many first-rate thoughts are lost in the mass of fiction and that is why they are not convincing!" I would like to know, did you really not see that this was just a "masquerade," or did you purposely shut your eyes to it all? If you shut them, that was not worthy either of you or of our usual candour. But I will never know this, it will remain on your conscience, for I do not know how to ask about things like that, and as for you, if you did not tell me then, then you will never be able to tell me, because it becomes more difficult as time goes by.

But it seems to me that you suspected something. With time you began conversations about the fact that I write too much, that it is hard on my health, drains my brain; that I ought not devote all my strength to belles lettres, because there was ever so much other work to be done, and there was no one to do it.

"So, give me some other work!" I blurted out once. "I'd like nothing more than some other kind of work."

You looked at me intently, but without surprise, as if you had been expecting what I said. However, you began to argue: "What kind of work am I 'to give' you, as you say. What have I to do with it? You're a member of the Party, and you have clearly defined obligations—if only you had the desire. But your comrades are complaining that you often lack the desire."

I flared up. "I would be curious to know if they would be eager to clean such Augean stalls as they create everyday in the editor's office with the assistance of what they call 'manuscripts.' Next time, tell them in reply that I'm amazed that they haven't lost the desire to bring me piles of rubbish for editing their 'style'—as if their writing had some kind of 'style' that was worth correcting! And the spelling! And the handwriting! It's worth taking a look at, just look!"

I grabbed the first manuscript that was handy on the table, all covered with my corrections. "How can they not be ashamed before the typesetters, if not before me! If they would read their own work at least once before rushing to have it printed!"

I tossed the manuscript disdainfully on the table.

An unkind flame flashed in your eyes, and there was "steel" in your voice when you started talking: "What can be done about it? They can be forgiven; they aren't professionals; they have to write this whenever they can tear themselves away from their work, and that's why it looks as if it's been tossed off in a hurry, in any old way. But it can't be helped, since 'more eminent writers' disdain writing on such prosaic themes—they prefer to criticize, which, by the way, is also easier to do."

My suffering must have been reflected in my gaze, because when your eyes met mine, you broke off suddenly, and blushing lightly, began to scribble with a pencil on my desk.

We were silent for some time.

"Halya," I said quietly, "you understand very well how accurately you've hit me right where it hurts, and so I won't say anything more about this . . . I'm asking only one thing of you— I have the right to ask you this—that you give me this kind of pain in some other way . . . This way . . . allusions . . . oblique glances . . . I can't tolerate . . . Perhaps I deserve to be treated this way . . . But it is unworthy of you; it is unworthy of what is holy in our relationship."

I was so hurt that I got up and headed for the balcony, so that you would not see my face at that moment. But you intercepted me, seized my hands, and—where had the "steel" in your voice disappeared?

"Forgive me, my friend! Forgive me, my dear! Yes, it truly is unworthy of me, and I'm ashamed of myself. But you know how I suffer, because your stubborn pen does not want to serve our cause like it should—and it is because of my anger at it that I wounded you. Forgive me!"

My soul drowned in your eyes as in a blue abyss . . . And I could smile sincerely once again.

"What can be done, Halya?" I defended myself without bitterness. "It seems that I'm a literary person 'who does not control his pen; rather his pen controls him,' as Mayakovsky said, and this is a hopeless situation . . . Well, enough about this. It would be better if you would advise me; I have seriously wanted to consult you for some time now."

You sat down and prepared to listen with that serious and tender expression that appeared on your face as soon as I began a conversation about "advice" of any kind. I do not recall a single time when you were inattentive at such a time, when you did not use all your ability to give an adequate reply to my troubled searches for advice. And even though I knew that you would not give me any fundamental, most needed advice, I no longer felt all alone, and I felt easier.

I began to say that belles lettres did not satisfy me completely, because I knew that our cause demanded another kind of service from me. But the "black work" of editing also did not satisfy me. It was actually a waste of my powers. This could be done by any educated professional person, any "teacher of grammar" could do this even better than a belletrist, and there were even complaints that I spoiled "the precision of the expression" with my "stylistic adornments."

"I think that, for example, Ovsiyenko could do a better job of it than I. I know that he is poor, and sick, and works hard to earn his daily bread, but I think he would not be hard done by if the Party gave him more pay for the time he spent editing, than what he earns for the time he spends chasing around "tutoring." If the Party does not have enough money, I could pay him, and I would ask for some different work for myself.

"Only I would prefer it if you would be the initiator of this 'change in roles.' For one thing, you have more influence on the Committee and, for another, it's awkward for me to begin a conversation about this myself. They'll say that he's hiring servants, and the like. Do you understand?"

You nodded your head silently. Then you asked: "What do you want to do instead of editing?"

At this point I gave rein to my feelings; I said that I wanted *to live* the work of the Party because I was ashamed "only to write," at a time when people "were living and dying." It was distressing to me that my work was overly safe compared to the work of the propagandists and conveyors, and other risky work that was undertaken mainly by untrained youth who were serving as a shield for us, "the older workers."

In my opinion it was embarrassing to live behind the protective backs of the youth. For some people it might be fine, but for me it was unforgivable. Obviously I was not born to be an ideologue, for I was not a publicist—it could not be helped; a fact was a fact! I also had not gained any influence in the Party as an orator or organizer, and it was likely that I never would; but at the same time I had the trait of courage—you once again nodded your head.

I knew how to think calmly at critical moments and keep my nerves steady; I had some talent for observation, was somewhat of a psychologist, ex officio, and knew how to figure out all kinds of possibilities and combinations. In addition, I was completely healthy, independent, and no one depended on me, at least not materially. All of these were "talents" of sorts, which, you would have to agree, should not be buried in the ground. Right?

I could feel that my face was burning, and that a cheerful despair was buzzing in my voice. You repeated, like an echo: "Right," but in a voice that seemed crestfallen, distant, and very sad. You were bent over, as if you had shrunk, while your eyes widened and looked so intently at a fixed point in the distance that your eyelids turned slightly red, and your gaze was damp.

Then you suddenly straightened up, looked me straight in the eye, and spoke in a different, firmer voice—not one with "steel," but a candid, friendly voice: "Right! You're worthy of better work than mere editing. And . . . forgive me not only for the form, but also for the content of my recent reproach."

Something about those words "disturbed" me, even though I could not take my eyes off you—you were so lovely when you uttered them. I felt that I was not being entirely honest in saying what I had said. However, I was speaking honestly with you, so everything that I said to you was the truth—because I sincerely believed in what I said. So it was the truth but not the whole truth! I was thinking frankly, but not only about this! And I was not sure if I would have found the words if I had *said everything* . . . I am not sure of this even now. I silenced "my misgivings" with the request that you "arrange for me to have a word" at the Committee hearings.

You thought in silence for some time.

Finally, you said distinctly, evenly, as if you were "hypnotizing" me: "Fine. I'll use all my influence to do this. But under one condition—if you're assigned to some risky task—I'll be with you always and everywhere. I also have the right to this and the 'talents.' Right?"

I wanted to say "right," but my throat was choking, and so I once again pressed your hand to my forehead and bowed very low.

You did not ask anything more, but your hand grew colder, as if you were expiring.

A Moment

(1905)

You know me—I'm a sensible man, and staid to the core. I'm unable to recall a time—even in my childhood or adolescence—when I was interested in religious or mystical matters. Nevertheless, I am able to understand even the strangest fanatic.

All I have to do is recall one moment in my life and imagine that this moment could have been prolonged for years, for all one's life. Granted, this would be impossible with the kind of nature that I possess, but this is not the point—the point is in the lengthening of the moment.

It should be said that, even though I related rather coolly to the religion into which I was born, nevertheless—if it is possible to put it this way—I treated it with respectful indifference.

At the same time, for example, Protestantism always presented itself to me in the guise of a chalkboard all scribbled over with writing; the Hebrew religion—in the guise of some kind of nightmare; and Catholicism—in the guise of a fat Polish priest, relishing a glass of liqueur and scrutinizing it as he held it up to the light. I cannot say if it was the widely-known, and, by now, boring, pictures on this theme that were to be blamed for this image, or if it was the one priest that I knew personally; however, Catholicism did not evoke any other images for me. As for the other religions, I admit that I had only the most vague knowledge of them, and as a rule never gave them much thought.

One time, a business matter took me to Poland where I had to spend a few days in a small city in which I did not know a single soul. My mornings were taken up with business dealings; during the remaining time, however, I wandered aimlessly through the city and its environs, trying in some manner to relieve my boredom—a goal that I was far from attaining.

The single notable attraction in the city was an old Polish Roman Catholic church. Constructed in the Gothic style, and much too big and grand for such a pitiful parish, it had been built in former times by a devout magnate. I seldom went there—the drone of the Latin and the company of teary-eyed old women did not attract me—and even when I did, it was only by chance, simply because the doors were always opened wide.

One day, however, weary and wilting both from boredom and heat—for I had wandered around for a couple of hours in the hot sun and the dust—I happened to walk past this church. As always, the hospitable doors were open, a semidarkness could be seen within, and the sounds of an organ could be heard. I thought it might be damp in there, but at least it would not be hot. And I had not listened to any music for a long time; let us assume, that these organs . . .

Yes, well, come what may! And so, I entered the church.

Just as I was walking in, the organ fell silent, and the priest began to read a long prayer. The church was almost empty—it was a work day, and only two or three figures were kneeling at the side altars decorated with floral arrangements.

There was a striking array of bouquets, because it was the month of May, when Catholics take special pains to adorn their churches. Notwithstanding the candles—that were lit, however, with a view to economy—these floral tributes seemed to be drowning in the semidarkness. It was only here and there that narrow bands of light, falling from the variegated panes of the lancet windows, painted the flowers with fabulous colours and endowed them with a strange, unearthly appearance.

These multicoloured rays glided over slender wooden columns and dark heads of angels sculpted out of wood, cast a rainbow on the white robe of the marble Madonna in a starry crown, and illuminated the pale face of the Crucified One, giving Him a strangely youthful appearance. From time to time the rays vanished or scattered—a breeze was probably stirring the tall trees beyond the windows—and when this happened, the angels disappeared entirely, the Madonna receded into the shadows, and the face of the Crucified One lost its glow and became totally lifeless.

"These Catholics have a strange way of doing things," I thought. "They're always introducing some theatrics. One can see that everything here is done for effect—these flowers, the lighting,

and even the realism with which Christ's suffering is depicted—
it all strangely affects the imagination. However, some of the
effects are quite grotesque."

And I looked with a smile at the sword piercing the breast of
the marble Madonna.

At that moment, a young woman, who by her attire appeared
to be a peasant, walked up to the foot of the statue. She was
dressed in a splendid, short green skirt, a white blouse with wide
sleeves, and a short, sleeveless red jacket. She was not wearing
anything on her head, but two thick blond braids were wound
around it like a wreath. She was carrying a large bouquet—almost
a sheaf—of common flowers found in fields and flower gardens.
They were tied inexpertly, but with obvious care.

The girl placed the flowers at the feet of the Madonna, gravely
pressed the palms of her hands together, and positioned them
edgewise against her breast. Her large, artless eyes were lifted
upwards, and her lips whispered a prayer.

"She looks like a Gretchen," I thought, and a strange tenderness
began to come over me, but I did not want to give in to it. At
that moment, a bell rang; the girl lowered her head and struck
her chest twice with a short, childish movement of her fist. The
bell fell silent, and the priest intoned a supplication in his nasal
voice. The girl's face lifted upwards, and her palms came together
again. Then the bell rang again, and once more there was the low
bow and the striking of the chest.

This praying by the bell struck me as comical, and I could
barely refrain from laughing. An old woman who was sharing the
bench with me tore herself away from her prayer book and
glanced at me sternly over the rim of her eyeglasses.

Suddenly, I started—as if from a thunderclap. Up above, the
organ, without any warning, had burst into sound—a powerful,
imperious pealing. It seemed to me that all the slender columns
were swaying, like a forest in a gust of wind, and that something
gloomy, like a rain cloud, was hovering over us high up under the
arches, and one's eyes, frightened by the threatening, mysterious
darkness, did not dare to look up.

I glanced down at the girl. She had thrown herself down in
reverence and humility in front of the Madonna, who seemed to
be moving away from her and drowning in the shadows. The face

of the girl was hidden in the flowers, and her hands were touching the marble pedestal. In that pose, I seemed to sense an infinite despair and a suffocating, zealous yearning.

Across from the Madonna, her crucified Son bowed His deathly pale face on His chest, as if He were exhaling His last breath. The sonorous droning of the organ was changing into a muffled, quiet rumble, through which throbbed a sobbing melody; suddenly, this melody and the rumbling blended into a chord.

Rays of sunlight that were festive, bright and, at that moment, rainbow-hued, began to quiver everywhere. The flowers blazed. The small heads of the angels peeped out from the thicket of columns. The Mother of God in her rainbow-coloured attire was pointing with one hand at the sword in her heart and, with the other one, at the girl lying at her feet. The Saviour's face, illuminated youthfully, smiled, and the girl raised her head above the flowers.

Tears were glistening in her guileless eyes, and her lips smiled as they whispered a prayer. She was no longer lying prostrated; she had raised herself up on one knee, and the folded palms of her hands almost touched the marble hands of the Madonna.

Something like a searingly hot wave surged through my chest, and I wanted to throw myself down on my knees alongside the girl, wrap my arms around the pedestal of the Madonna, and burst into song, or begin weeping, or die in an incomprehensible ecstasy.

All this lasted only a moment, and then, the ringing of a lay-brother's bell abruptly shattered the spell.

Translated from Russian

The Conversation

(1908)

"A great, fatal love is a simoom—a hot desert wind—that fills large, calm lakes and quiet, oasal streamlets with sand, and clogs with silt the clamorous mountain streams that have raced down so courageously from the mountains, bearing tidings about the freedom of the highlands into the valleys; it heaps up unexpected hilly ramparts that head off the imperious sea, which, affronted and indignant, is forced to retreat and alter the boundaries of its domain . . ."

This passage was being read aloud by a young poet who had bent his head, thickly covered with curls, over a notebook filled with cramped handwriting.

He was sitting near the feet of an ill, "retired" actress, and she, weak and apathetic, was lying on a sofa and listening to his reading in the same way that hopelessly ill people listen to the sound of the restless waves of the sea, as they lie on a beach made searingly hot by the sun.

Suddenly, she burst out laughing, and—perhaps because it sounded either too sincere, or too false—this laughter struck the poet disagreeably.

"You find it amusing?" he asked in a shocked voice. Then he added, far too humbly and guiltily: "You're right. I probably forgot to consider mundane matters of geography when I wrote this passage . . ."

The actress smiled more calmly. "I know even less about geography than you."

"Then may I ask why you laughed?"

"Why not? Only it's difficult to explain . . . It seemed to me it was the beginning of my obituary, or something like that . . . And it's strange to listen to it when one is still alive."

The poet flushed and flung the manuscript down on the sofa at her feet.

"Your obituary? Yours? In what way? Why? Even if it were an obituary, then it certainly isn't yours. Oh, no, it's not yours; I know this only too well . . ." There was a harsh and unkind ring to the poet's voice.

"My dear boy!" the actress's voice even though slightly mocking in tone, was, in contrast, tender and kind. "Don't always think just about yourself!"

The poet did not say anything; he only threw a reproachful look, full of love and injury, at her faded face.

"Don't reproach me, and don't be offended, because it's true. You *care* about me, but you are neglecting yourself; you look after me, bring me offerings that can never be repaid"—the poet made an abrupt movement to interrupt her, but she stopped him by shaking her head—"yes, offerings that cannot be repaid, but you're *thinking* only about yourself; you aren't thinking about me at all."

"I do more than just think about you!" The words flew out of him.

"That well may be . . . Indeed, I know it is so; but you still don't think about me, and you don't understand me, and that makes me sad. No one understands me, and it's not because I am so enigmatic or incomprehensible by nature. No, I'm quite easy to understand. All it would require is to think a little bit and become just slightly acquainted with me, but it seems this does not interest anyone.

"At one time, people gazed upon me and were 'in ecstasy'; they said I was a 'star,' that I was 'incomparable,' and so on and so on. Many things were said, as you know, and much was written, but when it comes to thinking about me—no one has done that, not even you."

The poet became thoughtful.

"Perhaps it's true," he stated quietly after a while. "Perhaps I haven't been thinking—that is, not until this very moment. But . . . that kind of thinking is pointless, for even though you may not be as you seem to me, I would still love you no matter what kind of a person you were—either flawed or flawless. You are my fate."

"Hm . . . 'Either flawed. . .'" she repeated thoughtfully, "but perhaps you would not love me, if I were flawless."

He stared at her in astonishment.

"Well, you see," she continued, "people like you are always searching for dissonance, broken strings, shattered harps; but when I was flawless, when there was nothing broken in me, not a shred of dissonance, you would been bored because of the harmony that then characterised my life!

"Take my photo album from over there; in it there are many pictures of me from my younger days. You can look them over. I won't stop you, for I'm not playing the coquette with you. Take a look at them."

One by one, he examined her earlier photographs, showing her in her "starring" roles, armed with her "on-stage" costumes. He looked at them for a long time, and then he silently closed the album and put it back in its place.

"Well?" she asked him nervously.

"Perhaps you're right," he answered, smiling tenderly and brightly.

For some reason she felt sorry for him.

"So, you see, my . . . I almost said 'my friend,' but isn't it true that this would be both unwise and unoriginal—and even cruel? There are situations when a woman is not permitted to use this word," she glanced at him worriedly and guiltily.

"Call me whatever you wish, whatever pleases you." He bent over, lifted her thin, pale hand that was even more emaciated than her face, and kissed it piously.

She closed her eyes, and after that kiss her hand lay inertly, awkwardly, as if she had forgotten about it.

A few minutes passed by in silence.

"Ah yes . . . What was it, exactly, that I wanted to tell you?" the actress murmured, as if slowly awakening from a half sleep.

"You wanted to tell me about something?"

"Yes, I think so . . . Here's what is was . . . What do you think: why did I become extinguished?"

"You? Extinguished?" The voice of the poet rang with too much astonishment.

"Now listen, I don't like reactions of that kind," she frowned as if she were experiencing physical pain. "Insincerity does not become you. You know very well what my decline was like, when it happened, and that it is irreversible."

"I don't know anything about irreversibility," the poet said, hiding the look on his face.

"Have it as you will. I'm not going to push you to the wall. And that's not the point. But what do you think: how did it happen that I went 'into retirement'?"

"Well, it's a well-known fact. You became ill . . . you were exhausted . . . and it's no wonder—you identified completely with all the roles that you played . . ."

"You know nothing!" she interrupted him impatiently. "Nothing at all! The whole point was that I had ceased identifying with the roles!"

"Because you had exhausted yourself earlier."

"Oh, do be quiet! It's not that," she interrupted capriciously; and she shifted her position impatiently several times.

"Have I made you angry?"

"Oh, no, no . . ."

She turned to the wall and, tracing them with her finger, began to count the squares on a Persian tapestry hanging by her bed. The expression on her face kept changing, her eyebrows twitched; at times it seemed as if she were about to speak, but then she pressed her lips together once again.

Finally, she turned abruptly to the poet and looked him straight in the face.

"Well, it doesn't matter now. I must tell you everything," she said with a kind of despair. "Even though I realize it isn't proper for me to tell you everything."

She emphasized the last 'me' and 'you'.

The poet repeated that emphasis: "You can tell me everything."

"Fine." She spoke decisively, but her voice was not very firm. "Here's what happened. I was once very much in love. 'Only once?' you're probably thinking."

"I'm not thinking anything," the poet said, quite crossly this time.

"I'm saying 'I was' in love, because in cases like this, it's the custom to say this instead of 'I am' in love . . ."

"It is?" the poet seemed to draw out his words in alarm.

"Yes, it is. Well, what of it? It's true that now you're thinking: 'Why, exactly, is she telling me all of this? She's just toying with the situation, after all—she's an actress!'"

She laughed her disagreeable laugh, and her face—ravaged by her illness and the cosmetics she had used on stage—broke out in a faint, blotchy blush.

"I would like to ask you—if you find it at all possible—not to laugh like that," the poet said softly and painfully, and he walked away to the window.

She stopped herself. "Well then, I won't, I won't. Come here, I can't speak loudly."

He sat down submissively in his usual spot in the low armchair at her feet.

"What I am about to tell you is very unoriginal; it's hardly worth relating, especially to a poet—it won't surprise you."

He shrugged his shoulders impatiently.

"But after all, you aren't expounding a 'theme' for me, are you?" he said in an offended tone.

"You must calm down; you have to understand it's not easy to strike a natural tone when one is talking about oneself."

"Forgive me; I'll be patient."

"But then again, there's nothing 'like that' in my story. I was only in love, and as they say, it never went any further than that. It's a very pedestrian romance—for an actress. Ha-ha! Oh, that's right, I promised not to laugh."

Seeing the tortured face of the poet, she abruptly interrupted her laughter.

"Does this mean he didn't love you?" the poet asked, when she had fallen silent.

"Why does it 'mean' anything? No, on the contrary, it's difficult to say who loved whom more."

"Then why . . ."

"Well, how is one not to laugh when one is with you? Surely you don't think that it's enough just to be in love in order to be united?

"How little you know! And for someone who is a poet! Surely you must know our old folk song:

> Not all the orchards fully bloom
> That in the spring begin to bud . . ."

"Who was he?" the poet asked, knitting his brows in anger.

"He was—and still is—a writer. Not the kind of writer you are, 'one chosen by God.'" The poet looked at her intently, but she did not pay any attention to him. "No, he is an ordinary 'rank and file' writer. He writes theatre reviews and heads one department or another in a provincial newspaper. At that time, he was head of 'Gleanings From Other Newspapers and Journals'; now, I think, he's been transferred to 'Local News.'

"There is no spark of genius in his writing; this was clear even to me. But, it seemed to me—no, I am certain of it—there is a spark of genius within him; it shines in his eyes, and what is lacking in his writing, one can hear in his voice. Because of this, I forgave him everything, even the unforgivably bad verses he once wrote in my honour.

"His reviews of my performances were always full of praise, but . . . may God forgive him for the style in which they were written—it proved distasteful at times even to an actor's undemanding taste.

"It always seemed to me that it was necessary to free his spark from that kind of writing, to ignite it within him, and I thought I could do that . . ."

She fell silent.

"Why didn't you do it?"

She swept her hand over her forehead. "Why? Because he didn't want to come with me, and I didn't want to go to him."

"Why?"

"Oh, how boring you are with your continual 'why's?'! I want to tell you all about it, even without them! It was very simple— he wanted me to become his wedded wife; otherwise, he didn't want to love me; he didn't want to share me with others—he was terribly jealous. I couldn't live forever in that town, and he couldn't find it within himself to be satisfied with having us meet only now and again; it was easier for him to part forever—as he himself said.

"But I didn't want to marry him."

The poet appeared to become happier. "I understand. You were reluctant to give up your precious freedom; the yoke of household responsibilities did not appeal to your artistic nature. Perhaps the thought of taking a vow that is like a constraint on love offended you. A legal wedding had an aura of Philistinism about it."

She gazed at him through narrowed eyes, and then smiled weakly. "No, that wasn't the point. I simply feared poverty, ordinary material indigence."

"You?"

"Yes, me."

"But I've rarely seen a person less greedy for money than you."

"I would not fear an actor's homeless poverty, because I have already experienced it, and I've come out of it unscathed; but matrimonial, familial poverty that one calls down upon oneself— I was afraid of it then, and I would be afraid of it now, irrespective of anything else!"

"Somehow I don't understand this," the poet spoke slowly, and an estranged, disillusioned look appeared on his face. "It seems to me your love was probably not as profound as you thought it to be."

"Then why am I now dying because of it?" These words, filled with a burning, genuine despair, flew out of her.

She raised herself on the sofa and clasped her hands in anguish. Her eyes widened and grew darker, as if they had been retouched.

The poet eased her back on to the pillow with a gentle movement, and she lay down once again and became calm.

Silence ensued.

The poet unconsciously flipped the pages of his manuscript.

"Do not think too badly of me, and try to understand me if you can," she spoke up once again. "When I feared *that* poverty, it was not because I feared hunger, the cold, ragged clothing, and worn shoes."

"You feared for your love? That it would fade in life's struggle?"

"Well . . . there was a little of that as well. Although it was not for my love I feared, but for his. Women are better able to maintain the poetry of their feelings in the prose of life than are men."

"Do you think so?"

"That's how it seems to me. But then, that's unimportant. Because that would not have stopped me. For his love could have vanished, if not because of poverty, then because of a long parting, or simply 'because'."

"You had no faith in him?"

"No, it wasn't that . . . Well, obviously one relies more on oneself. So it seemed to me that my love was 'as strong as death itself' . . ."

"But nevertheless?" the poet asked with hope in his voice.

She smiled sadly and ironically. "But nevertheless—death is stronger; unfortunately, I must admit it. It is even stronger than that which I thought was more powerful than my love, more powerful and more dear to me than my love—yes, more dear."

"What was it?"

"You mean you can't guess? Oh, poets are wiser on paper than in real life! My talent, of course! It was my *talent* which feared that poverty."

The poet was now staring at her with his former look, and he did not even attempt to hide it. "But you yourself said you were earning fairly good money," he insisted.

"Being the kind of migratory bird that I was—and that I had to be, given the state of our theatre—I could earn money only by being continuously in flight. I had no financial reserves and never did know how to accumulate them; but if I had made a permanent nest, I would have had to give up even those earnings.

"If he had been an actor, it would have been different . . . but it was not possible for a chronicler from a small newspaper to find a job with a different newspaper in every little town. It's not that easy."

"That's true."

"Of course, we both could have lived on the earnings that I was making at that time—perhaps even with a family—if he had been willing to give up his job and live at my expense while travelling with me. But he didn't even want to hear about that."

"That's understandable," the poet observed.

The actress flared up. "Of course! It's understandable to you! That a man can break his own heart and that of his beloved because of some Philistine superstitions—that's understandable to you!"

"These are not superstitions; this is elementary good form."

"Exactly, 'elementary'! For men, everything is 'elementary'! Well, what if I had been living on his meagre 'allowance,' having renounced my profession for love? Would that have been 'elementary good form'?"

"That would have been a completely different matter. In today's circumstances . . ."

The actress waved her hands impatiently. "I know, I know, I know! I've heard it more than a thousand times! It's tiresome. Elementary. That's enough. That's exactly what he said. I hated him at those times."

The poet decided not to pursue this theme.

"Perhaps he could have had some kind of job in your company?" he hesitantly suggested.

"What kind? To be a prompter? Or perhaps a 'leg-kicking dancer' of some kind? He wasn't even capable of singing in the chorus, and our troupe did not take bit players on tour. Perhaps he would have agreed to something like that. But that would have been too much. Our artistic superstitions do not permit something like that.

"'The wedded husband' of the leading 'star,' 'of our famous actress,' or something similar to that—and he was to 'stand like a post on the stage' as a bit player, take silent roles, serve as a drudge, 'shore up the walls'. . .

"No, no, it may be difficult for you to understand this, but this would be im-po-ssi-ble! I'm telling you. He would have been 'an utter failure' on the stage . . . Just as you would be!" she added suddenly.

The poet turned red. "What has this to do with me? I haven't ever appeared on a stage—how do you know, perhaps . . ."

"No, no, there's no 'perhaps'! I have an unfailing sixth sense for this. 'An utter failure', I tell you," she looked him daringly in the eyes. "Brrr . . . I don't know, but perhaps even my love could not withstand that!"

An angry flame flashed in the poet's eyes. "In any event, that . . . your acquaintance, it seems, also did not reveal any special 'talent' in his writing, as you yourself have said."

"But that's an entirely different matter!"

The poet shrugged his shoulders scornfully: "I don't understand why. What's the difference?"

"A newspaper writer may be untalented three times over, and he will still be called 'an honest worker of the press,' and not a 'good-for-nothing.'"

"Well, if it's all a matter of semantics to you . . ."

"And why not? I want to believe that you will not be the one to teach me to have a contempt for words."

"Well, there is also the word 'scribbler'!"

Red blotches flamed on her face, and she flashed her eyes at him: "How dare you!"

"Forgive me . . ."

"No matter what his status was in the literary field, those nearest to me would not have been in a position to measure and compare it to mine. Even if he were the worst writer in an editorial office, or even if he had no career at all, backstage he would have been only my husband, and not a theatrical drudge."

"An extremely pleasant status: 'the husband of the queen!'" the poet could not resist saying.

"Not any worse than 'the wife of her husband.'"

They looked at one another sharply, and with hostility. A period of silence ensued once again, this time a longer one.

"Give me a cigarette," the actress spoke up at last in a weary, indifferent tone of voice.

The poet had already calmed down, and he even felt guilty to some degree.

"I can't." He refused to comply with her request. "It's harmful for you to smoke."

"But isn't it all the same what's harmful to me, and what isn't?"

"To whom are you saying this?" the poet inquired in a gently reproachful voice. Then he added unexpectedly: "Have I offended you?"

"No. It's just that I don't feel like talking any more."

The poet looked intently at her face. Her eyes were lowered, but even so she could not withstand his intent gaze. She turned towards the wall.

He took her hand in both of his. "Don't be angry. I myself don't know where that quarrelsome spark that has come between us originated. Now it's no longer here—am I right?"

"You're right . . ."

She turned back to him and began speaking as if there had not been any interruption: "In any event, we parted. That is, I left him. I transferred into another, worse troupe, into worse conditions, just to leave the town and go off to the ends of the earth. Yes, I went all the way to Siberia, in order to avoid the temptation 'to visit' my friend—the friend who was not destined for me . . ."

"Not destined? Perhaps not accepted by you?"

"It's all the same. This was not some kind of whim on my part. I'm telling you, I feared for my talent, for it truly would not have been able to withstand petty, familial poverty; it would have been checkmated. That is, I thought so then, that only in that instance could my talent have been checkmated.

"As it turned out, however, no matter which way you turn, this way or that way, death is always hovering over you! Ha-ha-ha!"

"Oh, Lord, that laughter!" The poet cracked his knuckles.

She shrieked: "Don't do that! I can't stand it!"

The poet folded his arms, but observed: "You see, I can't do what is unpleasant for you, but you . . ."

"That's understandable! Because you're healthy, and I'm sick. Don't interrupt. I can't talk when you do that . . . So I went to Siberia. I thought that having made such a sacrifice to my god, I would become forever a great priestess of his."

"And that's just what happened!" the poet observed passionately.

"No. That's not what happened. I know this better than you. From that time on, I didn't feel like a priestess; I felt like a slave. It seemed to me that some kind of chains were binding me, that it was I who had bound myself with these chains—and I cursed some kind of unknown power . . . But then, perhaps it really was some unknown power that had split in two both my heart and my soul . . ."

"It is the fate of artists and poets that they must pave the way to their immortality with blood from their own hearts," the poet said somewhat pathetically.

The actress grimaced. "Oh, rubbish! But then, I won't speak for poets, for you would know more about them than I do. I'm not a poet. As for an artist . . . Well, first of all, what exactly is our artistic immortality? A few words included in the 'history of talented people'? Whose heart will beat faster upon reading these few words, even ten years down the road?"

"Well now, you've put too short a time limit on it."

"It's all the same. It suffices that such 'immortality' may in fact be measured . . . No, no, no! We have to live, and not hope for immortality. Only then will we feel ourselves to be both great and immortal.

"While I lived without any worries, in harmony with both myself and my talent, I was happy and truly worth something on the stage. As long as I had not experienced great misfortune and that grief which enslaves the soul completely, I could 'put myself' sincerely into my roles—as you know, my forte was strong, dramatic characters—because I had within me an inexhaustible reserve of emotions that I had not wasted on my own life.

"I knew only the grief found in dramas, and I believed it was like that in real life as well. On the stage, I lived with that grief; and off the stage, I rested from it and recouped my strength. Formerly, I used to be a very merry 'great companion.' You may not know . . ."

"No, I've heard . . ."

"Well, it's all the same. That's not the point . . . But then . . . when I personally experienced grief in the real world, and realized how people become victims, my roles suddenly became inconsequential to me. The slightest bit of falseness cut me to the quick, and I agonized for hours as I tried to find 'a natural' tone for those false banalities which filled my entire repertoire—and those are not the worst plays! I stopped acting intuitively and began studying my roles."

"But this is the highest stage of dramatic art!" the poet shouted.

He wanted to begin a lengthy exposition of his assertion, but she stopped him with her hand.

"Perhaps you're right. That's not the point. If I had reached this stage back then, when I was still happy, perhaps it might have worked to my advantage, but this way . . . this was only endless torture. I always compared the written grief to my own, and this was the measure for all my studying. I recalled how people *truly* cry when they part, how they *truly* lose consciousness from grief, and this tore my heart apart, and the roles seemed to me to be a caricature both of me and my grief.

"I often went out on the stage in fear, and with despair in my heart. How was I to act out this unadulterated lie? I swear, at times I was covered in sweat like a Gypsy. But my 'studying' saved me, and for a long time no one noticed it. But, you know, this wasn't exactly acting, it was hypocrisy . . .

"After such spectacles, I returned home completely unstrung, exhausted, discouraged, and I no longer knew why and to whom I was bringing my offering. My talent appeared to me then as something soulless, painted with fading colours on an idol, and I began to hate it. And nothing was more terrifying to me than that hatred; it was some kind of abyss, and I was flying into it head first . . ."

The poet's eyes shone with both sympathy and pity for her, but he forced himself to state calmly: "But not everything was that false in your roles. I know your repertoire. There are at least some passages, and even complete roles, that appear to be taken in their entirety from real life. Did it not seem that way to you?"

"It was even worse," she said without answering him directly, "when such passages occurred; then I acted neither 'intuitively,' or 'with my mind.' I wept publicly and nearly perished with grief, forgetting more than once about my audience, the play, and even the words of my role.

"Indeed, there were times when I should have been 'swept from the stage with a broom,' chased off for such a 'performance,' but the audience and the critics forgave everything, and chalked it up to hysterics. When the female half of the audience agonized along with me in the pangs of hysteria, this was considered to be my 'triumph,' and the wealthy men of Siberia presented me with sables and jewels.

"But for me, the 'triumph' did not end on the stage; I often relived the 'acting' throughout the entire night at home, until a deathly exhaustion or dangerous doses of narcotics made me lose consciousness.

"Oh, those nights! Those terrible nights! If it had not been for the distances, I most certainly would have run to him barefooted, fallen before him, and begged him to take me away and hide me from my 'talent'. . .

"But the next day I would be 'studying' again . . . And thus a few years went by."

"A few years? You could withstand all these tortures for a few years?"

"Oh, I could do a lot then, at least I thought I could . . . And my pride helped me in that as well. I did not want to admit to myself that I had made a mistake, that I was defeated."

A harsh look once again appeared on the poet's face. He felt this, and tried to stop himself, but could not.

He spoke, therefore, in a voice purposely devoid of expression: "I don't quite understand this. You accused me of not *thinking* about you, but even so I could not abandon you because of some pride, as you abandoned . . . Well, did it ever occur to you that you were not the only one who was experiencing such suffering? No, you truly are hardhearted."

She looked askance at him, and her voice rang with sarcasm: "And you, you're so incredibly compassionate! Who ever heard of defending the interests of one's—what would one call him? Well, it doesn't matter . . . Only, you see, 'to justify myself' I can say I did not know anything—what kind of suffering someone else besides me was experiencing—because no one ever wrote me anything about it . . . It is true, of course, that I had asked him not to write to me . . ."

The poet had a response ready to throw out at her, but he held it back, and even pressed his lips together disdainfully.

"Yes, I asked him, but he should not have listened to my request, if . . . You're probably going to say: there's a woman's logic for you."

"I'm not saying anything," the poet replied gloomily, and he once again began rifling through his manuscript.

She thought for a moment, and then she said simply—without any sarcasm, and without anger—in a genuinely amicable tone: "You know, let's drop this topic of conversation. Obviously my story is upsetting you."

"No, no," he cried, painfully furrowing his brow, "if you find it at all possible, please finish your story. Tell me everything, everything, to the very end. Otherwise I will suffer unbearably. Don't pay any attention to my behaviour . . . perhaps I spoke incorrectly and badly . . . but I . . . Try to understand me . . . It's some kind of duality, or even more . . . It's very difficult for me . . . Everyone in my position would . . . No, I'm not saying what I want to . . ."

She gathered her strength, and with a soft groan raised herself in order to reach him with her hand. She stroked his hand, and then, moaning softly, once again lowered herself. "No, it is I who am more to blame . . . But then, no one is to blame. Who knows if it's harder to listen to, or to narrate such things . . . But once it's been started—it would be even more difficult not to hear it all, or to tell it all. However, I'll shorten what I'm saying, and I'll relate it without lyricism . . . Is that fine with you?"

"Anything that makes you feel good," the poet said, and he became completely agreeable.

"Only give me my medicine first, and place the pillow under my head—it seems to have slipped down a bit. That's good . . . Thanks. So, you see, I did not stick it out to the very end. Perhaps I would have found peace eventually, perhaps I would even have forgotten about my love—in our day it doesn't seem quite right to believe in eternal love—if it had not been for those roles with their lies and their truth, but it was as if my wounds were constantly being reopened . . .

"Well, to make a long story short, I finally returned to that town. But he was already married . . ."

"Really?" the poet gasped in surprise. "He could forget you?"

She smiled sadly. "Who can say? Perhaps he didn't forget me."

"Then how . . ."

"Oh, don't pretend to be so naive! It's quite customary for men, in addition to a great, and as you have said, fatal love, to have at least a dozen or so, if not more, smaller loves that are not fatal."

"I think this is often true of women as well."

She turned her eyes away from him indifferently: "As you like."

"Did you see his wife?" the poet asked somewhat enigmatically.

"Of course. I was in their home."

"You were in their home?"

"Do you find that strange? Well it may be strange, or not so strange, but I was in his home.

"On the very first evening, I saw him with his wife at the theatre. I realized at once it was his wife; she was sitting next to him, and it was possible to guess immediately she had come to the theatre on a complimentary ticket: she was too poorly dressed to be in the front rows of the seats on the main floor . . . And then, there's something peculiar in the behaviour of a married couple, the interaction between a man and wife—it's always easy to spot.

"During the first intermission, I called him backstage and asked him to introduce me to his wife. He could not think of an excuse not to. This was happening in public. None of my friends even guessed at anything, because no one knew about us. And so we became acquainted with one another."

"What was she like?" the poet was unable to hide his curiosity.

"What was she like? Different from me, completely different. Is that good enough for you?"

"But who was she?" the poet, slightly abashed, responded with a question.

"She used to be 'a lady in the office' at the newspaper where he worked, and now she was—'the wife of her husband,' or 'a married woman.' Who else could she be?"

"Well, she could have continued serving . . ."

"She's in another service now!" the actress replied with a short laugh that resembled a cough. "When I came to their home, she was in the middle of bathing the smallest child, and two more were crawling about at her feet, fighting with one another, screaming, and bringing her to the brink of despair.

"I quickly realized I had come at an inopportune moment, just when the children were being put to sleep. Her husband should have been helping her, because his wife and their teenage servant were fully occupied with the bathing. He tried to pretend that all this did not embarrass him in any way, that it even amused him, but—the poor fellow—there is no doubt he would have made a very poor actor! He even mopped his brow a couple of times.

"They had only two little rooms in all, and the older children slept in the room where I was sitting. I should have gone home, but I didn't."

"Why?"

She laughed once again. "What do you mean 'why'? I had come for a visit, and I was invited 'to stay, to sit down for a while,' and so I stayed, and I sat for a while; I sat for the entire evening."

Her face took on a very unpleasant expression as she said this.

The poet once again felt something disagreeable stirring in his heart. "But they most certainly invited you just out of politeness, because you yourself said that you had come at an inopportune time."

"But what did that concern me? I wanted to, and I had the right, to look things over carefully, to see how my ex-fiancé and his wife lived. For that's how I would have been living if . . ."

"Well, I did have a good look. The children didn't want to fall asleep for a long time, and there was a problem until they were given some milk, and so on. The smallest was a trifle ill as well, and had to carried until it fell asleep. After all the children had fallen asleep, they were separated from us by a curtain, and we sat down at the table to have tea.

"But before tea was served, the maid called the mistress several times into the tiny kitchen through which I had passed on my way in, for that was the only entrance into their home. Then the mistress called the master into the kitchen, and they whispered there for quite some time. Then the servant ran someplace a few times, called my hosts out again, and once more there were secret consultations. Then the mistress went into the kitchen for a long time. I suspect she was the main cook and nanny, and that the girl who was about twelve years of age was only her helper.

"In the meantime, I was 'entertained' by the master, or rather, I entertained him."

"What did you talk about?" the poet asked dully.

She glanced at him in amusement. "About all sorts of matters."

"Happy ones?"

"Well, what do you think—that in the absence of his wife we tried 'to renew our old memories,' or that I 'fell weeping into his arms,' or that he was 'possessed by a demoniac force to abandon everything and follow me like a faithful dog'? Oh, my little darling, things like that happen only in plays.

"No, that evening I told him about my merry 'sleigh rides on a troika' with the rich gentlemen of Siberia, about the *portebouquets [bouquet-holders]* stuffed with hundred-ruble notes that were presented to me, about how I learned to sing Gypsy romances and to dance on tables.

"When the lady of the house finally came in with a dish of dumplings, and the servant finally brought in the samovar, the buns and the traditional 'tea' sausage, I was right in the middle of describing the gourmet 'Lucullian banquet' that had been held in my honour in Irkutsk.

"After pouring the tea, the lady took up some mending—a child's jacket—and one could see that it was a truly urgent job. I complimented her dexterity, and she replied that she sewed everything for herself and the children. It seemed to me the gentleman's clothing was also made by her. I promised to bring her the pattern for a dress in the latest fashion, like the one I was wearing . . . and the poor soul had to thank me. Ha-ha! She had torn elbows; she probably had no time to mend them."

"I never thought you could be so unkind," the poet said in a trembling voice.

"And I never thought you were so sentimental! But after all, it suits you—you're a poet, and a lyrical one at that. But what am I? I'm just an 'actress'! All the same, I acted out my role with talent that evening, only it was my final one . . ."

The poet stared at her, but he did not say anything.

"Then our conversation moved on to literature—you see how well I have remembered the 'program' of that evening! It appears they didn't read anything, he—because he had to write so much, and she—well, how could she read!

"He at least knew about the new plays because 'in his line of work' he attended the theatre. She, however, didn't even know that, because she went only rarely, 'when there was someone with whom to leave the children,' and perhaps if there was an extra complimentary ticket.

"So we talked about the new plays and some more about my roles. I assured them that nothing can be as satisfying as an artistic career."

The poet gazed at her sadly. "Was this said sincerely?"

"I didn't expect that one would have to point out every dot over every 'i' to you! 'Sincerely? Insincerely?' I don't like these questions! How am I to know? Perhaps it was both, the one and the other together!"

"I thought that at that moment you could truly say it sincerely. Formerly, you were so frightened by the prospect of poverty, and now you could see it with your very own eyes."

She interrupted him impatiently: "Yes, but so what? Did this change anything? Well, it was poverty, true poverty, perhaps even worse than I had once imagined. But do you think that the 'spark of genius' had been extinguished completely in his eyes? That his voice had changed completely? Not at all! Only his writing had deteriorated even further . . . I understood only too well that it was still possible 'to ignite' that spark within him, only not in such mundane surroundings.

"However, there were not going to be any other surroundings for him, nor could there have been. *His* family could not have been different, do you understand? No matter what his wife was like, her fate could not have been any different.

"Do you understand?" she raised herself without a groan this time and, trembling, squeezed his hand.

He once again eased her carefully back on to her pillow and said—he himself did not know why: "But a man sometimes finds happiness and love outside of the family, and not with his wedded wife."

She shut her eyes wearily. "It's no use talking about that," she said softly. "This has no place here . . . he's not like that."

"How did he treat his wife?"

"In a friendly manner, it seemed . . . but . . . somehow, they appeared to be guilty before one another. This is all so senseless."

Her head tipped to one side, as if it had fallen by itself, so wearily, so weakly. "Well, I finished playing my role . . ."

"What kind of role?" the poet asked in alarm. It seemed to him she was losing consciousness.

"What kind? Well, the visit of 'a friend who was not fated to be' . . . Then I returned home, and I no longer thought about anything, and I no longer felt anything; it was as if I had ceased to exist in the world. Formerly, there had still been something like repentance, like pride, like hope, but now there was nothing left.

"The next day I had to appear on stage, and the play was a really disgusting one, some kind of melodrama. Oh, what torture this was! To be completely numb, to act like some kind of a parody of a living person.

"In this instance, even my 'studying' was of no help to me; I no longer felt either falseness, or truth: I was extinguished, I was one of the living dead. This was finally noticed. I disintegrated. Then I became ill. But you already know about this."

"And you never saw him again?"

"No. What for? It was all the same to me . . . I later left the town . . . Not on purpose, because that was all the same to me, as well . . . The troupe moved to another town, and I went along with it . . ."

She fell silent and seemed to fall asleep; the rays of the western sun fell on her closed eyes, but she did not notice them.

The poet sat quietly and held his breath so as not to disturb the silence. A ray trembled on the wall in tiny blotches, and then it faded . . .

The actress slowly opened her eyes . . . "How could you have fallen in love with such a dead person like me?"

"I fell in love with you a long time ago, while you were still in Kharkiv."

"Ah, yes, that's right . . . That was just before I left for Siberia . . . I was still alive then . . . It's not good of me to keep you with me, is it?" she asked somehow seriously, in an almost businesslike manner.

"You aren't keeping me," the poet said, and he leaned over.

"Yes . . . you say: I am your fate. I believe this. It happens. Perhaps. At least as long as I exist in this world. But I will soon die, and you will be free."

"Then I too will die!"

Her lips barely moved. "A poet should speak like that . . ."

"Do you think that I . . ."

"No, I don't think that; I'm not thinking about anything. Unless it's this: if he had died way back *then*, I would still be free, and I would not have become extinguished . . . But then, I don't know . . . Enough about this . . . Read something to me."

"What?"

"Something of your own, obviously."

The poet flipped through his manuscript indecisively, and remained silent.

"Finish what you started earlier."

"That?"

"Yes, of course. It will feel so good. Do read. Begin at the beginning, because I interrupted you."

The poet smoothed back his bushy hair and began: "A great, fatal love is a simoom . . ."

The poet dissipated himself in comparisons; the actress lay quietly, and slowly wound a strand of her dark, copious hair on her pale slender finger; she wound it and rewound it for a long, long time . . .

The Enemies
(1909)

Fiat lux!
[Let there be light!]

"O God! What kind of a life is this? Why have I condemned myself to this harsh sentence?" a young woman exclaimed, flinging herself in utter exhaustion and despair on the couch in front of the burning fireplace.

Her husband glanced at her with unconcealed loathing and continued pacing with long strides from one corner of the room to the other.

Finally, he stopped in front of his wife and touched her roughly on the shoulder.

"Why don't you abandon this dramatic pose once and for all—it's positively ridiculous. Sit down properly, and let's have—at least once in our lives—a conversation like normal people."

She glanced up at him in alarm, quickly raised herself to a sitting position, and folded her hands on her knees; however, she did make an observation: "Of what concern is my pose to you? It's just petty tyranny on your part."

He was stung, but he controlled himself.

"You're saying that you don't know why you've condemned yourself to such a harsh sentence—I could ask myself the same question. The fact is that we . . ." He wanted to say that they never had been able to stand one another, but confined himself to saying: "We have always tormented each other. So, wouldn't it be better if we . . ."

She did not let him finish speaking. "Why yes, of course, that would be the easiest of all—to worry a wife to death, exhaust her completely, and then say: 'Go away, I no longer want you.'"

"Well, what do you propose? What is the way out?"

In reply, an incoherent litany poured forth—complaints, reproaches, demands, concessions—and finally everything was drowned in tears.

"Well, what is it that is keeping us together?" her husband interjected, trying hard to remain calm. "We have no children, we are materially independent of one another, and as for love . . ." He laughed tensely: "It's ridiculous even to speak of it."

"Do you realize how revolting this laughter is—I can't stand it any more!" His wife rushed impetuously from the room and locked herself up in her bedroom.

All her husband's efforts—either to call her out for an explanation, or at least to get her to come out of the room—were futile.

He sat down by the fireplace and lost himself in his gloomy thoughts.

It was true that they could not stand one another. From the moment they became acquainted, their conversations assumed the character of arguments that inevitably crossed over into the personal domain. Even when they were out of sight of each other, they always spoke about one another in a mocking tone.

He had even proposed to her in the strangest fashion: "This will probably seem amusing to you—and it actually is amusing—but I love you."

"If you find it amusing," she answered in an offended tone, "then what is this all about? If that's the case . . ."

She wanted to walk out of the room, genuinely indignant, but when he caught hold of her hand and asked her if she would be his wife, she replied: "Yes!"

Then she burst into tears, rushed to her room, and would not see him again that day.

During their engagement, their presence always embarrassed the company in which they happened to be. They exchanged the most insulting, stinging gibes and reproaches in spite of their declared status—indeed, it was as if they were emphasizing it.

But the idea of parting never crossed their minds. It seemed to them that there was no turning back, and it was with a kind of irony that they went to the altar. And from then on, the "harsh sentence"—as she had just called it—began to drag on.

Engrossed in these painful memories, he did not notice when she re-entered the room.

She was pale, but calm; her eyes were lowered and teary.

"Yes, you're right," she stated so unexpectedly that he was startled. "There is no reason for us to live together; it's pointless to remain together when you can't stand me."

"Did I ever say that?"

"Yes."

"It's not true; you're outrageously misconstruing my words, as always."

"It's not the words that matter . . ."

But he began to make his point—maliciously, and in an irritated tone—that it was not true that he could not stand her, that it was she who had always hated and tormented him.

"Well, it's all the same; we're poisoning each other's lives. Regardless of who is to blame, this is intolerable. This absurd comedy must be ended."

At this point, he observed that if she considered marriage to be a comedy, then he was truly amazed how she could call herself a respectable woman.

And, after saying a lot of things to each other that were horrifying in their undisguised cruelty, they parted and went to their separate rooms.

These scenes, like fits of madness in hopelessly ill people, were repeated with increasing frequency.

One evening, exhausted and worn out by their futile struggle, they sat in silence—he with a book, and she with her handiwork—avoiding all conversation, and fearing a new storm.

Oh, how weary they both were of those storms.

Suddenly, he raised his head from his book and looked at his wife.

She was sitting quietly. Her hand that was holding the needle had fallen on her knees, and she was gazing at him with eyes full of tears, and in them, along with the customary hatred, a deep sadness was shining, and, it seemed, even tenderness.

"What are you thinking about?" he asked her, and he was surprised how gentle his words sounded.

"I'm thinking that we must . . . we must part, my dearest." She blushed as she uttered this uncustomary endearment.

His eyes blazed, but not with malice.

Walking up to her, he took her by the hand, and a tenderness flooded his chest.

Many, many, such uncustomary endearments moaned in his thoughts, but he did not utter them.

Slowly, gently, and softly—but in a tone of unshakable determination—he said: "Yes, we must part."

Translated from Russian